nickelodeon

降击神通

AVATAR

THE LAST AIRBENDER

SMOKE AND SHADOW

Created by
BRYAN KONIETZKO
MICHAEL DANTE DiMARTINO

script
GENE LUEN YANG

art and cover
GURIHIRU

lettering
MICHAEL HEISLER

DARK HORSE BOOKS

publisher
MIKE RICHARDSON

editor
RACHEL ROBERTS

assistant editor
JENNY BLENK

designer
SARAH TERRY

digital art technician
SAMANTHA HUMMER

Special thanks to Linda Lee, James Salerno, and Joan Hilty at
Nickelodeon, to Dave Marshall at Dark Horse, and to Bryan Konietzko,
Michael Dante DiMartino, and Tim Hedrick.

This book collects *Avatar: The Last Airbender—Smoke and Shadow* parts one through three.

Published by
Dark Horse Books
A division of
Dark Horse Comics LLC
10956 SE Main Street
Milwaukie, OR 97222

DarkHorse.com
Nick.com

To find a comics shop in your area,
visit ComicShopLocator.com

First edition: September 2021
eBOOK ISBN 978-1-50672-175-0
ISBN 978-1-50672-168-2
T# 857966

1 3 5 7 9 10 8 6 4 2
Printed in China

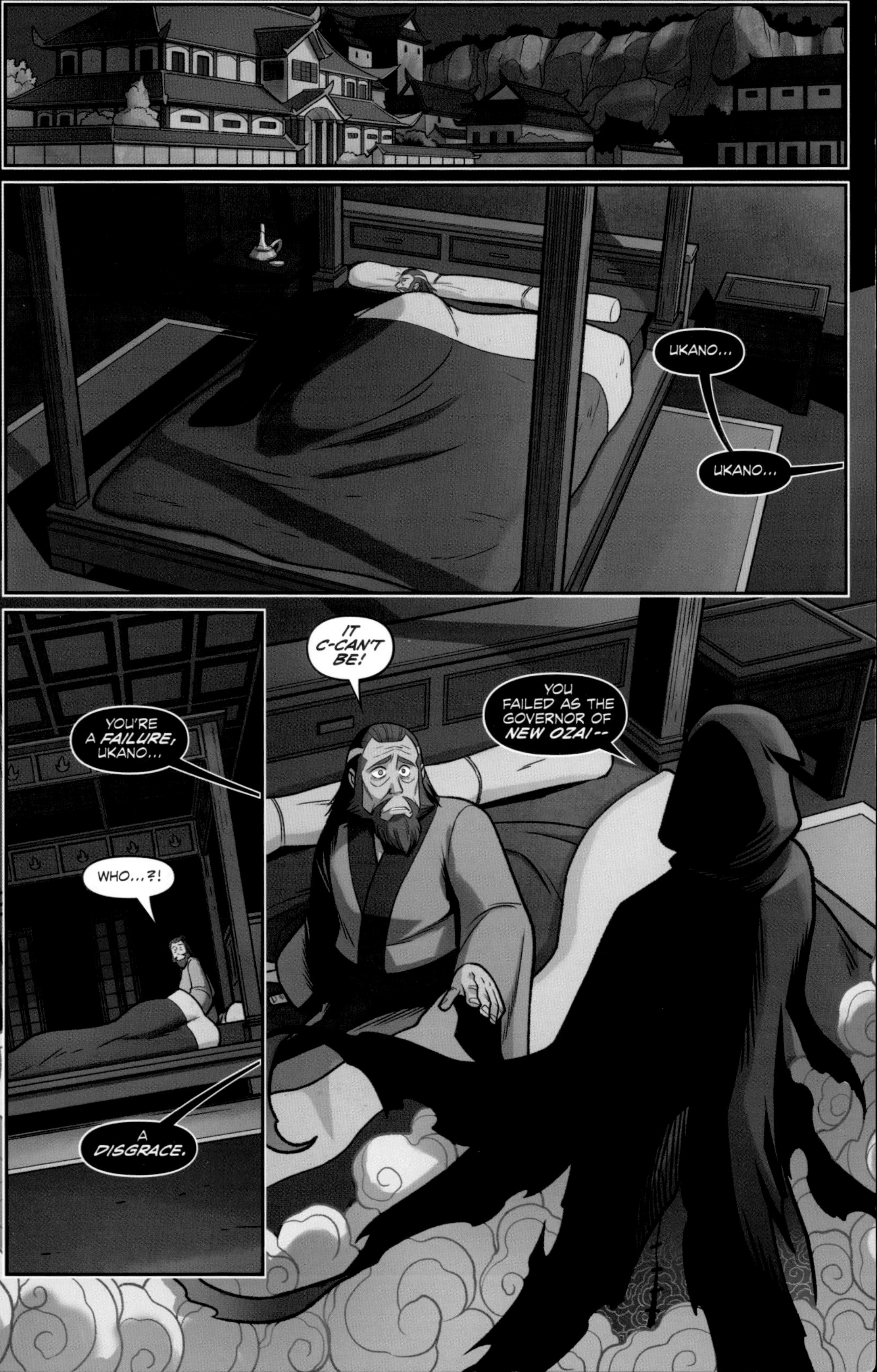
UKANO...
UKANO...
YOU'RE A FAILURE, UKANO...
WHO...?!
A DISGRACE.
IT C-CAN'T BE!
YOU FAILED AS THE GOVERNOR OF NEW OZAI--

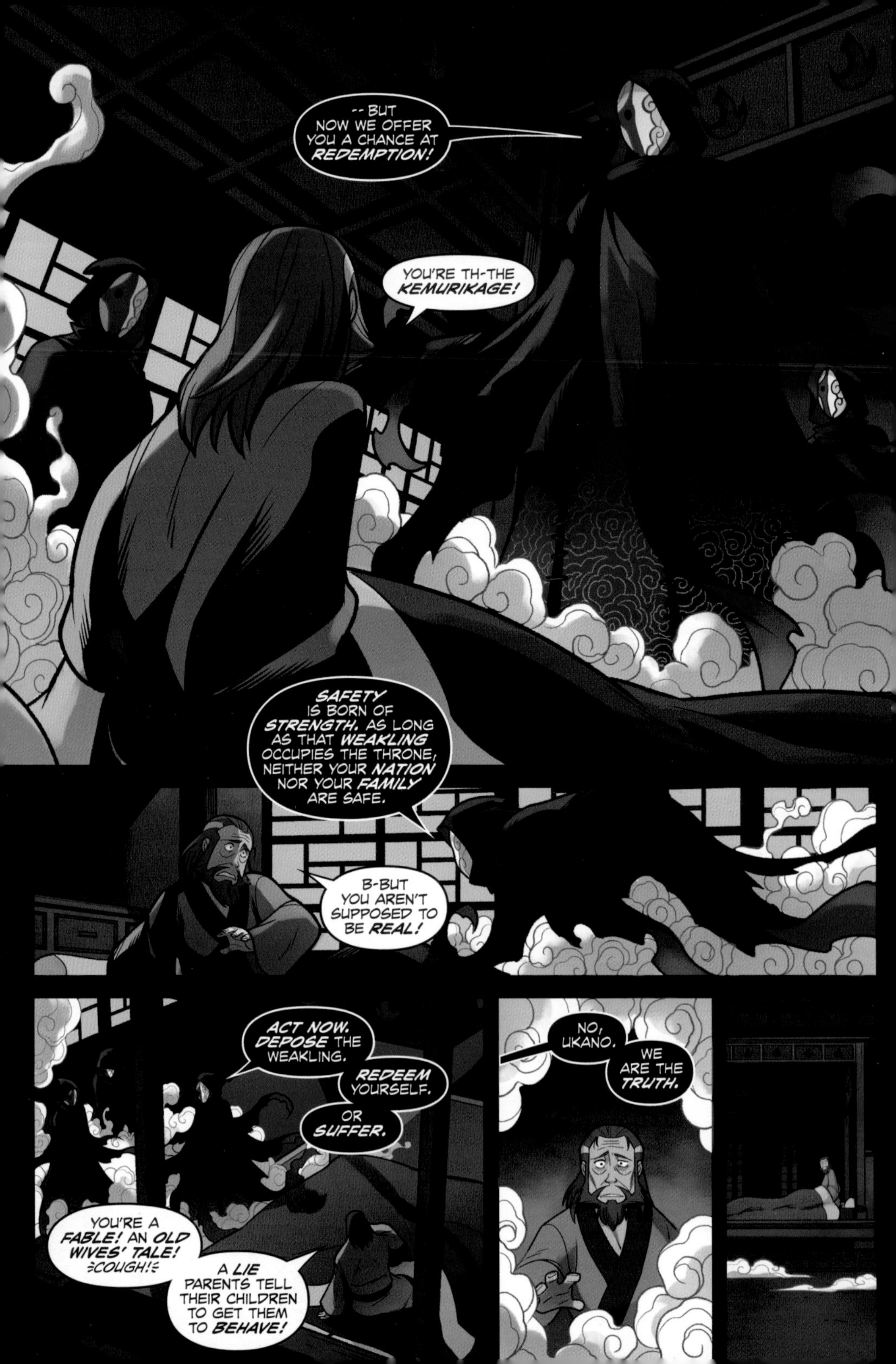

-- BUT NOW WE OFFER YOU A CHANCE AT *REDEMPTION!*
YOU'RE TH-THE *KEMURIKAGE!*
SAFETY IS BORN OF *STRENGTH.* AS LONG AS THAT *WEAKLING* OCCUPIES THE THRONE, NEITHER YOUR *NATION* NOR YOUR *FAMILY* ARE SAFE.
B-BUT YOU AREN'T SUPPOSED TO BE *REAL!*
ACT NOW. DEPOSE THE WEAKLING.
REDEEM YOURSELF.
OR *SUFFER.*
YOU'RE A *FABLE!* AN *OLD WIVES' TALE!* *COUGH!*
A *LIE* PARENTS TELL THEIR CHILDREN TO GET THEM TO *BEHAVE!*
NO, UKANO.
WE ARE THE *TRUTH.*

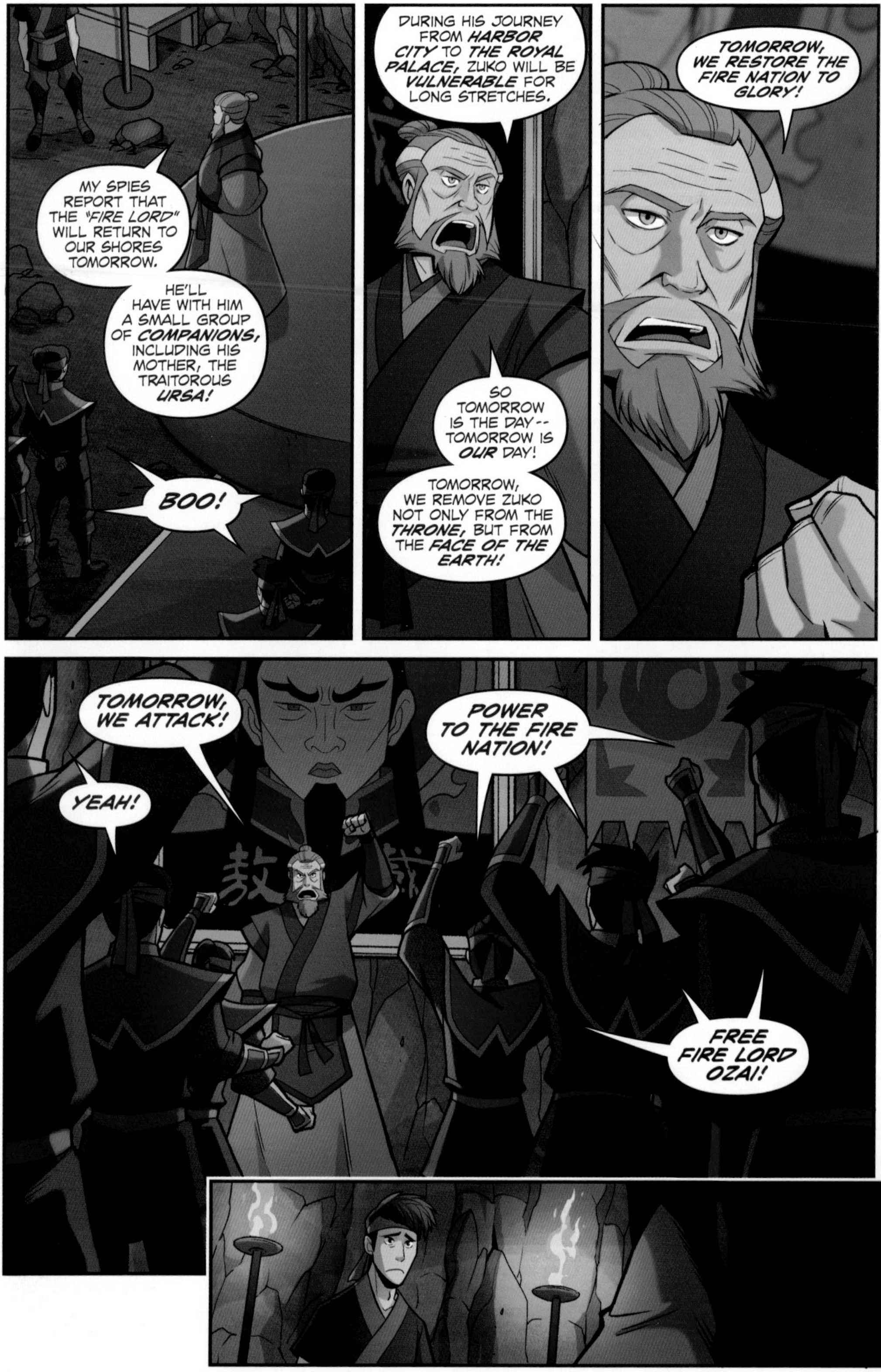
MY SPIES REPORT THAT THE "FIRE LORD" WILL RETURN TO OUR SHORES TOMORROW.
HE'LL HAVE WITH HIM A SMALL GROUP OF COMPANIONS, INCLUDING HIS MOTHER, THE TRAITOROUS URSA!
BOO!
DURING HIS JOURNEY FROM HARBOR CITY TO THE ROYAL PALACE, ZUKO WILL BE VULNERABLE FOR LONG STRETCHES.
SO TOMORROW IS THE DAY-- TOMORROW IS OUR DAY!
TOMORROW, WE REMOVE ZUKO NOT ONLY FROM THE THRONE, BUT FROM THE FACE OF THE EARTH!
TOMORROW, WE RESTORE THE FIRE NATION TO GLORY!
TOMORROW, WE ATTACK!
YEAH!
POWER TO THE FIRE NATION!
FREE FIRE LORD OZAI!

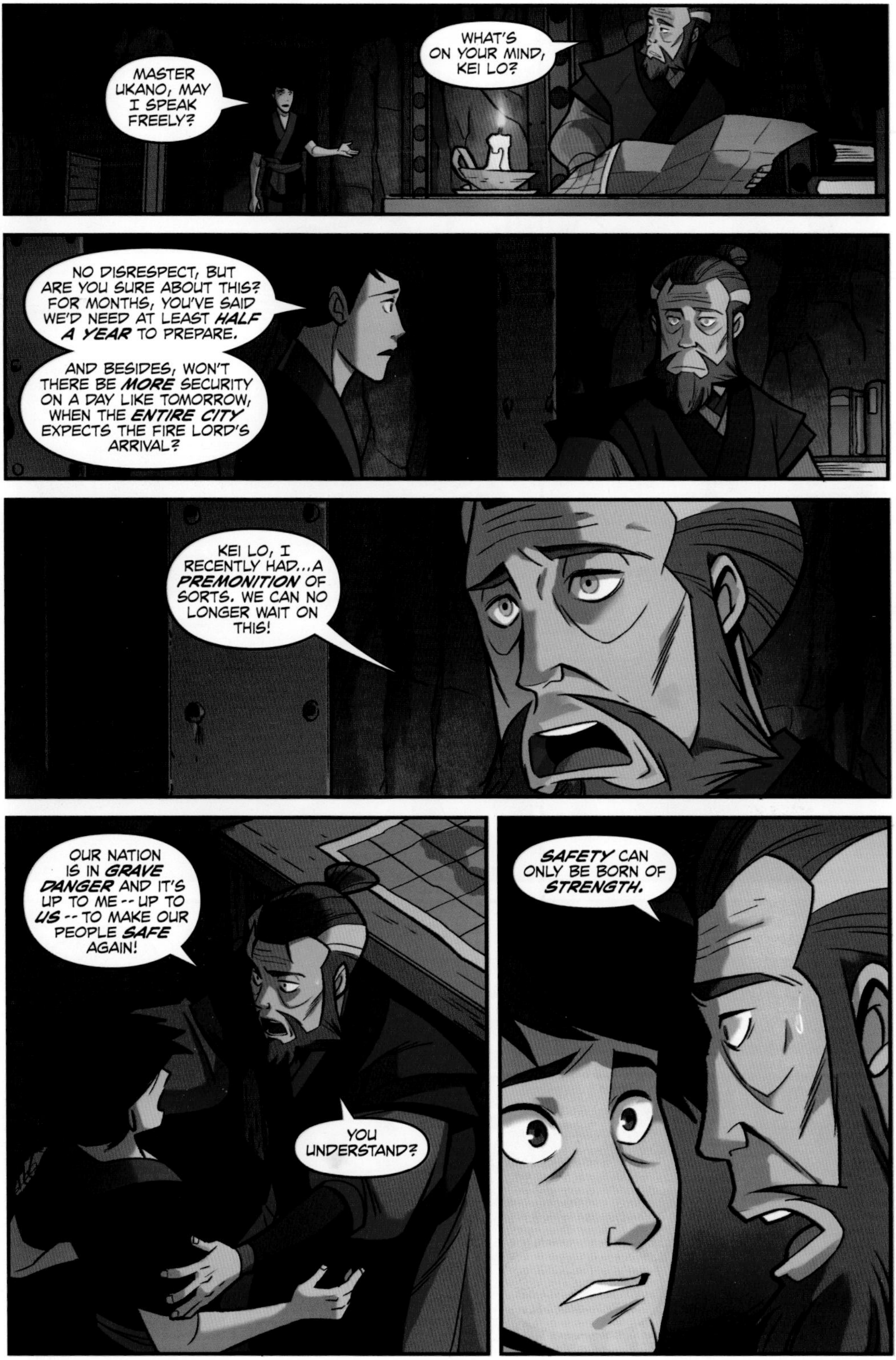
MASTER UKANO, MAY I SPEAK FREELY?
WHAT'S ON YOUR MIND, KEI LO?
NO DISRESPECT, BUT ARE YOU SURE ABOUT THIS? FOR MONTHS, YOU'VE SAID WE'D NEED AT LEAST HALF A YEAR TO PREPARE.
AND BESIDES, WON'T THERE BE MORE SECURITY ON A DAY LIKE TOMORROW, WHEN THE ENTIRE CITY EXPECTS THE FIRE LORD'S ARRIVAL?
KEI LO, I RECENTLY HAD...A PREMONITION OF SORTS. WE CAN NO LONGER WAIT ON THIS!
OUR NATION IS IN GRAVE DANGER AND IT'S UP TO ME -- UP TO US -- TO MAKE OUR PEOPLE SAFE AGAIN!
YOU UNDERSTAND?
SAFETY CAN ONLY BE BORN OF STRENGTH.

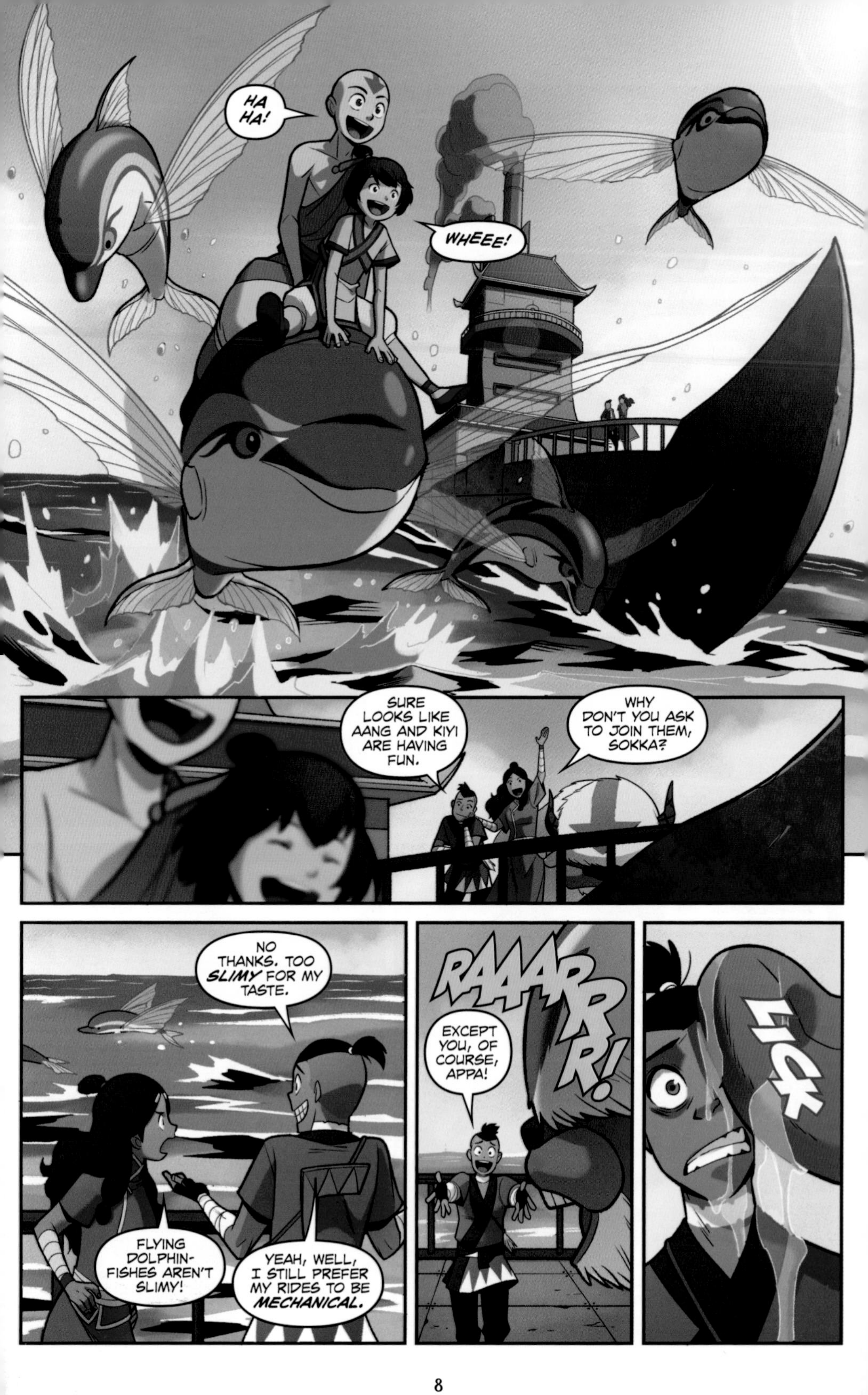
HA HA!
WHEEE!
SURE LOOKS LIKE AANG AND KIYI ARE HAVING FUN.
WHY DON'T YOU ASK TO JOIN THEM, SOKKA?
NO THANKS. TOO SLIMY FOR MY TASTE.
FLYING DOLPHIN-FISHES AREN'T SLIMY!
YEAH, WELL, I STILL PREFER MY RIDES TO BE MECHANICAL.
RAAARRR!
EXCEPT YOU, OF COURSE, APPA!
LICK

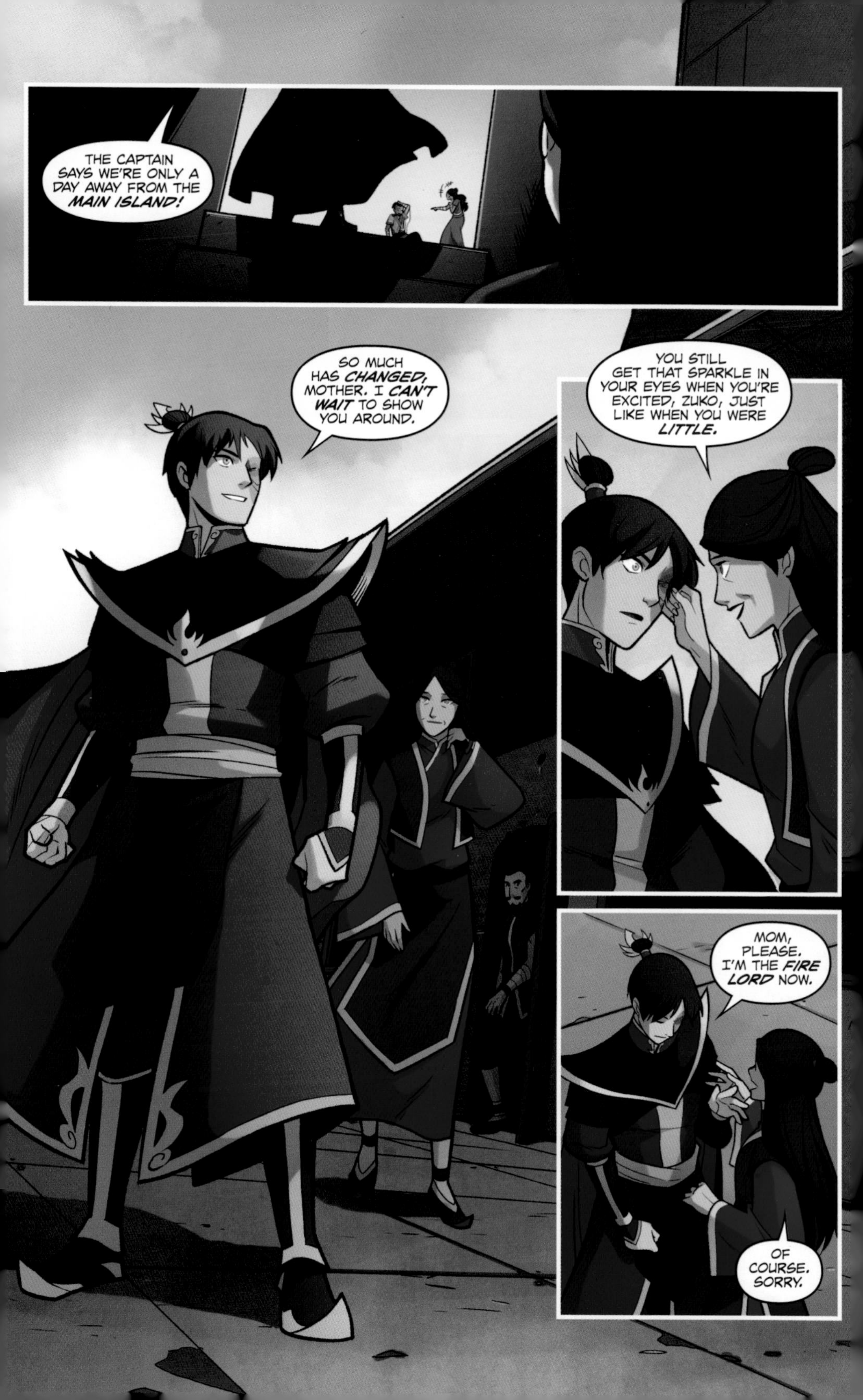
THE CAPTAIN SAYS WE'RE ONLY A DAY AWAY FROM THE MAIN ISLAND!
SO MUCH HAS CHANGED, MOTHER. I CAN'T WAIT TO SHOW YOU AROUND.
YOU STILL GET THAT SPARKLE IN YOUR EYES WHEN YOU'RE EXCITED, ZUKO, JUST LIKE WHEN YOU WERE LITTLE.
MOM, PLEASE. I'M THE FIRE LORD NOW.
OF COURSE. SORRY.

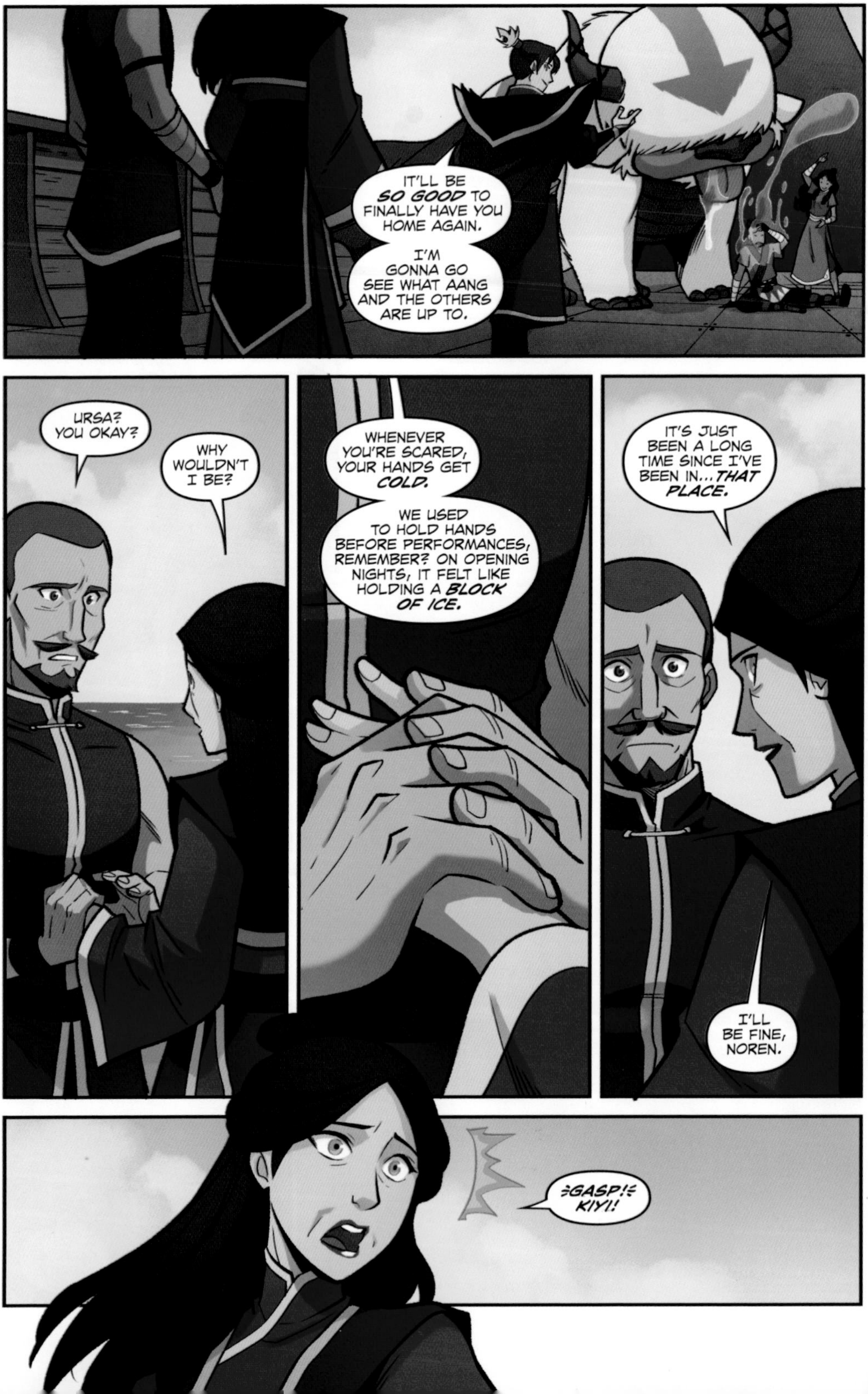
IT'LL BE SO GOOD TO FINALLY HAVE YOU HOME AGAIN.
I'M GONNA GO SEE WHAT AANG AND THE OTHERS ARE UP TO.
URSA? YOU OKAY?
WHY WOULDN'T I BE?
WHENEVER YOU'RE SCARED, YOUR HANDS GET COLD.
WE USED TO HOLD HANDS BEFORE PERFORMANCES, REMEMBER? ON OPENING NIGHTS, IT FELT LIKE HOLDING A BLOCK OF ICE.
IT'S JUST BEEN A LONG TIME SINCE I'VE BEEN IN... THAT PLACE.
I'LL BE FINE, NOREN.
GASP! KIYI!

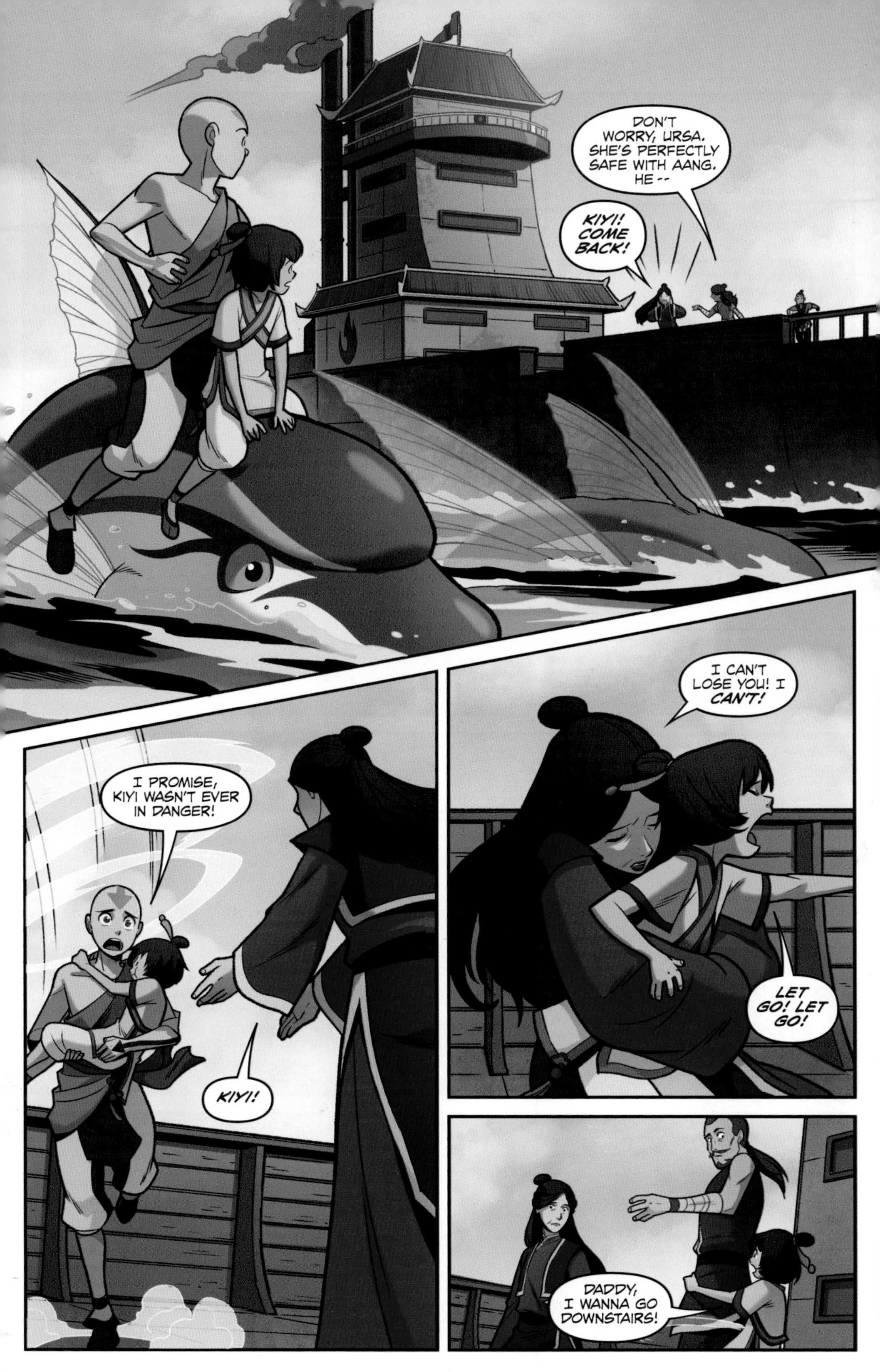
DON'T WORRY, URSA. SHE'S PERFECTLY SAFE WITH AANG. HE --
KIYI! COME BACK!
I PROMISE, KIYI WASN'T EVER IN DANGER!
KIYI!
I CAN'T LOSE YOU! I CAN'T!
LET GO! LET GO!
DADDY, I WANNA GO DOWNSTAIRS!

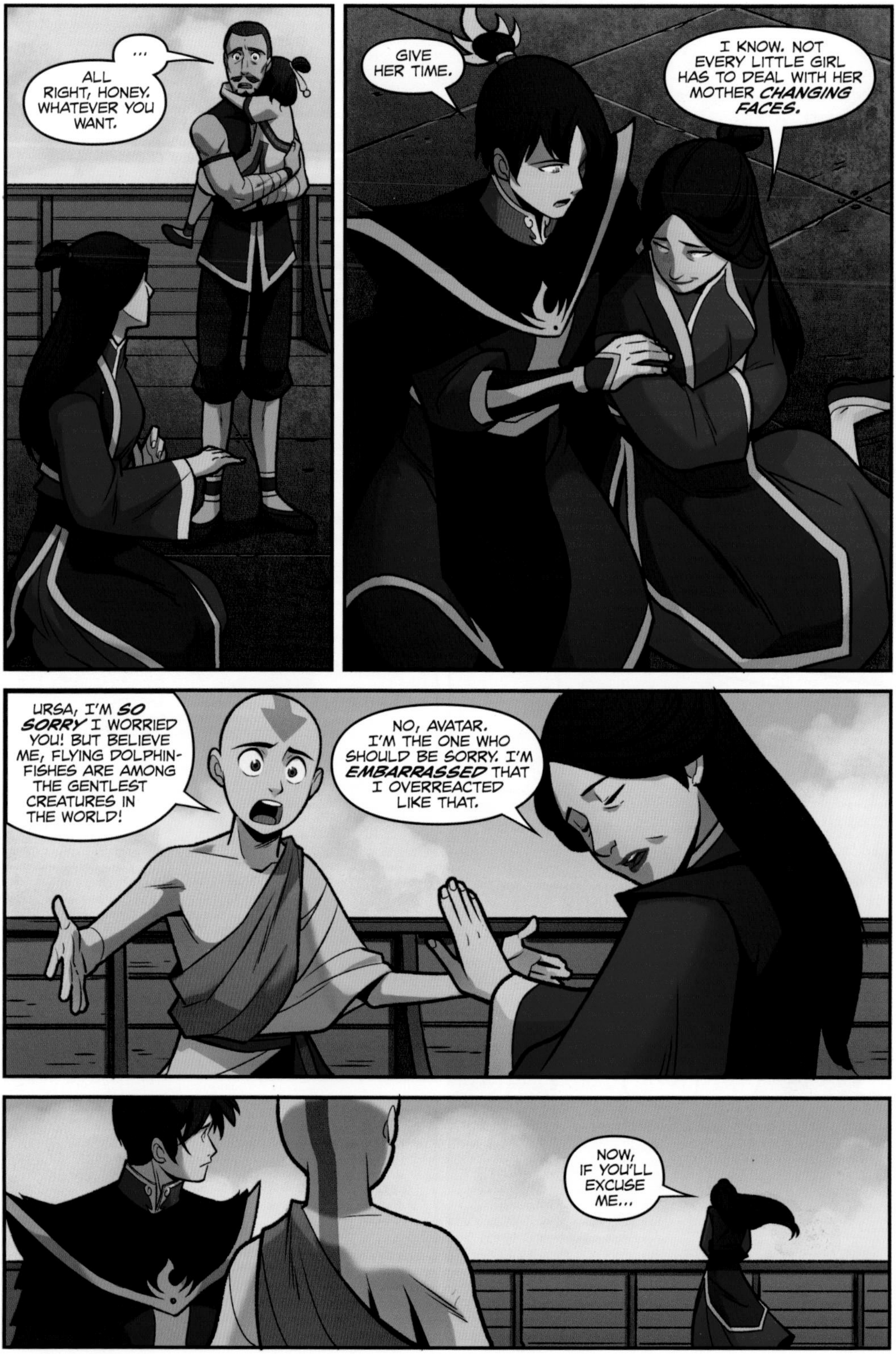
...
ALL RIGHT, HONEY. WHATEVER YOU WANT.
GIVE HER TIME.
I KNOW. NOT EVERY LITTLE GIRL HAS TO DEAL WITH HER MOTHER CHANGING FACES.
URSA, I'M SO SORRY I WORRIED YOU! BUT BELIEVE ME, FLYING DOLPHIN-FISHES ARE AMONG THE GENTLEST CREATURES IN THE WORLD!
NO, AVATAR. I'M THE ONE WHO SHOULD BE SORRY. I'M EMBARRASSED THAT I OVERREACTED LIKE THAT.
NOW, IF YOU'LL EXCUSE ME...

ding!
ding!

TY LEE! IT'S BEEN SO LONG!

MICHI! TOM-TOM! I DIDN'T KNOW YOU GUYS WOULD BE HERE! DOES THAT MEAN MASTER UKANO IS HERE TOO?

NO. NO, HE'S *NOT.*

THE END OF THE WAR WAS HARD ON HIM -- ON ALL OF US, REALLY -- BUT HE *CROSSED THE LINE.* I FINALLY REALIZED THAT HE CARES MORE ABOUT *POLITICS* THAN HIS OWN CHILDREN'S *SAFETY.*

SO WE'RE HERE NOW, ON OUR OWN.

OH. I'M SORRY.

DON'T BE. LIVING WITH MURA HAS BEEN WONDERFUL!

OH, THE PLEASURE'S ALL MINE! NICE HAVING SOME COMPANY FOR A CHANGE!

FLOWERS AREN'T FOR EATING, TOM-TOM.

THEN HOW COME THEY'RE SO *YUMMY?*

13

14

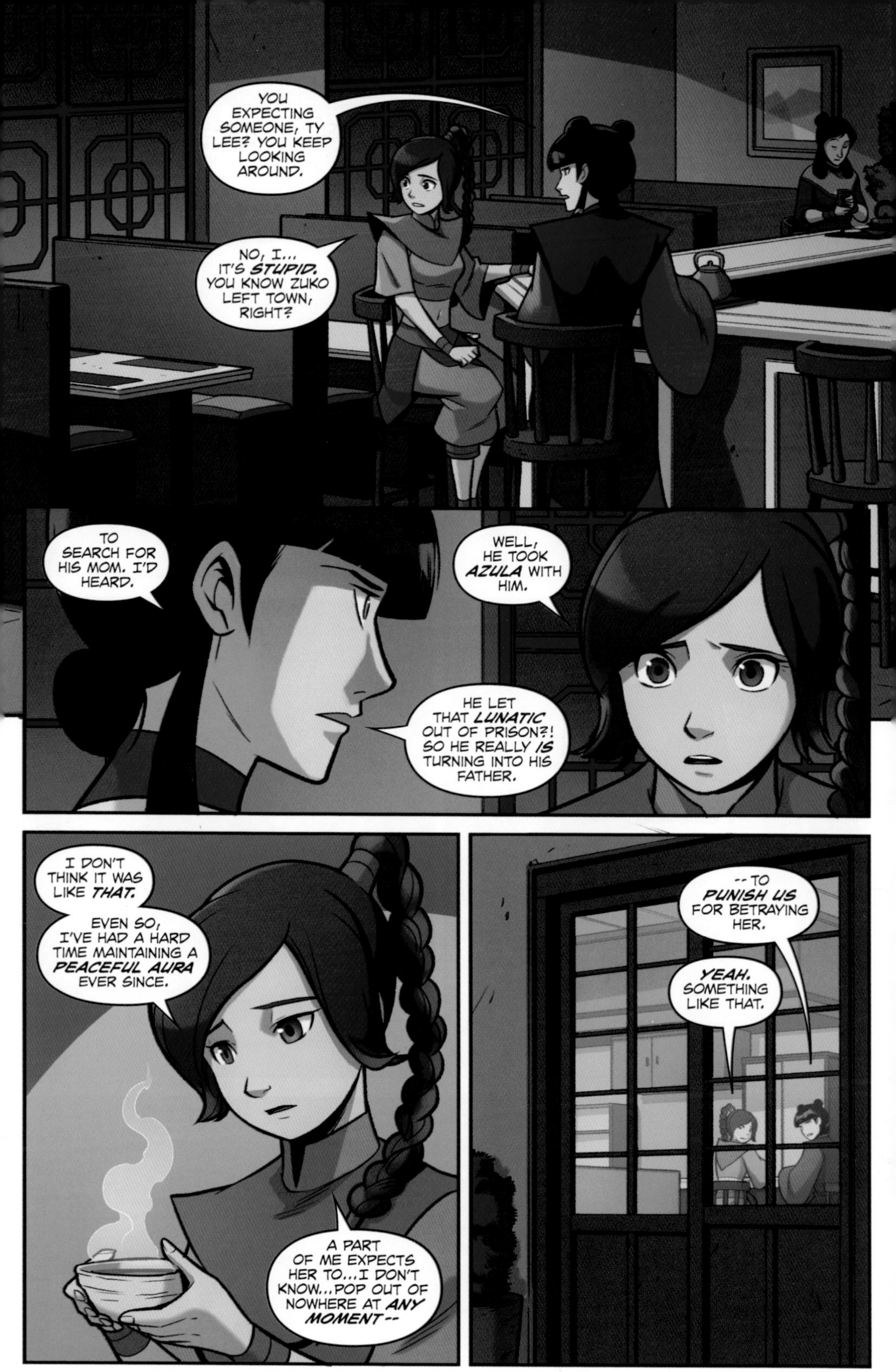

YOU EXPECTING SOMEONE, TY LEE? YOU KEEP LOOKING AROUND.
NO, I... IT'S STUPID. YOU KNOW ZUKO LEFT TOWN, RIGHT?
TO SEARCH FOR HIS MOM. I'D HEARD.
WELL, HE TOOK AZULA WITH HIM.
HE LET THAT LUNATIC OUT OF PRISON?! SO HE REALLY IS TURNING INTO HIS FATHER.
I DON'T THINK IT WAS LIKE THAT.
EVEN SO, I'VE HAD A HARD TIME MAINTAINING A PEACEFUL AURA EVER SINCE.
A PART OF ME EXPECTS HER TO...I DON'T KNOW...POP OUT OF NOWHERE AT ANY MOMENT--
--TO PUNISH US FOR BETRAYING HER.
YEAH. SOMETHING LIKE THAT.

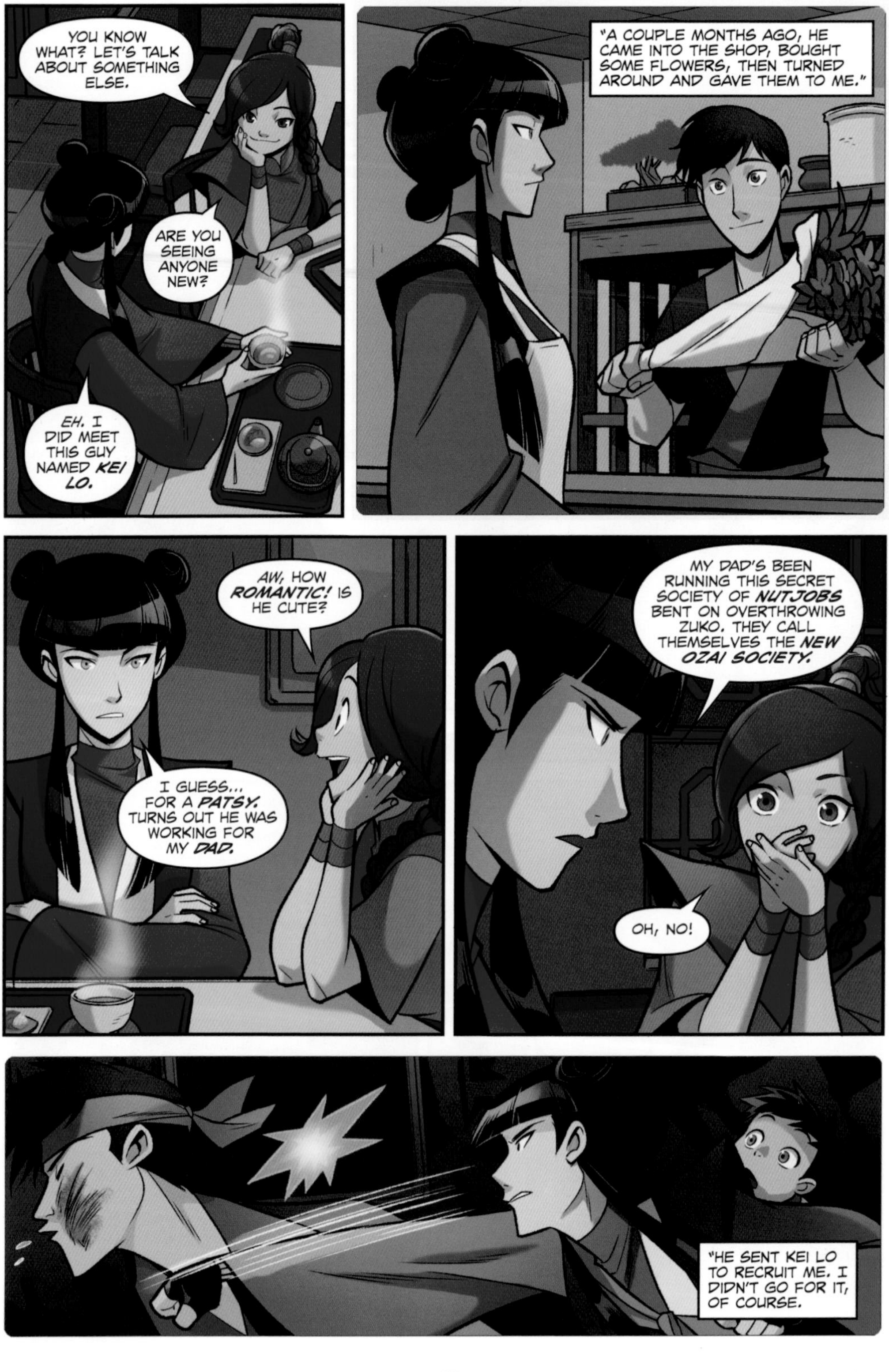
YOU KNOW WHAT? LET'S TALK ABOUT SOMETHING ELSE.
ARE YOU SEEING ANYONE NEW?
EH. I DID MEET THIS GUY NAMED KEI LO.
"A COUPLE MONTHS AGO, HE CAME INTO THE SHOP, BOUGHT SOME FLOWERS, THEN TURNED AROUND AND GAVE THEM TO ME."
AW, HOW ROMANTIC! IS HE CUTE?
I GUESS... FOR A PATSY. TURNS OUT HE WAS WORKING FOR MY DAD.
MY DAD'S BEEN RUNNING THIS SECRET SOCIETY OF NUTJOBS BENT ON OVERTHROWING ZUKO. THEY CALL THEMSELVES THE NEW OZAI SOCIETY.
OH, NO!
"HE SENT KEI LO TO RECRUIT ME. I DIDN'T GO FOR IT, OF COURSE.

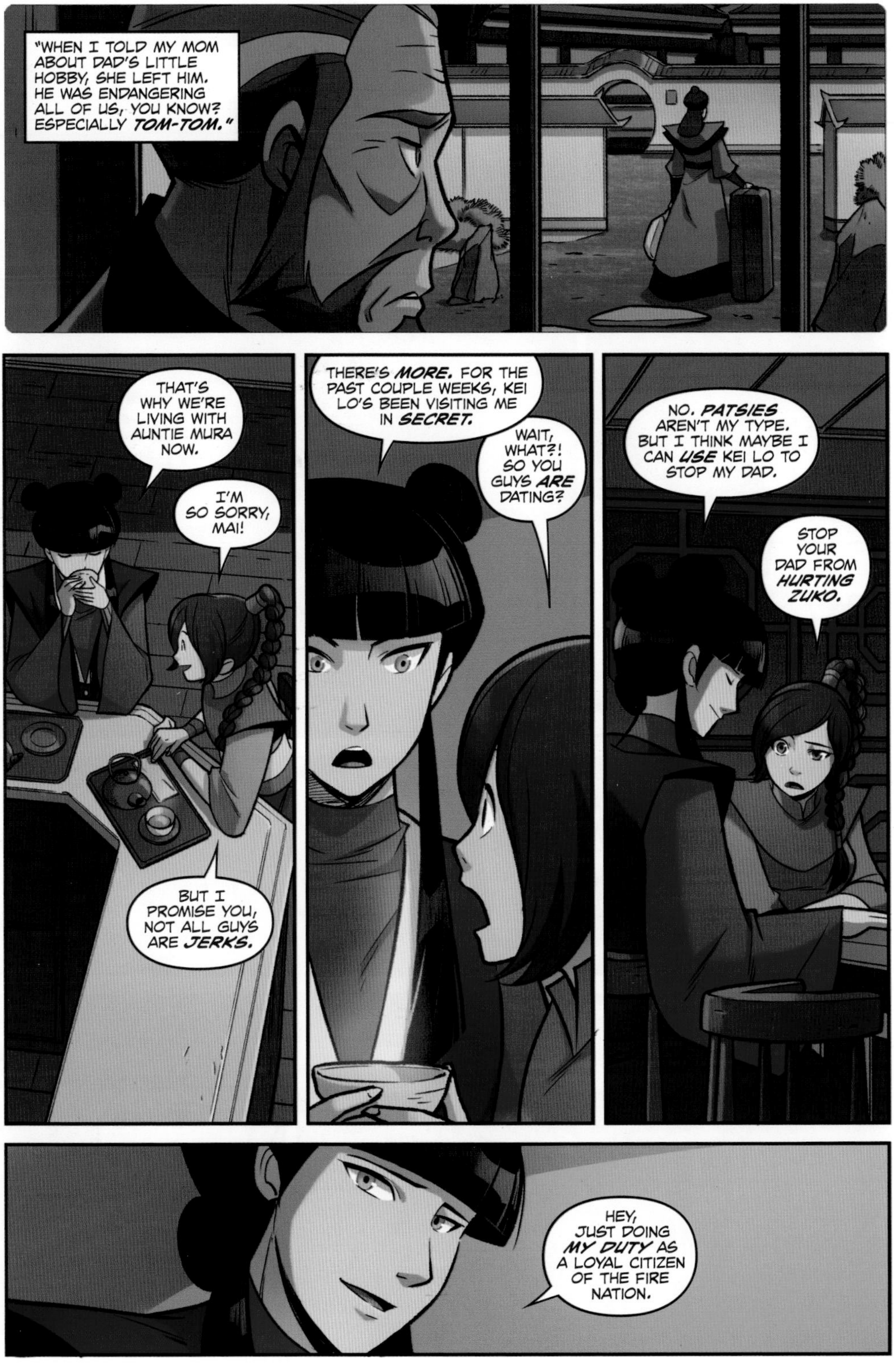
"WHEN I TOLD MY MOM ABOUT DAD'S LITTLE HOBBY, SHE LEFT HIM. HE WAS ENDANGERING ALL OF US, YOU KNOW? ESPECIALLY TOM-TOM."
THAT'S WHY WE'RE LIVING WITH AUNTIE MURA NOW.
I'M SO SORRY, MAI!
BUT I PROMISE YOU, NOT ALL GUYS ARE JERKS.
THERE'S MORE. FOR THE PAST COUPLE WEEKS, KEI LO'S BEEN VISITING ME IN SECRET.
WAIT, WHAT?! SO YOU GUYS ARE DATING?
NO. PATSIES AREN'T MY TYPE. BUT I THINK MAYBE I CAN USE KEI LO TO STOP MY DAD.
STOP YOUR DAD FROM HURTING ZUKO.
HEY, JUST DOING MY DUTY AS A LOYAL CITIZEN OF THE FIRE NATION.

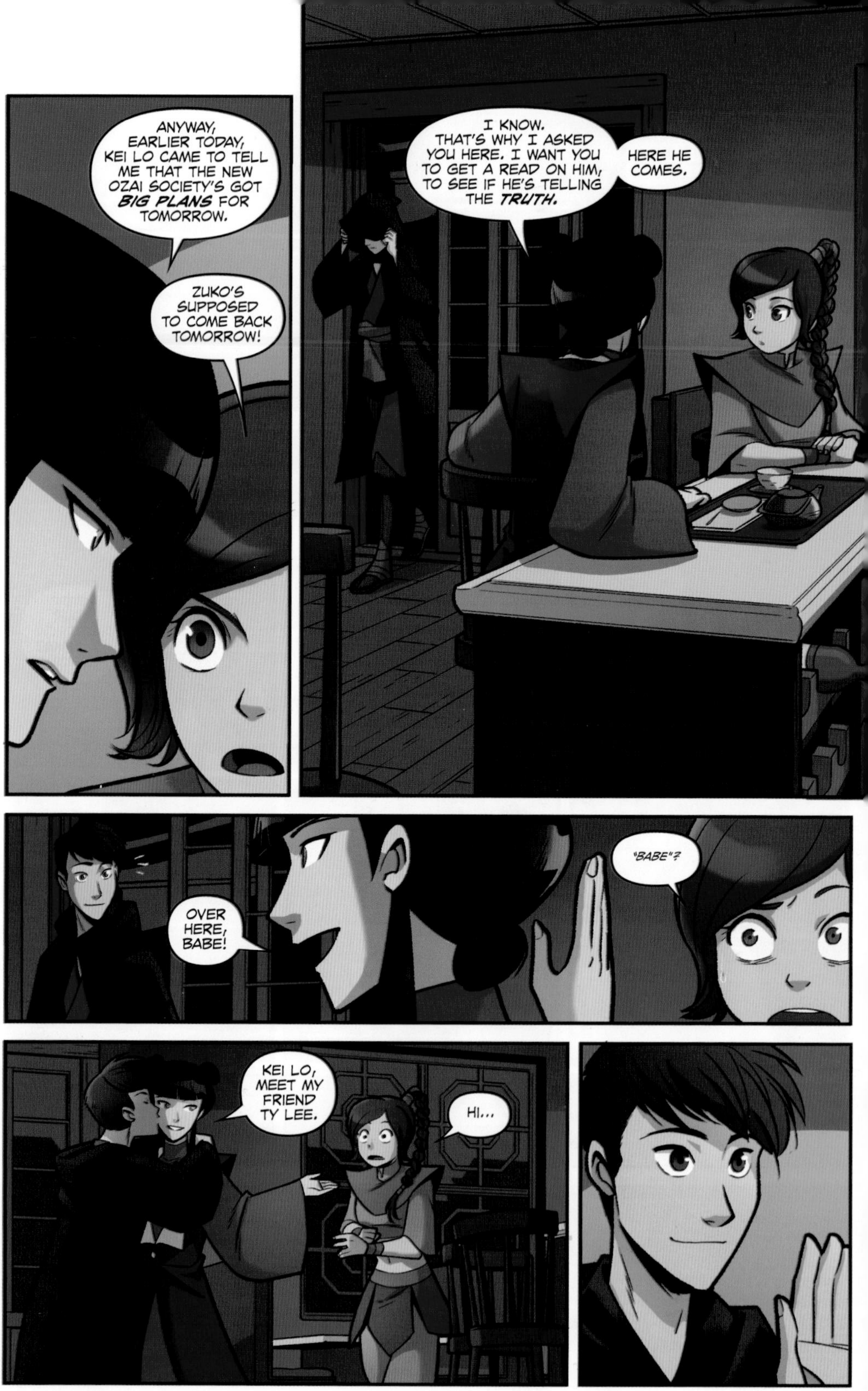
ANYWAY, EARLIER TODAY, KEI LO CAME TO TELL ME THAT THE NEW OZAI SOCIETY'S GOT BIG PLANS FOR TOMORROW.
ZUKO'S SUPPOSED TO COME BACK TOMORROW!
I KNOW. THAT'S WHY I ASKED YOU HERE. I WANT YOU TO GET A READ ON HIM, TO SEE IF HE'S TELLING THE TRUTH.
HERE HE COMES.
OVER HERE, BABE!
"BABE"?
KEI LO, MEET MY FRIEND TY LEE.
HI...

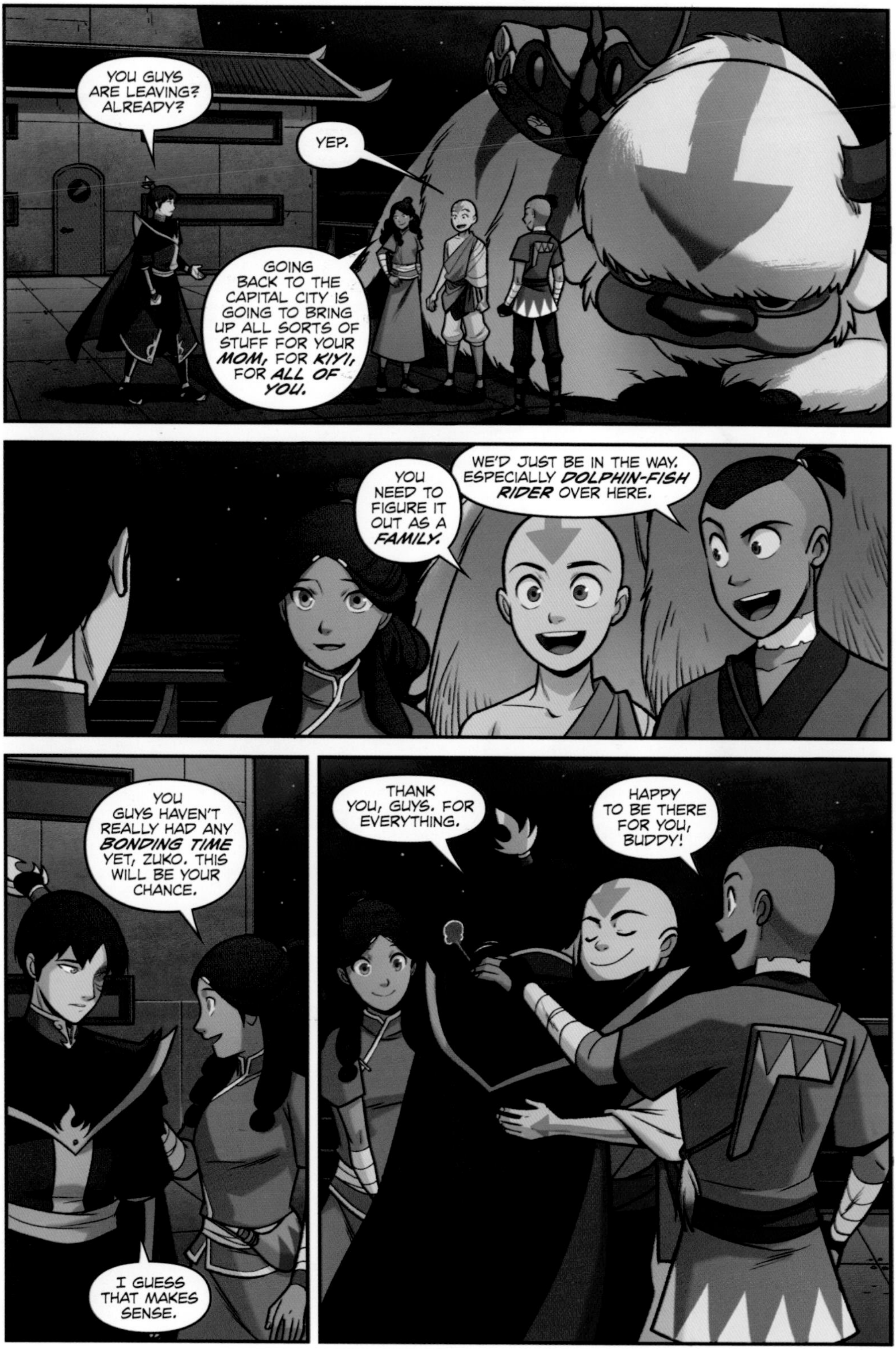
YOU GUYS ARE LEAVING? ALREADY?
YEP.
GOING BACK TO THE CAPITAL CITY IS GOING TO BRING UP ALL SORTS OF STUFF FOR YOUR MOM, FOR KIYI, FOR ALL OF YOU.
YOU NEED TO FIGURE IT OUT AS A FAMILY.
WE'D JUST BE IN THE WAY. ESPECIALLY DOLPHIN-FISH RIDER OVER HERE.
YOU GUYS HAVEN'T REALLY HAD ANY BONDING TIME YET, ZUKO. THIS WILL BE YOUR CHANCE.
I GUESS THAT MAKES SENSE.
THANK YOU, GUYS. FOR EVERYTHING.
HAPPY TO BE THERE FOR YOU, BUDDY!

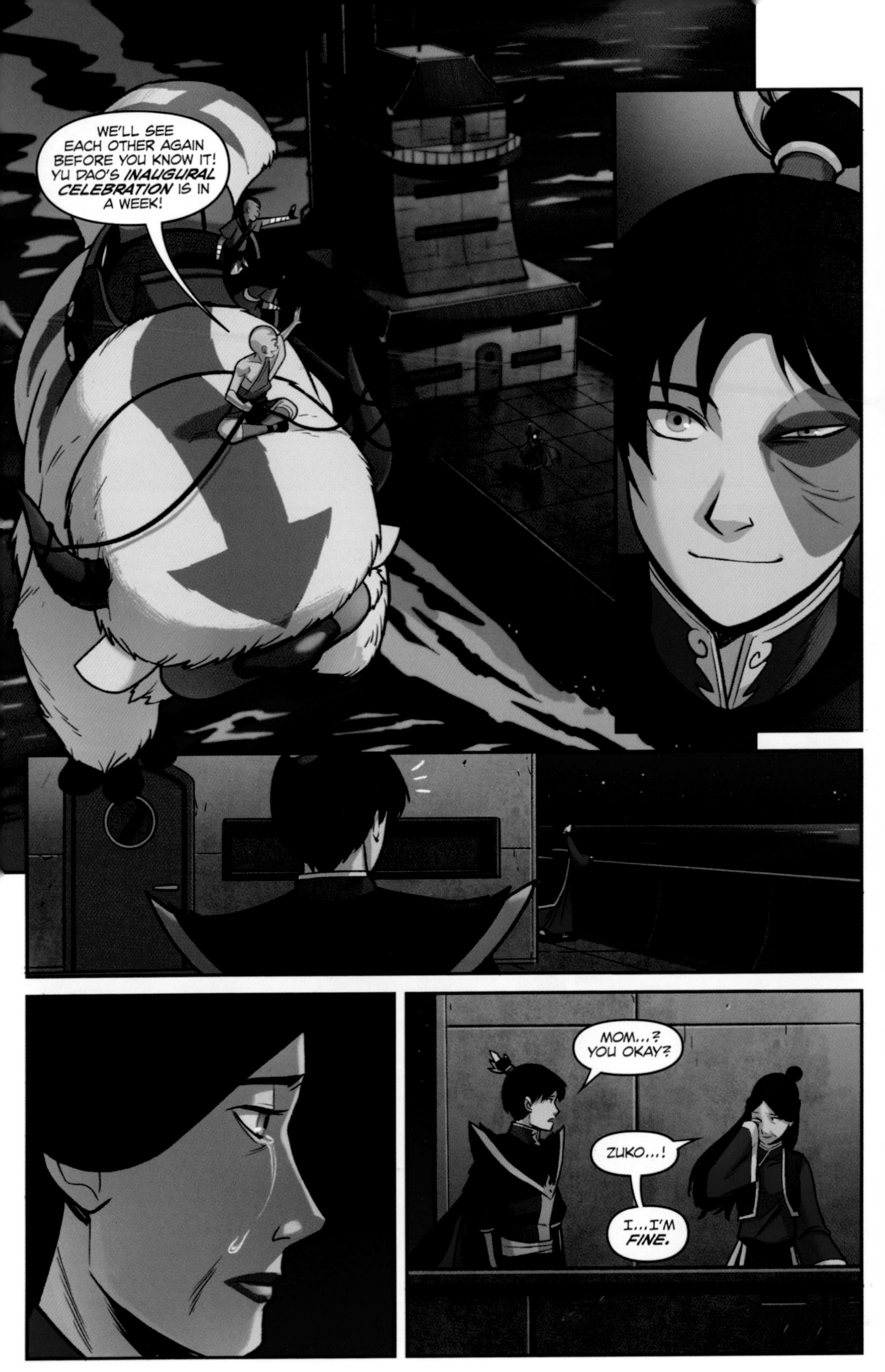
WE'LL SEE EACH OTHER AGAIN BEFORE YOU KNOW IT! YU DAO'S INAUGURAL CELEBRATION IS IN A WEEK!
MOM...? YOU OKAY?
ZUKO...!
I...I'M FINE.

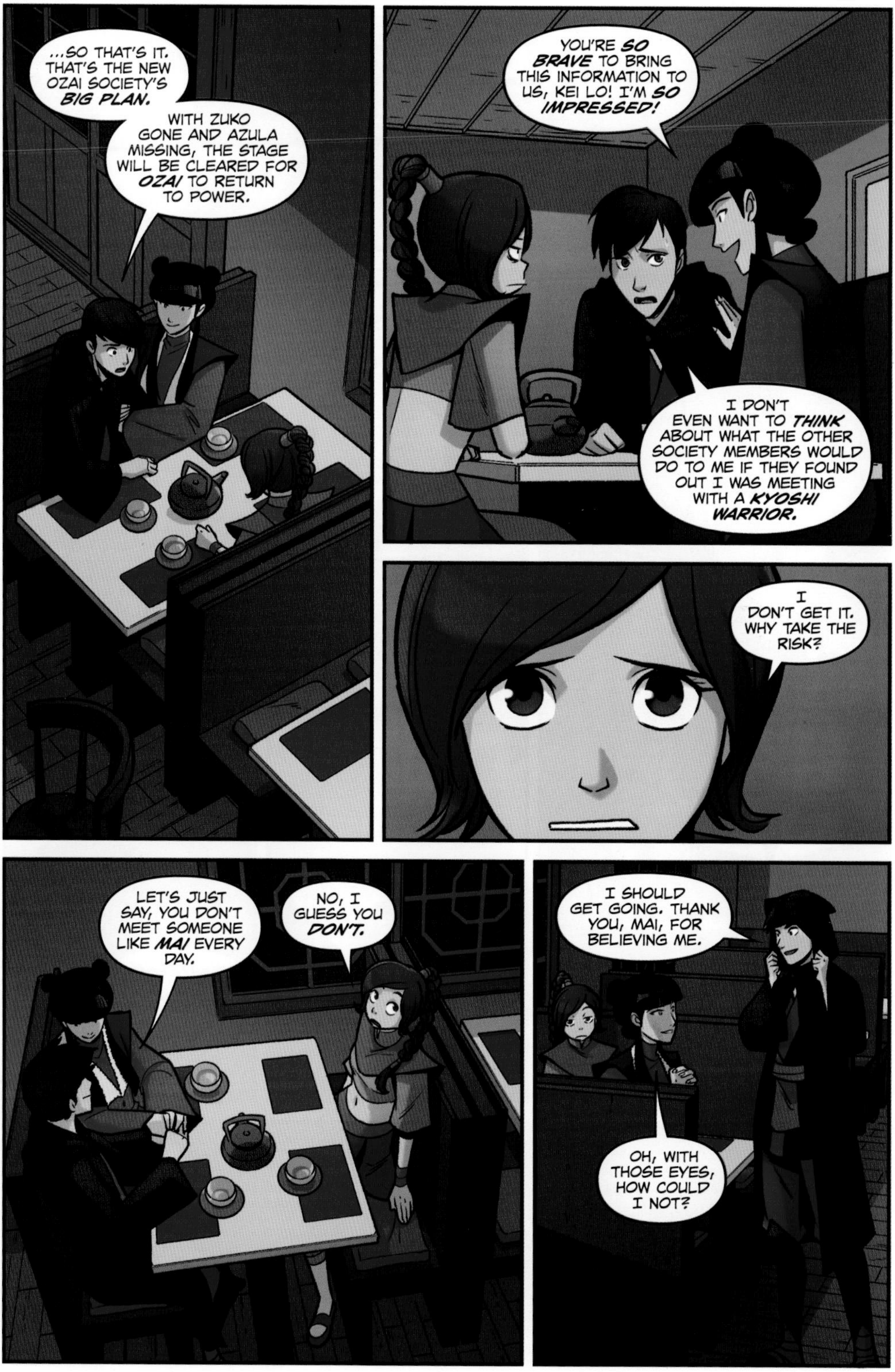
...SO THAT'S IT. THAT'S THE NEW OZAI SOCIETY'S BIG PLAN.
WITH ZUKO GONE AND AZULA MISSING, THE STAGE WILL BE CLEARED FOR OZAI TO RETURN TO POWER.
YOU'RE SO BRAVE TO BRING THIS INFORMATION TO US, KEI LO! I'M SO IMPRESSED!
I DON'T EVEN WANT TO THINK ABOUT WHAT THE OTHER SOCIETY MEMBERS WOULD DO TO ME IF THEY FOUND OUT I WAS MEETING WITH A KYOSHI WARRIOR.
I DON'T GET IT. WHY TAKE THE RISK?
LET'S JUST SAY, YOU DON'T MEET SOMEONE LIKE MAI EVERY DAY.
NO, I GUESS YOU DON'T.
I SHOULD GET GOING. THANK YOU, MAI, FOR BELIEVING ME.
OH, WITH THOSE EYES, HOW COULD I NOT?

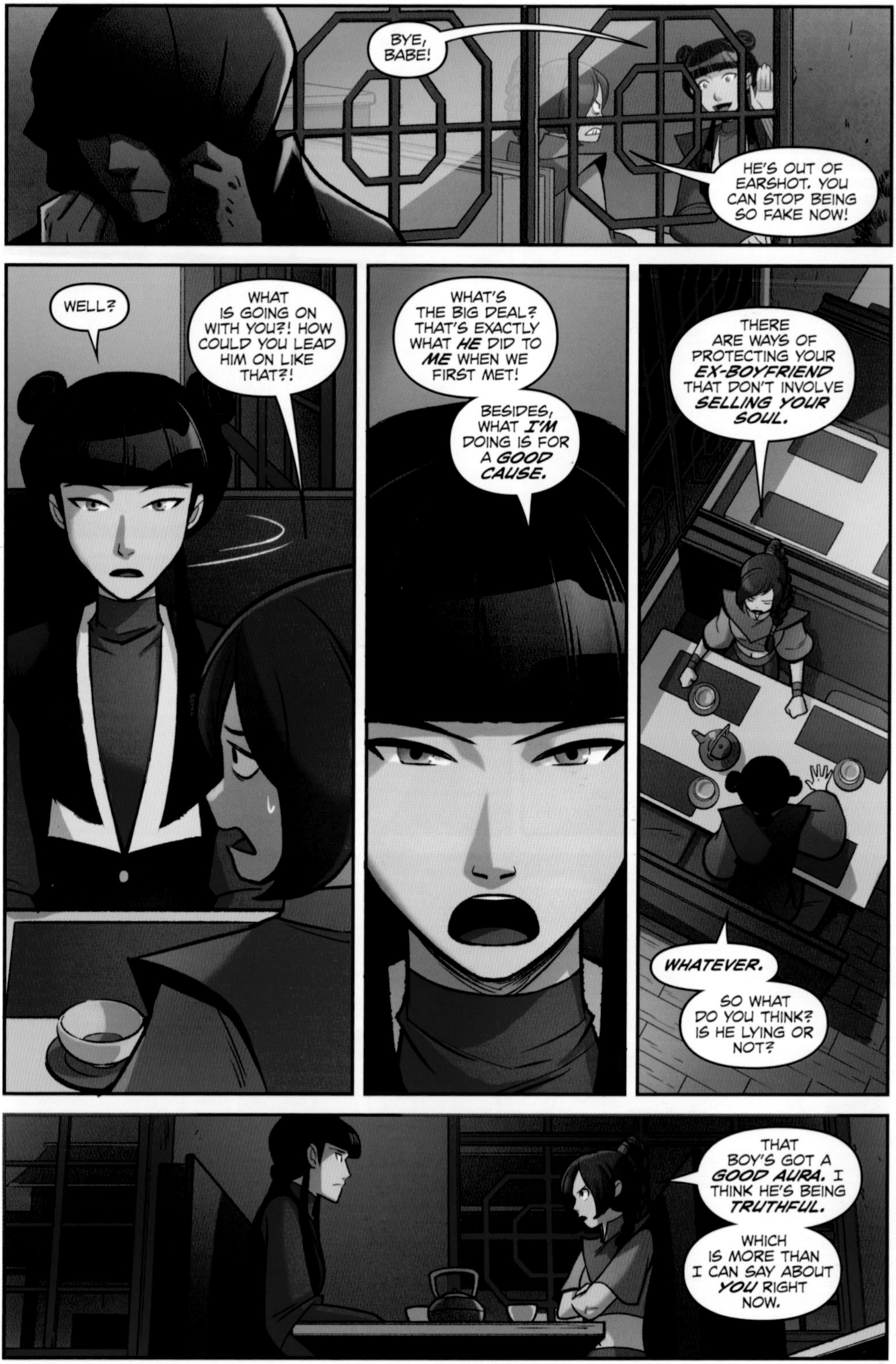
BYE, BABE!
HE'S OUT OF EARSHOT. YOU CAN STOP BEING SO FAKE NOW!
WELL?
WHAT IS GOING ON WITH YOU?! HOW COULD YOU LEAD HIM ON LIKE THAT?!
WHAT'S THE BIG DEAL? THAT'S EXACTLY WHAT HE DID TO ME WHEN WE FIRST MET!
BESIDES, WHAT I'M DOING IS FOR A GOOD CAUSE.
THERE ARE WAYS OF PROTECTING YOUR EX-BOYFRIEND THAT DON'T INVOLVE SELLING YOUR SOUL.
WHATEVER.
SO WHAT DO YOU THINK? IS HE LYING OR NOT?
THAT BOY'S GOT A GOOD AURA. I THINK HE'S BEING TRUTHFUL.
WHICH IS MORE THAN I CAN SAY ABOUT YOU RIGHT NOW.

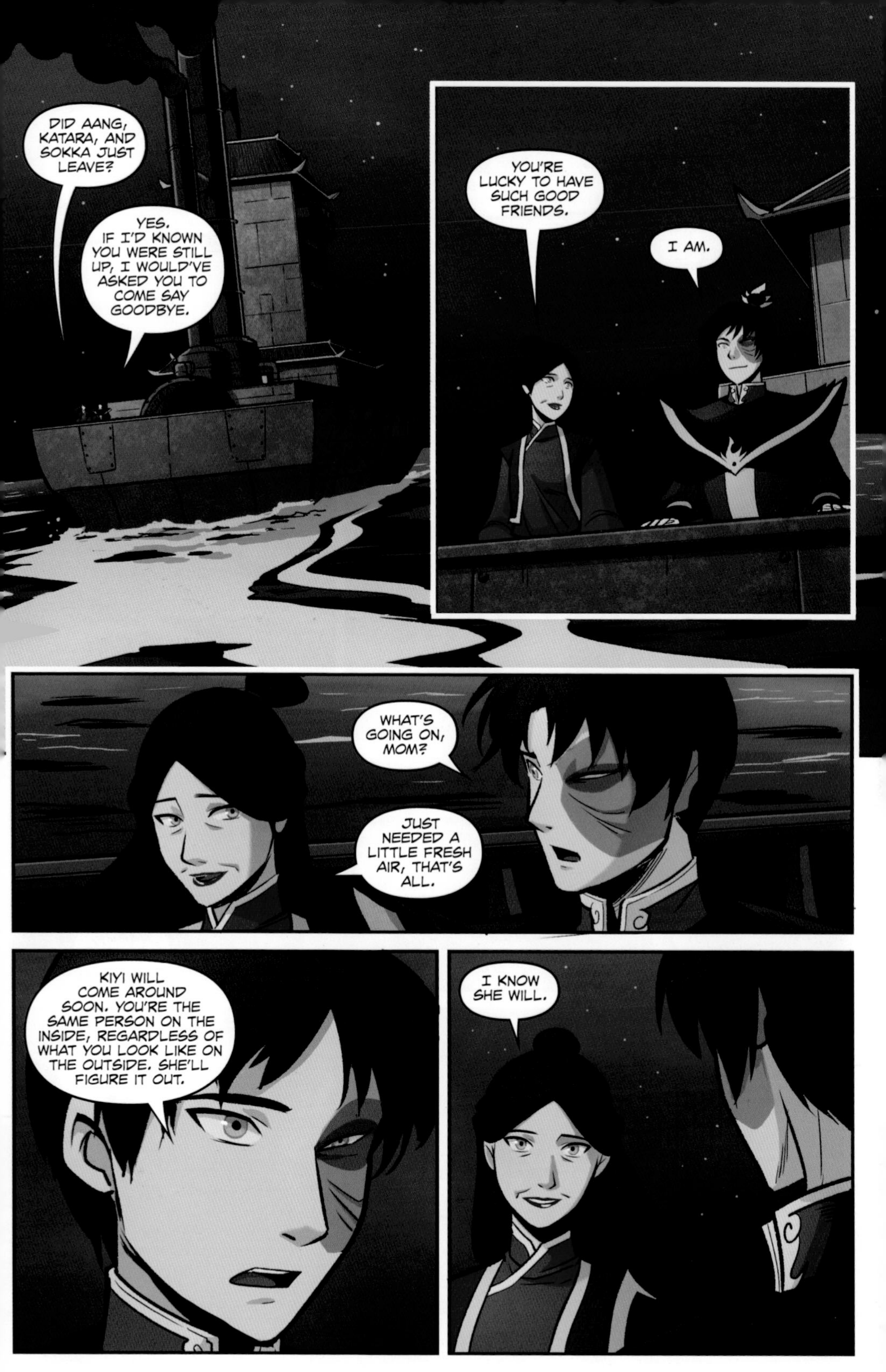
DID AANG, KATARA, AND SOKKA JUST LEAVE?
YES. IF I'D KNOWN YOU WERE STILL UP, I WOULD'VE ASKED YOU TO COME SAY GOODBYE.
YOU'RE LUCKY TO HAVE SUCH GOOD FRIENDS.
I AM.
WHAT'S GOING ON, MOM?
JUST NEEDED A LITTLE FRESH AIR, THAT'S ALL.
KIYI WILL COME AROUND SOON. YOU'RE THE SAME PERSON ON THE INSIDE, REGARDLESS OF WHAT YOU LOOK LIKE ON THE OUTSIDE. SHE'LL FIGURE IT OUT.
I KNOW SHE WILL.

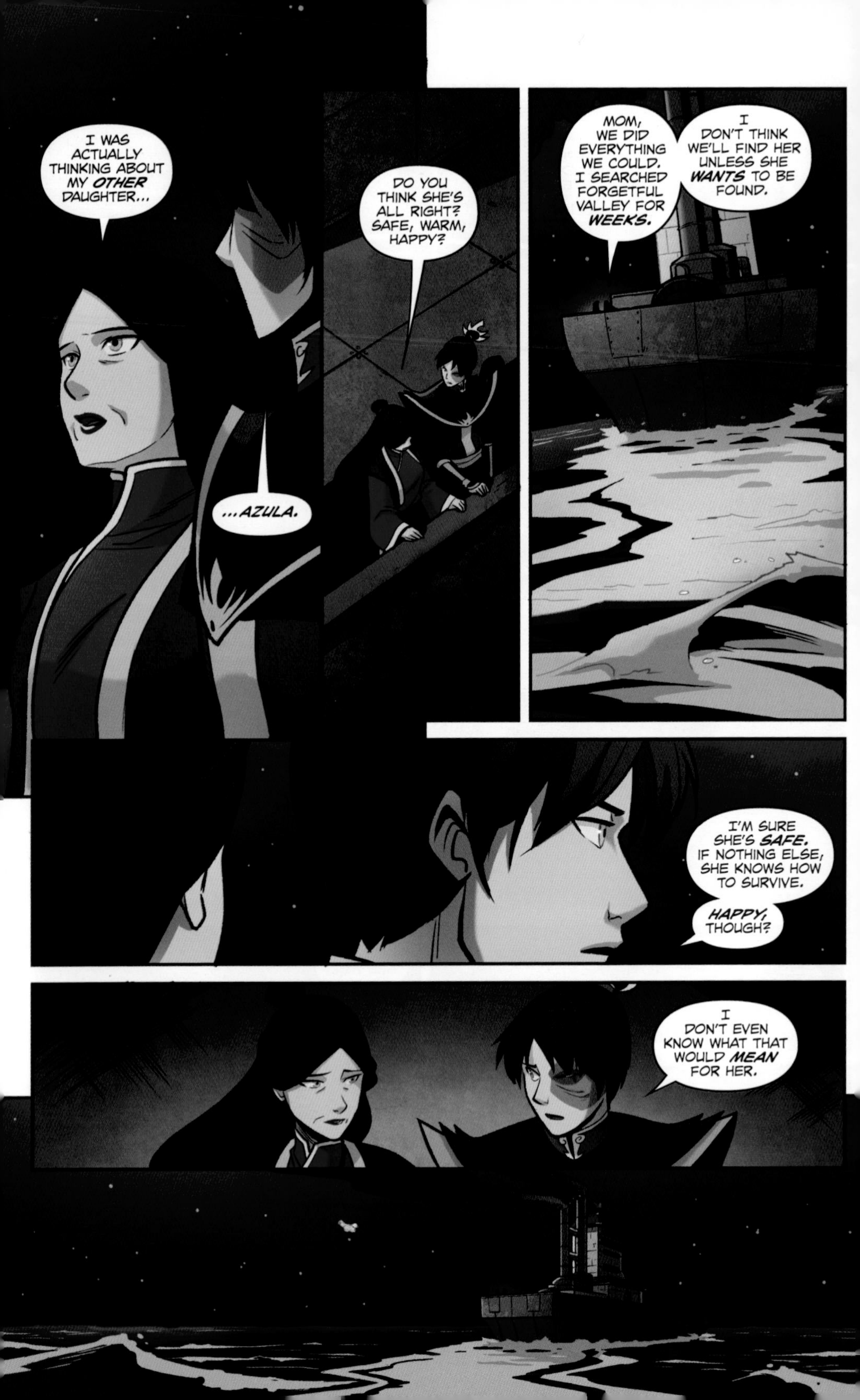
I WAS ACTUALLY THINKING ABOUT MY *OTHER* DAUGHTER...
...*AZULA.*
DO YOU THINK SHE'S ALL RIGHT? SAFE, WARM, HAPPY?
MOM, WE DID EVERYTHING WE COULD. I SEARCHED FORGETFUL VALLEY FOR *WEEKS.*
I DON'T THINK WE'LL FIND HER UNLESS SHE *WANTS* TO BE FOUND.
I'M SURE SHE'S *SAFE.* IF NOTHING ELSE, SHE KNOWS HOW TO SURVIVE.
HAPPY, THOUGH?
I DON'T EVEN KNOW WHAT THAT WOULD *MEAN* FOR HER.

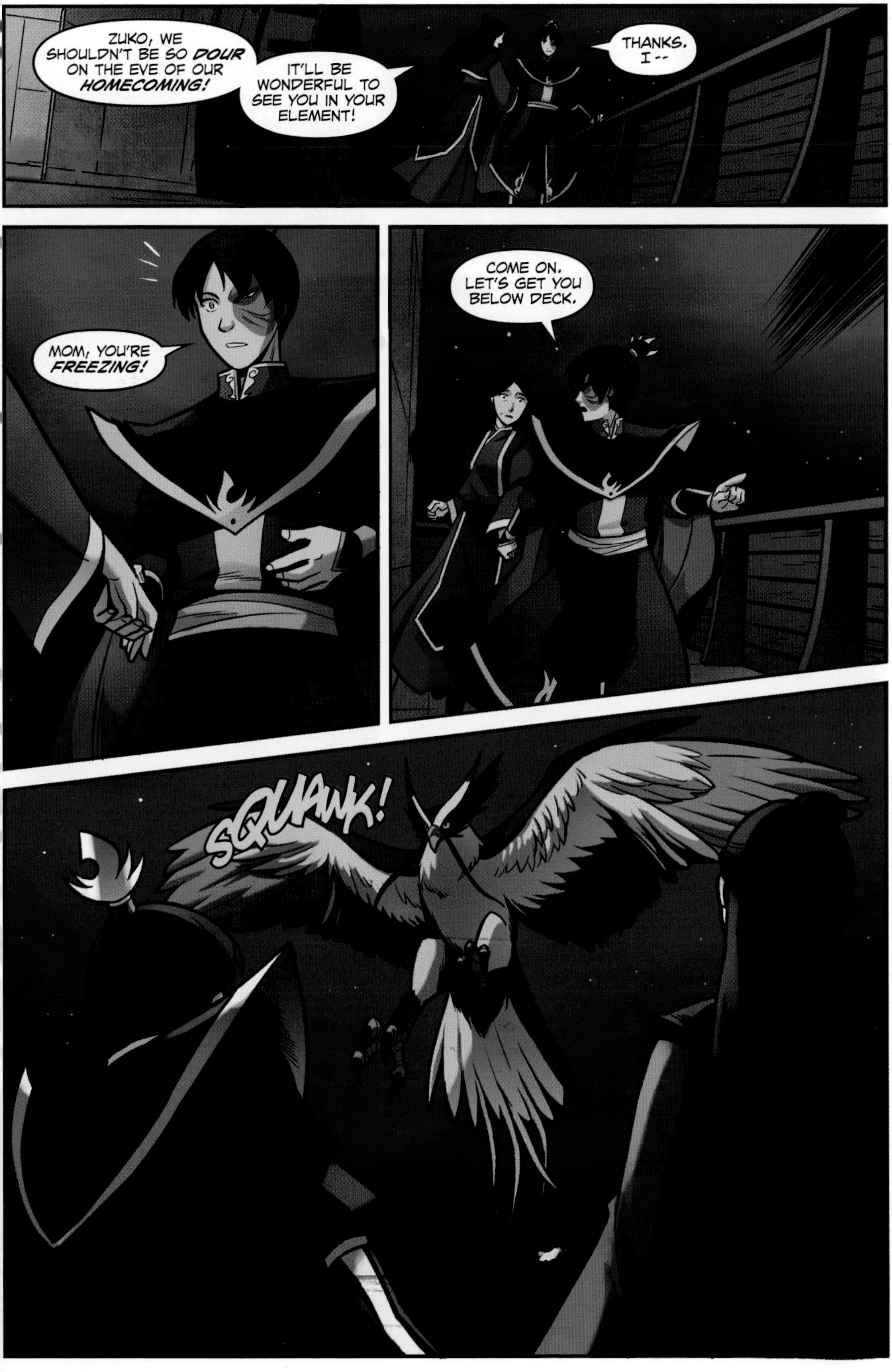
ZUKO, WE SHOULDN'T BE SO DOUR ON THE EVE OF OUR HOMECOMING!
IT'LL BE WONDERFUL TO SEE YOU IN YOUR ELEMENT!
THANKS. I--
MOM, YOU'RE FREEZING!
COME ON. LET'S GET YOU BELOW DECK.
SQUAWK!

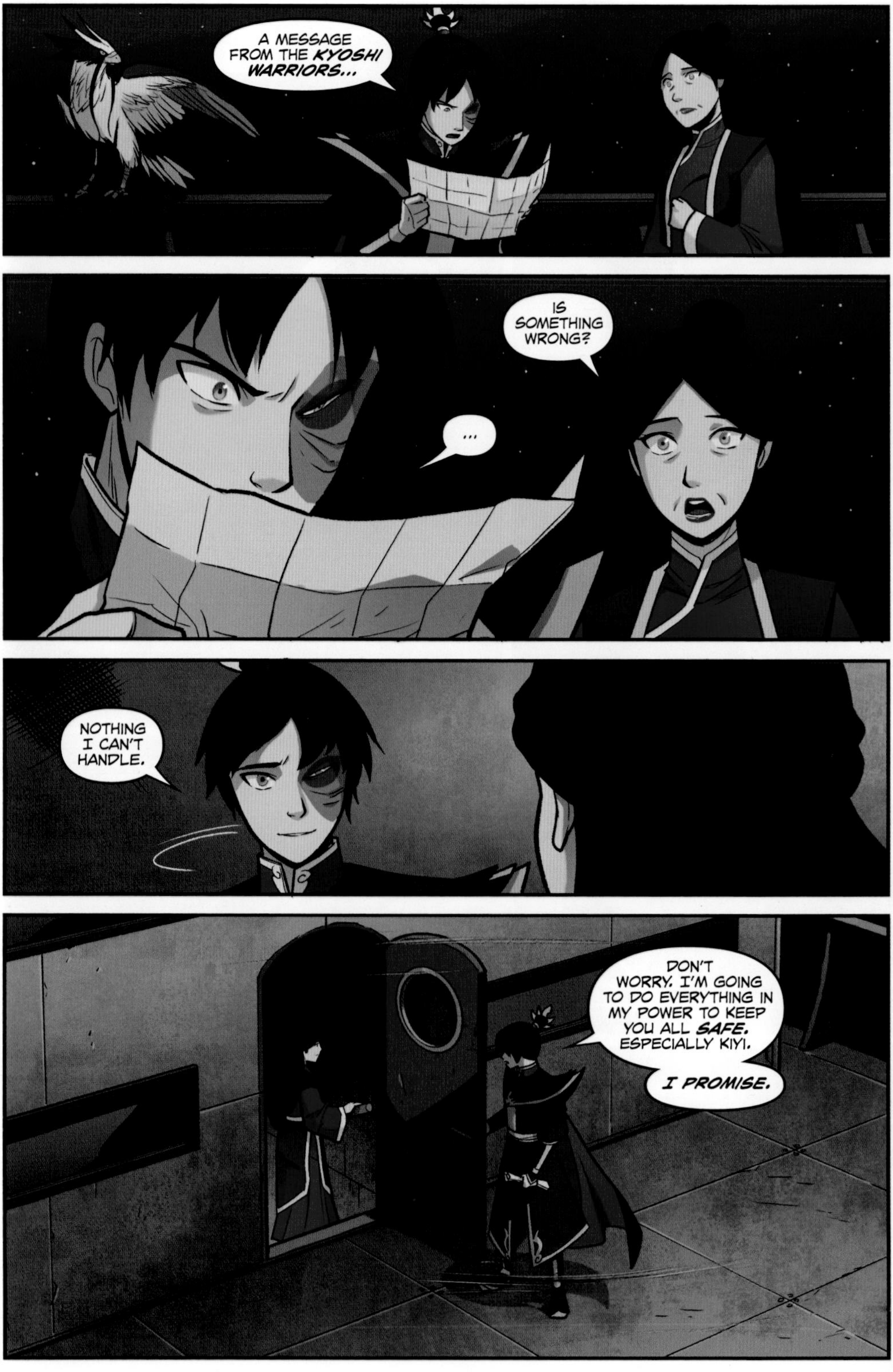
A MESSAGE FROM THE KYOSHI WARRIORS...
IS SOMETHING WRONG?
...
NOTHING I CAN'T HANDLE.
DON'T WORRY. I'M GOING TO DO EVERYTHING IN MY POWER TO KEEP YOU ALL SAFE. ESPECIALLY KIYI.
I PROMISE.

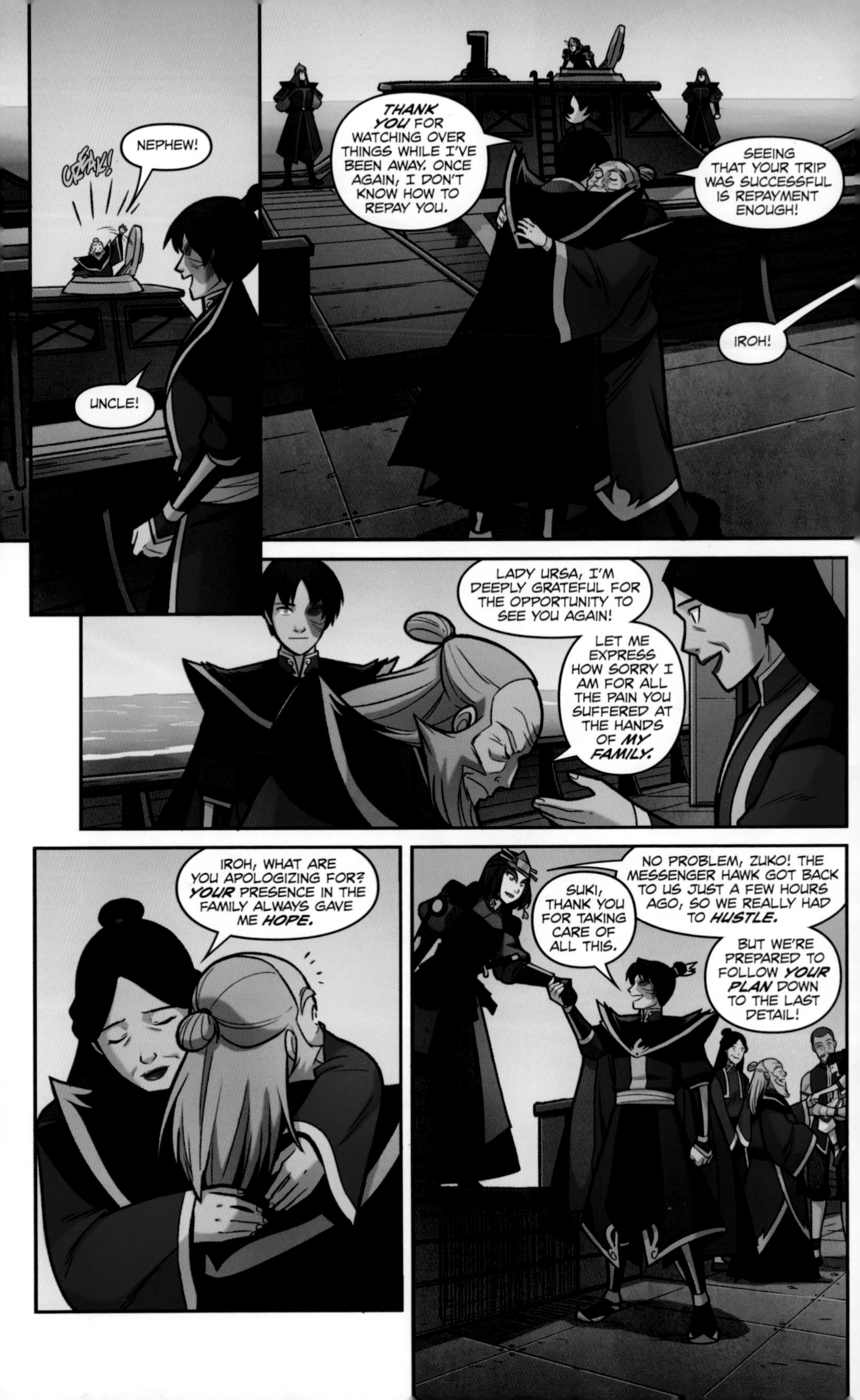
CREAK!
NEPHEW!
UNCLE!
THANK YOU FOR WATCHING OVER THINGS WHILE I'VE BEEN AWAY. ONCE AGAIN, I DON'T KNOW HOW TO REPAY YOU.
SEEING THAT YOUR TRIP WAS SUCCESSFUL IS REPAYMENT ENOUGH!
IROH!
LADY URSA, I'M DEEPLY GRATEFUL FOR THE OPPORTUNITY TO SEE YOU AGAIN!
LET ME EXPRESS HOW SORRY I AM FOR ALL THE PAIN YOU SUFFERED AT THE HANDS OF MY FAMILY.
IROH, WHAT ARE YOU APOLOGIZING FOR? YOUR PRESENCE IN THE FAMILY ALWAYS GAVE ME HOPE.
SUKI, THANK YOU FOR TAKING CARE OF ALL THIS.
NO PROBLEM, ZUKO! THE MESSENGER HAWK GOT BACK TO US JUST A FEW HOURS AGO, SO WE REALLY HAD TO HUSTLE.
BUT WE'RE PREPARED TO FOLLOW YOUR PLAN DOWN TO THE LAST DETAIL!

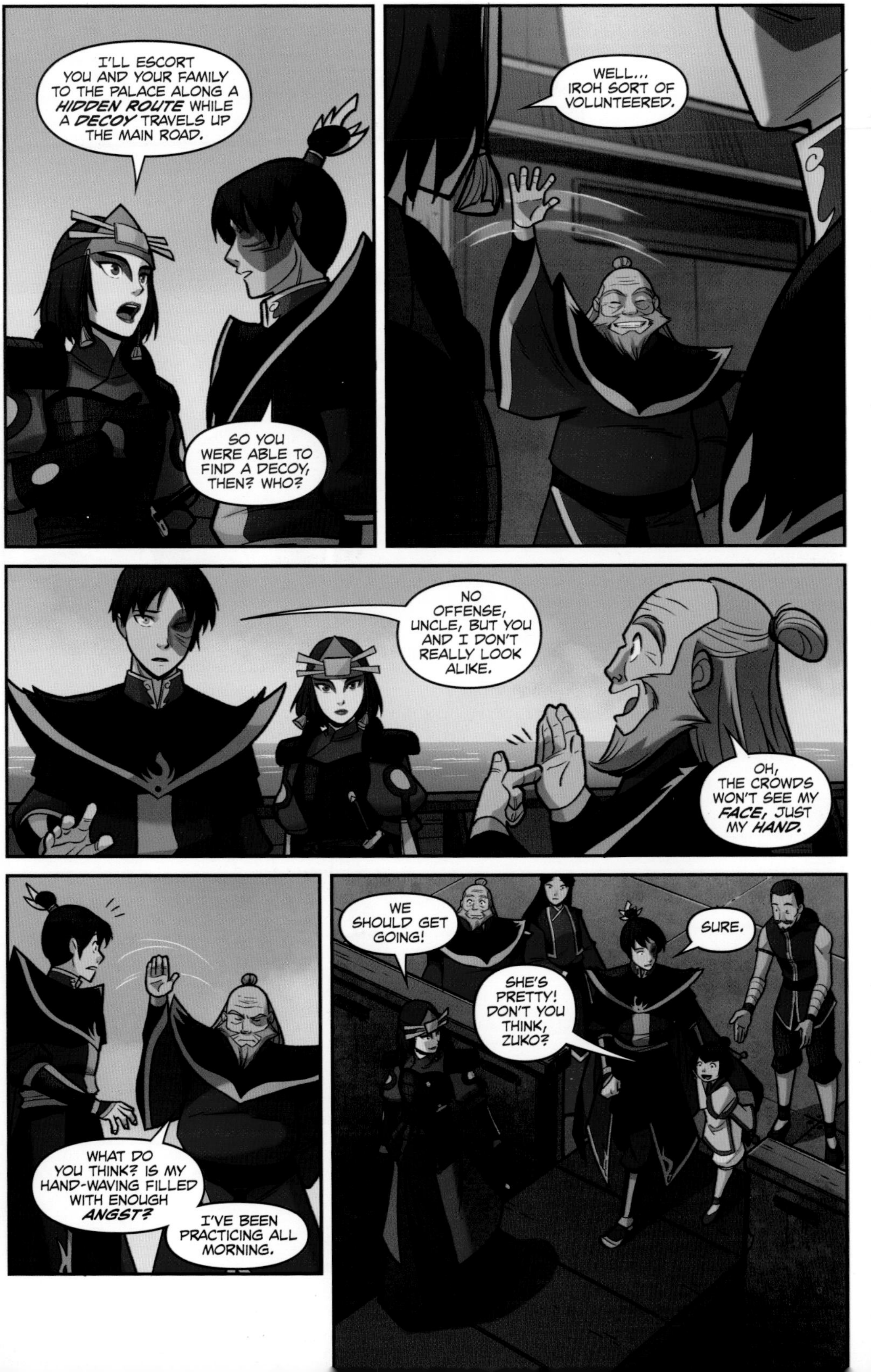
I'LL ESCORT YOU AND YOUR FAMILY TO THE PALACE ALONG A HIDDEN ROUTE WHILE A DECOY TRAVELS UP THE MAIN ROAD.
SO YOU WERE ABLE TO FIND A DECOY, THEN? WHO?
WELL... IROH SORT OF VOLUNTEERED.
NO OFFENSE, UNCLE, BUT YOU AND I DON'T REALLY LOOK ALIKE.
OH, THE CROWDS WON'T SEE MY FACE, JUST MY HAND.
WHAT DO YOU THINK? IS MY HAND-WAVING FILLED WITH ENOUGH ANGST?
I'VE BEEN PRACTICING ALL MORNING.
WE SHOULD GET GOING!
SURE.
SHE'S PRETTY! DON'T YOU THINK, ZUKO?

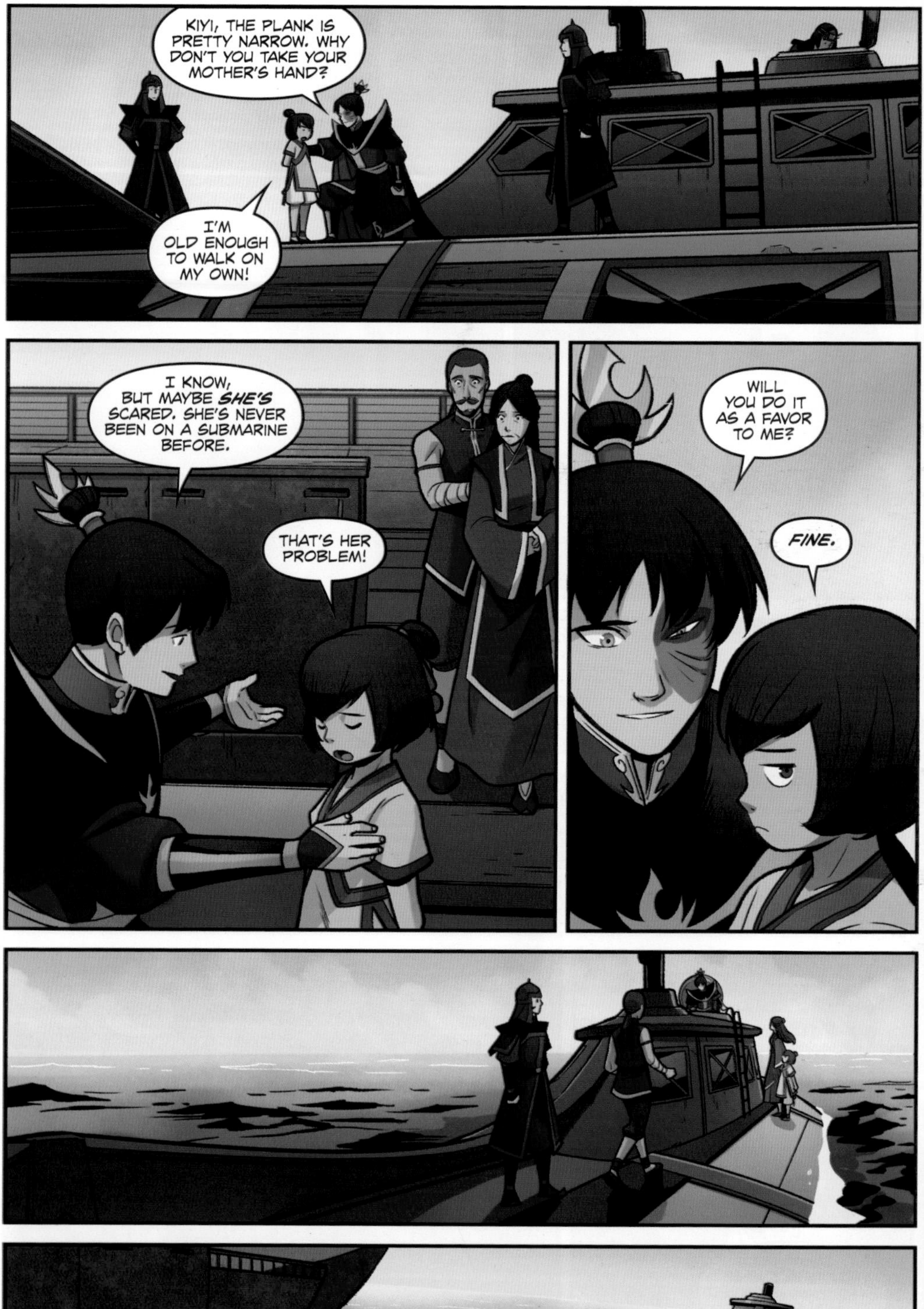
KIYI, THE PLANK IS PRETTY NARROW. WHY DON'T YOU TAKE YOUR MOTHER'S HAND?
I'M OLD ENOUGH TO WALK ON MY OWN!
I KNOW, BUT MAYBE SHE'S SCARED. SHE'S NEVER BEEN ON A SUBMARINE BEFORE.
THAT'S HER PROBLEM!
WILL YOU DO IT AS A FAVOR TO ME?
FINE.

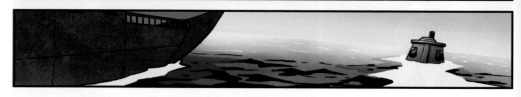

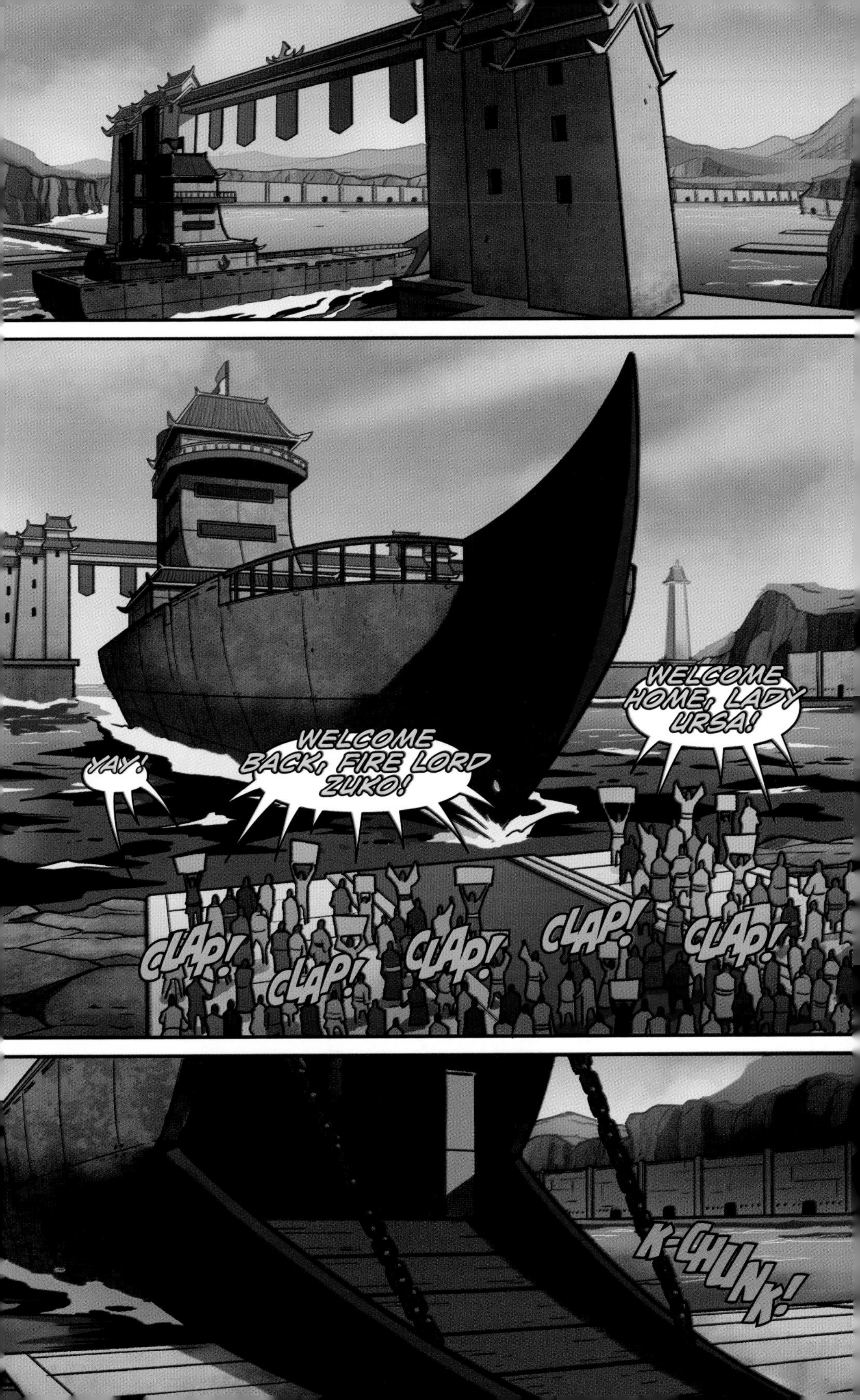
YAY!
WELCOME BACK, FIRE LORD ZUKO!
WELCOME HOME, LADY URSA!
CLAP! CLAP! CLAP! CLAP! CLAP!
K-CHUNK!

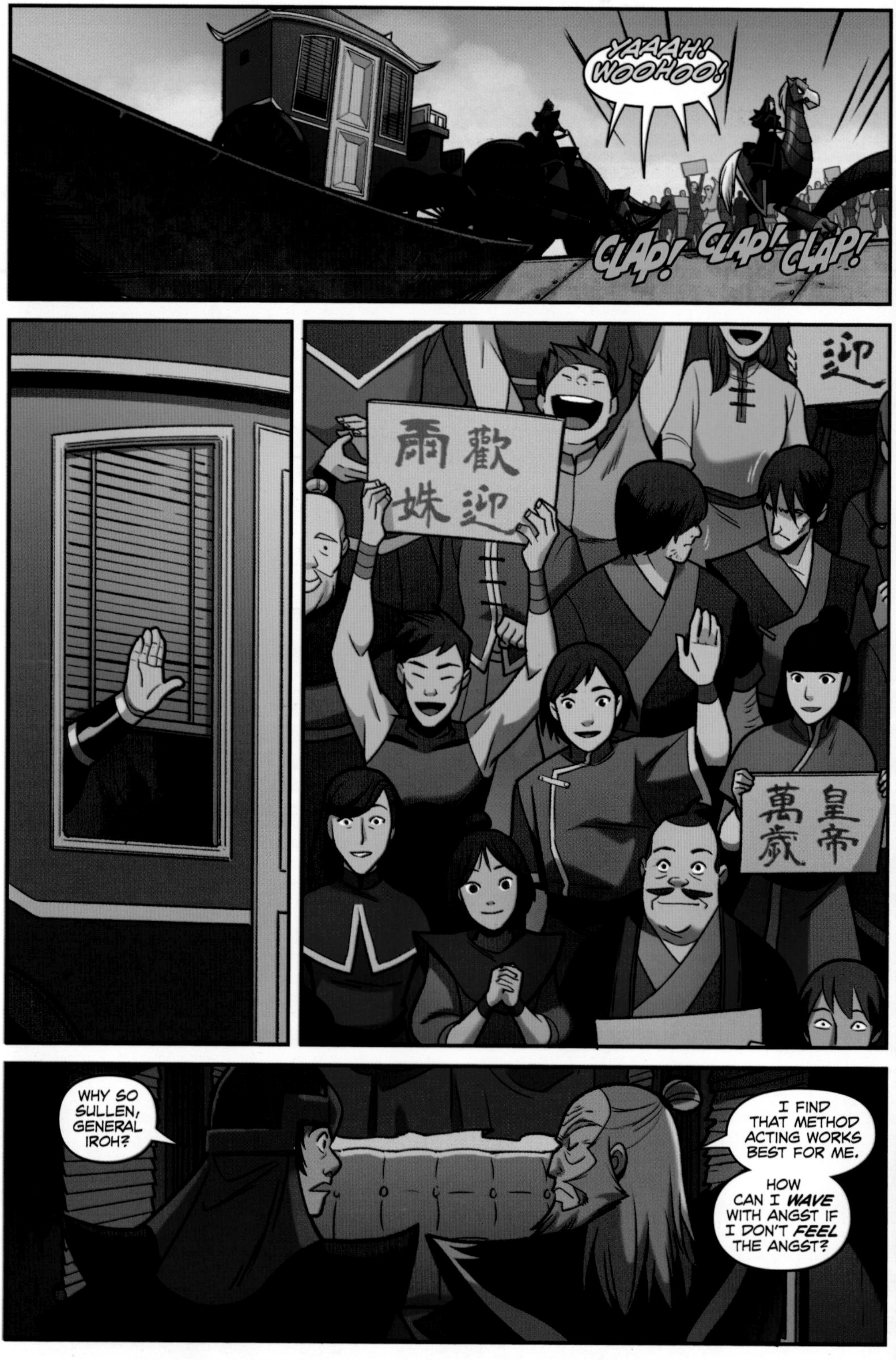
YAAAH! WOOHOO!
CLAP! CLAP! CLAP!
迎
歡迎
雨姝
皇帝
萬歲
WHY SO SULLEN, GENERAL IROH?
I FIND THAT METHOD ACTING WORKS BEST FOR ME.
HOW CAN I **WAVE** WITH ANGST IF I DON'T **FEEL** THE ANGST?

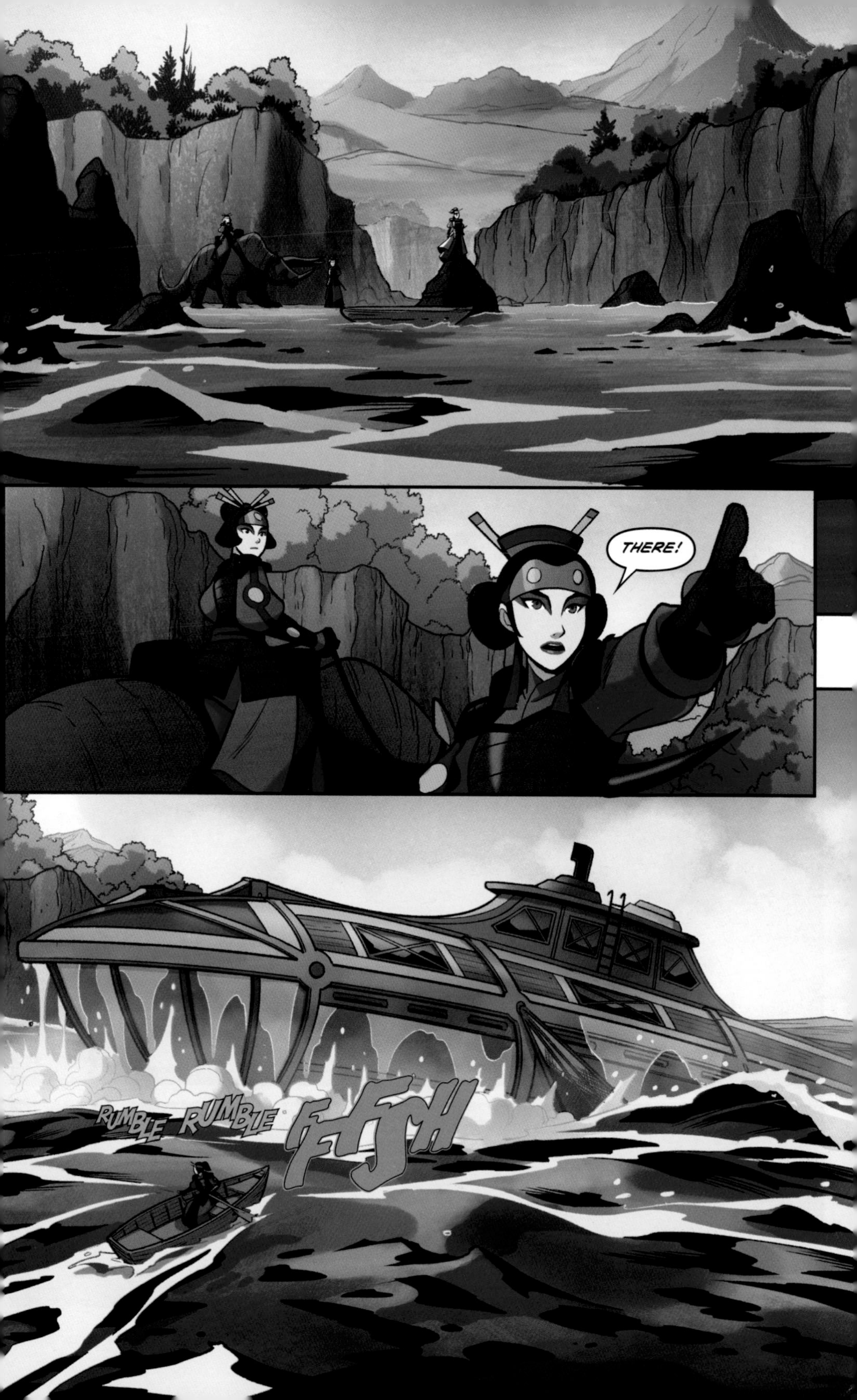
THERE!
RUMBLE RUMBLE
FFFSH

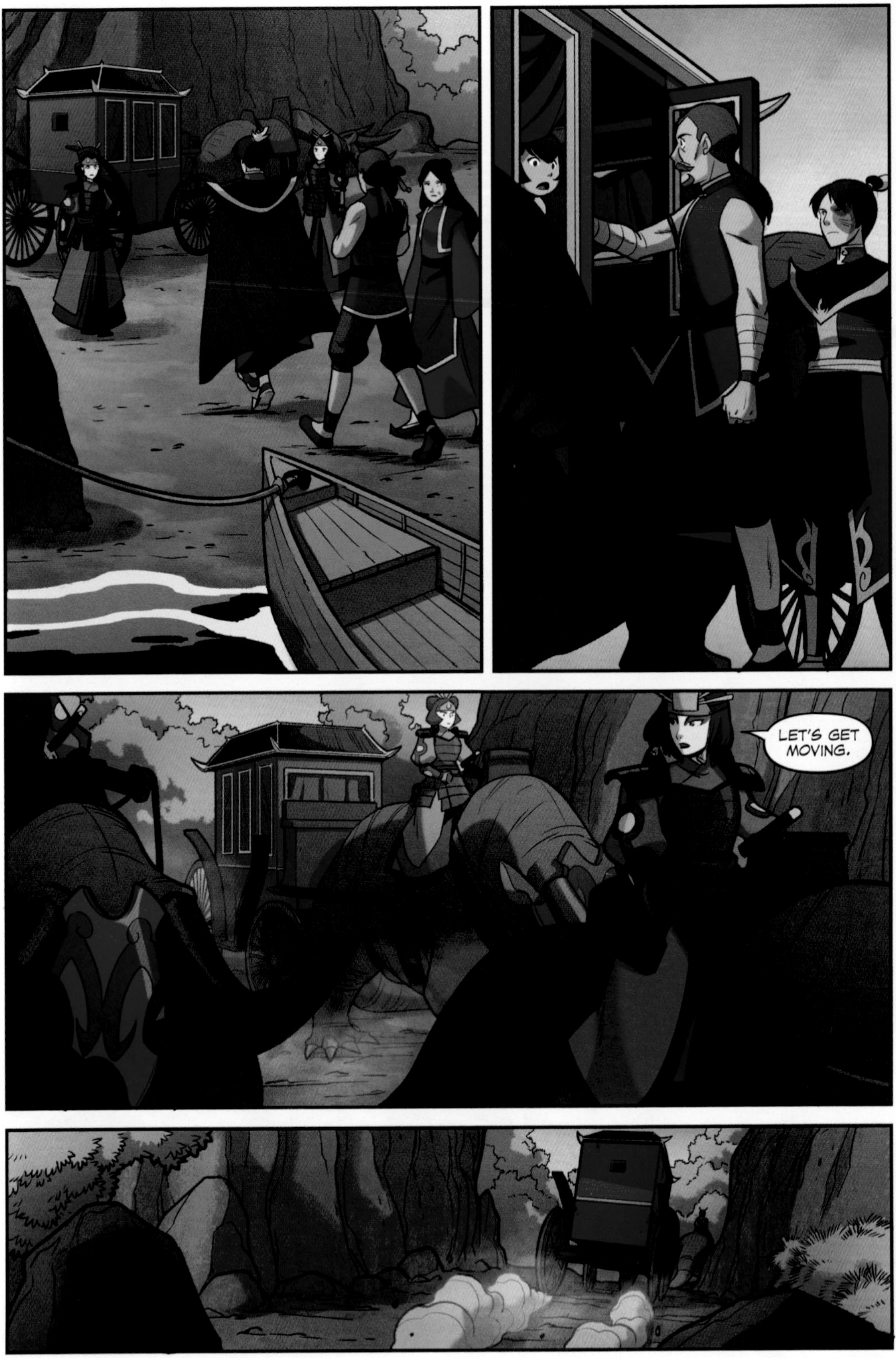
LET'S GET MOVING.

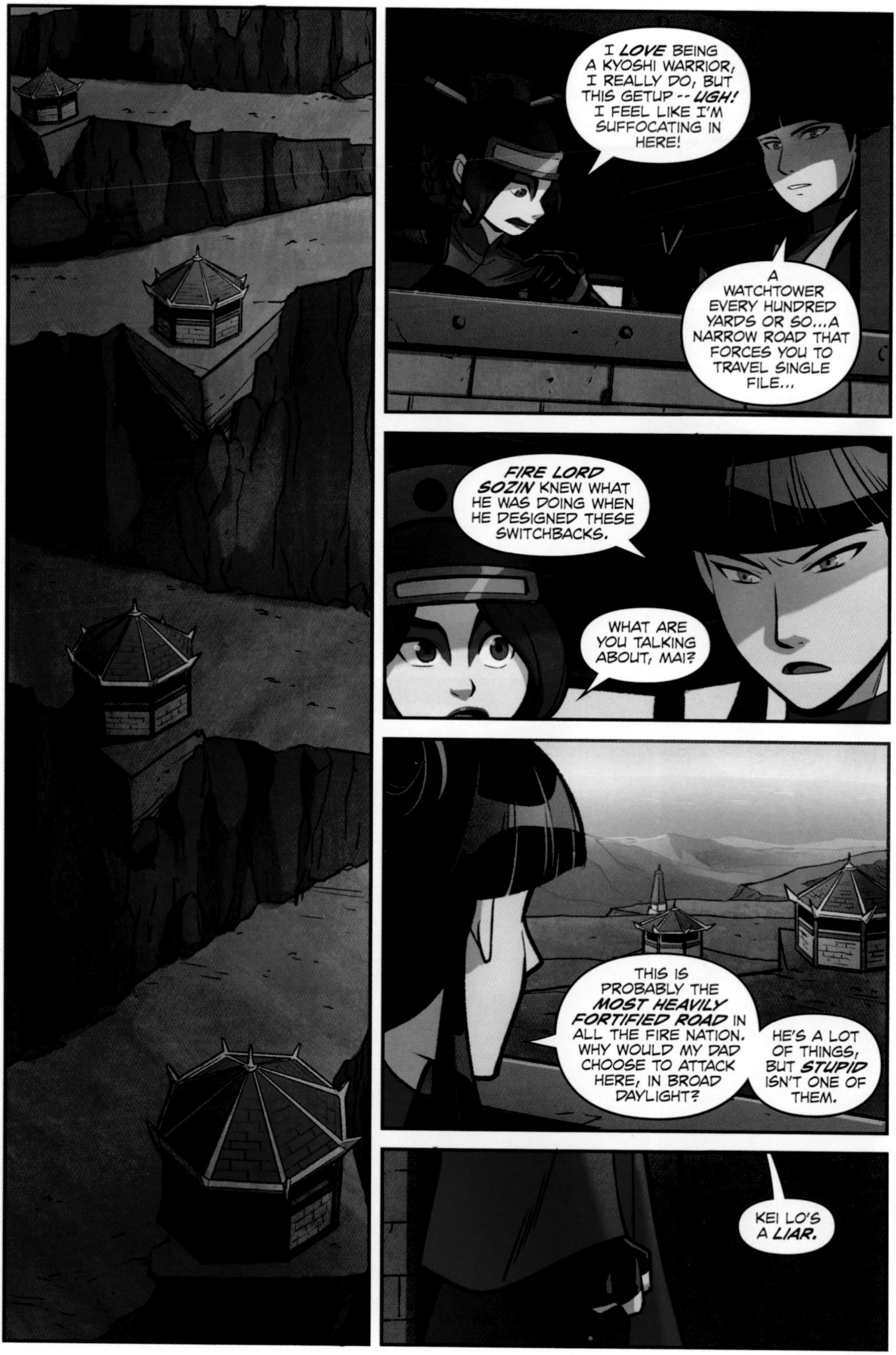
I LOVE BEING A KYOSHI WARRIOR, I REALLY DO, BUT THIS GETUP -- UGH! I FEEL LIKE I'M SUFFOCATING IN HERE!
A WATCHTOWER EVERY HUNDRED YARDS OR SO...A NARROW ROAD THAT FORCES YOU TO TRAVEL SINGLE FILE...
FIRE LORD SOZIN KNEW WHAT HE WAS DOING WHEN HE DESIGNED THESE SWITCHBACKS.
WHAT ARE YOU TALKING ABOUT, MAI?
THIS IS PROBABLY THE MOST HEAVILY FORTIFIED ROAD IN ALL THE FIRE NATION. WHY WOULD MY DAD CHOOSE TO ATTACK HERE, IN BROAD DAYLIGHT?
HE'S A LOT OF THINGS, BUT STUPID ISN'T ONE OF THEM.
KEI LO'S A LIAR.

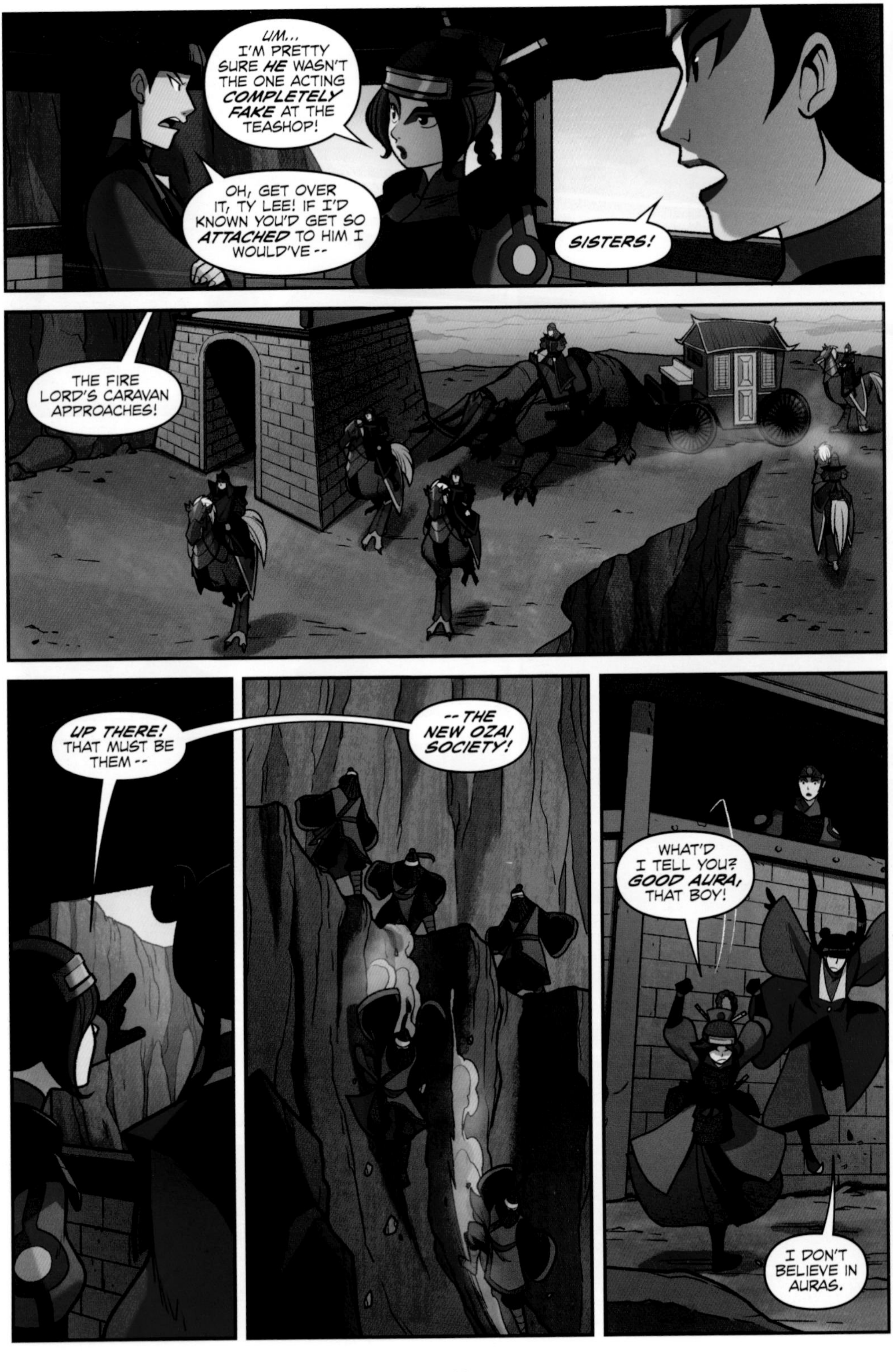
UM... I'M PRETTY SURE HE WASN'T THE ONE ACTING COMPLETELY FAKE AT THE TEASHOP!
OH, GET OVER IT, TY LEE! IF I'D KNOWN YOU'D GET SO ATTACHED TO HIM I WOULD'VE --
SISTERS!
THE FIRE LORD'S CARAVAN APPROACHES!
UP THERE! THAT MUST BE THEM --
-- THE NEW OZAI SOCIETY!
WHAT'D I TELL YOU? GOOD AURA, THAT BOY!
I DON'T BELIEVE IN AURAS.

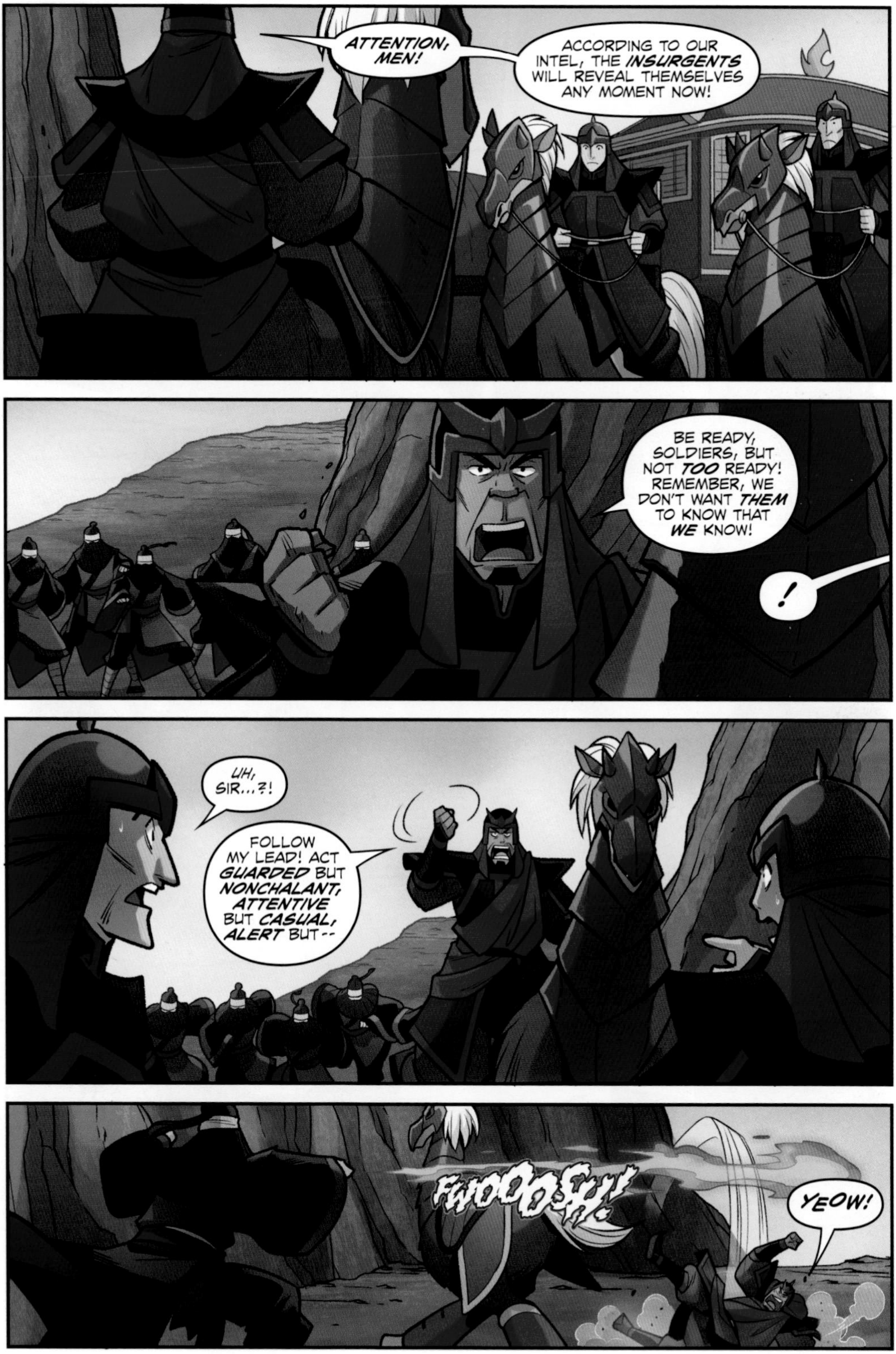
ATTENTION, MEN!
ACCORDING TO OUR INTEL, THE INSURGENTS WILL REVEAL THEMSELVES ANY MOMENT NOW!
BE READY, SOLDIERS, BUT NOT TOO READY! REMEMBER, WE DON'T WANT THEM TO KNOW THAT WE KNOW!
!
UH, SIR...?!
FOLLOW MY LEAD! ACT GUARDED BUT NONCHALANT, ATTENTIVE BUT CASUAL, ALERT BUT--
FWOOOSH!
YEOW!

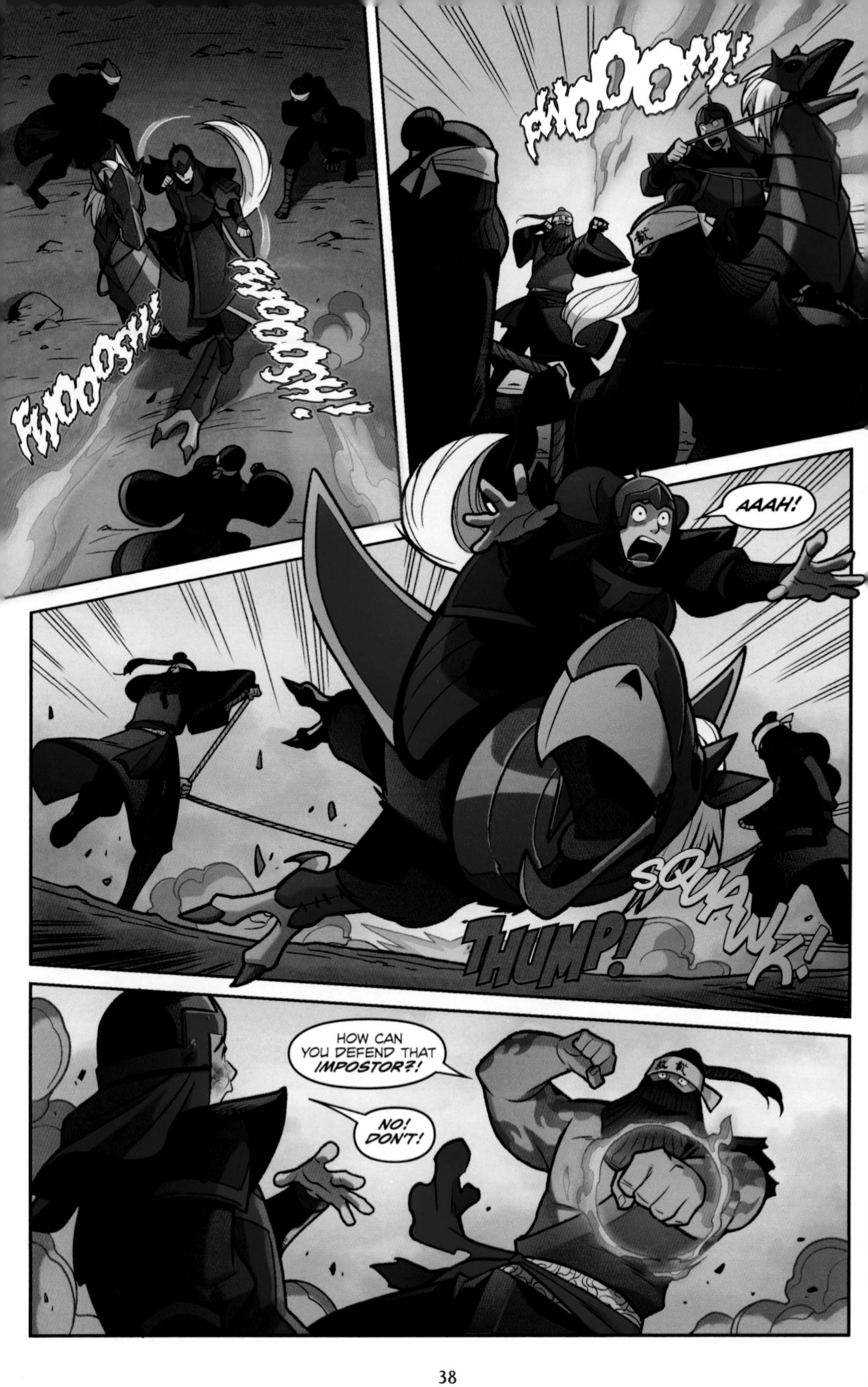
FWOOOSH!
FWOOOSH!
FWOOOM!
AAAH!
SQUAWK!
THUMP!
HOW CAN YOU DEFEND THAT *IMPOSTOR*?!
NO! DON'T!

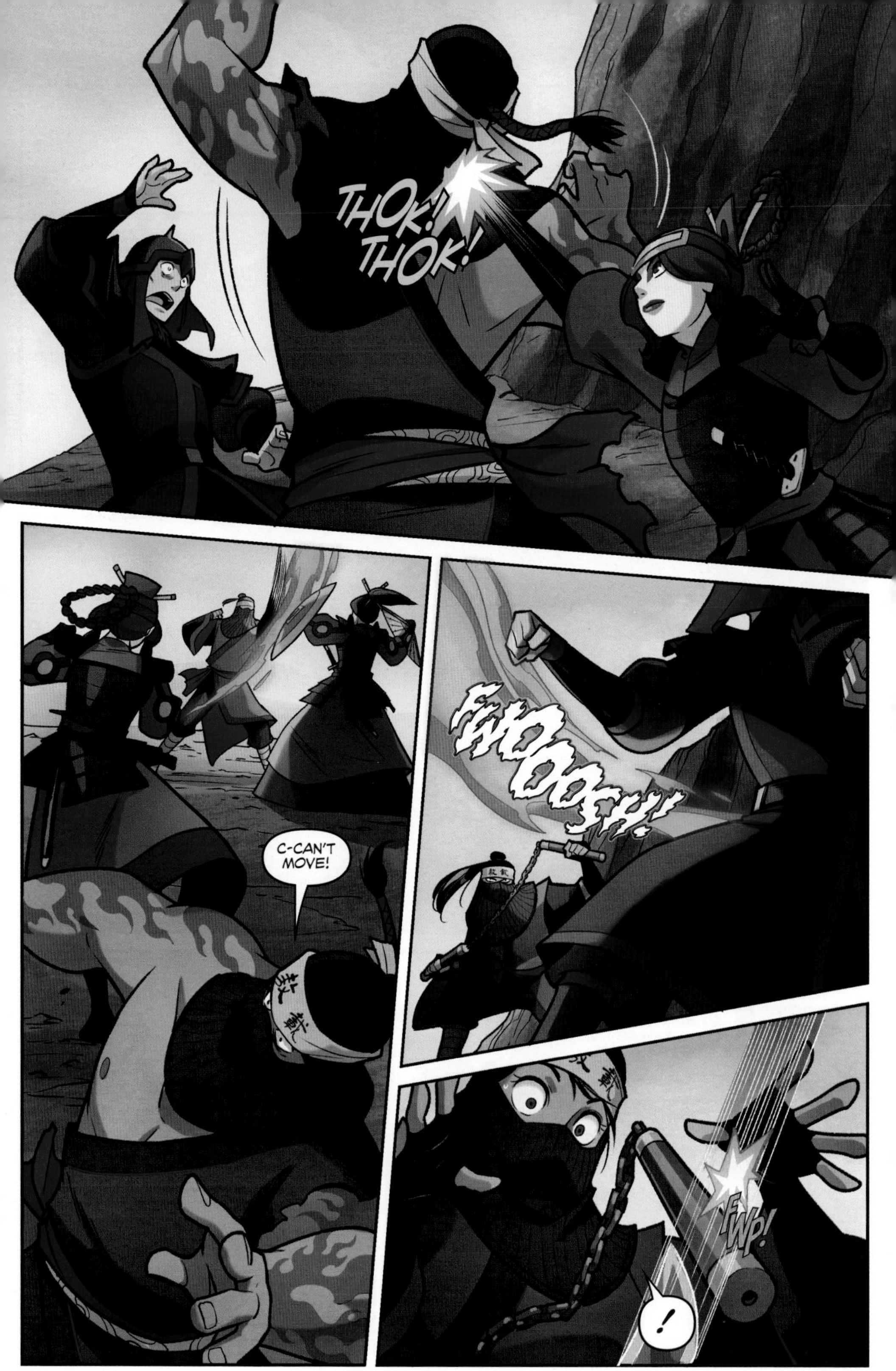
THOK! THOK!
C-CAN'T MOVE!
FWOOOSH!
FWP!
!

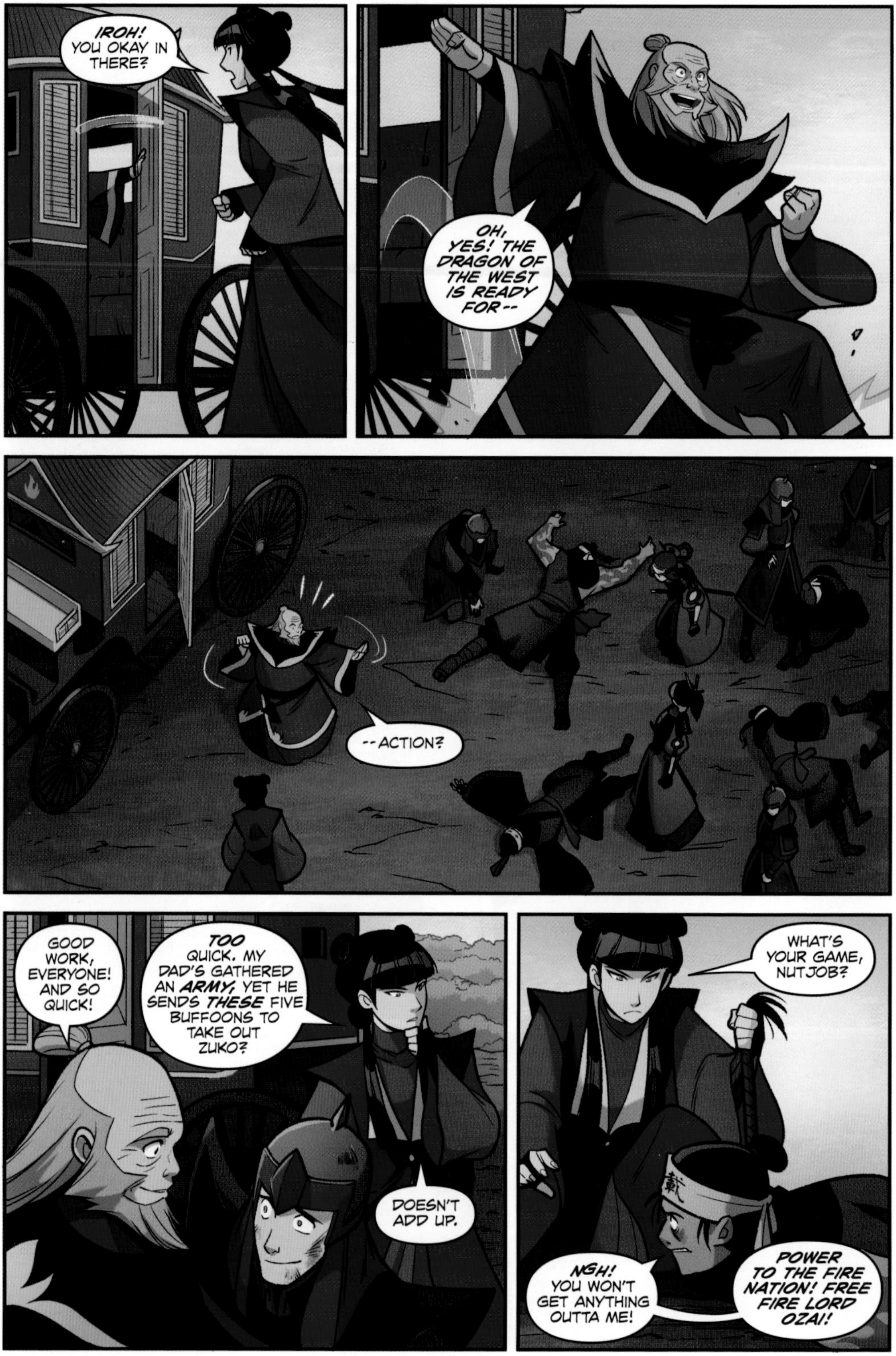
IROH! YOU OKAY IN THERE?
OH, YES! THE DRAGON OF THE WEST IS READY FOR--
--ACTION?
GOOD WORK, EVERYONE! AND SO QUICK!
TOO QUICK. MY DAD'S GATHERED AN ARMY, YET HE SENDS THESE FIVE BUFFOONS TO TAKE OUT ZUKO?
DOESN'T ADD UP.
WHAT'S YOUR GAME, NUTJOB?
NGH! YOU WON'T GET ANYTHING OUTTA ME!
POWER TO THE FIRE NATION! FREE FIRE LORD OZAI!

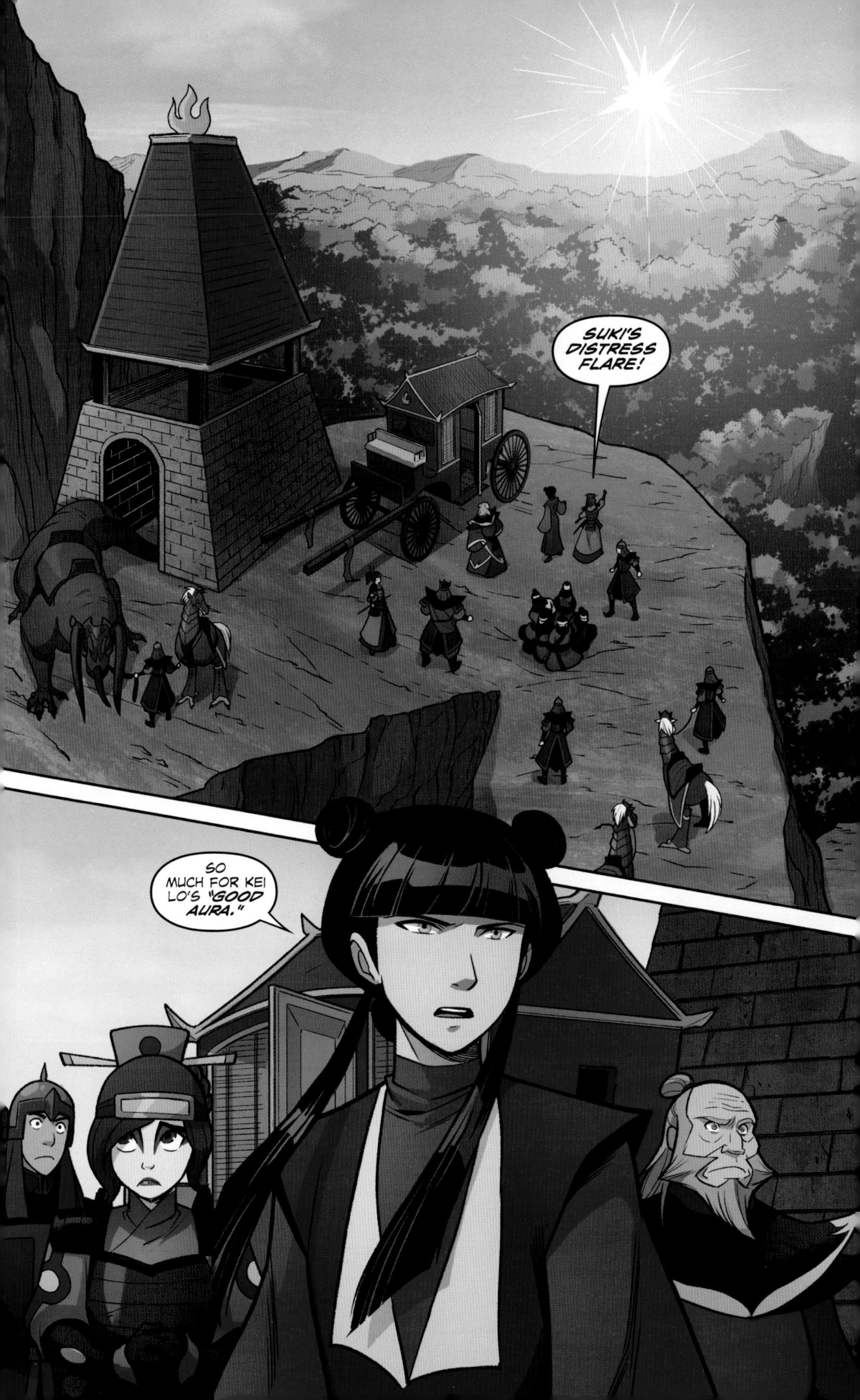
SUKI'S DISTRESS FLARE!
SO MUCH FOR KEI LO'S "GOOD AURA."

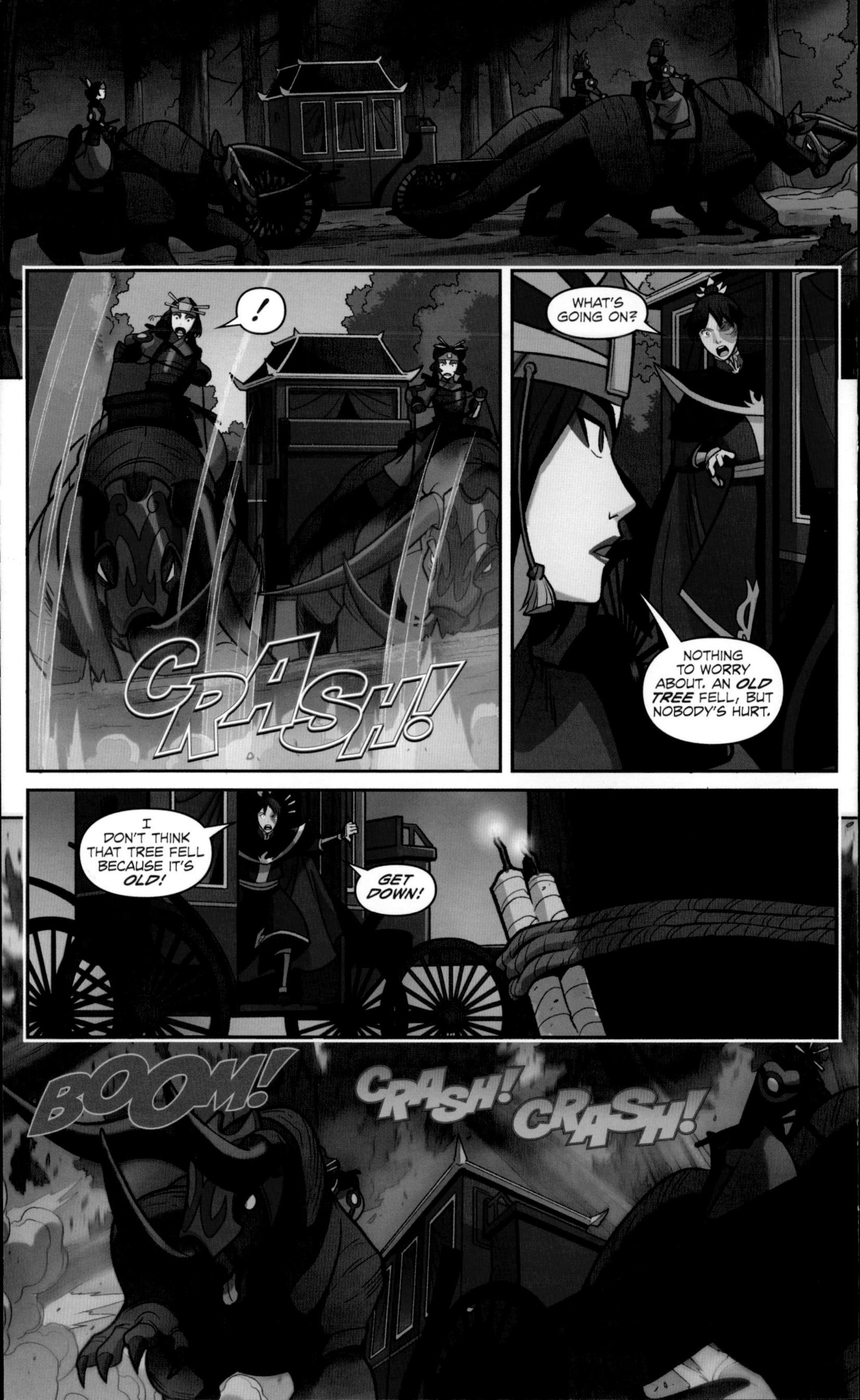
!
CRASH!
WHAT'S GOING ON?
NOTHING TO WORRY ABOUT. AN *OLD TREE* FELL, BUT NOBODY'S HURT.
I DON'T THINK THAT TREE FELL BECAUSE IT'S *OLD!*
GET DOWN!
BOOM!
CRASH! CRASH!

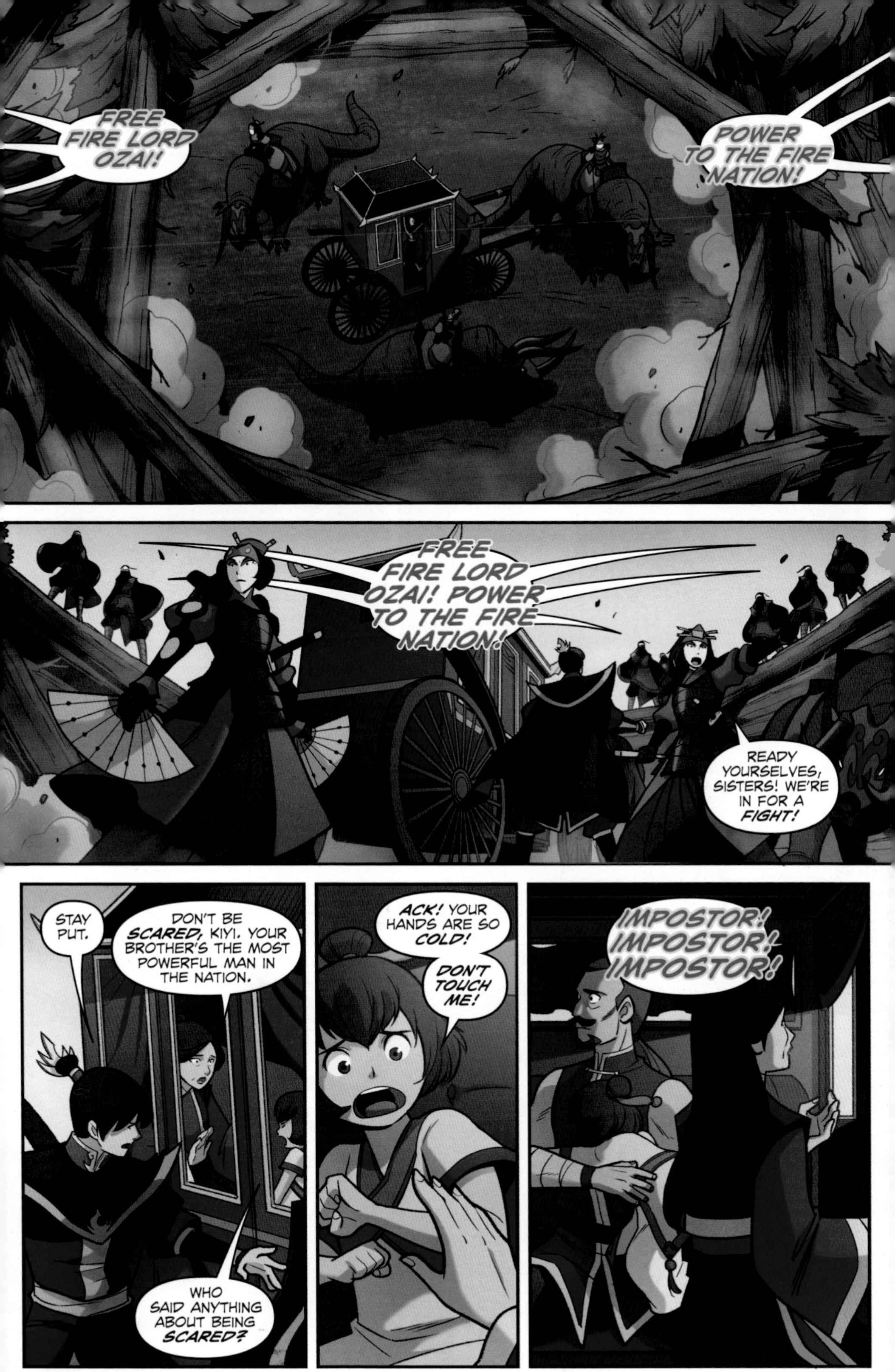
FREE FIRE LORD OZAI!
POWER TO THE FIRE NATION!
FREE FIRE LORD OZAI! POWER TO THE FIRE NATION!
READY YOURSELVES, SISTERS! WE'RE IN FOR A FIGHT!
STAY PUT.
DON'T BE SCARED, KIYI. YOUR BROTHER'S THE MOST POWERFUL MAN IN THE NATION.
WHO SAID ANYTHING ABOUT BEING SCARED?
ACK! YOUR HANDS ARE SO COLD!
DON'T TOUCH ME!
IMPOSTOR! IMPOSTOR! IMPOSTOR!

IMPOSTOR! IMPOSTOR!

ZUKO! THE TIME HAS COME FOR YOU TO RETURN THE THRONE TO THE *ONE TRUE FIRE LORD!*

WE *DEMAND* THAT YOU STEP DOWN *AT ONCE!*

DO SO *PEACEFULLY* AND *NO HARM* SHALL COME TO YOUR FAMILY!

LET ME GET THIS STRAIGHT.

YOU EXPECT ME TO GIVE UP MY *DESTINY* -- MY *RIGHTFUL PLACE* IN THE NATION -- JUST BECAUSE A BUNCH OF *THUGS* TOO COWARDLY TO SHOW THEIR FACES ASKED ME TO?

RIDICULOUS.

WELL... YES.

FWOOOM!

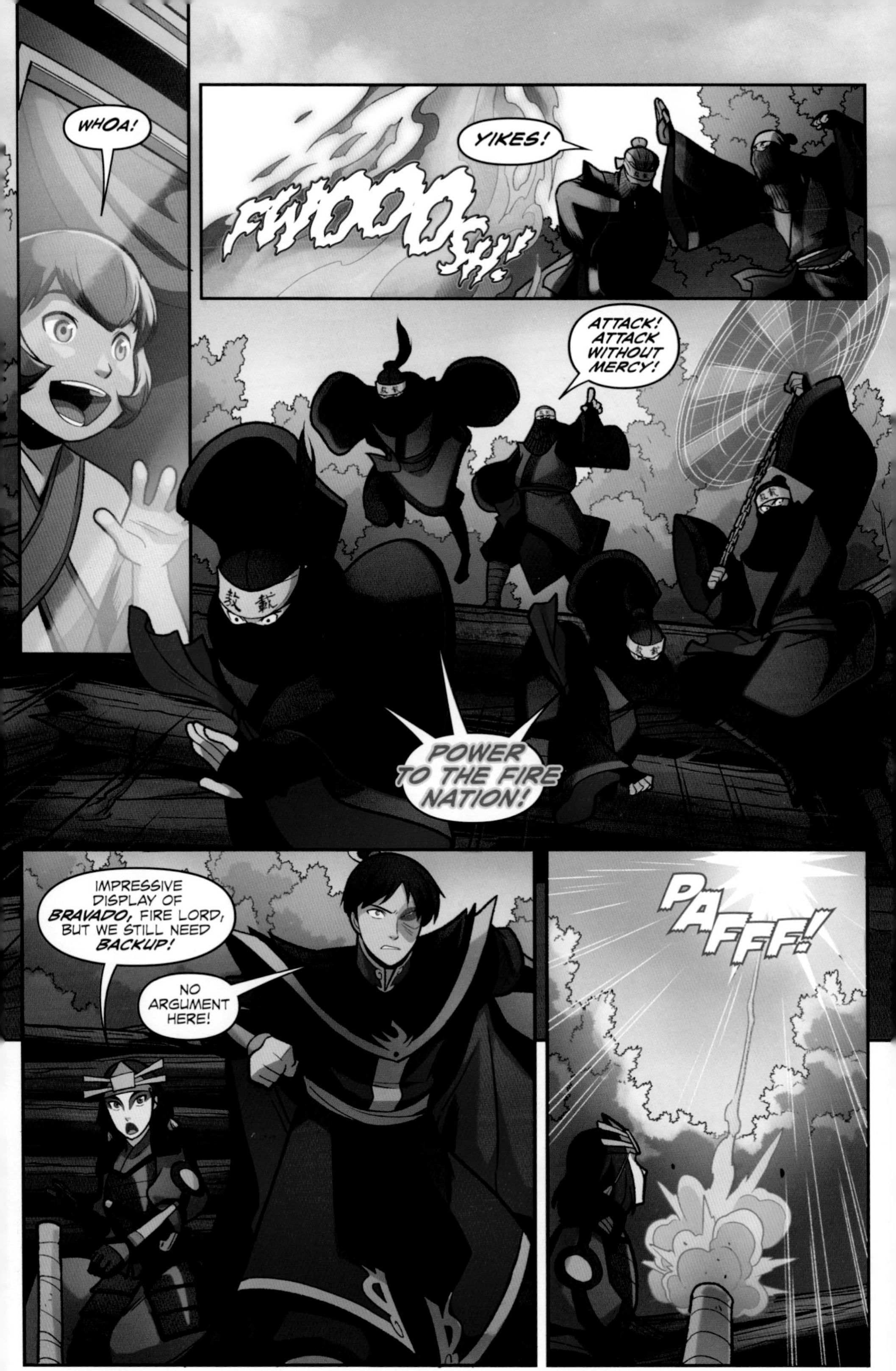
WHOA!
YIKES!
FWOOOSH!
ATTACK! ATTACK WITHOUT MERCY!
POWER TO THE FIRE NATION!
IMPRESSIVE DISPLAY OF BRAVADO, FIRE LORD, BUT WE STILL NEED BACKUP!
NO ARGUMENT HERE!
PAFFF!

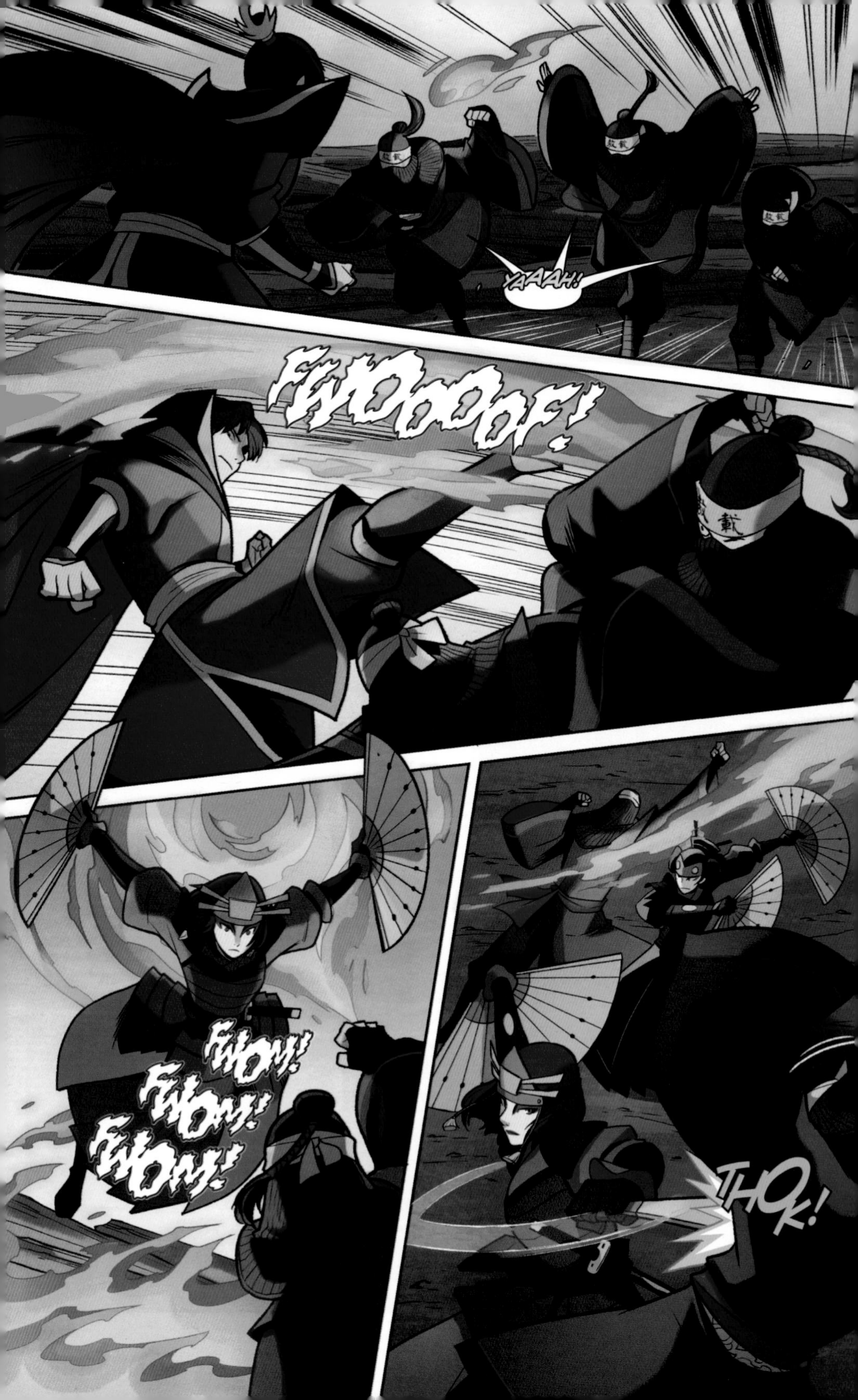
YAAAH!
FWOOOOF!
FWOM!
FWOM!
FWOM!
THOK!

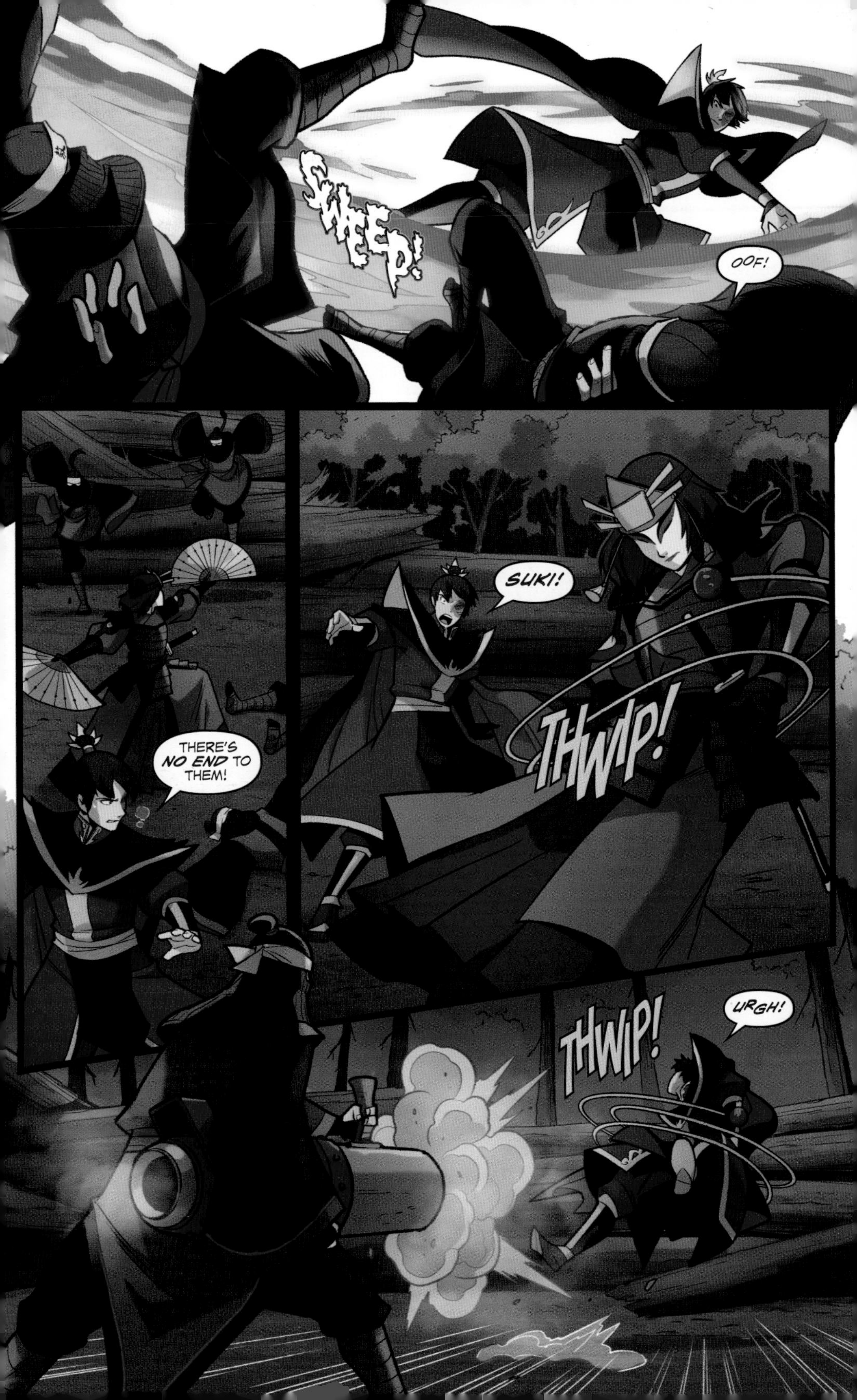
SWEEP!
OOF!
THERE'S NO END TO THEM!
SUKI!
THWIP!
THWIP!
URGH!

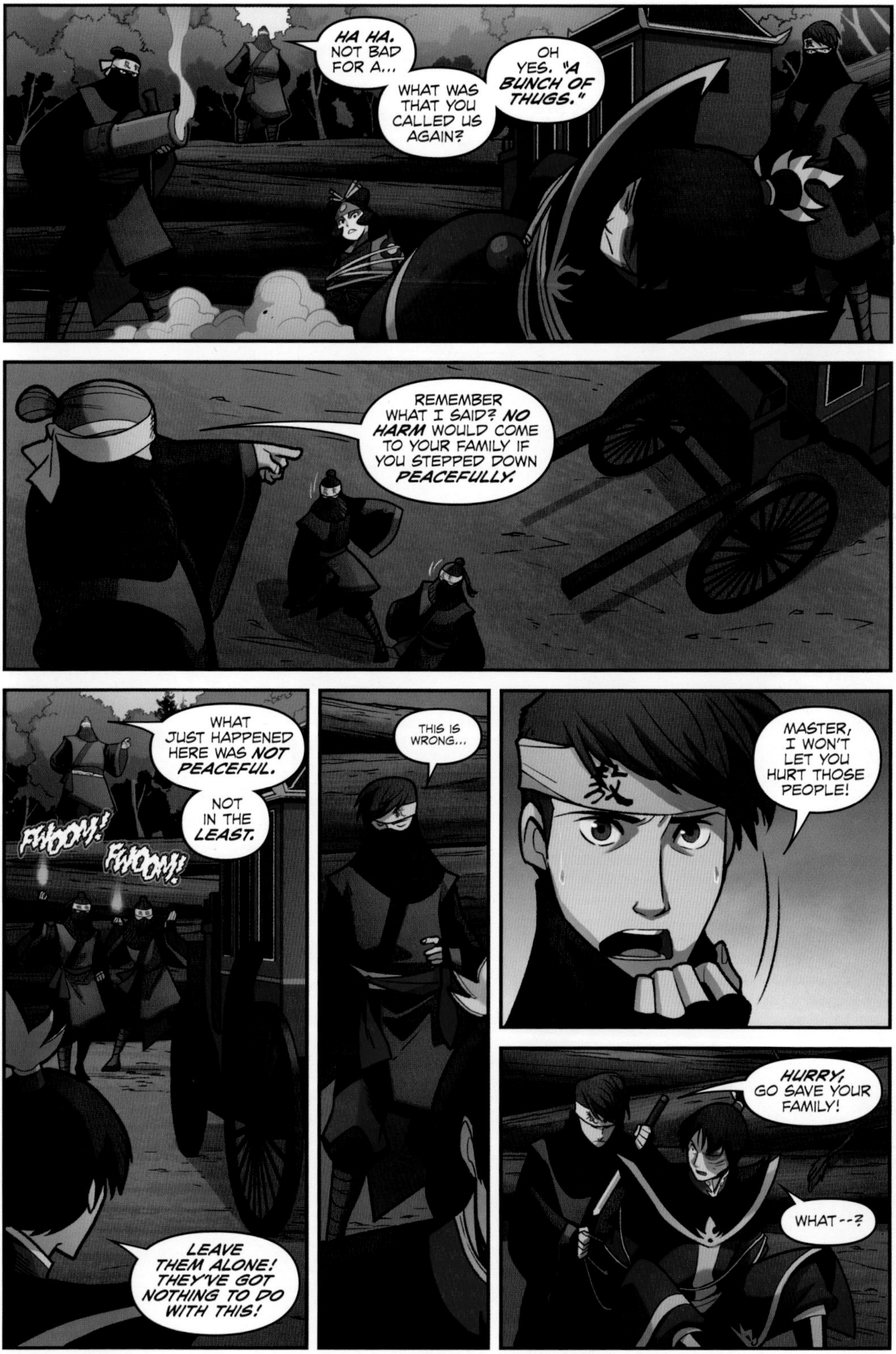
HA HA. NOT BAD FOR A...
WHAT WAS THAT YOU CALLED US AGAIN?
OH YES. "A BUNCH OF THUGS."
REMEMBER WHAT I SAID? NO HARM WOULD COME TO YOUR FAMILY IF YOU STEPPED DOWN PEACEFULLY.
WHAT JUST HAPPENED HERE WAS NOT PEACEFUL.
NOT IN THE LEAST.
FWOOM! FWOOM!
LEAVE THEM ALONE! THEY'VE GOT NOTHING TO DO WITH THIS!
THIS IS WRONG...
MASTER, I WON'T LET YOU HURT THOSE PEOPLE!
HURRY, GO SAVE YOUR FAMILY!
WHAT--?

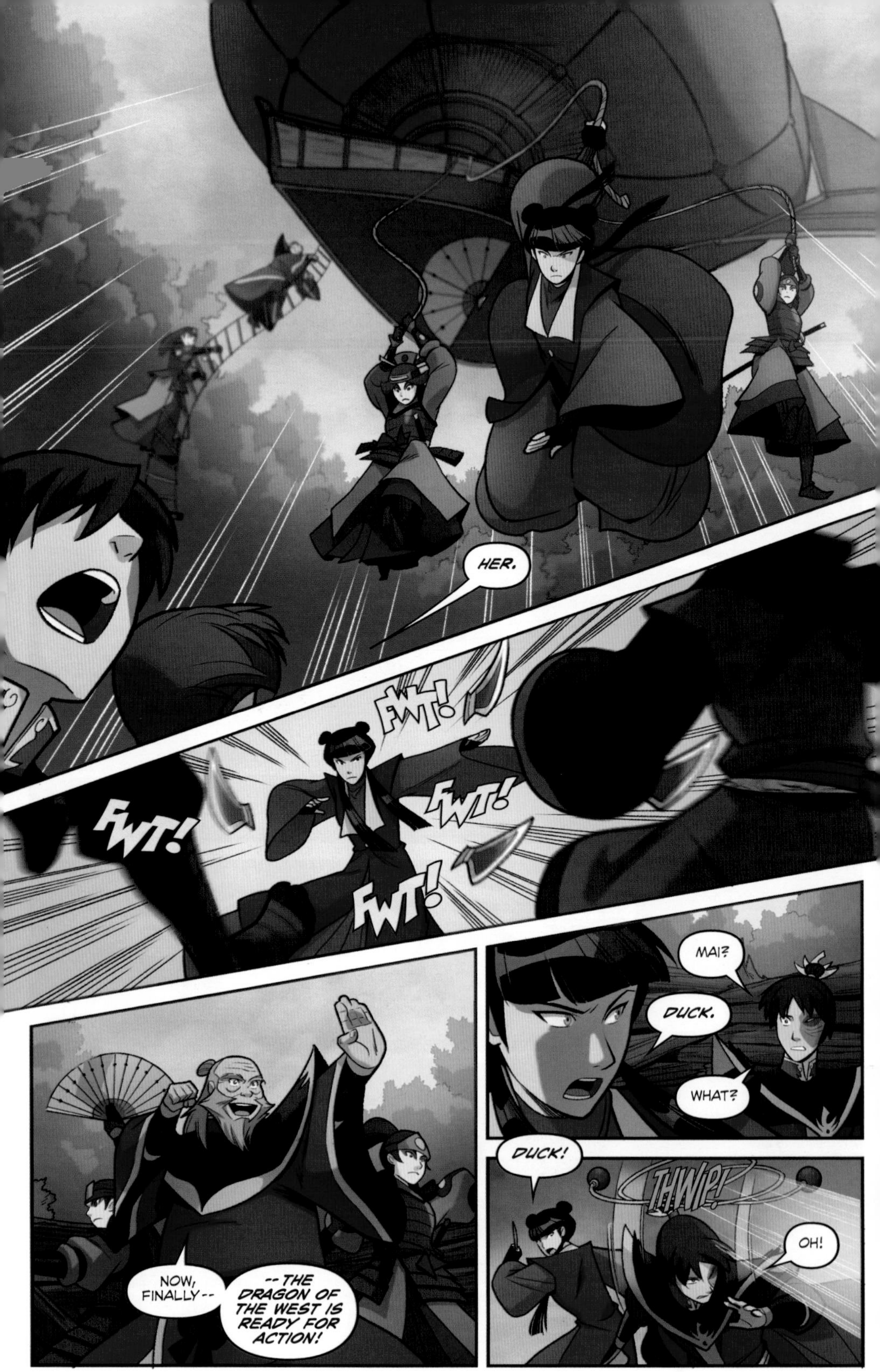
HER.
FWT!
FWT!
FWT!
FWT!
MAI?
DUCK.
WHAT?
NOW, FINALLY--
--THE DRAGON OF THE WEST IS READY FOR ACTION!
DUCK!
THWIP!
OH!

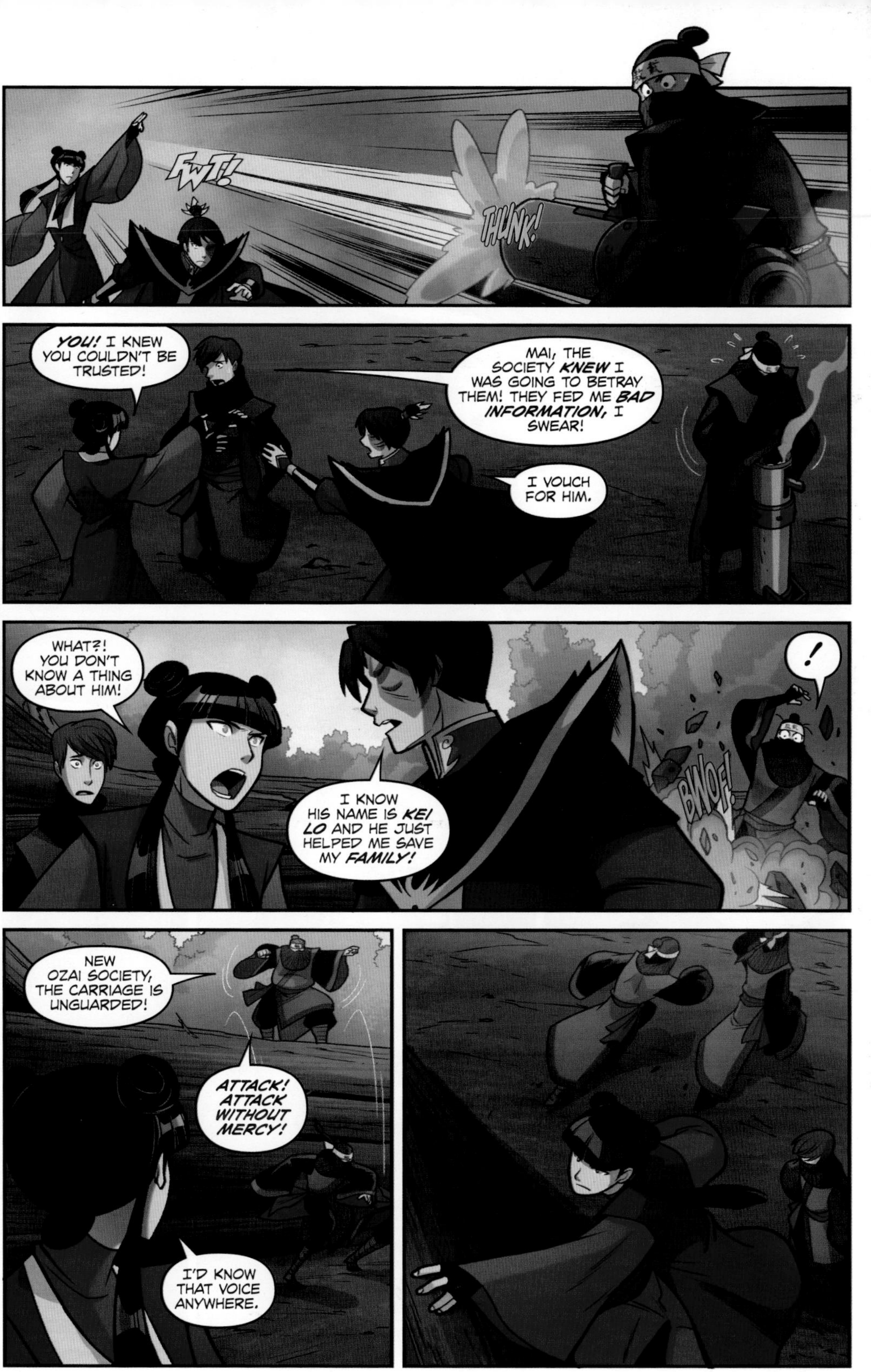
FWT!
THUNK!
YOU! I KNEW YOU COULDN'T BE TRUSTED!
MAI, THE SOCIETY KNEW I WAS GOING TO BETRAY THEM! THEY FED ME BAD INFORMATION, I SWEAR!
I VOUCH FOR HIM.
WHAT?! YOU DON'T KNOW A THING ABOUT HIM!
I KNOW HIS NAME IS KEI LO AND HE JUST HELPED ME SAVE MY FAMILY!
!
BWOF!
NEW OZAI SOCIETY, THE CARRIAGE IS UNGUARDED!
ATTACK! ATTACK WITHOUT MERCY!
I'D KNOW THAT VOICE ANYWHERE.

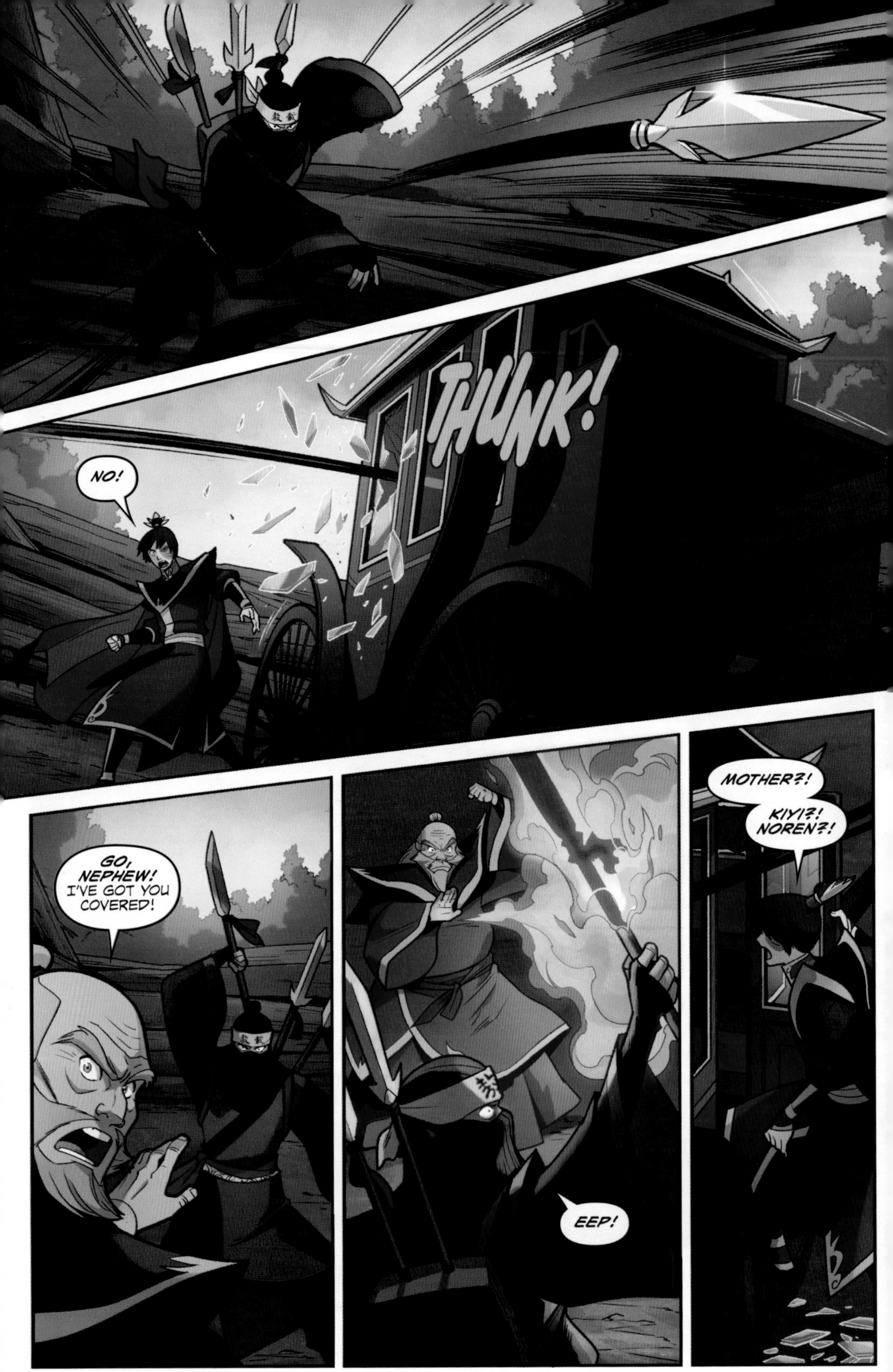
THUNK!
NO!
GO, NEPHEW! I'VE GOT YOU COVERED!
EEP!
MOTHER?!
KIYI?! NOREN?!

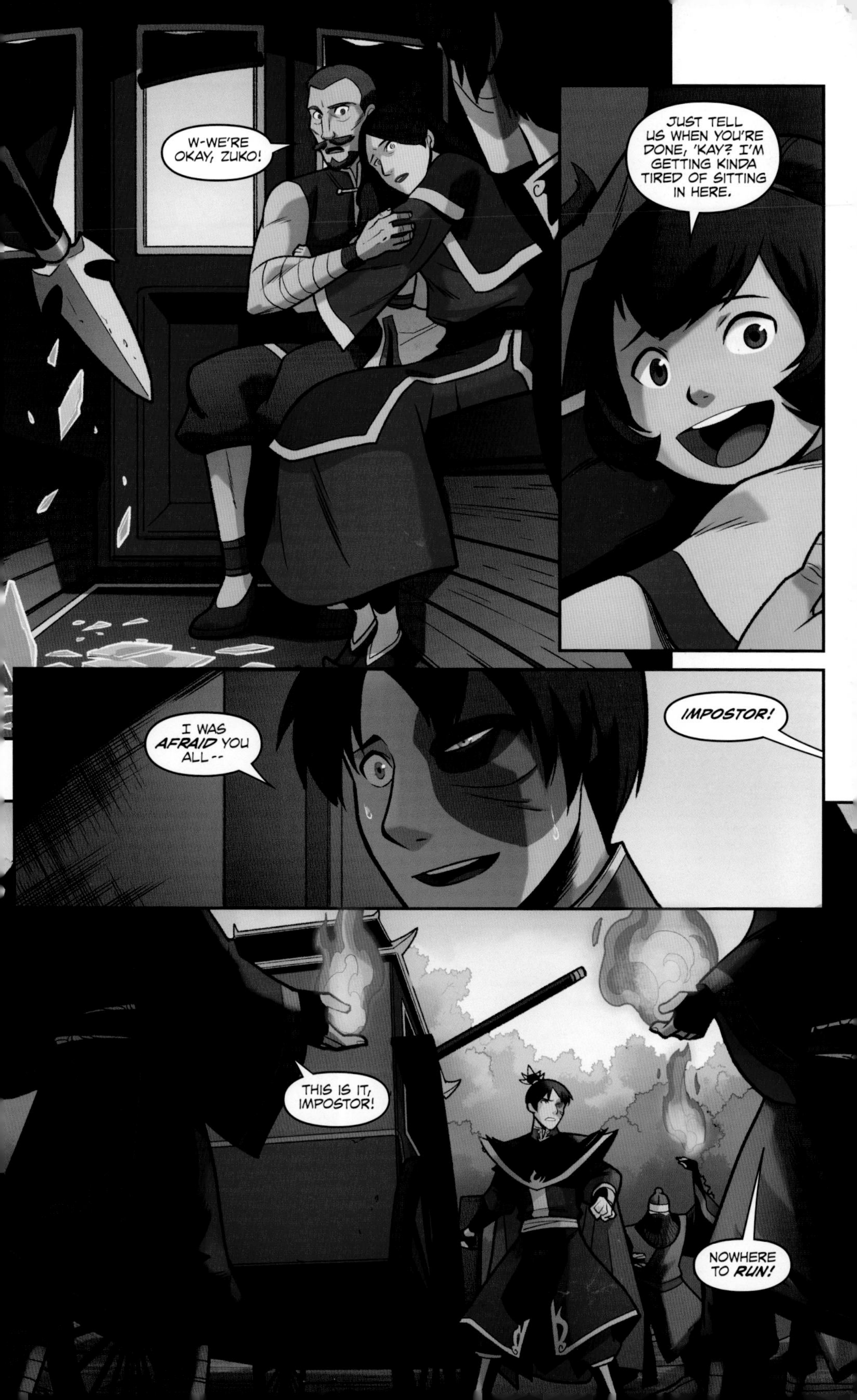
W-WE'RE OKAY, ZUKO!
JUST TELL US WHEN YOU'RE DONE, 'KAY? I'M GETTING KINDA TIRED OF SITTING IN HERE.
I WAS *AFRAID* YOU ALL--
IMPOSTOR!
THIS IS IT, IMPOSTOR!
NOWHERE TO *RUN!*

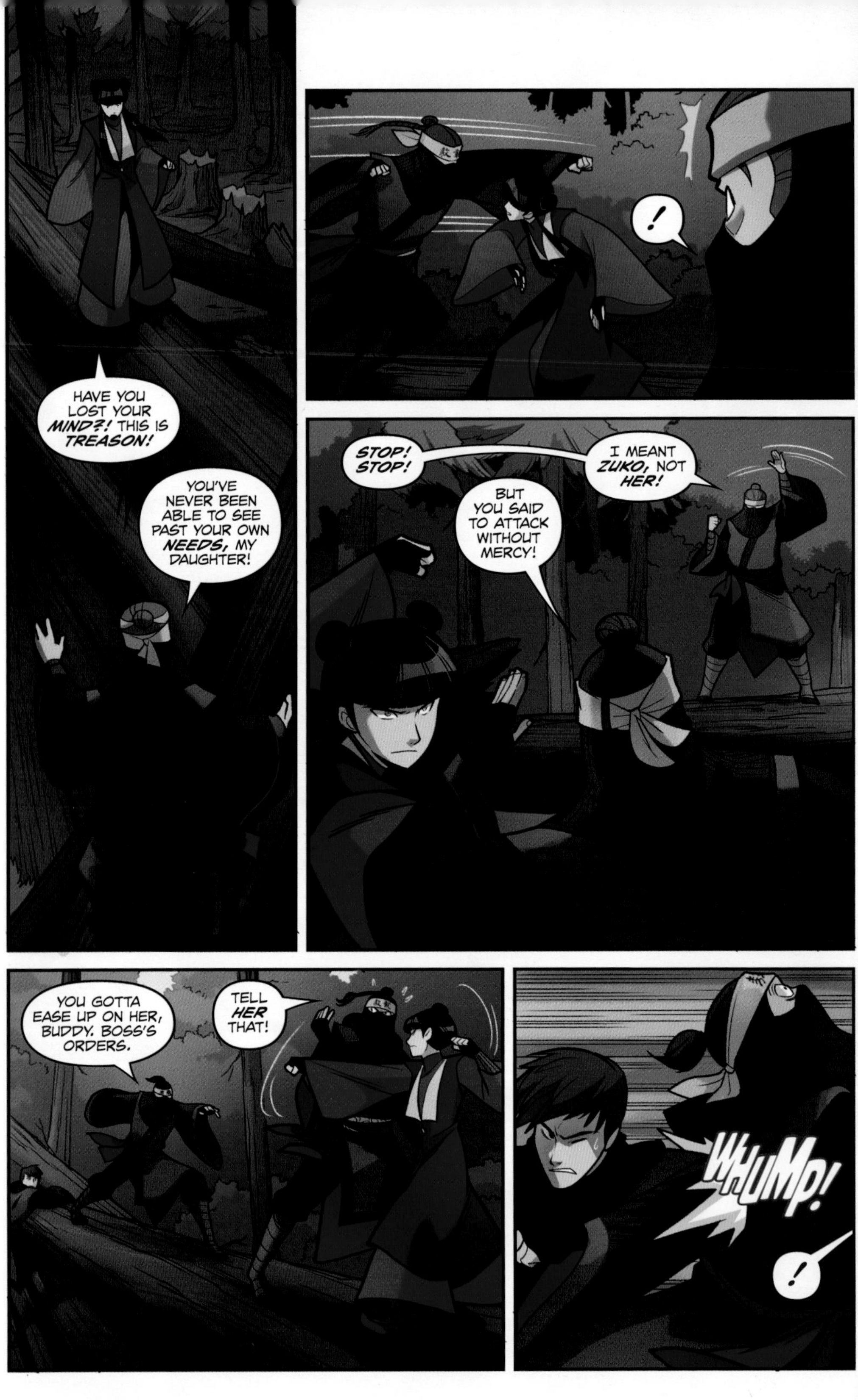
!
HAVE YOU LOST YOUR MIND?! THIS IS TREASON!
YOU'VE NEVER BEEN ABLE TO SEE PAST YOUR OWN NEEDS, MY DAUGHTER!
STOP! STOP!
I MEANT ZUKO, NOT HER!
BUT YOU SAID TO ATTACK WITHOUT MERCY!
YOU GOTTA EASE UP ON HER, BUDDY. BOSS'S ORDERS.
TELL HER THAT!
WHUMP!
!

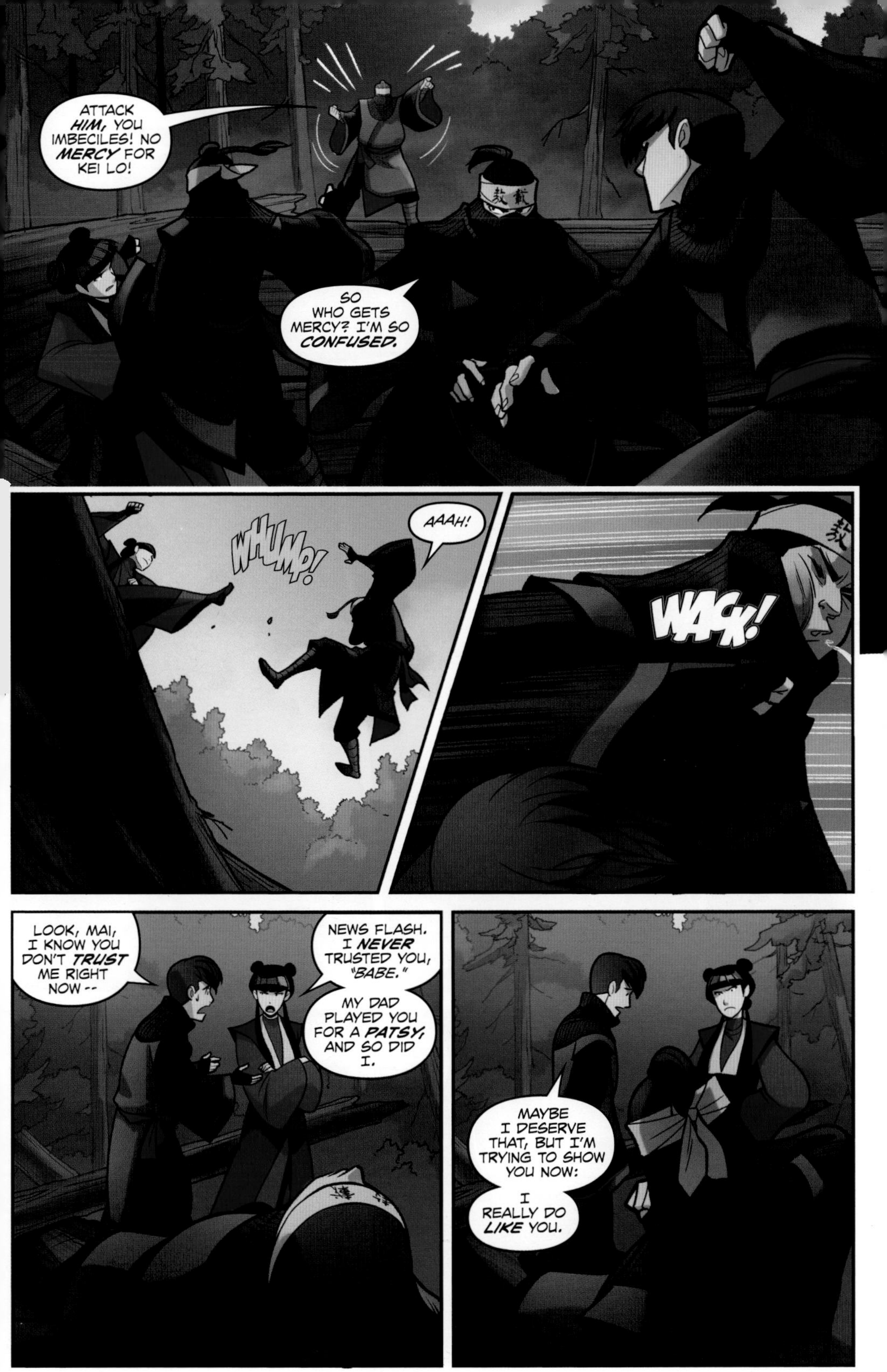
ATTACK HIM, YOU IMBECILES! NO MERCY FOR KEI LO!
SO WHO GETS MERCY? I'M SO CONFUSED.
WHUMP!
AAAH!
WACK!
LOOK, MAI, I KNOW YOU DON'T TRUST ME RIGHT NOW --
NEWS FLASH. I NEVER TRUSTED YOU, "BABE."
MY DAD PLAYED YOU FOR A PATSY, AND SO DID I.
MAYBE I DESERVE THAT, BUT I'M TRYING TO SHOW YOU NOW:
I REALLY DO LIKE YOU.

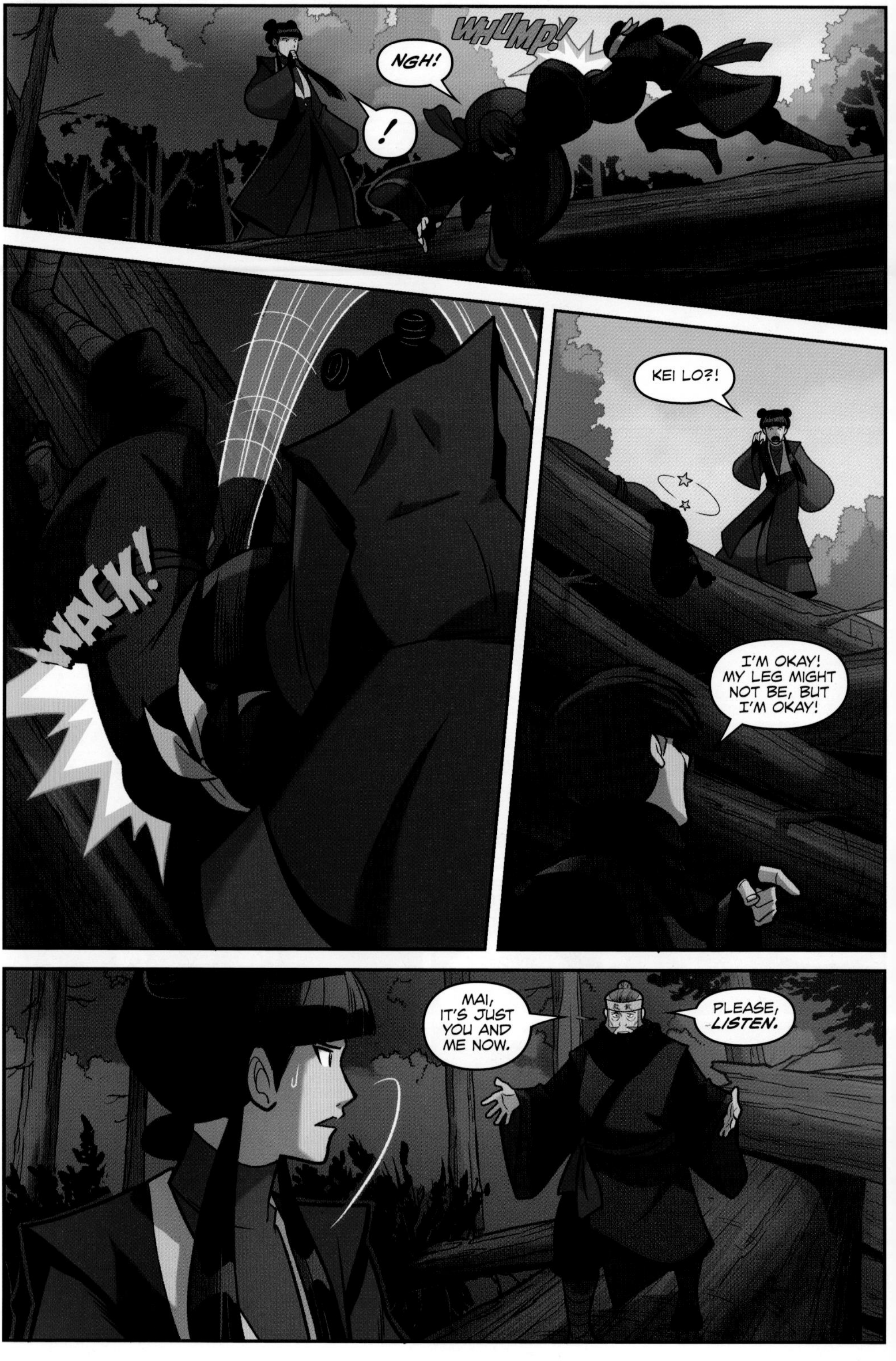
WHUMP!
NGH!
!
WACK!
KEI LO?!
I'M OKAY! MY LEG MIGHT NOT BE, BUT I'M OKAY!
MAI, IT'S JUST YOU AND ME NOW.
PLEASE, LISTEN.

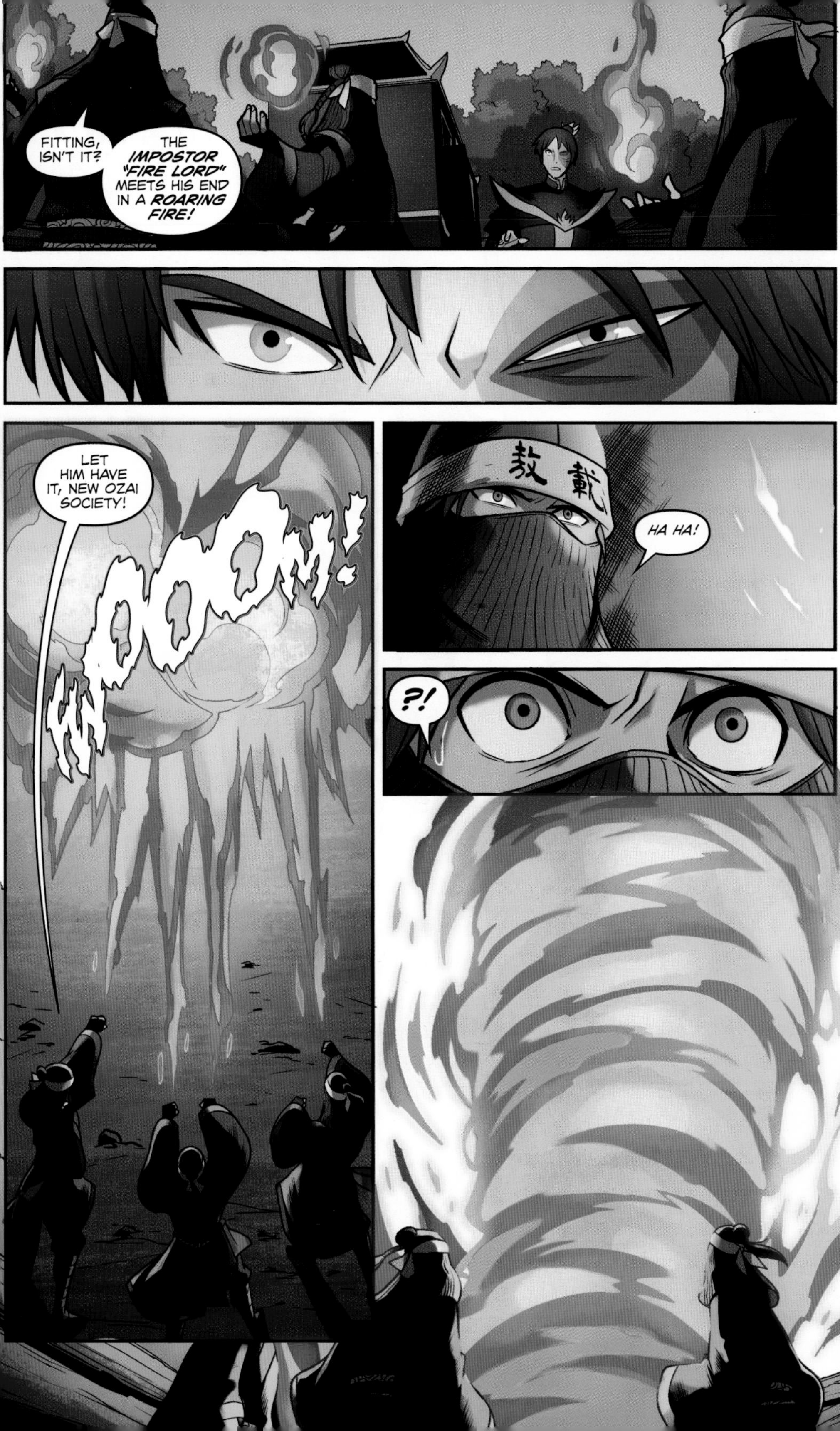
FITTING, ISN'T IT?
THE IMPOSTOR "FIRE LORD" MEETS HIS END IN A ROARING FIRE!
LET HIM HAVE IT, NEW OZAI SOCIETY!
WHOOOM!
HA HA!
?!

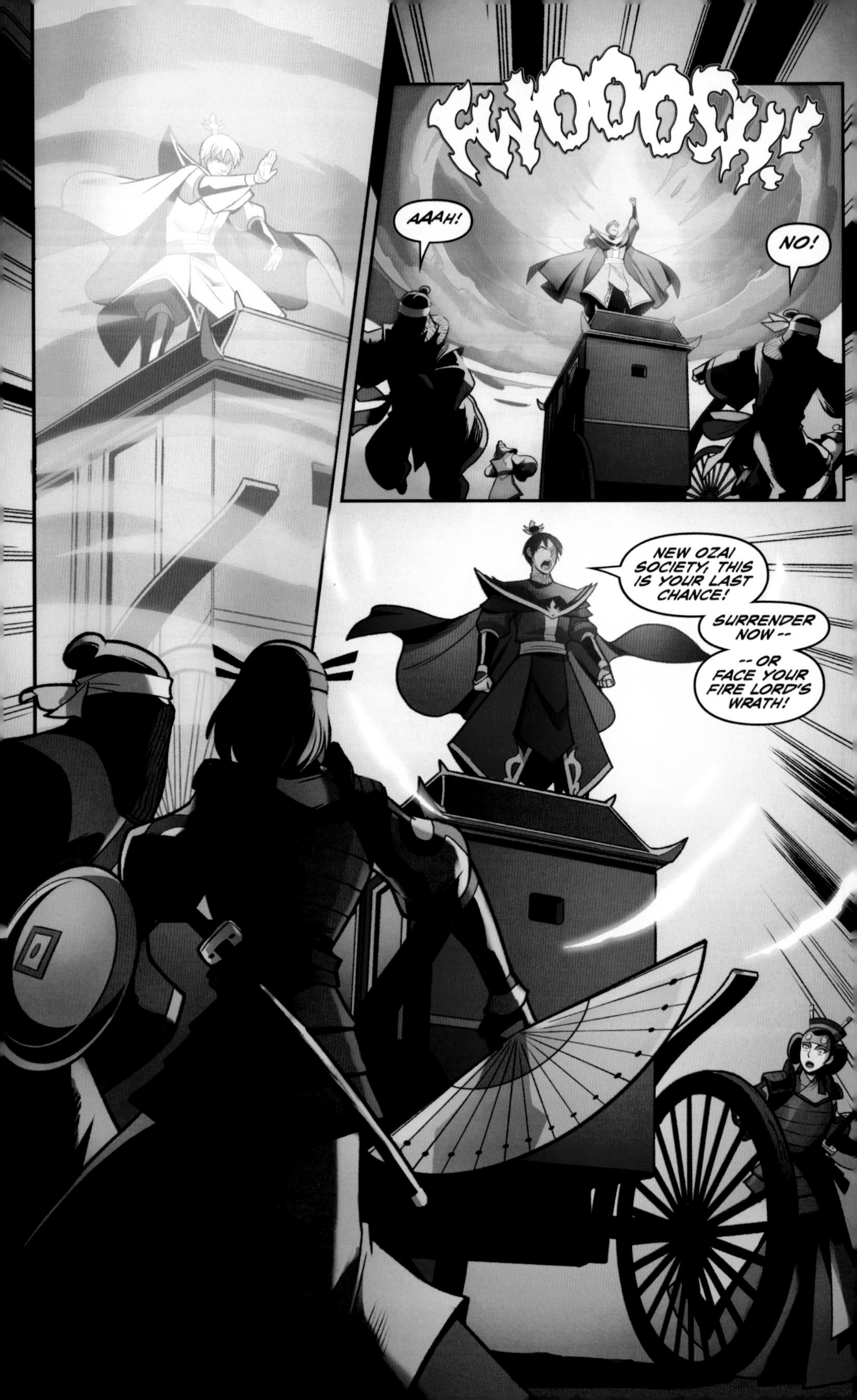
FWOOOSH!
AAAH!
NO!
NEW OZAI SOCIETY, THIS IS YOUR LAST CHANCE!
SURRENDER NOW --
-- OR FACE YOUR FIRE LORD'S WRATH!

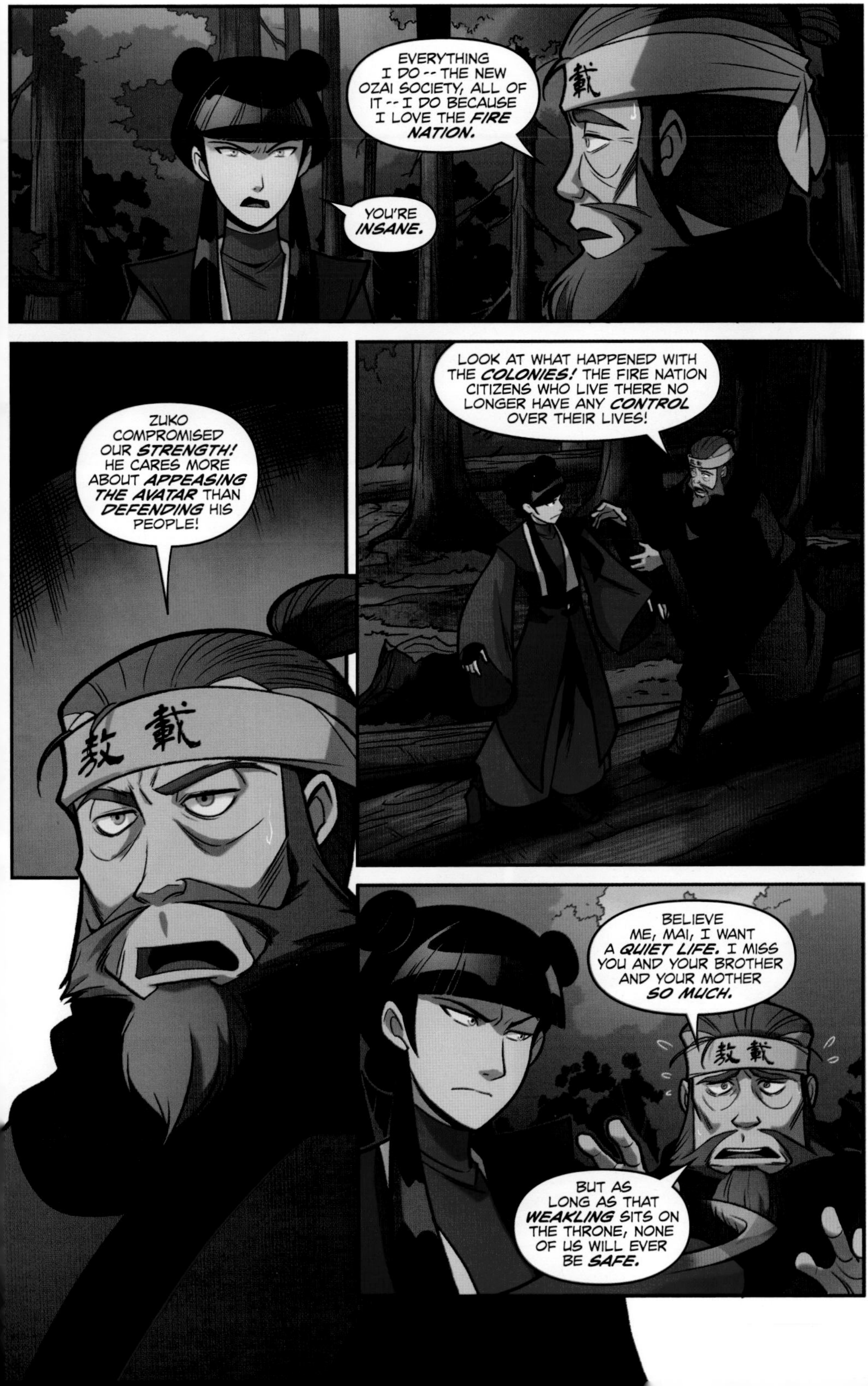
EVERYTHING I DO -- THE NEW OZAI SOCIETY, ALL OF IT -- I DO BECAUSE I LOVE THE *FIRE NATION.*
YOU'RE *INSANE.*
ZUKO COMPROMISED OUR *STRENGTH!* HE CARES MORE ABOUT *APPEASING THE AVATAR* THAN *DEFENDING* HIS PEOPLE!
LOOK AT WHAT HAPPENED WITH THE *COLONIES!* THE FIRE NATION CITIZENS WHO LIVE THERE NO LONGER HAVE ANY *CONTROL* OVER THEIR LIVES!
BELIEVE ME, MAI, I WANT A *QUIET LIFE.* I MISS YOU AND YOUR BROTHER AND YOUR MOTHER *SO MUCH.*
BUT AS LONG AS THAT *WEAKLING* SITS ON THE THRONE, NONE OF US WILL EVER BE *SAFE.*

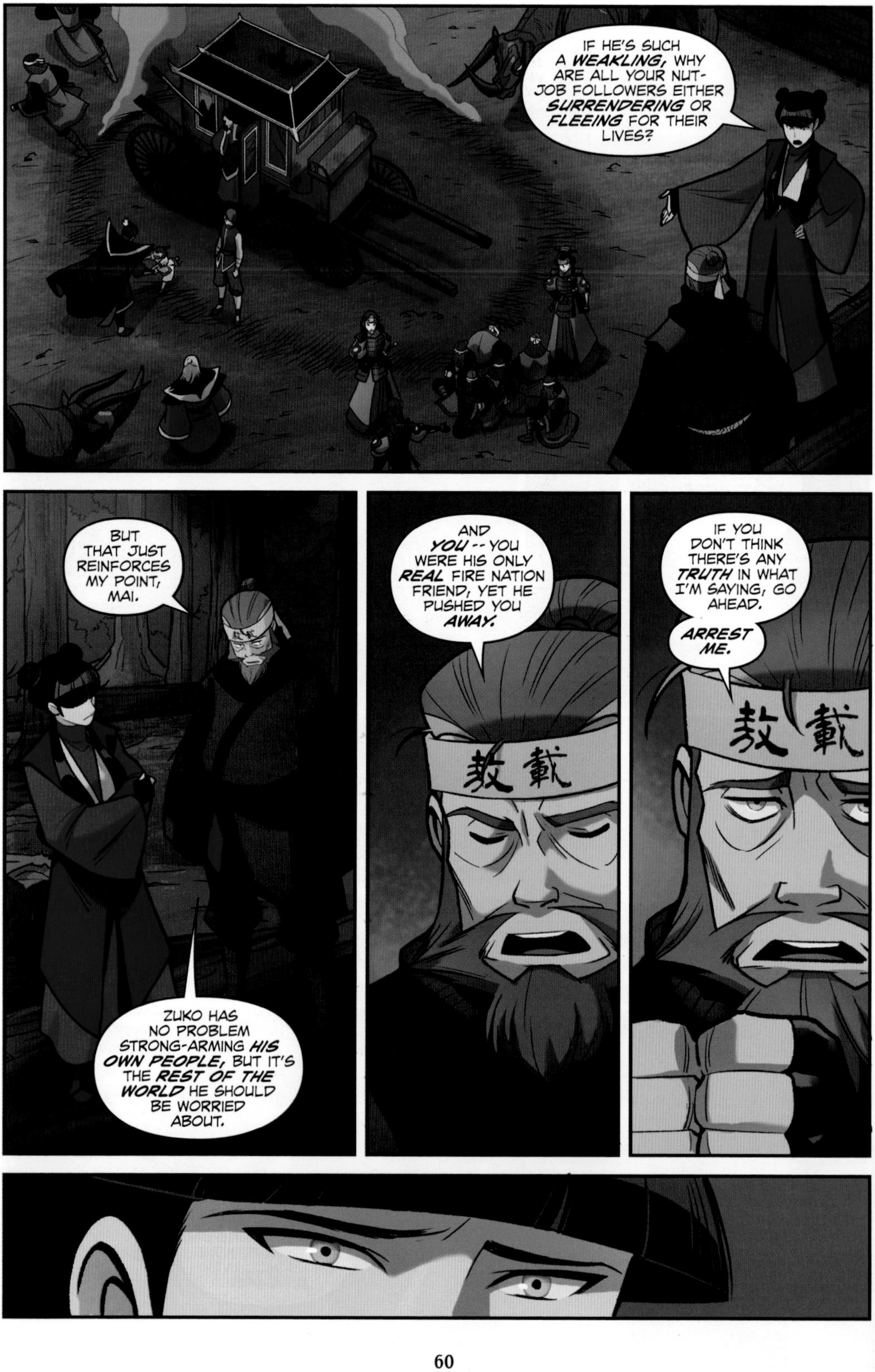
IF HE'S SUCH A WEAKLING, WHY ARE ALL YOUR NUT-JOB FOLLOWERS EITHER SURRENDERING OR FLEEING FOR THEIR LIVES?
BUT THAT JUST REINFORCES MY POINT, MAI.
ZUKO HAS NO PROBLEM STRONG-ARMING HIS OWN PEOPLE, BUT IT'S THE REST OF THE WORLD HE SHOULD BE WORRIED ABOUT.
AND YOU -- YOU WERE HIS ONLY REAL FIRE NATION FRIEND, YET HE PUSHED YOU AWAY.
IF YOU DON'T THINK THERE'S ANY TRUTH IN WHAT I'M SAYING, GO AHEAD.
ARREST ME.

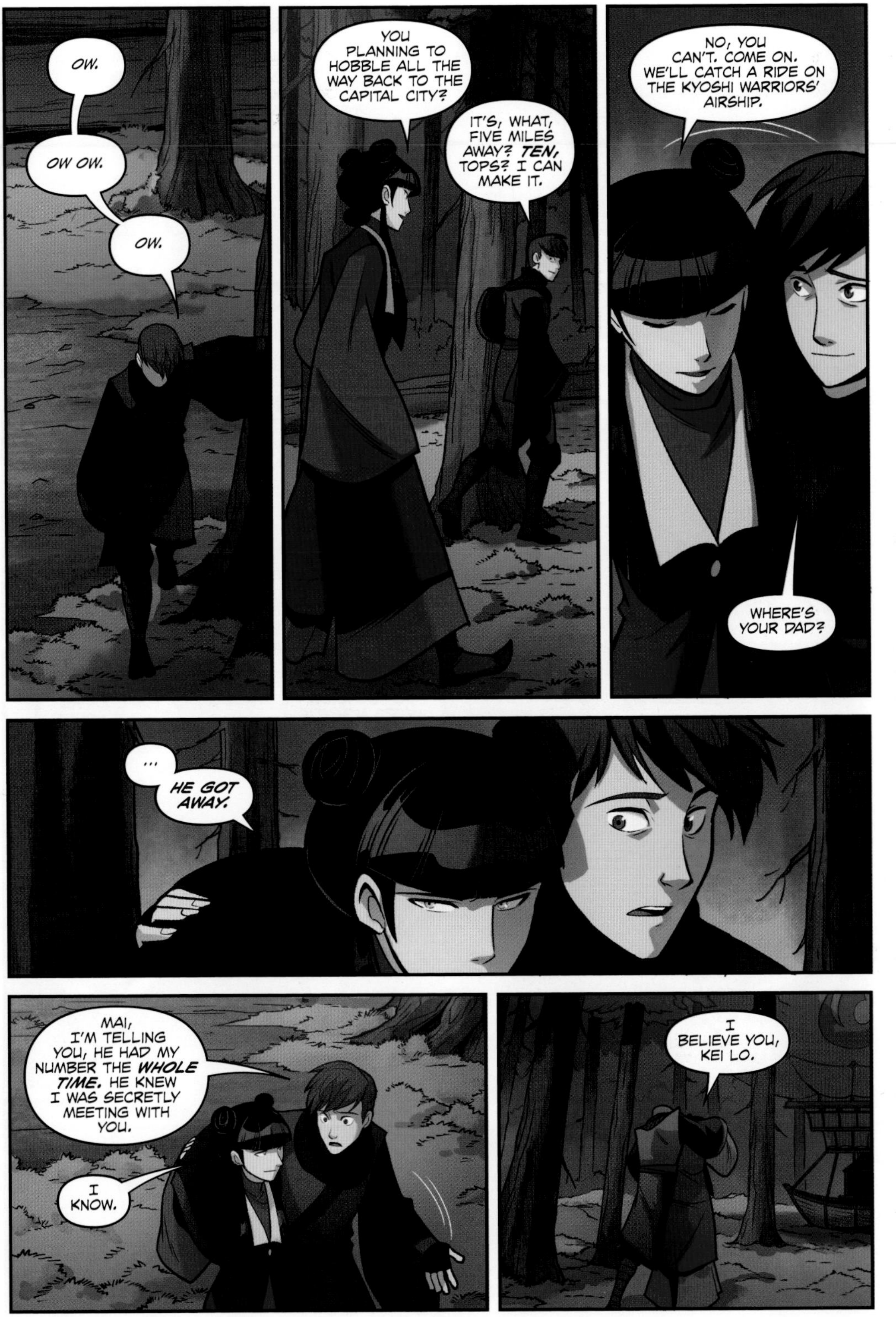
OW.
OW OW.
OW.
YOU PLANNING TO HOBBLE ALL THE WAY BACK TO THE CAPITAL CITY?
IT'S, WHAT, FIVE MILES AWAY? TEN, TOPS? I CAN MAKE IT.
NO, YOU CAN'T. COME ON. WE'LL CATCH A RIDE ON THE KYOSHI WARRIORS' AIRSHIP.
WHERE'S YOUR DAD?
... HE GOT AWAY.
MAI, I'M TELLING YOU, HE HAD MY NUMBER THE WHOLE TIME. HE KNEW I WAS SECRETLY MEETING WITH YOU.
I KNOW.
I BELIEVE YOU, KEI LO.

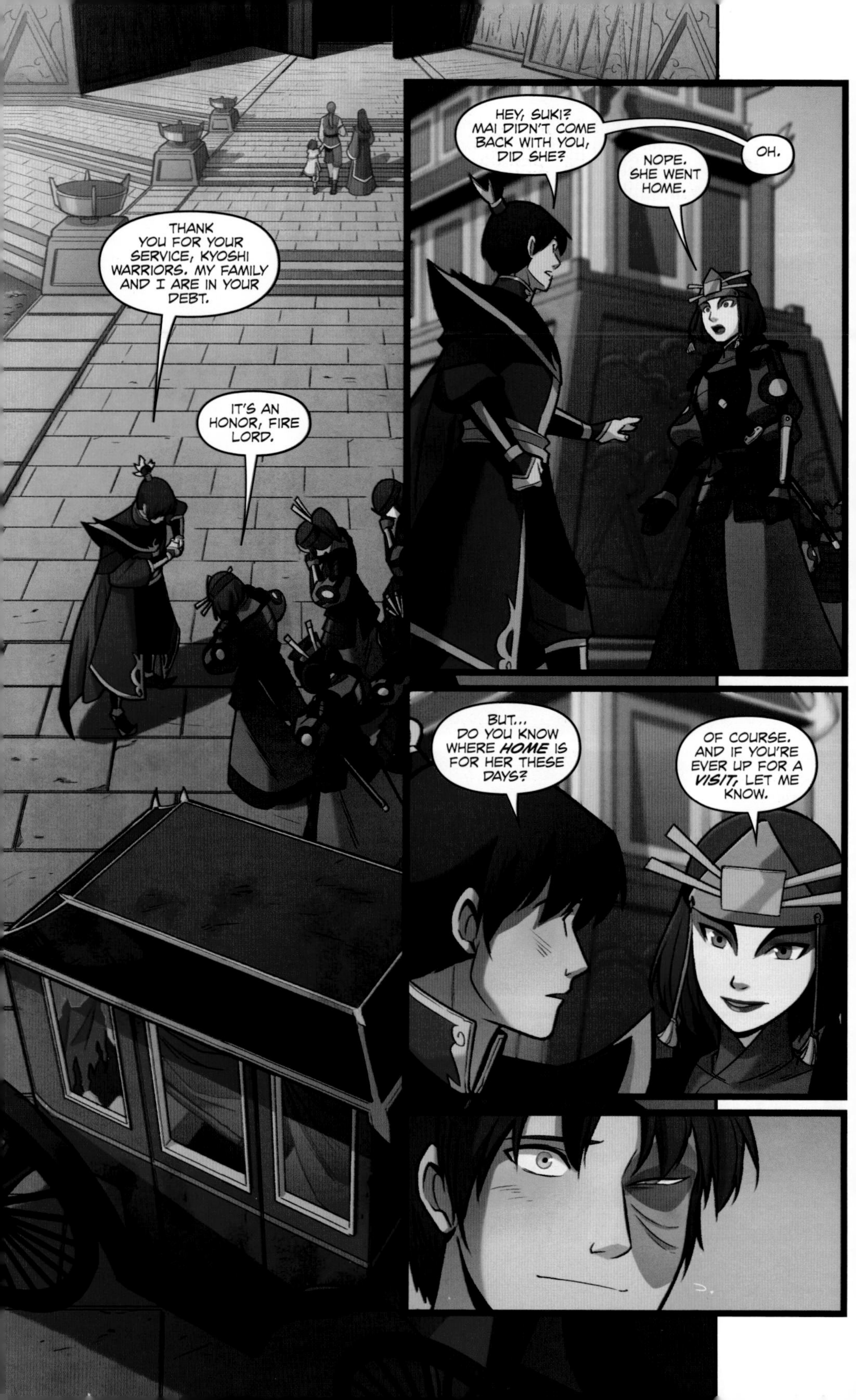

THANK YOU FOR YOUR SERVICE, KYOSHI WARRIORS. MY FAMILY AND I ARE IN YOUR DEBT.
IT'S AN HONOR, FIRE LORD.
HEY, SUKI? MAI DIDN'T COME BACK WITH YOU, DID SHE?
NOPE. SHE WENT HOME.
OH.
BUT... DO YOU KNOW WHERE *HOME* IS FOR HER THESE DAYS?
OF COURSE. AND IF YOU'RE EVER UP FOR A *VISIT,* LET ME KNOW.

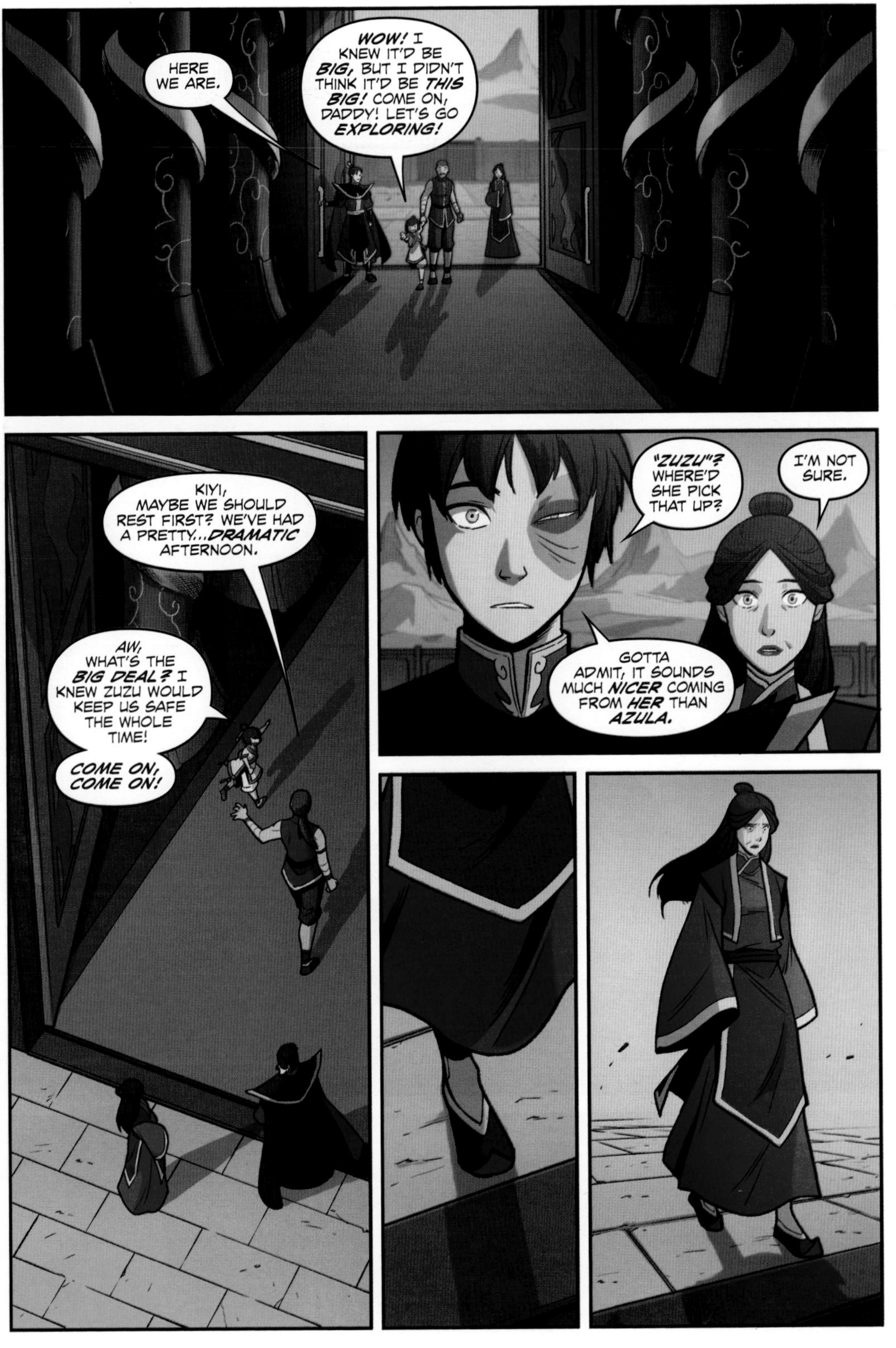
HERE WE ARE.
WOW! I KNEW IT'D BE BIG, BUT I DIDN'T THINK IT'D BE THIS BIG! COME ON, DADDY! LET'S GO EXPLORING!
KIYI, MAYBE WE SHOULD REST FIRST? WE'VE HAD A PRETTY...DRAMATIC AFTERNOON.
AW, WHAT'S THE BIG DEAL? I KNEW ZUZU WOULD KEEP US SAFE THE WHOLE TIME!
COME ON, COME ON!
"ZUZU"? WHERE'D SHE PICK THAT UP?
I'M NOT SURE.
GOTTA ADMIT, IT SOUNDS MUCH NICER COMING FROM HER THAN AZULA.

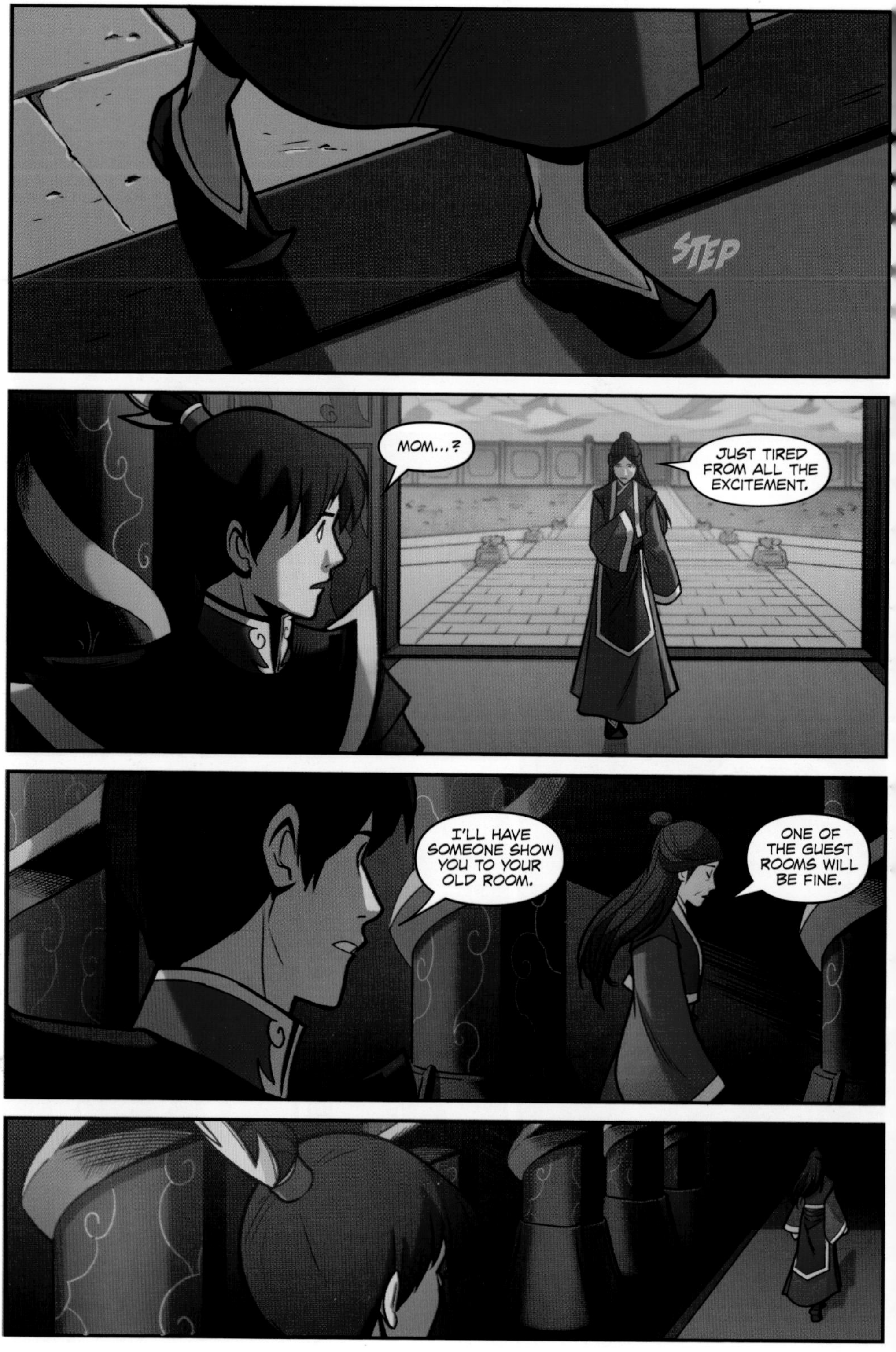
STEP
MOM...?
JUST TIRED FROM ALL THE EXCITEMENT.
I'LL HAVE SOMEONE SHOW YOU TO YOUR OLD ROOM.
ONE OF THE GUEST ROOMS WILL BE FINE.

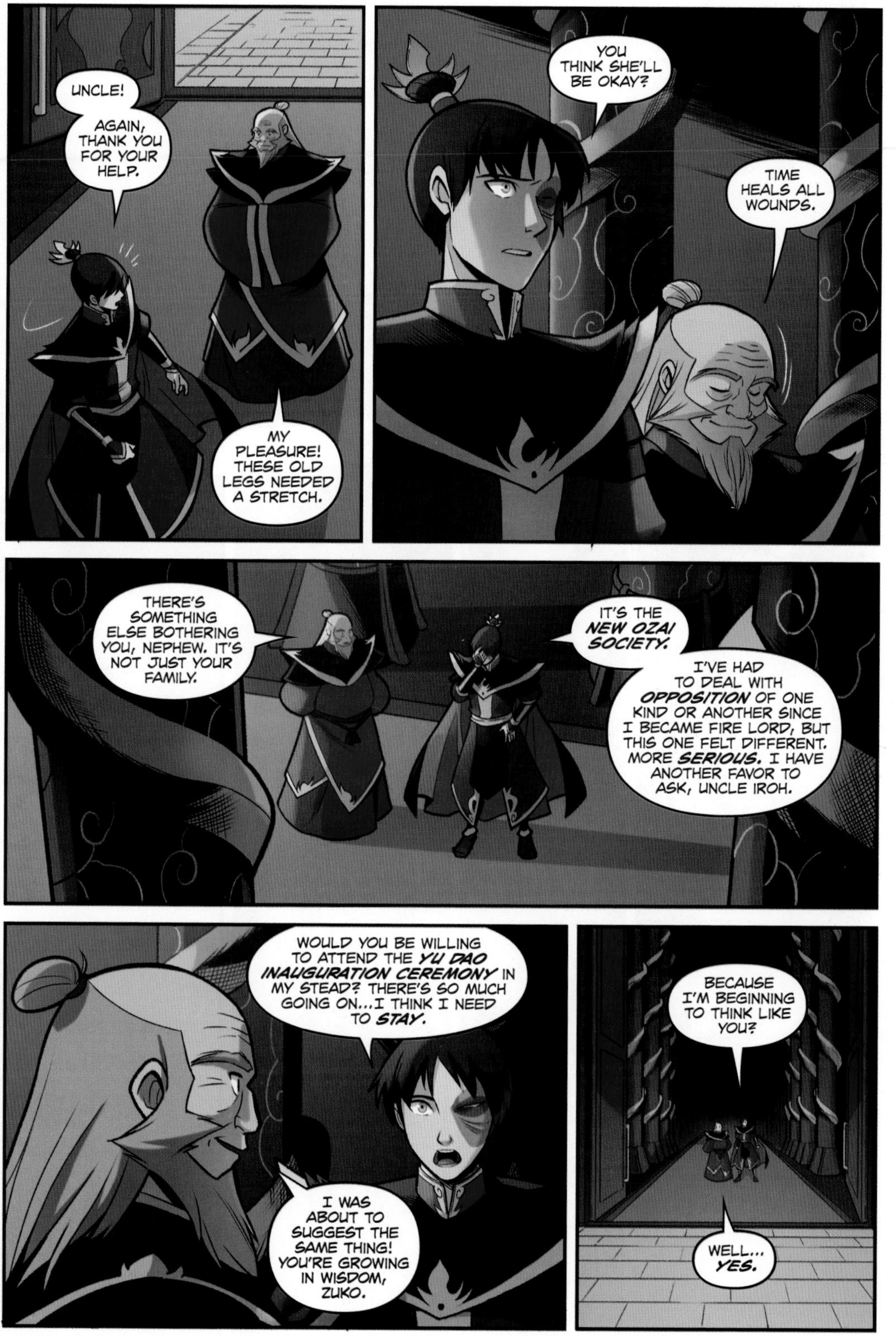
UNCLE!
AGAIN, THANK YOU FOR YOUR HELP.
MY PLEASURE! THESE OLD LEGS NEEDED A STRETCH.
YOU THINK SHE'LL BE OKAY?
TIME HEALS ALL WOUNDS.
THERE'S SOMETHING ELSE BOTHERING YOU, NEPHEW. IT'S NOT JUST YOUR FAMILY.
IT'S THE NEW OZAI SOCIETY.
I'VE HAD TO DEAL WITH OPPOSITION OF ONE KIND OR ANOTHER SINCE I BECAME FIRE LORD, BUT THIS ONE FELT DIFFERENT. MORE SERIOUS. I HAVE ANOTHER FAVOR TO ASK, UNCLE IROH.
WOULD YOU BE WILLING TO ATTEND THE YU DAO INAUGURATION CEREMONY IN MY STEAD? THERE'S SO MUCH GOING ON...I THINK I NEED TO STAY.
I WAS ABOUT TO SUGGEST THE SAME THING! YOU'RE GROWING IN WISDOM, ZUKO.
BECAUSE I'M BEGINNING TO THINK LIKE YOU?
WELL... YES.

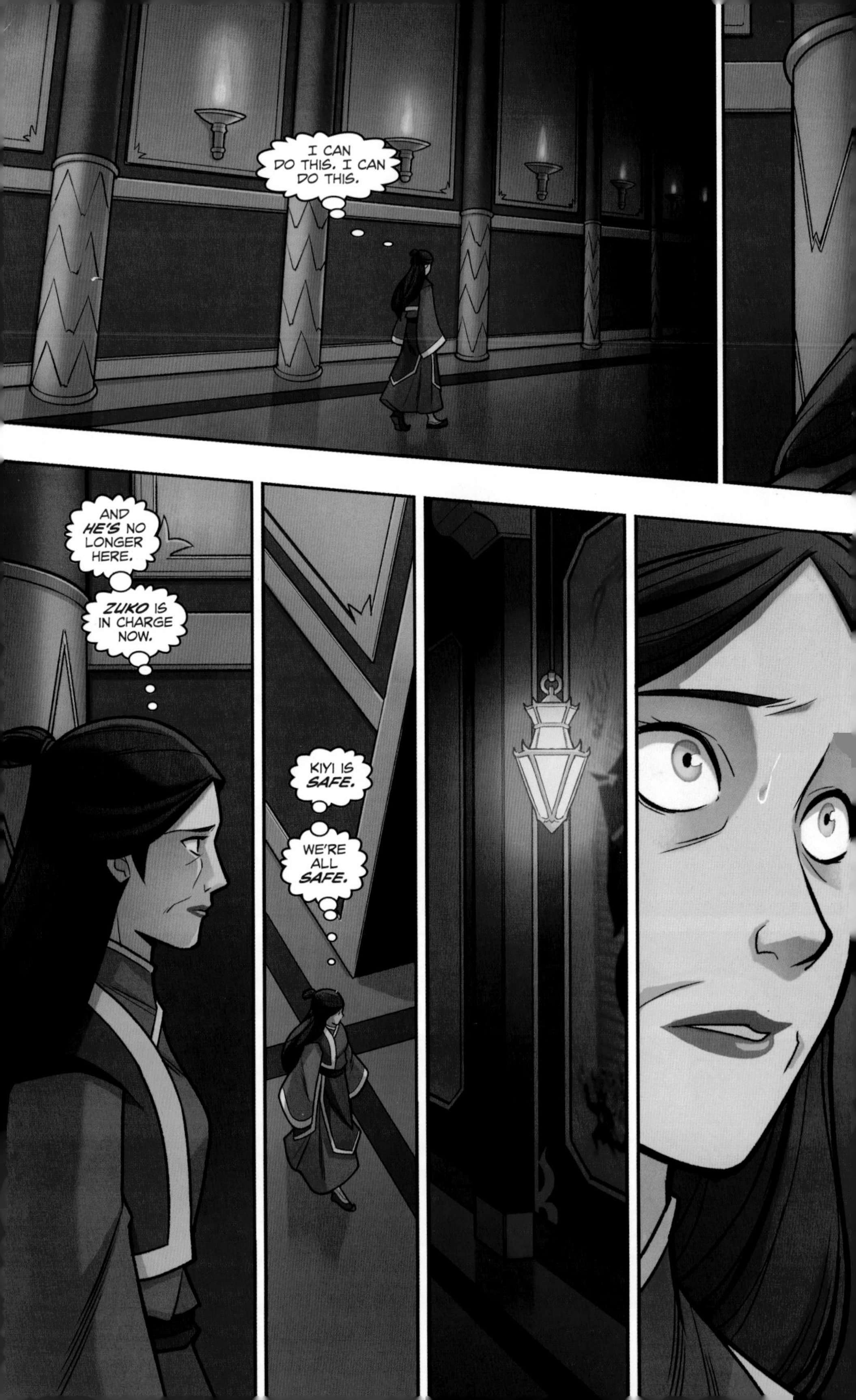
I CAN DO THIS. I CAN DO THIS.
AND HE'S NO LONGER HERE.
ZUKO IS IN CHARGE NOW.
KIYI IS SAFE.
WE'RE ALL SAFE.

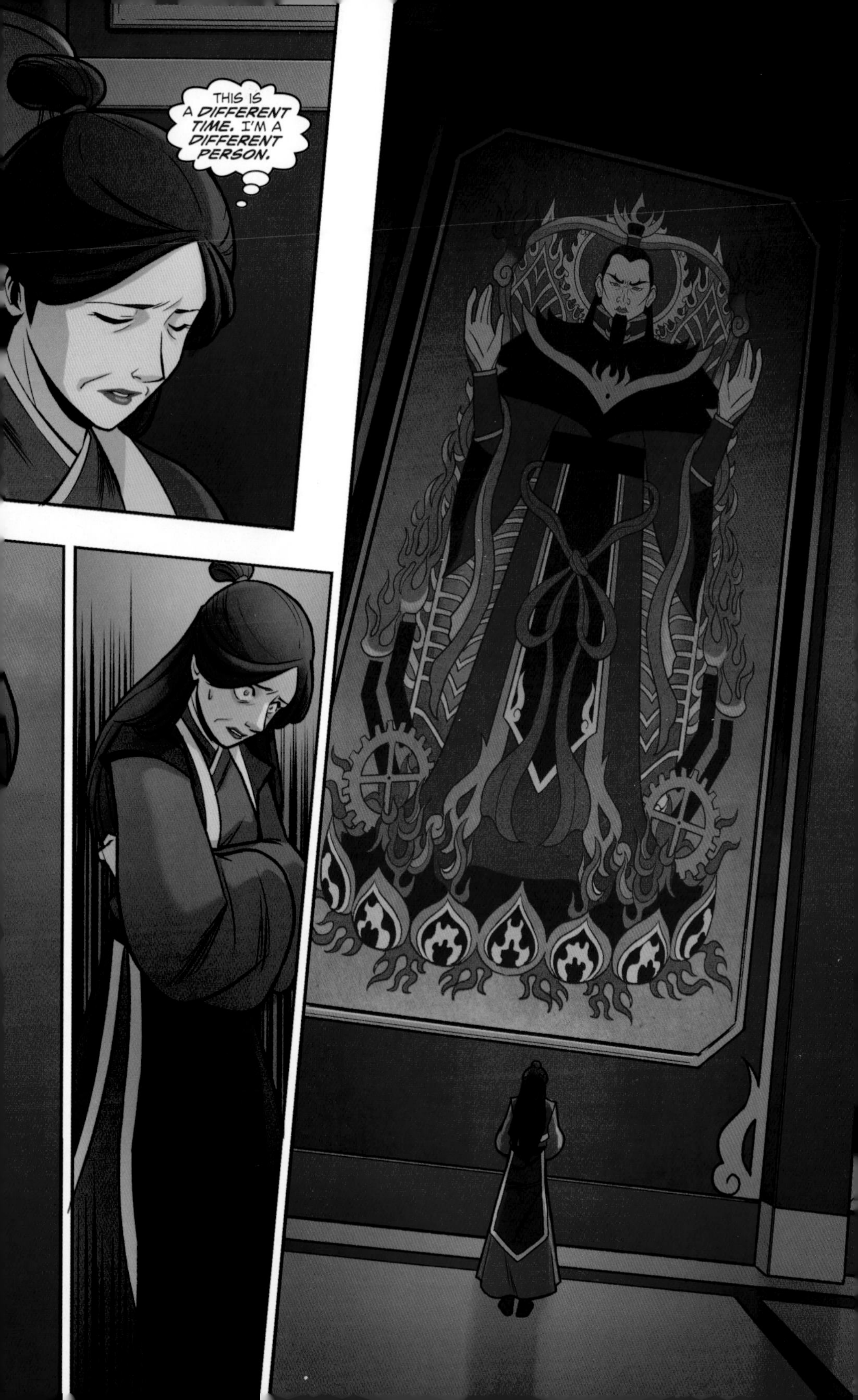
THIS IS A DIFFERENT TIME. I'M A DIFFERENT PERSON.

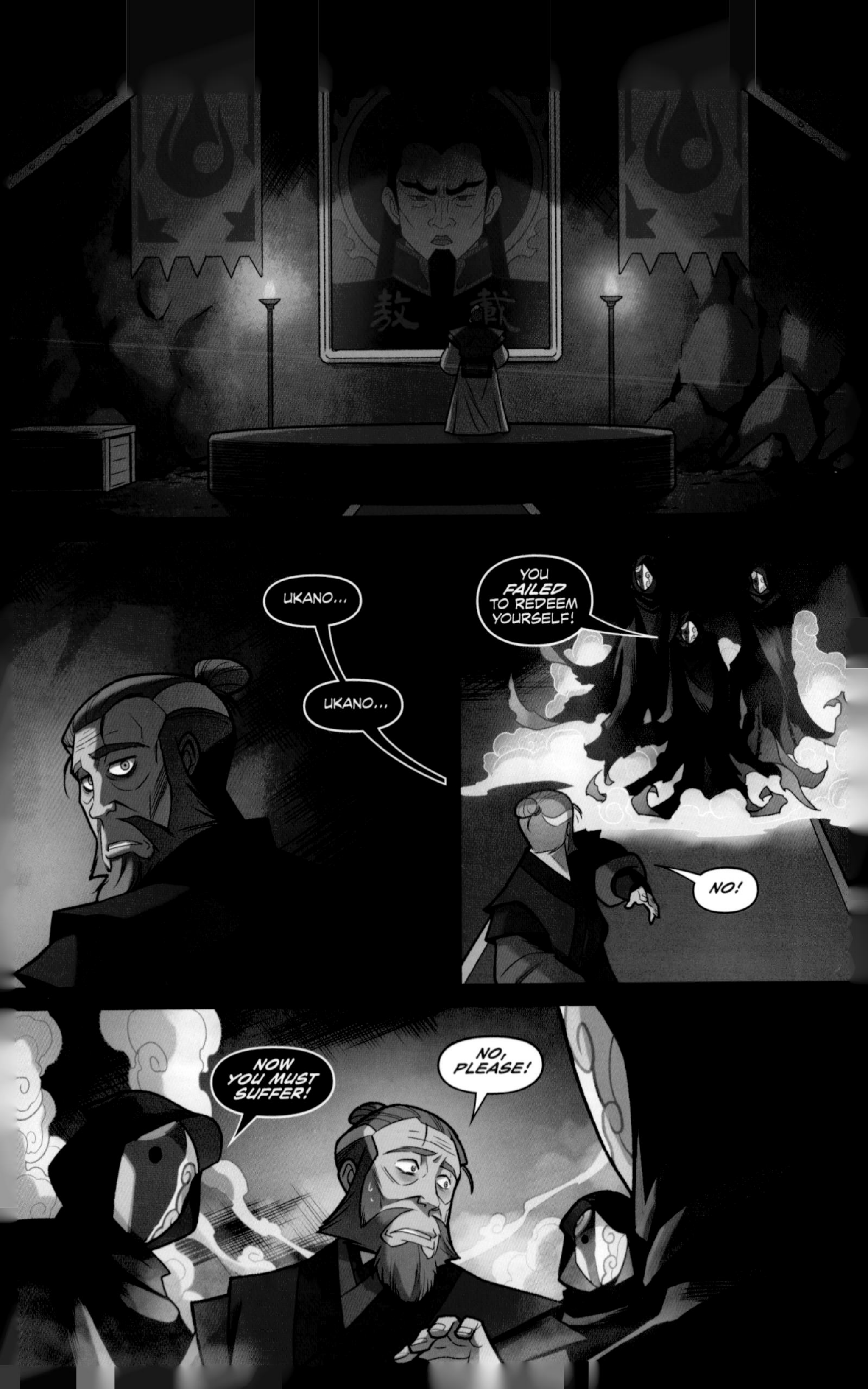
UKANO...
UKANO...
YOU *FAILED* TO REDEEM YOURSELF!
NO!
NOW YOU MUST SUFFER!
NO, PLEASE!

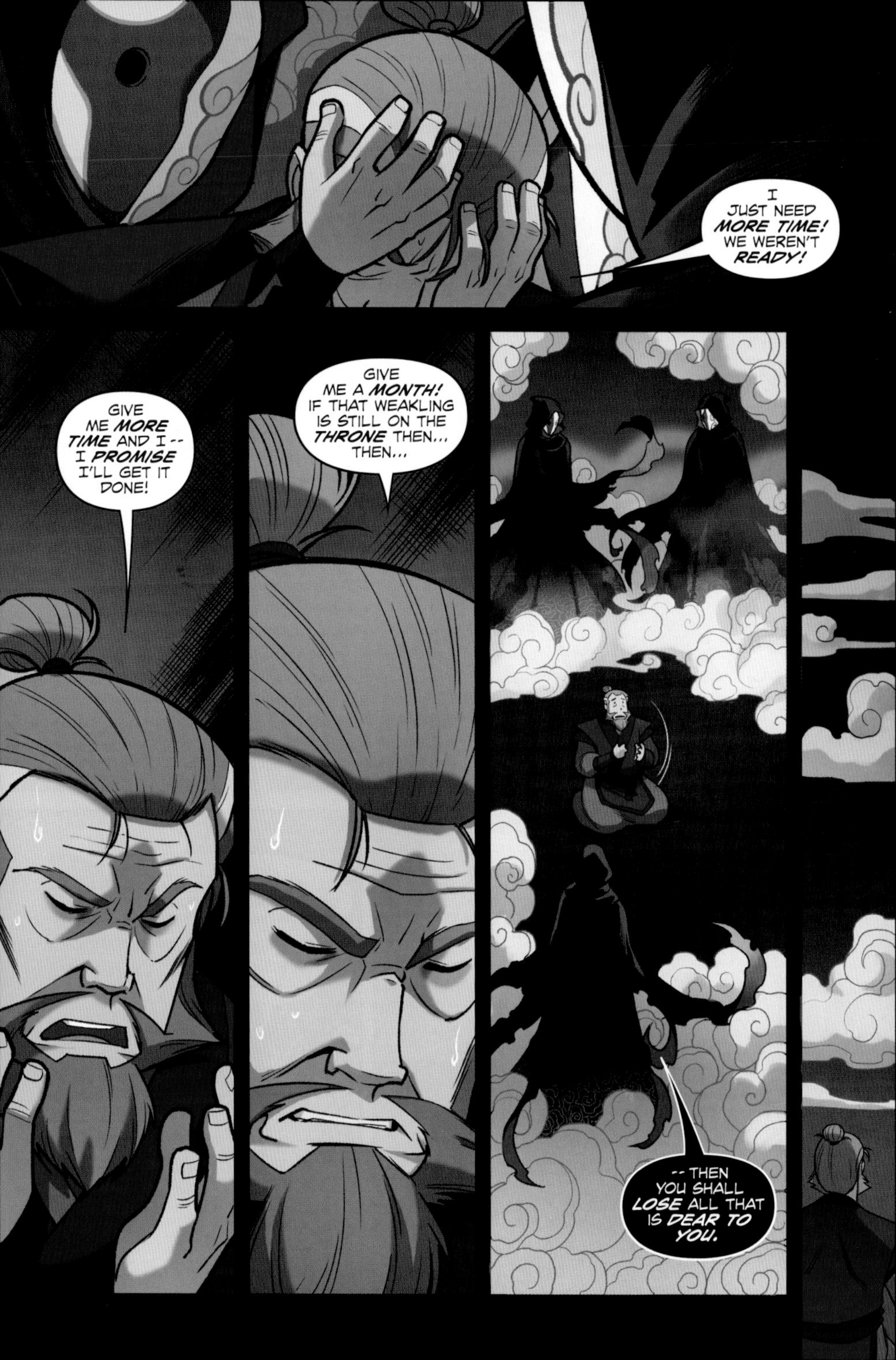
I JUST NEED MORE TIME! WE WEREN'T READY!
GIVE ME MORE TIME AND I -- I PROMISE I'LL GET IT DONE!
GIVE ME A MONTH! IF THAT WEAKLING IS STILL ON THE THRONE THEN... THEN...
-- THEN YOU SHALL LOSE ALL THAT IS DEAR TO YOU.

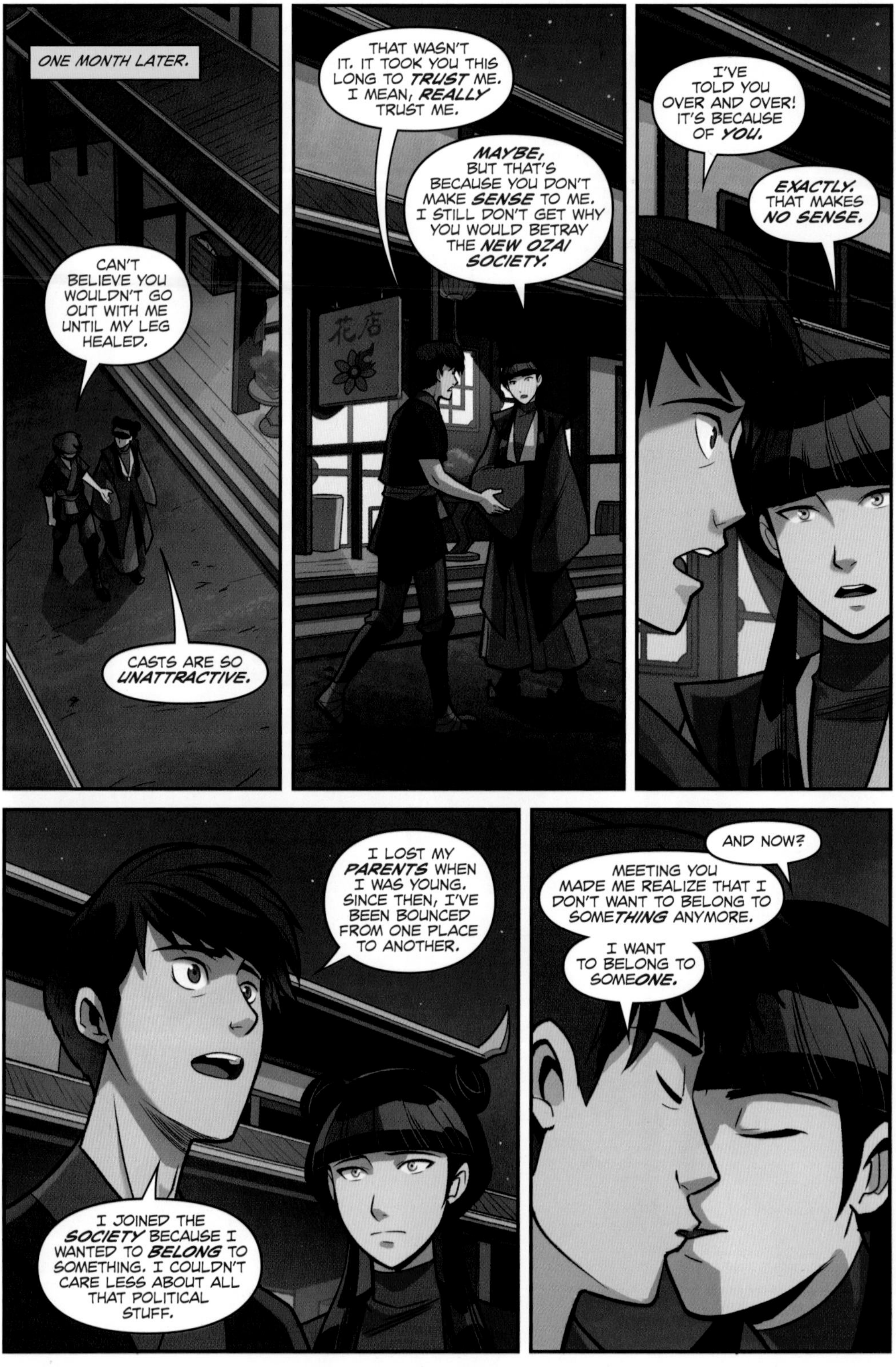
ONE MONTH LATER.
CAN'T BELIEVE YOU WOULDN'T GO OUT WITH ME UNTIL MY LEG HEALED.
CASTS ARE SO UNATTRACTIVE.
THAT WASN'T IT. IT TOOK YOU THIS LONG TO TRUST ME. I MEAN, REALLY TRUST ME.
MAYBE, BUT THAT'S BECAUSE YOU DON'T MAKE SENSE TO ME. I STILL DON'T GET WHY YOU WOULD BETRAY THE NEW OZAI SOCIETY.
花店
I'VE TOLD YOU OVER AND OVER! IT'S BECAUSE OF YOU.
EXACTLY. THAT MAKES NO SENSE.
I LOST MY PARENTS WHEN I WAS YOUNG. SINCE THEN, I'VE BEEN BOUNCED FROM ONE PLACE TO ANOTHER.
I JOINED THE SOCIETY BECAUSE I WANTED TO BELONG TO SOMETHING. I COULDN'T CARE LESS ABOUT ALL THAT POLITICAL STUFF.
AND NOW?
MEETING YOU MADE ME REALIZE THAT I DON'T WANT TO BELONG TO SOMETHING ANYMORE.
I WANT TO BELONG TO SOMEONE.

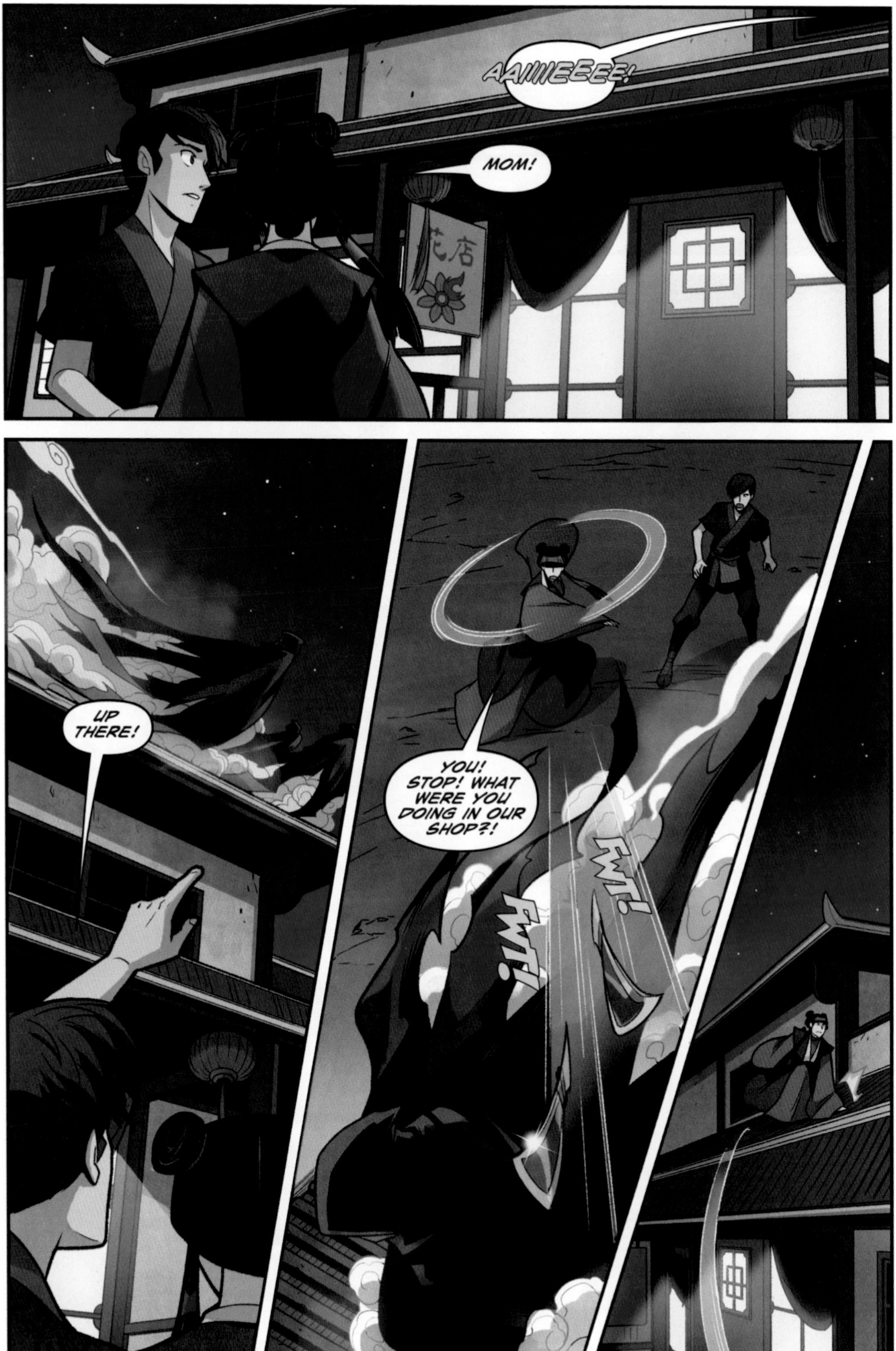
AAIIIEEEEE!
MOM!
UP THERE!
YOU! STOP! WHAT WERE YOU DOING IN OUR SHOP?!
FWT!
FWT!

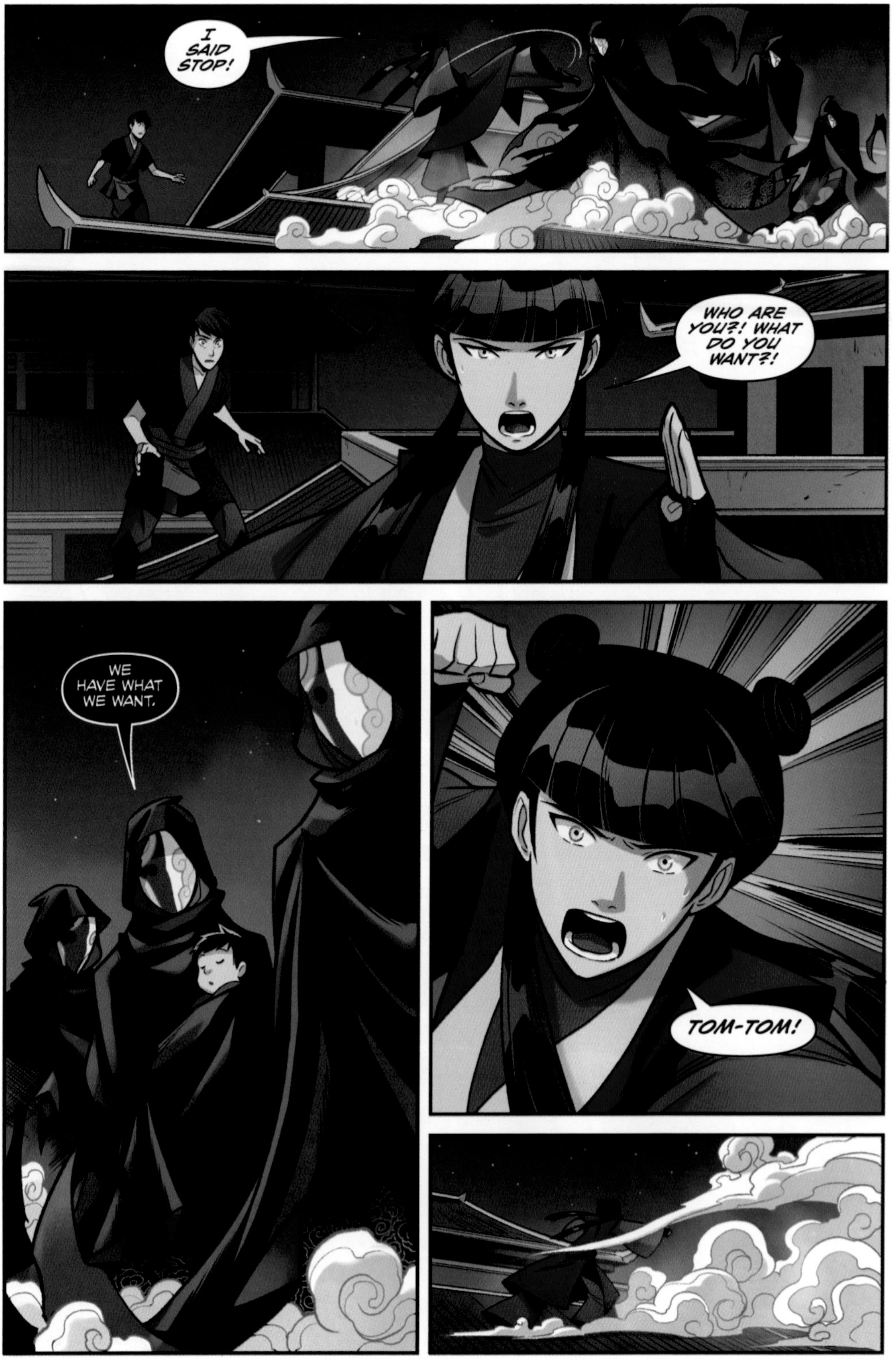
I SAID STOP!
WHO ARE YOU?! WHAT DO YOU WANT?!
WE HAVE WHAT WE WANT.
TOM-TOM!

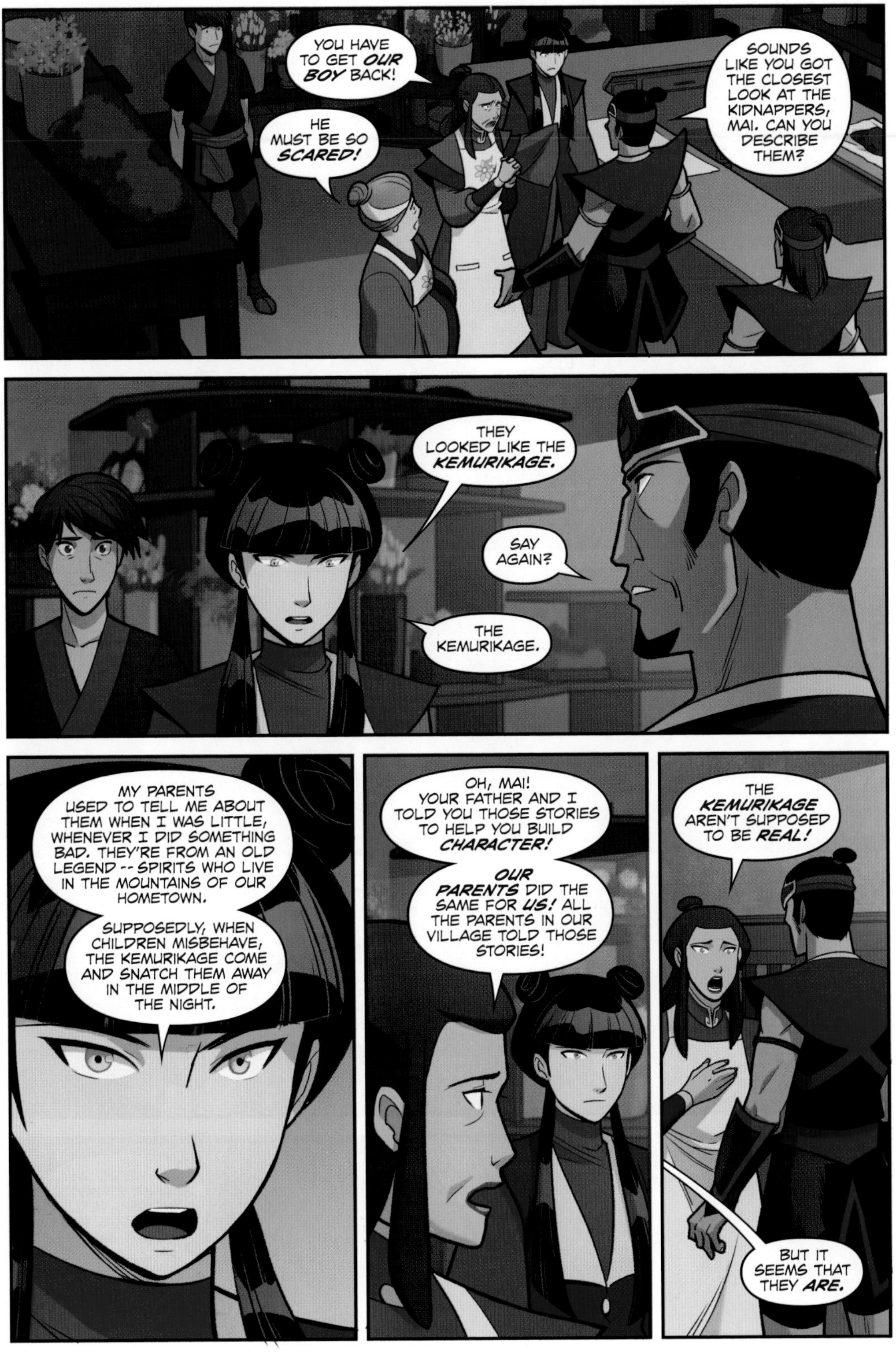
YOU HAVE TO GET OUR BOY BACK!
HE MUST BE SO SCARED!
SOUNDS LIKE YOU GOT THE CLOSEST LOOK AT THE KIDNAPPERS, MAI. CAN YOU DESCRIBE THEM?
THEY LOOKED LIKE THE KEMURIKAGE.
SAY AGAIN?
THE KEMURIKAGE.
MY PARENTS USED TO TELL ME ABOUT THEM WHEN I WAS LITTLE, WHENEVER I DID SOMETHING BAD. THEY'RE FROM AN OLD LEGEND -- SPIRITS WHO LIVE IN THE MOUNTAINS OF OUR HOMETOWN.
SUPPOSEDLY, WHEN CHILDREN MISBEHAVE, THE KEMURIKAGE COME AND SNATCH THEM AWAY IN THE MIDDLE OF THE NIGHT.
OH, MAI! YOUR FATHER AND I TOLD YOU THOSE STORIES TO HELP YOU BUILD CHARACTER!
OUR PARENTS DID THE SAME FOR US! ALL THE PARENTS IN OUR VILLAGE TOLD THOSE STORIES!
THE KEMURIKAGE AREN'T SUPPOSED TO BE REAL!
BUT IT SEEMS THAT THEY ARE.

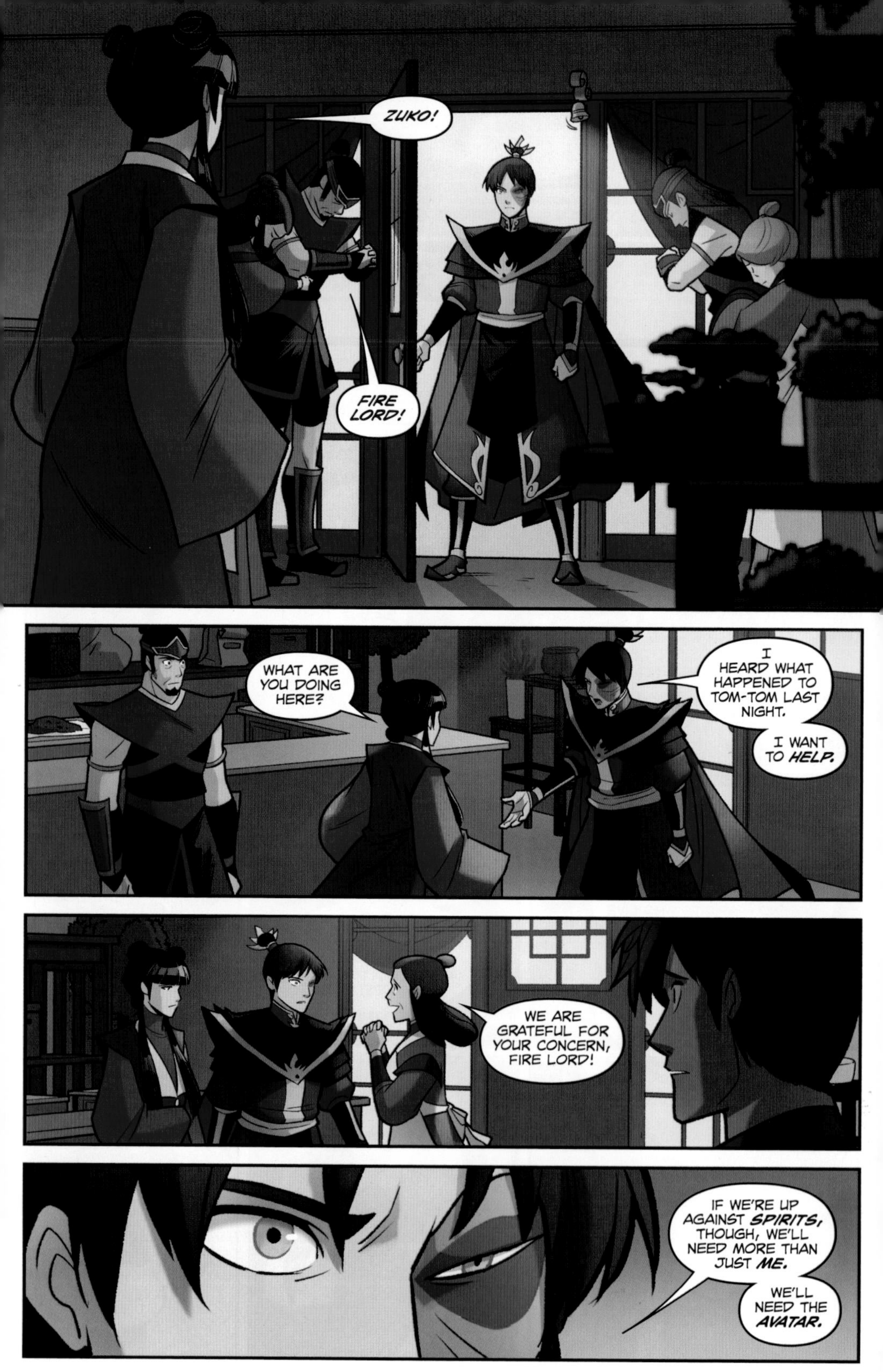
ZUKO!
FIRE LORD!
WHAT ARE YOU DOING HERE?
I HEARD WHAT HAPPENED TO TOM-TOM LAST NIGHT.
I WANT TO HELP.
WE ARE GRATEFUL FOR YOUR CONCERN, FIRE LORD!
IF WE'RE UP AGAINST SPIRITS, THOUGH, WE'LL NEED MORE THAN JUST ME.
WE'LL NEED THE AVATAR.

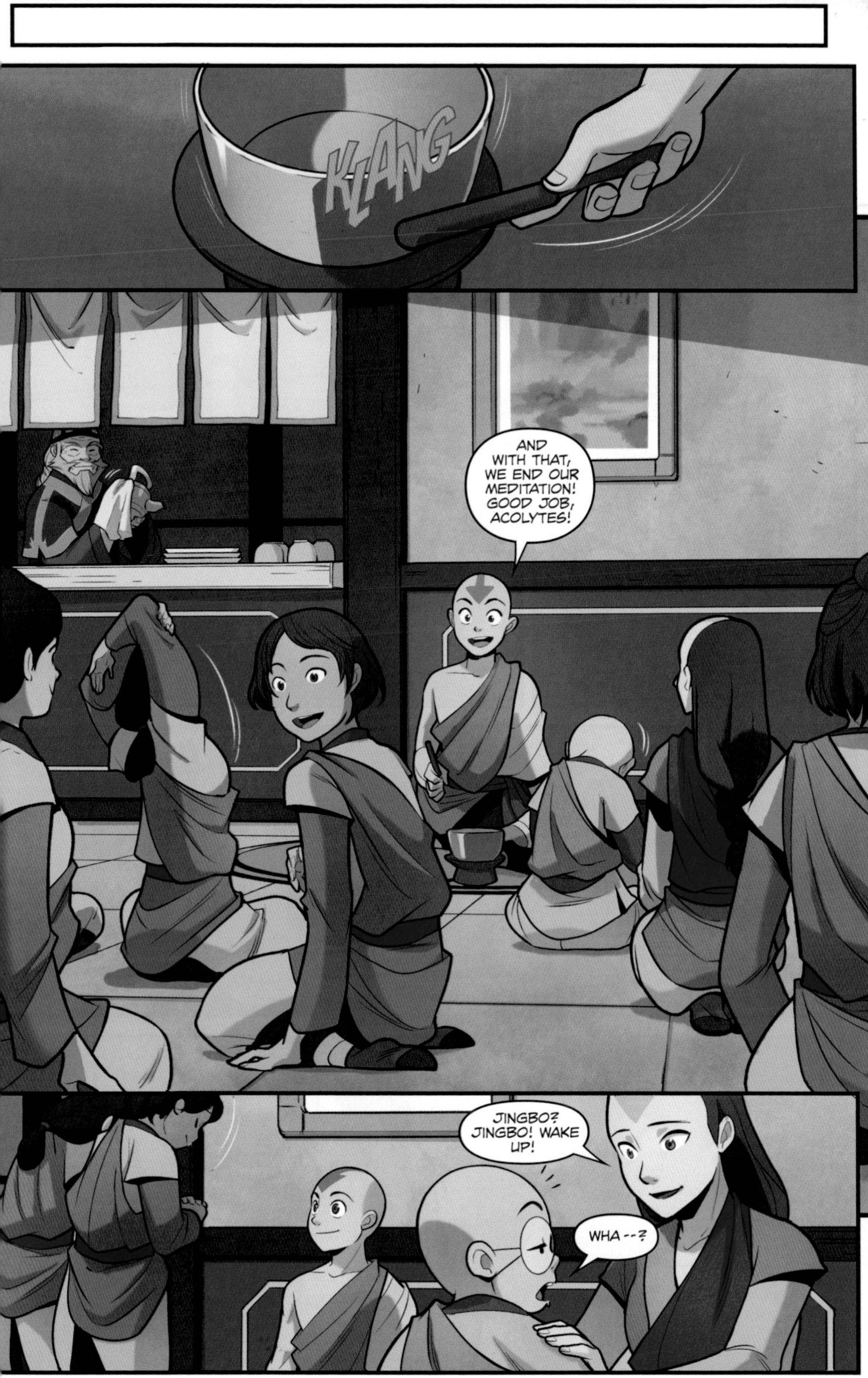
KLANG
AND WITH THAT, WE END OUR MEDITATION! GOOD JOB, ACOLYTES!
JINGBO? JINGBO! WAKE UP!
WHA--?

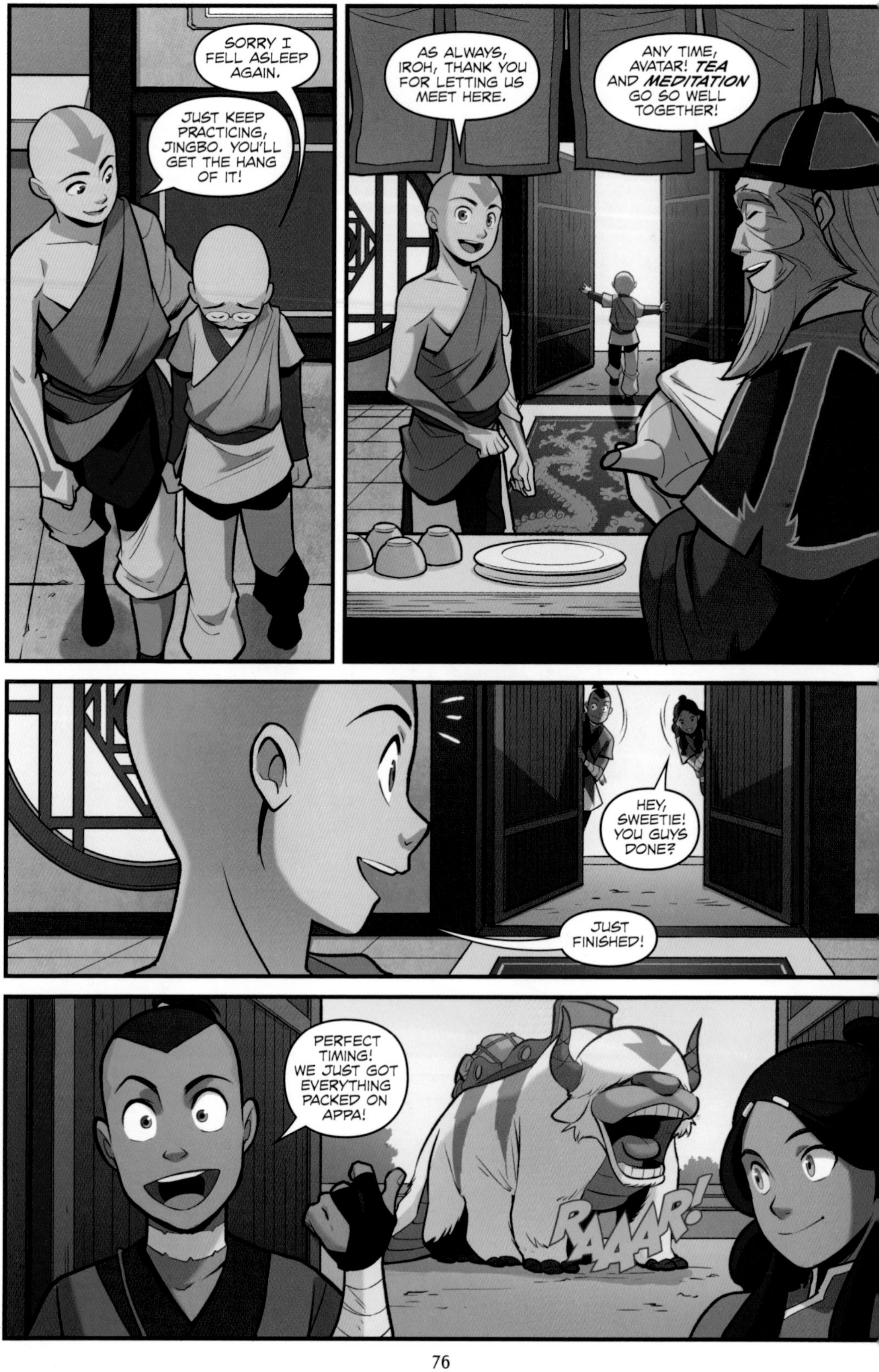

SORRY I FELL ASLEEP AGAIN.
JUST KEEP PRACTICING, JINGBO. YOU'LL GET THE HANG OF IT!
AS ALWAYS, IROH, THANK YOU FOR LETTING US MEET HERE.
ANY TIME, AVATAR! *TEA* AND *MEDITATION* GO SO WELL TOGETHER!
HEY, SWEETIE! YOU GUYS DONE?
JUST FINISHED!
PERFECT TIMING! WE JUST GOT EVERYTHING PACKED ON APPA!
RAAAR!

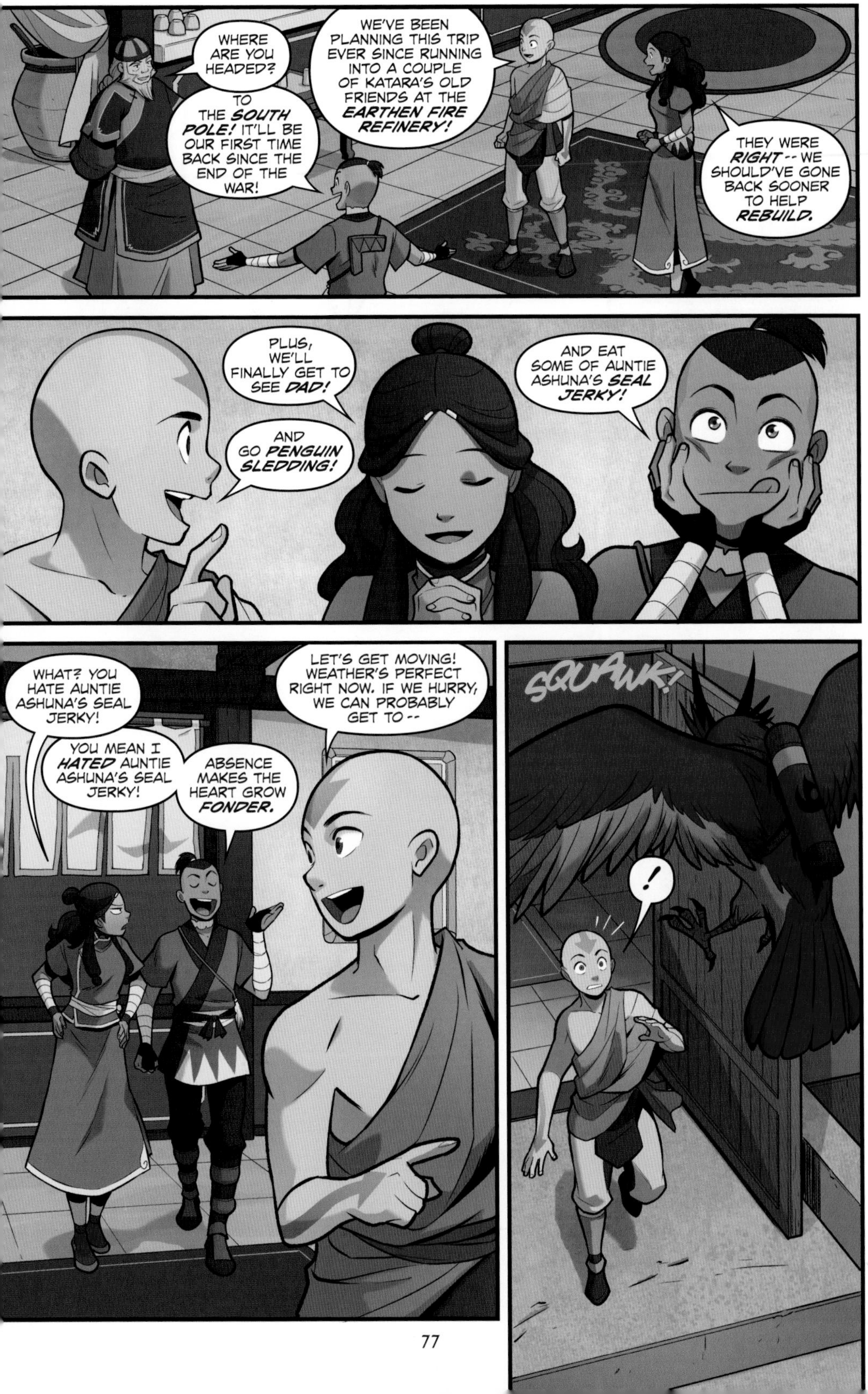
WHERE ARE YOU HEADED?
TO THE SOUTH POLE! IT'LL BE OUR FIRST TIME BACK SINCE THE END OF THE WAR!
WE'VE BEEN PLANNING THIS TRIP EVER SINCE RUNNING INTO A COUPLE OF KATARA'S OLD FRIENDS AT THE EARTHEN FIRE REFINERY!
THEY WERE RIGHT -- WE SHOULD'VE GONE BACK SOONER TO HELP REBUILD.
PLUS, WE'LL FINALLY GET TO SEE DAD!
AND GO PENGUIN SLEDDING!
AND EAT SOME OF AUNTIE ASHUNA'S SEAL JERKY!
WHAT? YOU HATE AUNTIE ASHUNA'S SEAL JERKY!
YOU MEAN I HATED AUNTIE ASHUNA'S SEAL JERKY!
ABSENCE MAKES THE HEART GROW FONDER.
LET'S GET MOVING! WEATHER'S PERFECT RIGHT NOW. IF WE HURRY, WE CAN PROBABLY GET TO --
SQUAWK!
!

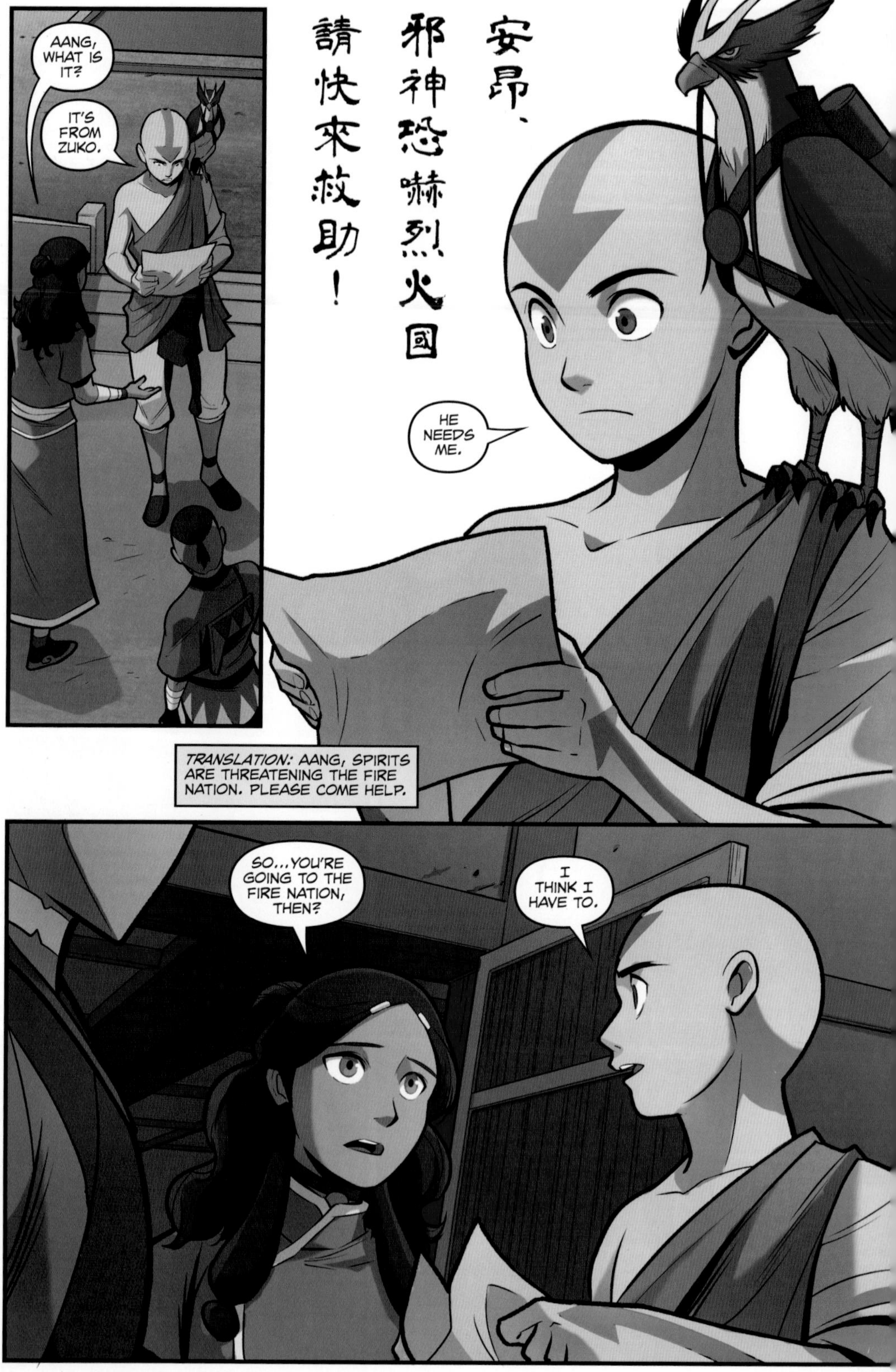
AANG, WHAT IS IT?
IT'S FROM ZUKO.
安昂、
邪神恐嚇烈火國
請快來救助！
HE NEEDS ME.
TRANSLATION: AANG, SPIRITS ARE THREATENING THE FIRE NATION. PLEASE COME HELP.
SO...YOU'RE GOING TO THE FIRE NATION, THEN?
I THINK I HAVE TO.

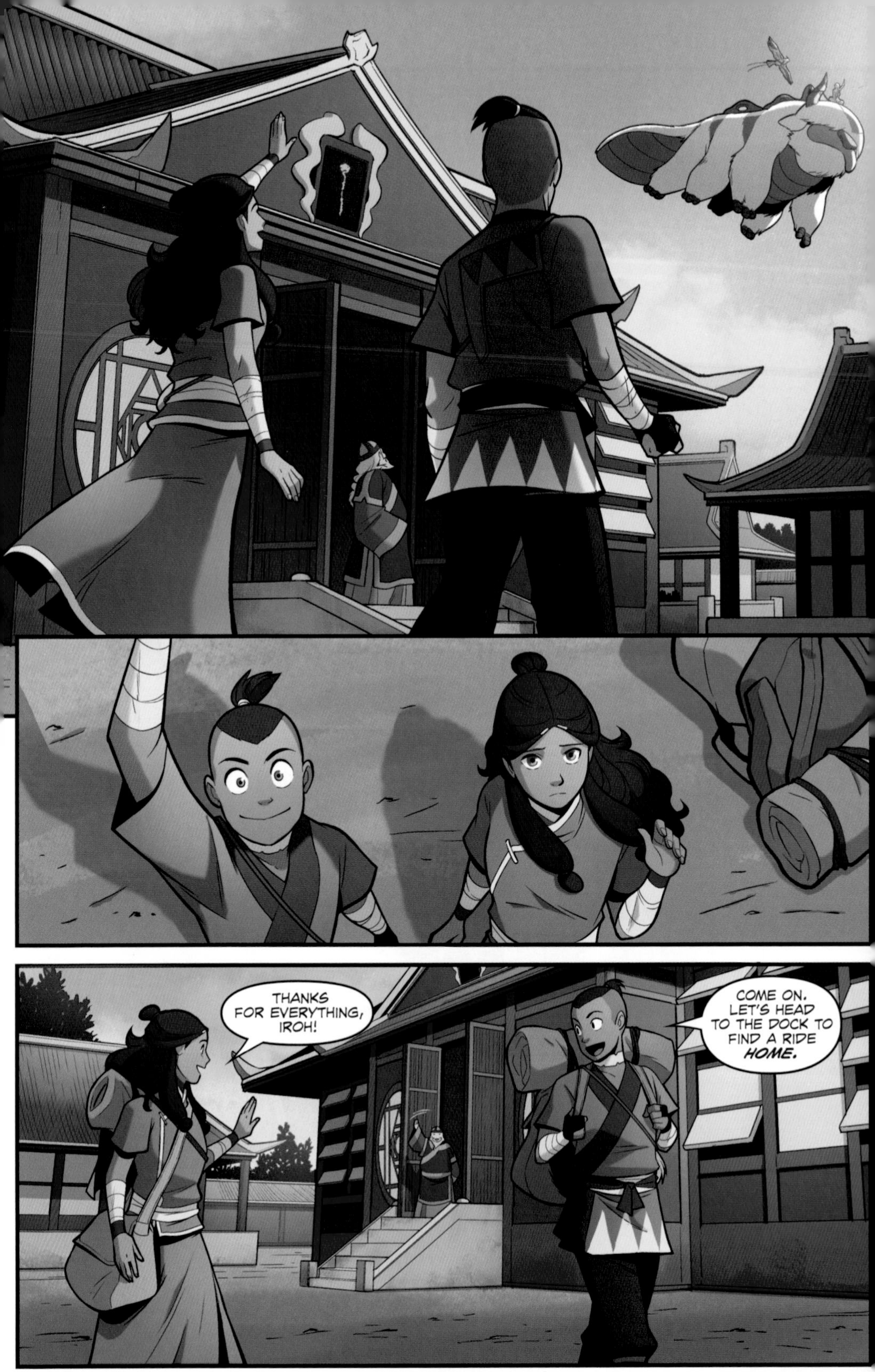
THANKS FOR EVERYTHING, IROH!
COME ON. LET'S HEAD TO THE DOCK TO FIND A RIDE HOME.

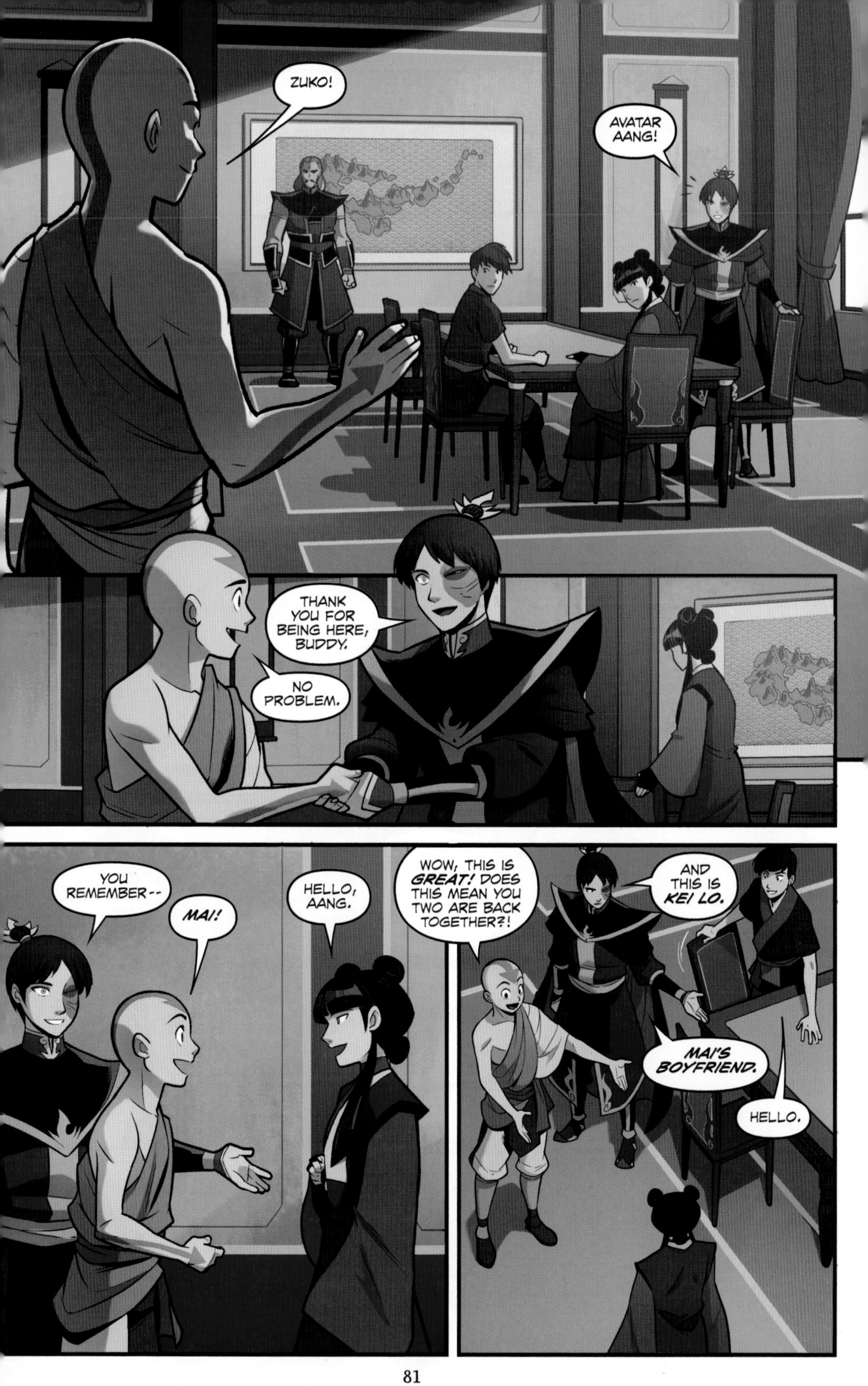
ZUKO!
AVATAR AANG!
THANK YOU FOR BEING HERE, BUDDY.
NO PROBLEM.
YOU REMEMBER--
MAI!
HELLO, AANG.
WOW, THIS IS GREAT! DOES THIS MEAN YOU TWO ARE BACK TOGETHER?!
AND THIS IS KEI LO.
MAI'S BOYFRIEND.
HELLO.

OH, I MEAN--YOU KNOW, I--

WHAT I SAID EARLIER--

BY **"BACK TOGETHER"** I MEANT, UM--

PLEASE, KEEP TALKING. BECAUSE THINGS AREN'T **AWKWARD** ENOUGH YET.

SORRY.

≶AHEM≷

AND FINALLY, AANG, PLEASE MEET **CONSTABLE SUNG.** HE'S LEADING THE INVESTIGATION INTO THE KIDNAPPING.

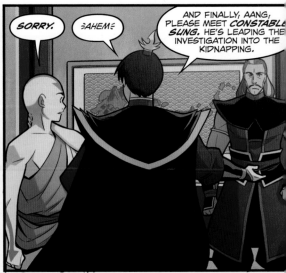

I'M HONORED, AVATAR.

NICE TO MEET YOU, CONSTABLE--

WAIT, **KIDNAPPING?!**

LAST NIGHT, MY LITTLE BROTHER **TOM-TOM** WAS TAKEN BY A BAND OF **DARK SPIRITS.**

YOU SAW THEM?

I **FOUGHT** THEM. THEY WERE THE **KEMURIKAGE.**

WHO?

DARK SPIRITS WHO SUPPOSEDLY HAUNT THE MOUNTAINS JUST OUTSIDE MY HOME VILLAGE. I RECOGNIZED THEM FROM STORIES MY PARENTS USED TO TELL ME.

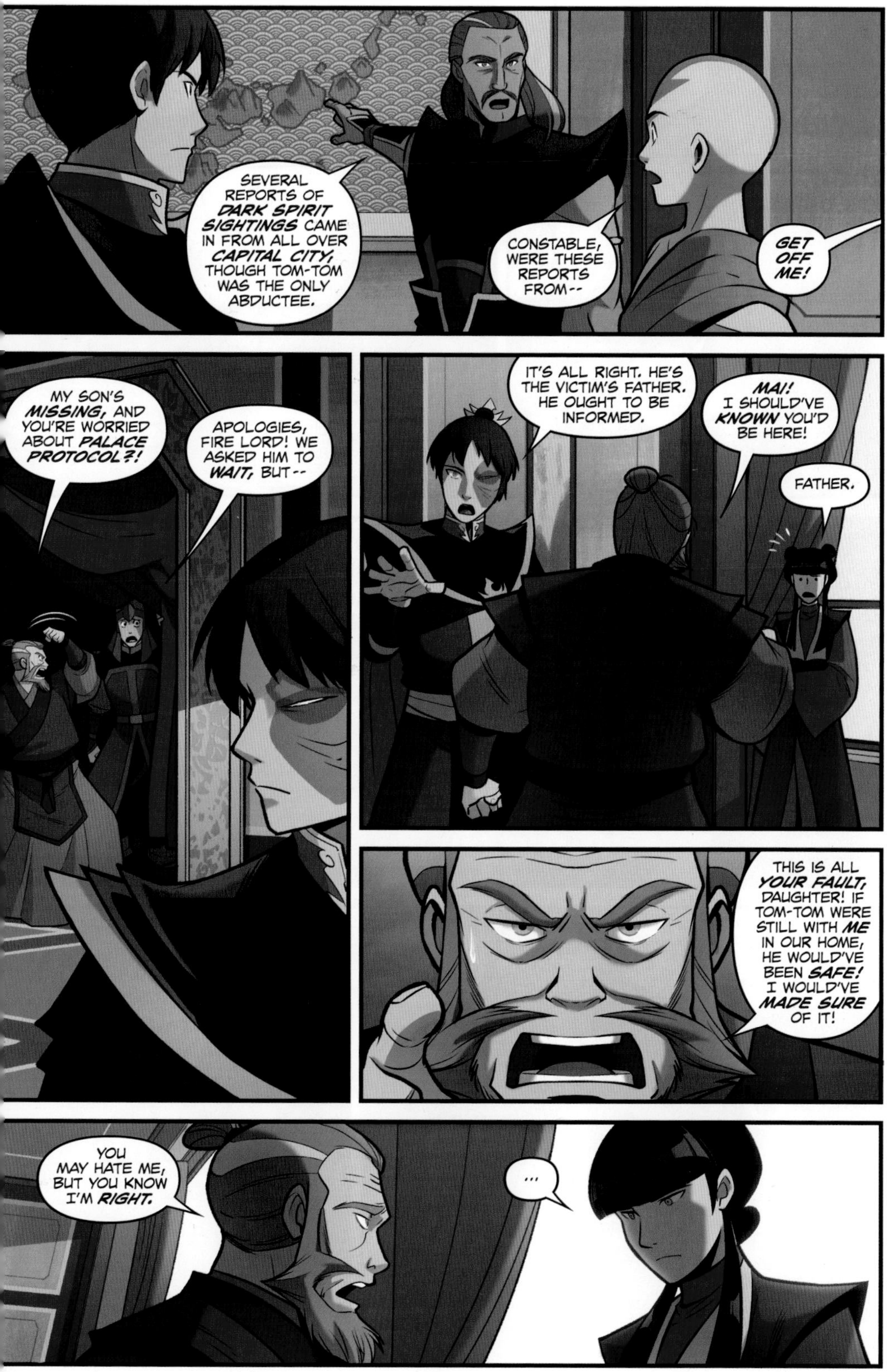
SEVERAL REPORTS OF DARK SPIRIT SIGHTINGS CAME IN FROM ALL OVER CAPITAL CITY, THOUGH TOM-TOM WAS THE ONLY ABDUCTEE.
CONSTABLE, WERE THESE REPORTS FROM--
GET OFF ME!
MY SON'S MISSING, AND YOU'RE WORRIED ABOUT PALACE PROTOCOL?!
APOLOGIES, FIRE LORD! WE ASKED HIM TO WAIT, BUT--
IT'S ALL RIGHT. HE'S THE VICTIM'S FATHER. HE OUGHT TO BE INFORMED.
MAI! I SHOULD'VE KNOWN YOU'D BE HERE!
FATHER.
THIS IS ALL YOUR FAULT, DAUGHTER! IF TOM-TOM WERE STILL WITH ME IN OUR HOME, HE WOULD'VE BEEN SAFE! I WOULD'VE MADE SURE OF IT!
YOU MAY HATE ME, BUT YOU KNOW I'M RIGHT.
...

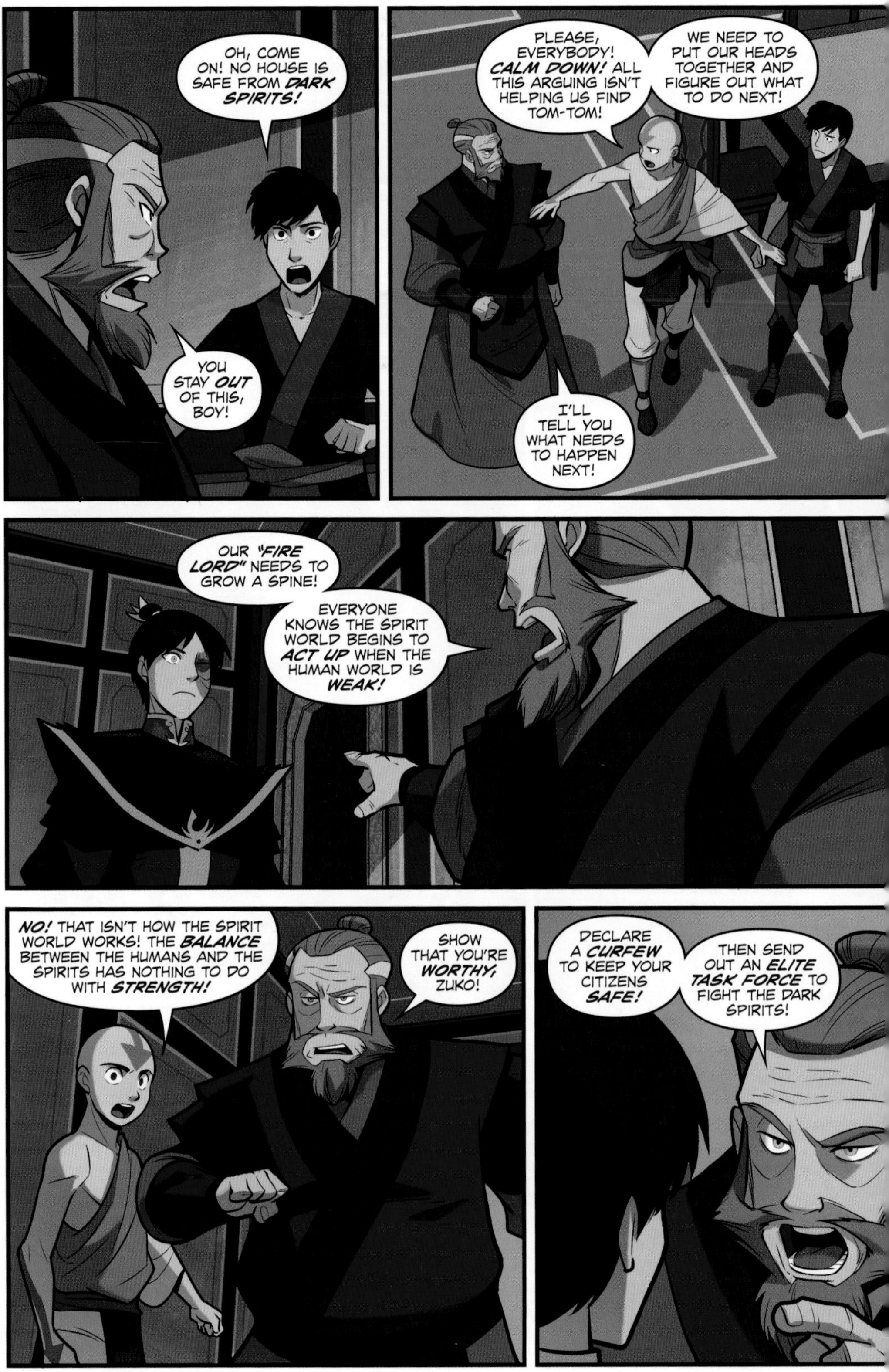
OH, COME ON! NO HOUSE IS SAFE FROM DARK SPIRITS!
YOU STAY OUT OF THIS, BOY!
PLEASE, EVERYBODY! CALM DOWN! ALL THIS ARGUING ISN'T HELPING US FIND TOM-TOM!
WE NEED TO PUT OUR HEADS TOGETHER AND FIGURE OUT WHAT TO DO NEXT!
I'LL TELL YOU WHAT NEEDS TO HAPPEN NEXT!
OUR "FIRE LORD" NEEDS TO GROW A SPINE!
EVERYONE KNOWS THE SPIRIT WORLD BEGINS TO ACT UP WHEN THE HUMAN WORLD IS WEAK!
NO! THAT ISN'T HOW THE SPIRIT WORLD WORKS! THE BALANCE BETWEEN THE HUMANS AND THE SPIRITS HAS NOTHING TO DO WITH STRENGTH!
SHOW THAT YOU'RE WORTHY, ZUKO!
DECLARE A CURFEW TO KEEP YOUR CITIZENS SAFE!
THEN SEND OUT AN ELITE TASK FORCE TO FIGHT THE DARK SPIRITS!

TAKE DOWN JUST *ONE* OF THEM AND WE'LL SHOW THE SPIRITS THAT HUMANS AREN'T TO BE *TRIFLED* WITH!

IF THAT IS YOUR WISH, FIRE LORD, I'LL BEGIN GATHERING A *TASK FORCE.* IT MAY TAKE SOME TIME, THOUGH.

DON'T DO IT, ZUKO! A CURFEW WOULD JUST MAKE FOLKS EVEN *MORE* FEARFUL!

PLUS, HOW'S A *"TASK FORCE"* SUPPOSED TO FIGHT *SPIRITS?* YOU CAN'T USE NORMAL BENDING!

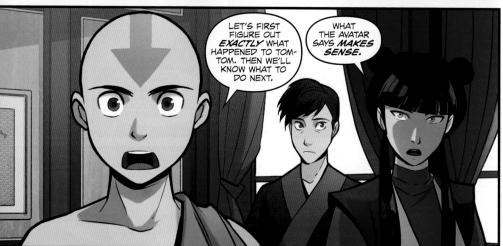

LET'S FIRST FIGURE OUT *EXACTLY* WHAT HAPPENED TO TOM-TOM. THEN WE'LL KNOW WHAT TO DO NEXT.

WHAT THE AVATAR SAYS *MAKES SENSE.*

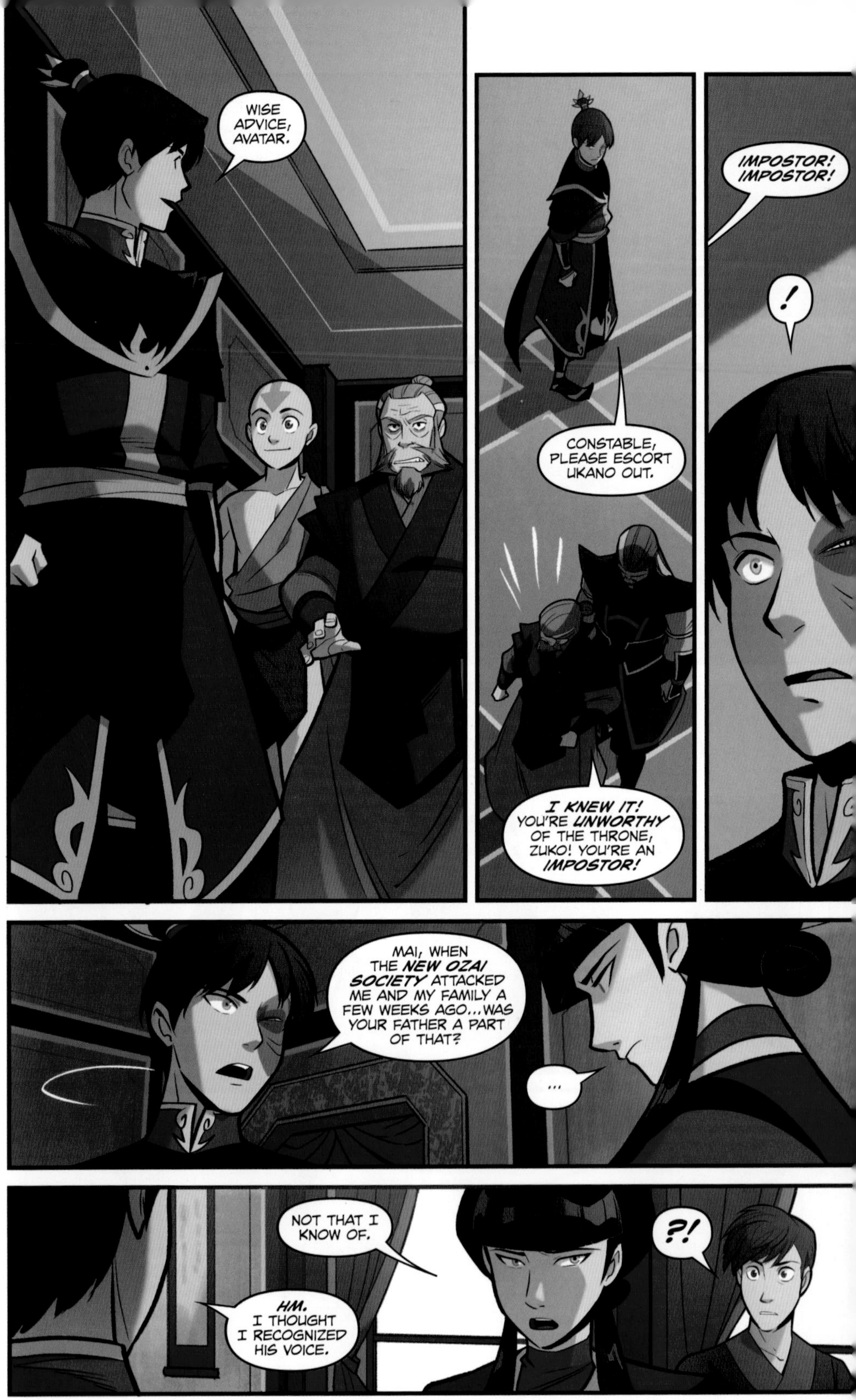
WISE ADVICE, AVATAR.
CONSTABLE, PLEASE ESCORT UKANO OUT.
I KNEW IT! YOU'RE UNWORTHY OF THE THRONE, ZUKO! YOU'RE AN IMPOSTOR!
IMPOSTOR! IMPOSTOR!
!
MAI, WHEN THE NEW OZAI SOCIETY ATTACKED ME AND MY FAMILY A FEW WEEKS AGO...WAS YOUR FATHER A PART OF THAT?
...
NOT THAT I KNOW OF.
HM. I THOUGHT I RECOGNIZED HIS VOICE.
?!

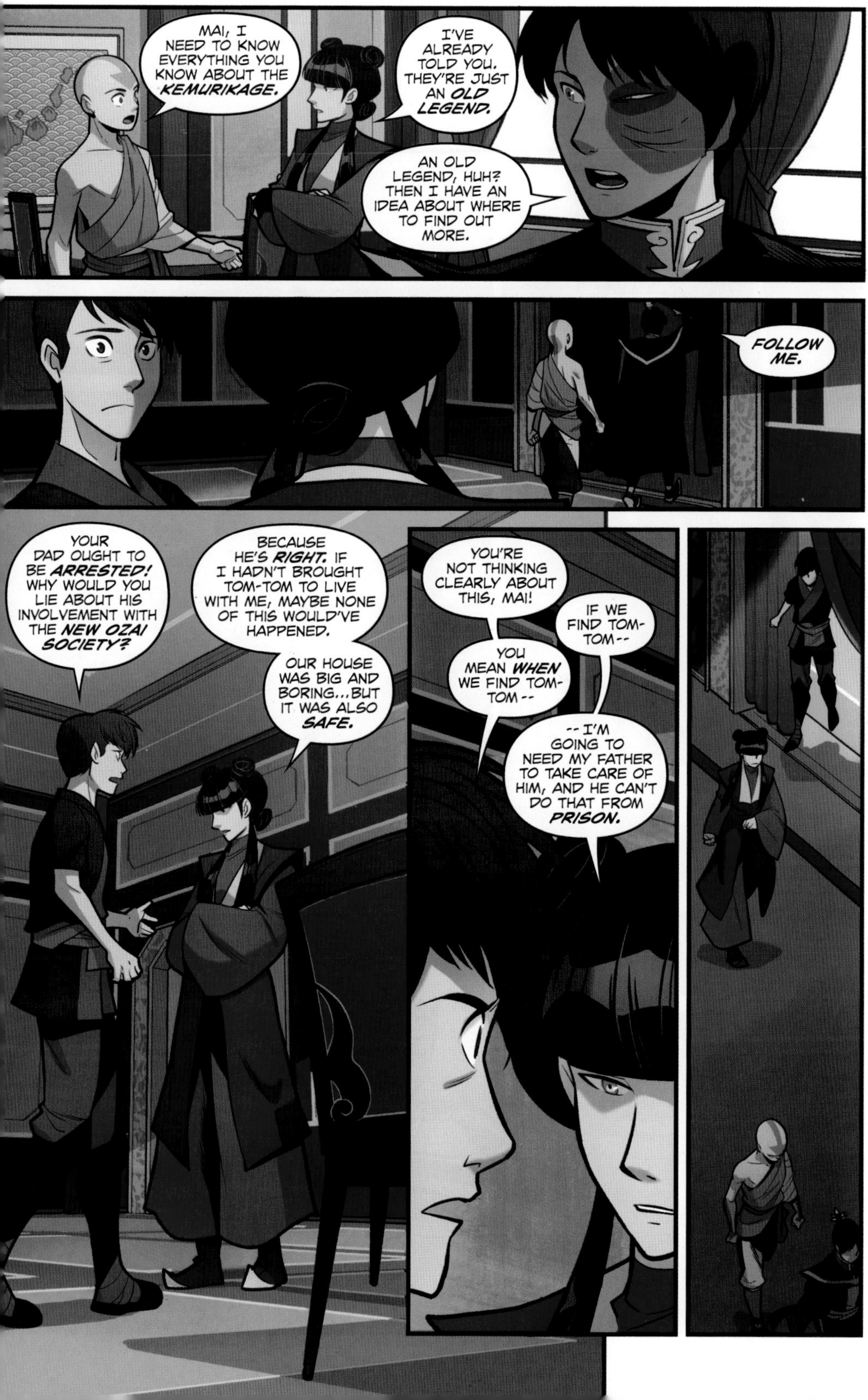
MAI, I NEED TO KNOW EVERYTHING YOU KNOW ABOUT THE *KEMURIKAGE.*
I'VE ALREADY TOLD YOU. THEY'RE JUST AN *OLD LEGEND.*
AN OLD LEGEND, HUH? THEN I HAVE AN IDEA ABOUT WHERE TO FIND OUT MORE.
FOLLOW ME.
YOUR DAD OUGHT TO BE *ARRESTED!* WHY WOULD YOU LIE ABOUT HIS INVOLVEMENT WITH THE *NEW OZAI SOCIETY?*
BECAUSE HE'S *RIGHT.* IF I HADN'T BROUGHT TOM-TOM TO LIVE WITH ME, MAYBE NONE OF THIS WOULD'VE HAPPENED.
OUR HOUSE WAS BIG AND BORING...BUT IT WAS ALSO *SAFE.*
YOU'RE NOT THINKING CLEARLY ABOUT THIS, MAI!
IF WE FIND TOM-TOM--
YOU MEAN *WHEN* WE FIND TOM-TOM--
--I'M GOING TO NEED MY FATHER TO TAKE CARE OF HIM, AND HE CAN'T DO THAT FROM *PRISON.*

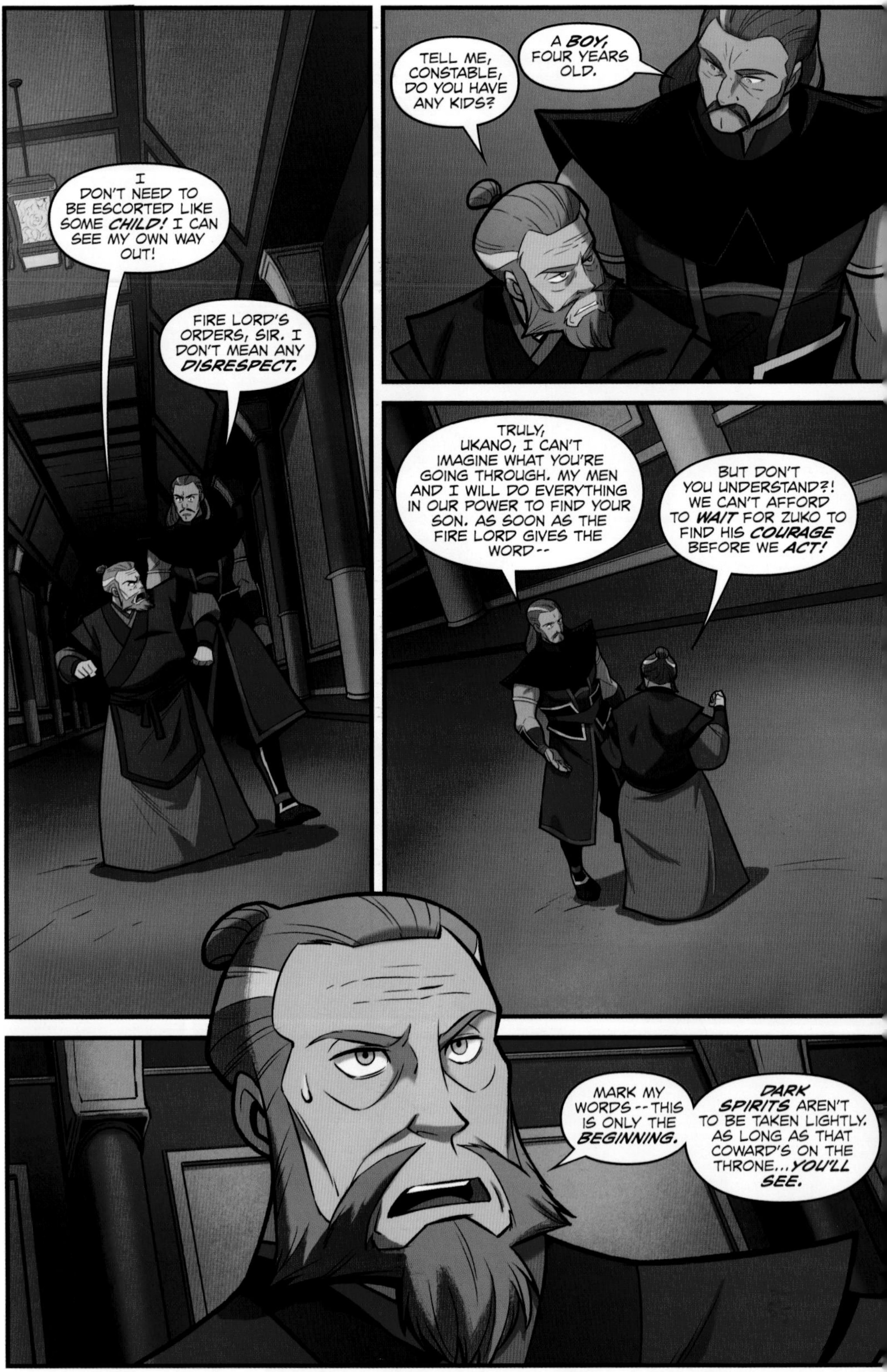
I DON'T NEED TO BE ESCORTED LIKE SOME CHILD! I CAN SEE MY OWN WAY OUT!
FIRE LORD'S ORDERS, SIR. I DON'T MEAN ANY DISRESPECT.
TELL ME, CONSTABLE, DO YOU HAVE ANY KIDS?
A BOY, FOUR YEARS OLD.
TRULY, UKANO, I CAN'T IMAGINE WHAT YOU'RE GOING THROUGH. MY MEN AND I WILL DO EVERYTHING IN OUR POWER TO FIND YOUR SON. AS SOON AS THE FIRE LORD GIVES THE WORD--
BUT DON'T YOU UNDERSTAND?! WE CAN'T AFFORD TO WAIT FOR ZUKO TO FIND HIS COURAGE BEFORE WE ACT!
MARK MY WORDS--THIS IS ONLY THE BEGINNING.
DARK SPIRITS AREN'T TO BE TAKEN LIGHTLY. AS LONG AS THAT COWARD'S ON THE THRONE...YOU'LL SEE.

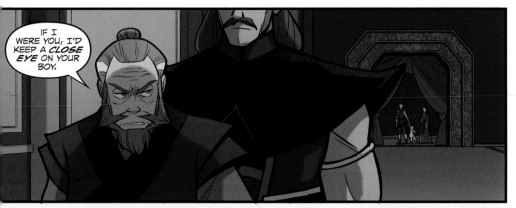

IF I WERE YOU, I'D KEEP A *CLOSE EYE* ON YOUR BOY.

IT'S WELL PAST YOUR BEDTIME, KIYI. IF YOU'RE TRYING TO STALL AGAIN...

DADDY, WHAT'S THAT GRUMPY MAN TALKING ABOUT?

I DON'T THINK IT'S ANY OF OUR BUSINESS.

IT'S NOTHING, DEAR. DON'T WORRY. THERE'S NO PLACE *SAFER* THAN THE *ROYAL PALACE.*

I WAS ASKING *DADDY,* NOT *YOU!* LET GO! YOU'RE *FREEZING!*

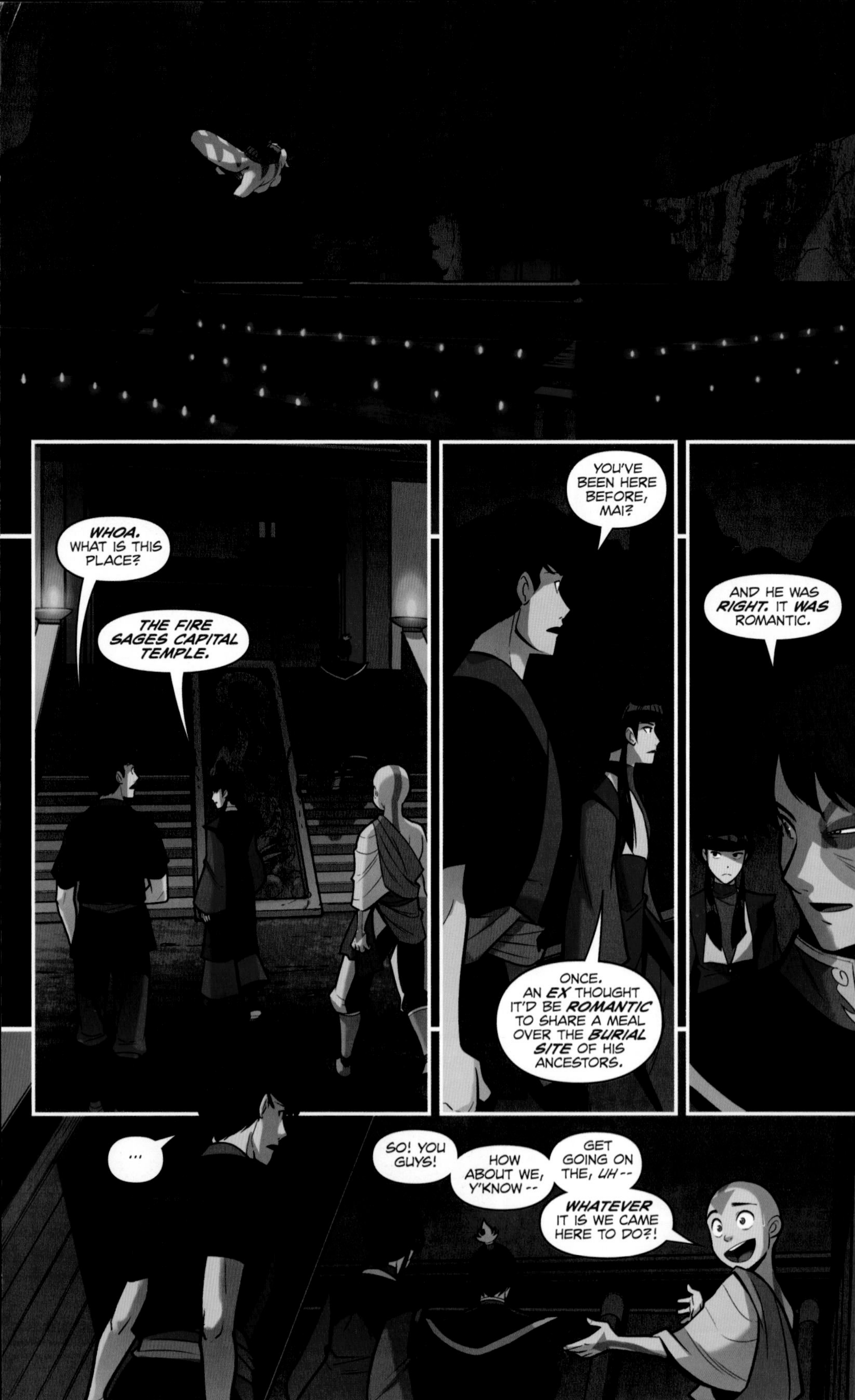

WHOA. WHAT IS THIS PLACE?
THE FIRE SAGES CAPITAL TEMPLE.
YOU'VE BEEN HERE BEFORE, MAI?
ONCE. AN EX THOUGHT IT'D BE ROMANTIC TO SHARE A MEAL OVER THE BURIAL SITE OF HIS ANCESTORS.
AND HE WAS RIGHT. IT WAS ROMANTIC.
...
SO! YOU GUYS!
HOW ABOUT WE, Y'KNOW --
GET GOING ON THE, UH --
WHATEVER IT IS WE CAME HERE TO DO?!

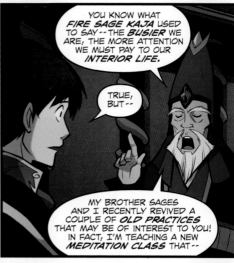

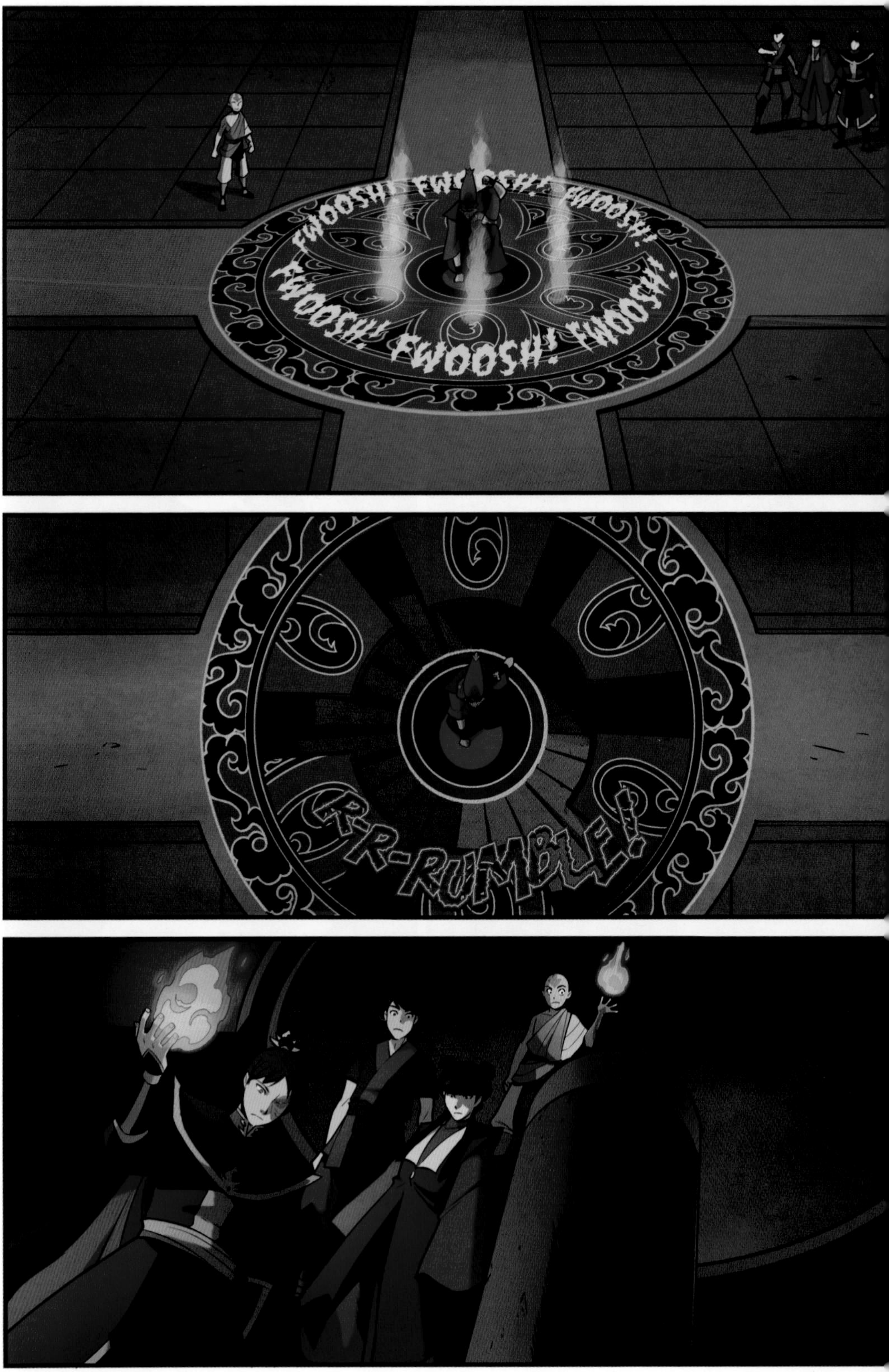
FWOOSH! FWOOSH! FWOOSH! FWOOSH! FWOOSH! FWOOSH!
R-R-RUMBLE!

94

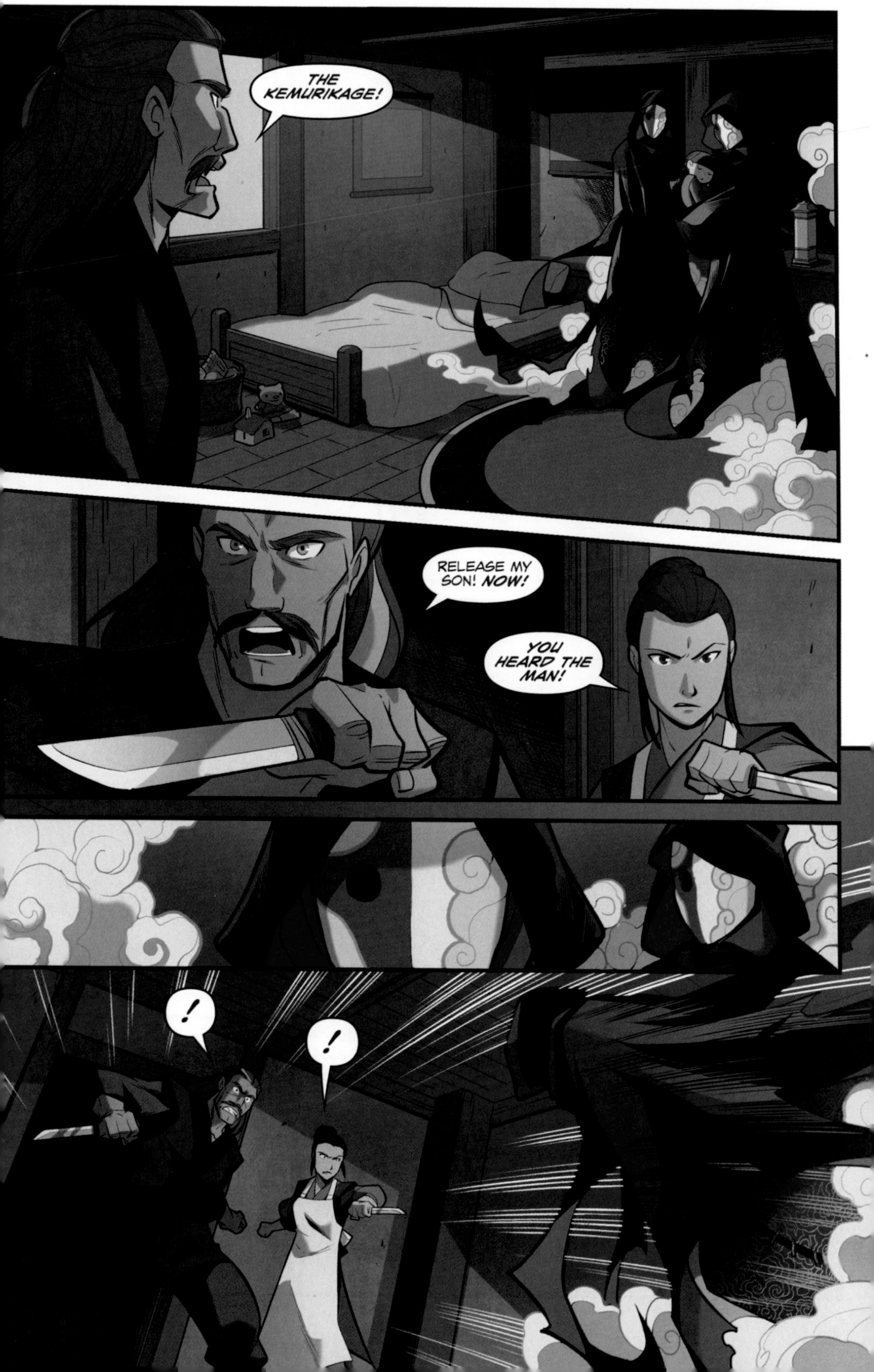
THE KEMURIKAGE!
RELEASE MY SON! NOW!
YOU HEARD THE MAN!
!
!

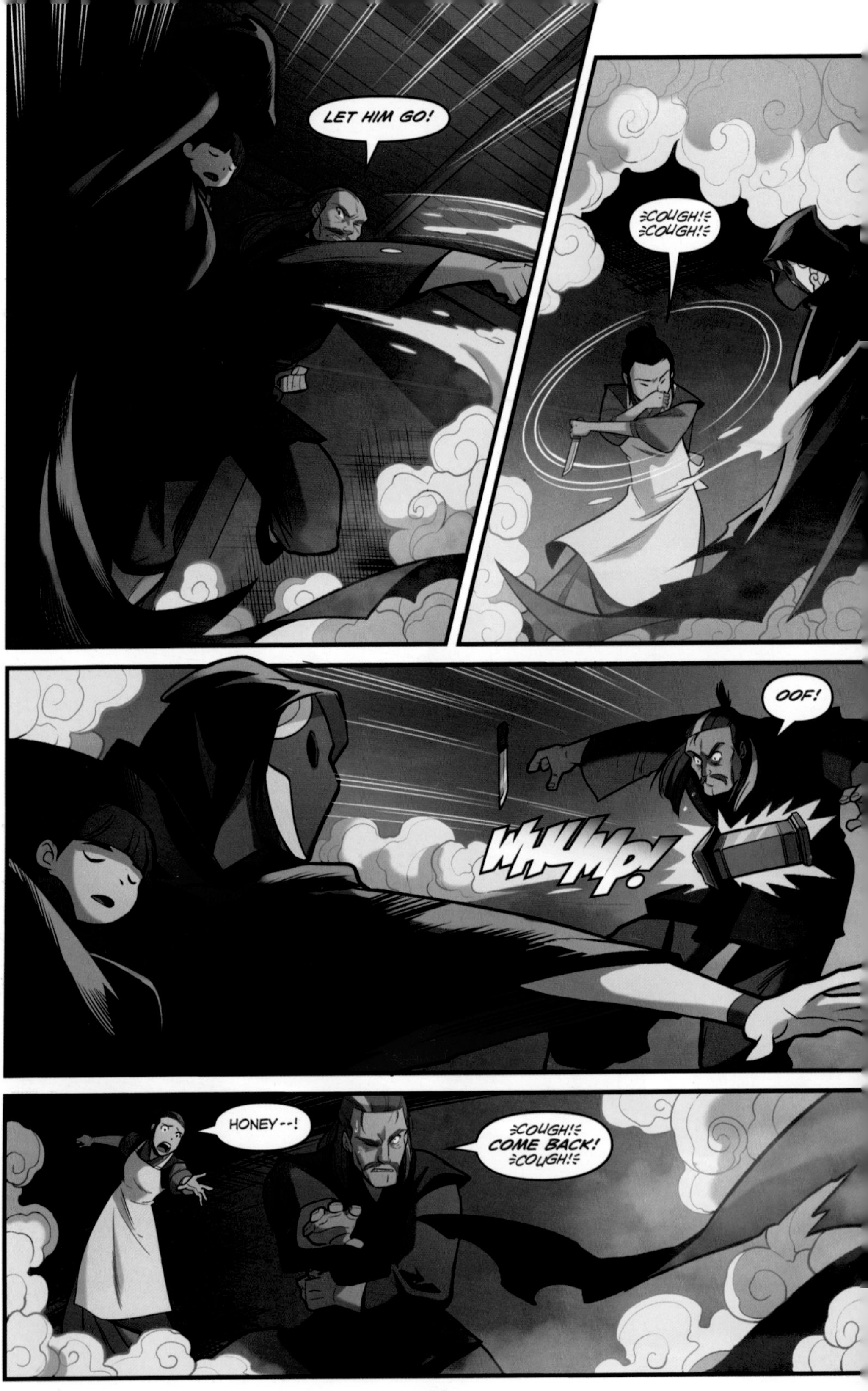
LET HIM GO!
COUGH! COUGH!
OOF!
WHUMP!
HONEY--!
COUGH! COME BACK! COUGH!

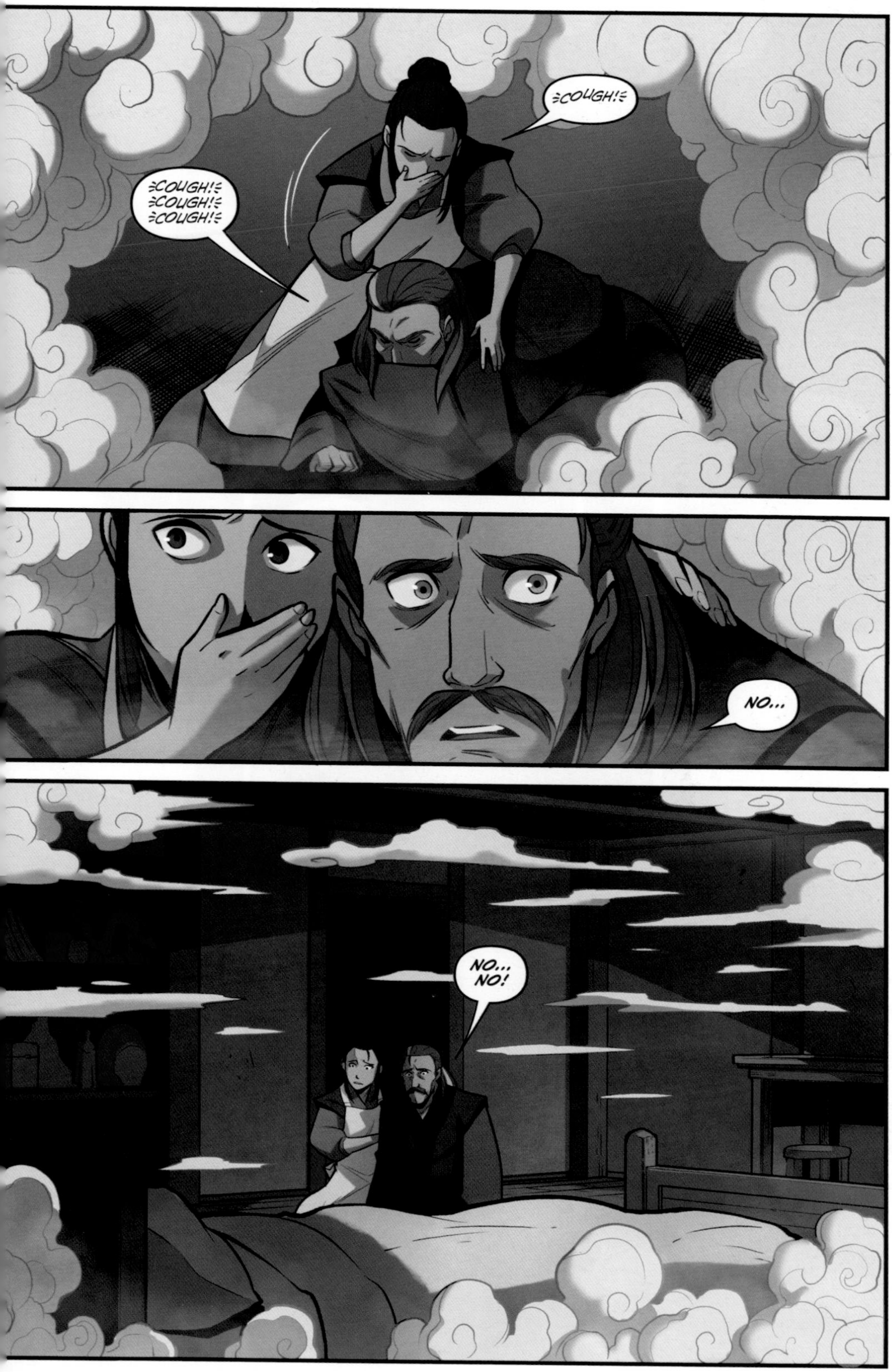

COUGH!
COUGH! COUGH! COUGH!
NO...
NO... NO!

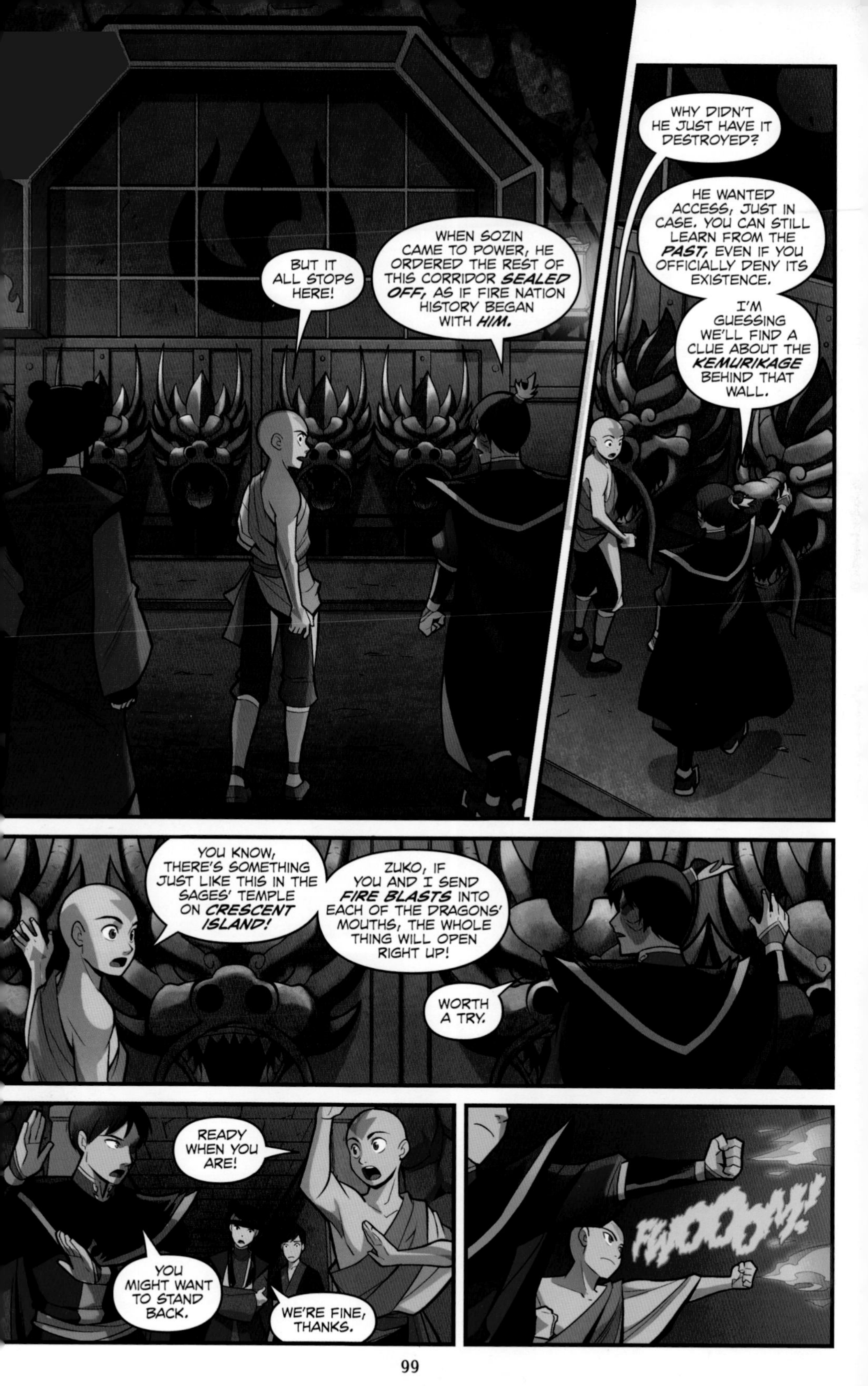
BUT IT ALL STOPS HERE!
WHEN SOZIN CAME TO POWER, HE ORDERED THE REST OF THIS CORRIDOR SEALED OFF, AS IF FIRE NATION HISTORY BEGAN WITH HIM.
WHY DIDN'T HE JUST HAVE IT DESTROYED?
HE WANTED ACCESS, JUST IN CASE. YOU CAN STILL LEARN FROM THE PAST, EVEN IF YOU OFFICIALLY DENY ITS EXISTENCE.
I'M GUESSING WE'LL FIND A CLUE ABOUT THE KEMURIKAGE BEHIND THAT WALL.
YOU KNOW, THERE'S SOMETHING JUST LIKE THIS IN THE SAGES' TEMPLE ON CRESCENT ISLAND!
ZUKO, IF YOU AND I SEND FIRE BLASTS INTO EACH OF THE DRAGONS' MOUTHS, THE WHOLE THING WILL OPEN RIGHT UP!
WORTH A TRY.
READY WHEN YOU ARE!
YOU MIGHT WANT TO STAND BACK.
WE'RE FINE, THANKS.
FWOOOM!

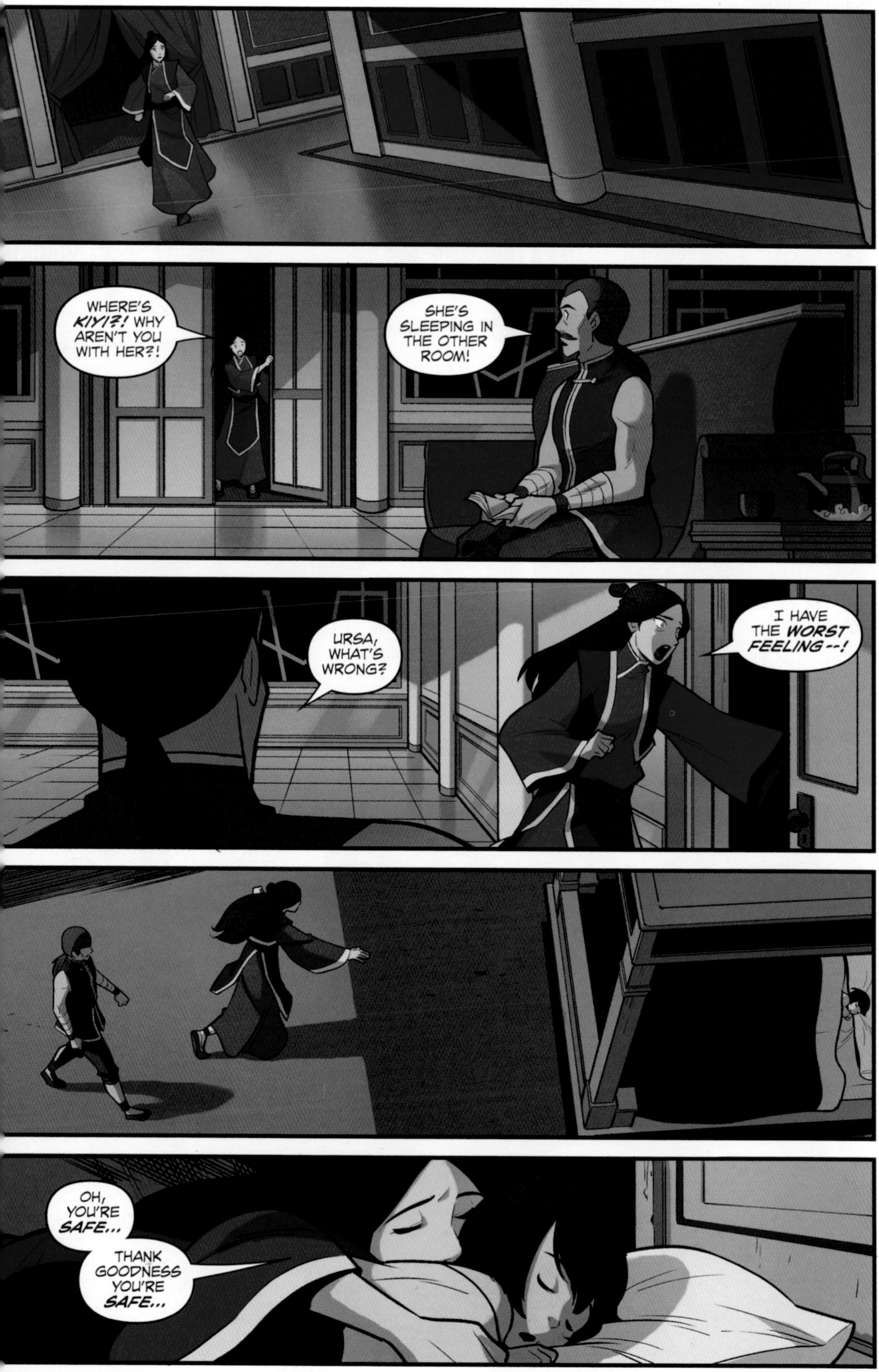
WHERE'S KIYI?! WHY AREN'T YOU WITH HER?!
SHE'S SLEEPING IN THE OTHER ROOM!
URSA, WHAT'S WRONG?
I HAVE THE WORST FEELING--!
OH, YOU'RE SAFE...
THANK GOODNESS YOU'RE SAFE...

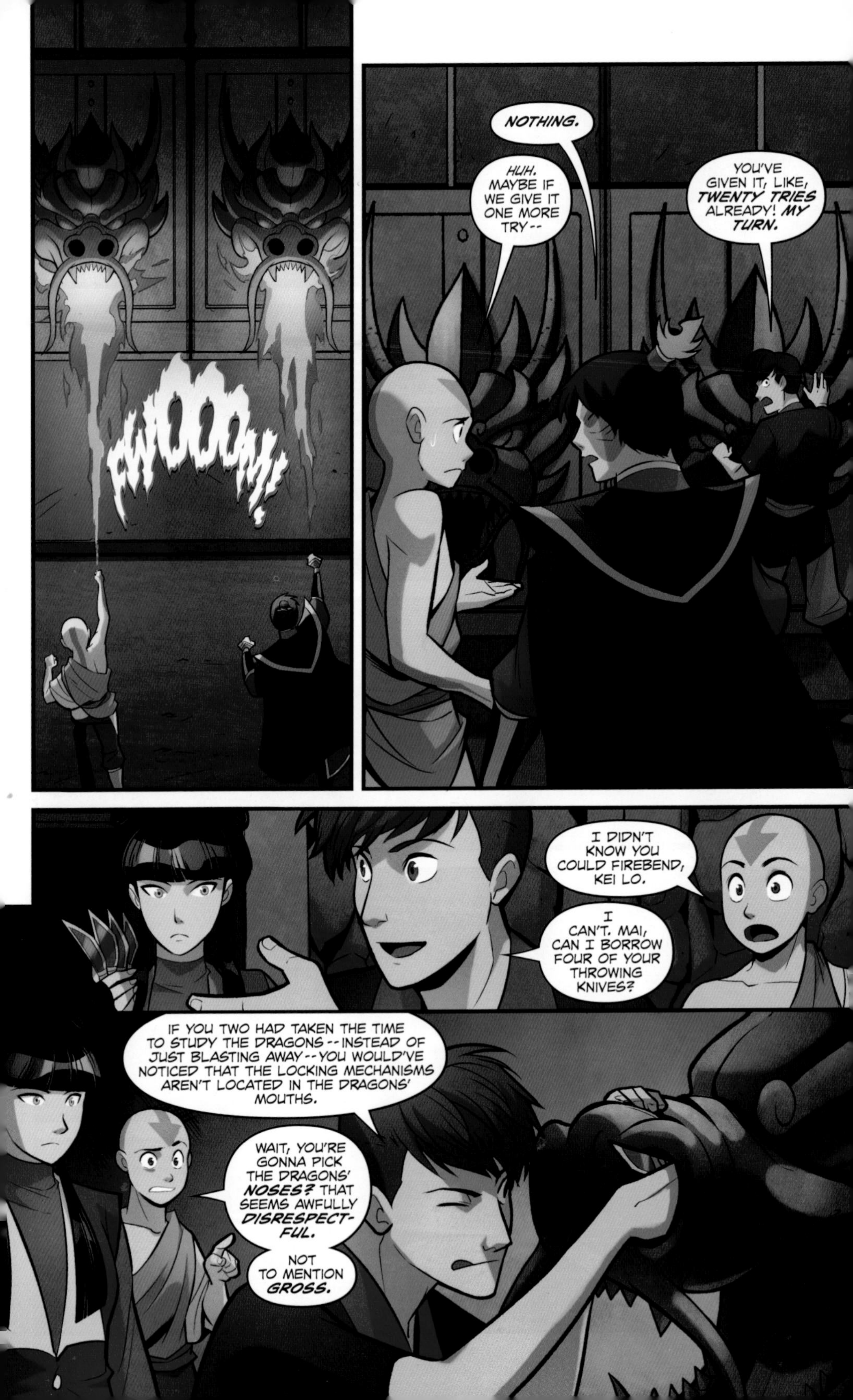
FWOOOM!
NOTHING.
HUH. MAYBE IF WE GIVE IT ONE MORE TRY--
YOU'VE GIVEN IT, LIKE, TWENTY TRIES ALREADY! MY TURN.
I DIDN'T KNOW YOU COULD FIREBEND, KEI LO.
I CAN'T. MAI, CAN I BORROW FOUR OF YOUR THROWING KNIVES?
IF YOU TWO HAD TAKEN THE TIME TO STUDY THE DRAGONS--INSTEAD OF JUST BLASTING AWAY--YOU WOULD'VE NOTICED THAT THE LOCKING MECHANISMS AREN'T LOCATED IN THE DRAGONS' MOUTHS.
WAIT, YOU'RE GONNA PICK THE DRAGONS' NOSES? THAT SEEMS AWFULLY DISRESPECTFUL.
NOT TO MENTION GROSS.

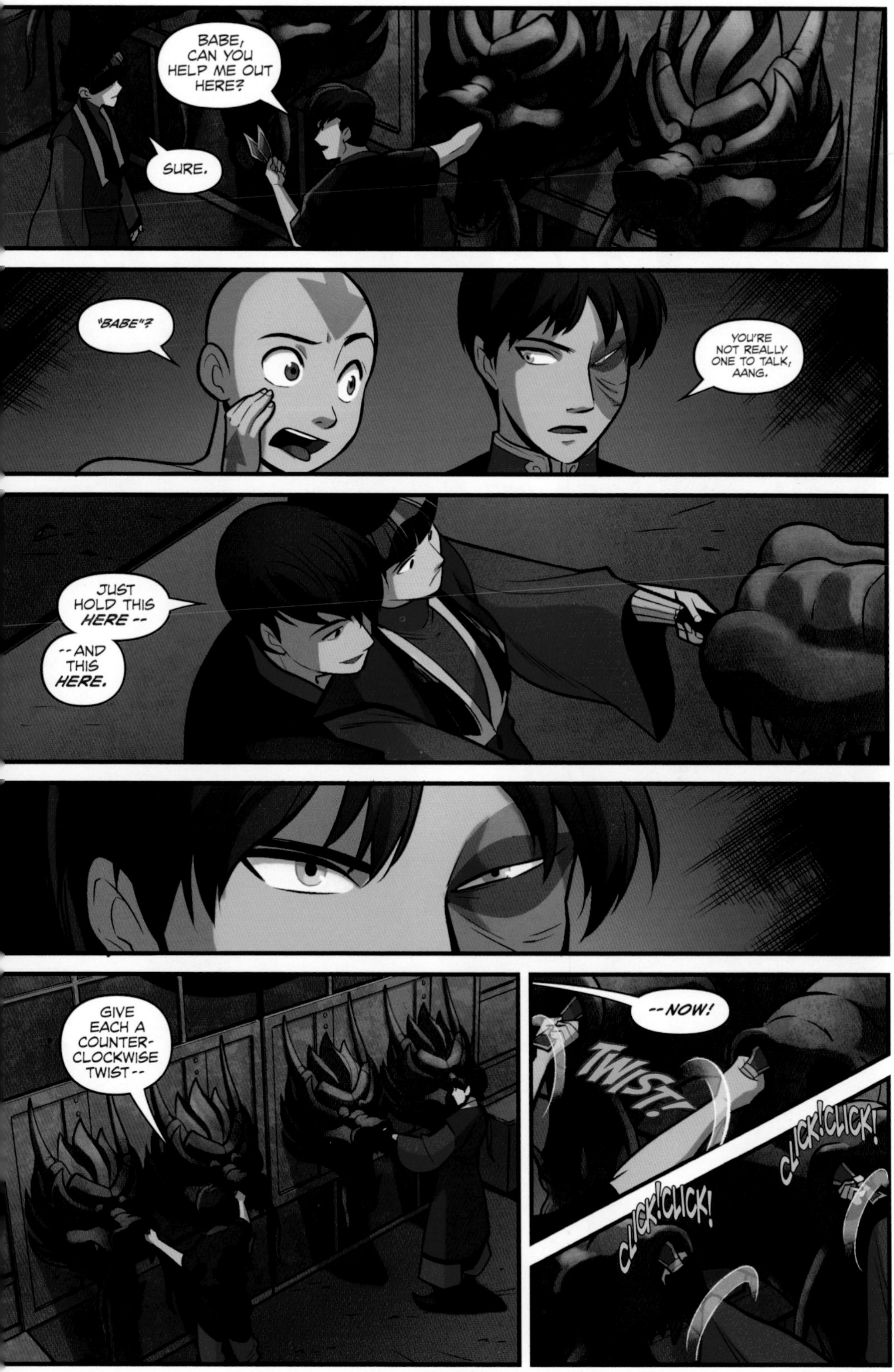
BABE, CAN YOU HELP ME OUT HERE?
SURE.
"BABE"?
YOU'RE NOT REALLY ONE TO TALK, AANG.
JUST HOLD THIS *HERE* --
-- AND THIS *HERE.*
GIVE EACH A COUNTER-CLOCKWISE TWIST --
-- *NOW!*
TWIST!
CLICK! CLICK!
CLICK! CLICK!

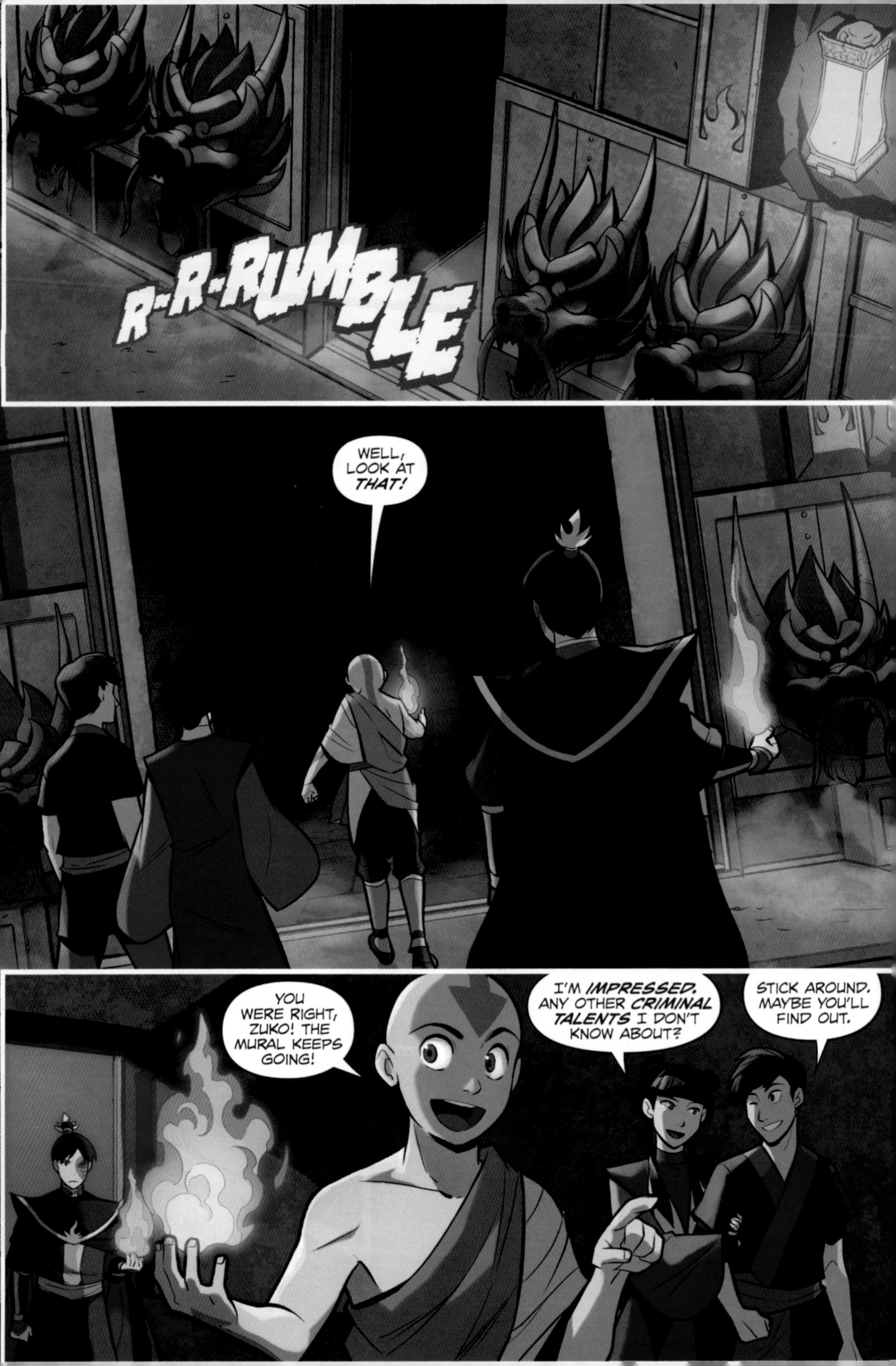
R-R-RUMBLE
WELL, LOOK AT THAT!
YOU WERE RIGHT, ZUKO! THE MURAL KEEPS GOING!
I'M IMPRESSED. ANY OTHER CRIMINAL TALENTS I DON'T KNOW ABOUT?
STICK AROUND. MAYBE YOU'LL FIND OUT.

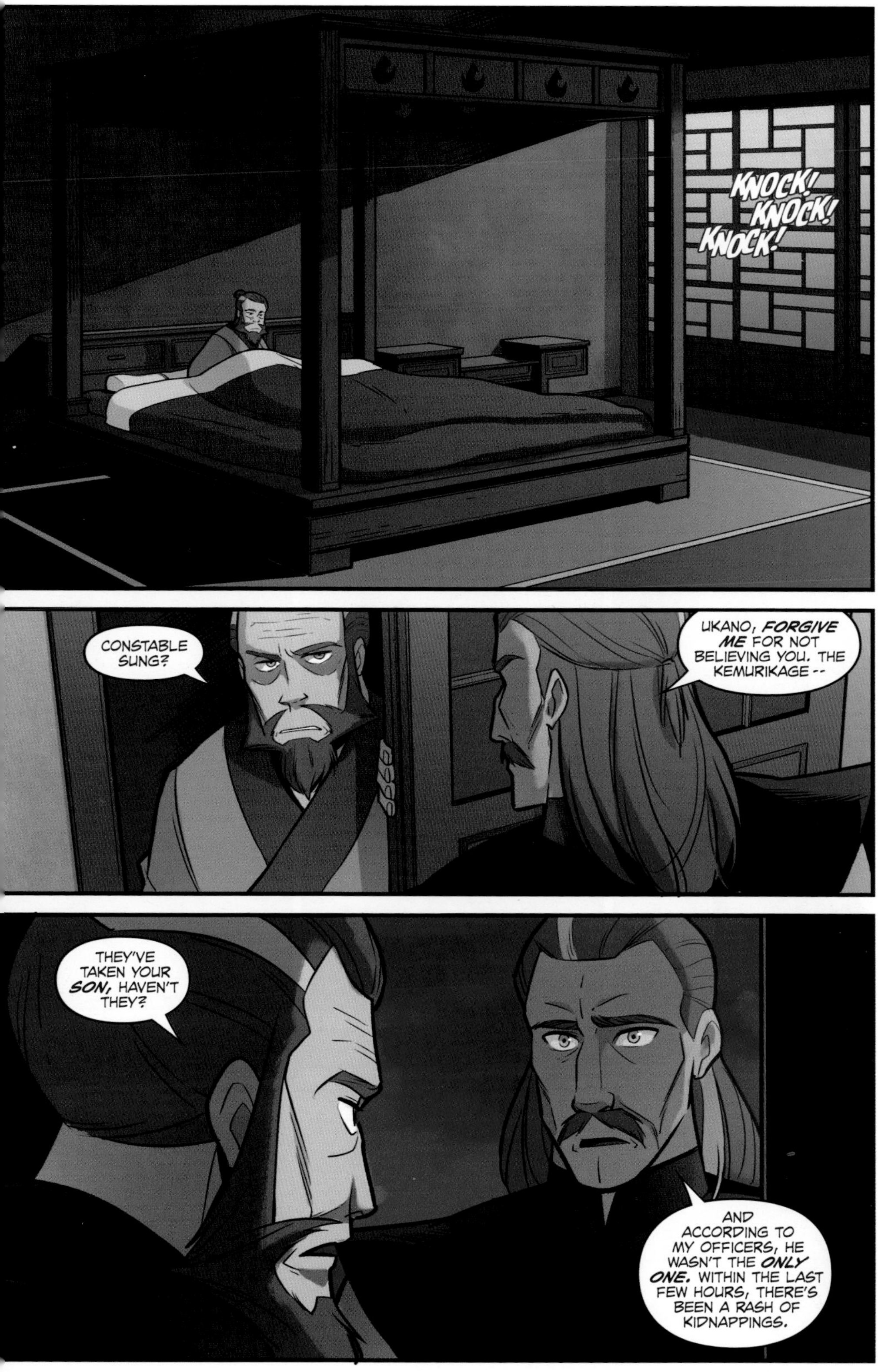
KNOCK! KNOCK! KNOCK!
CONSTABLE SUNG?
UKANO, FORGIVE ME FOR NOT BELIEVING YOU. THE KEMURIKAGE --
THEY'VE TAKEN YOUR SON, HAVEN'T THEY?
AND ACCORDING TO MY OFFICERS, HE WASN'T THE ONLY ONE. WITHIN THE LAST FEW HOURS, THERE'S BEEN A RASH OF KIDNAPPINGS.

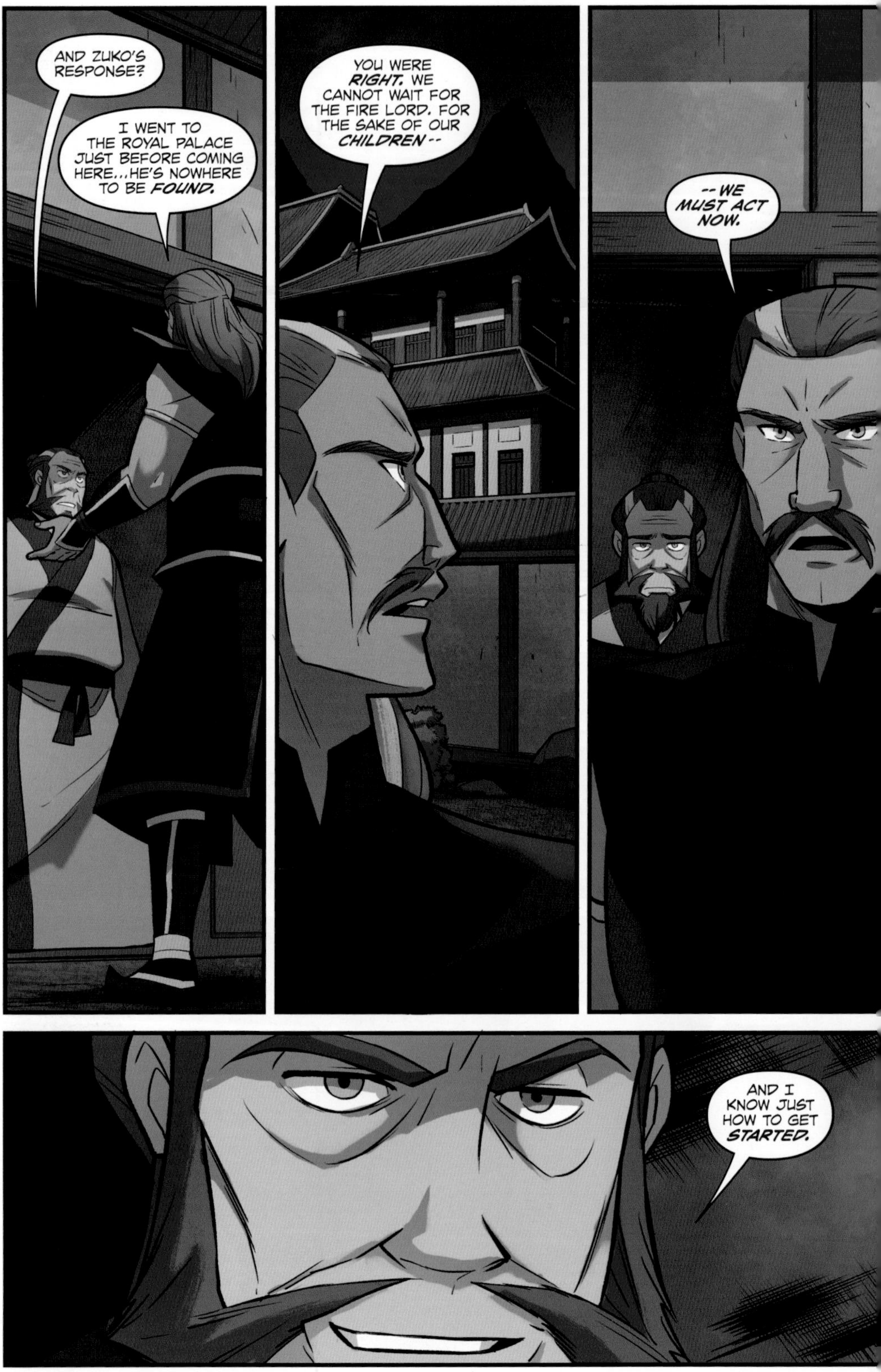
AND ZUKO'S RESPONSE?
I WENT TO THE ROYAL PALACE JUST BEFORE COMING HERE...HE'S NOWHERE TO BE FOUND.
YOU WERE RIGHT. WE CANNOT WAIT FOR THE FIRE LORD. FOR THE SAKE OF OUR CHILDREN --
-- WE MUST ACT NOW.
AND I KNOW JUST HOW TO GET STARTED.

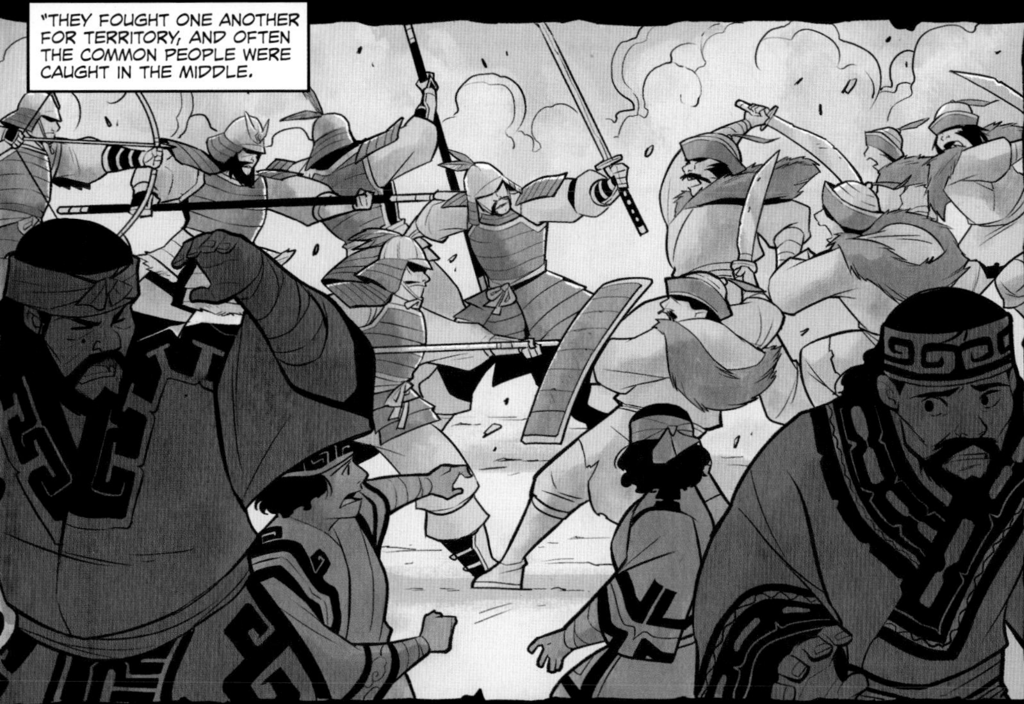
"THEY FOUGHT ONE ANOTHER FOR TERRITORY, AND OFTEN THE COMMON PEOPLE WERE CAUGHT IN THE MIDDLE.
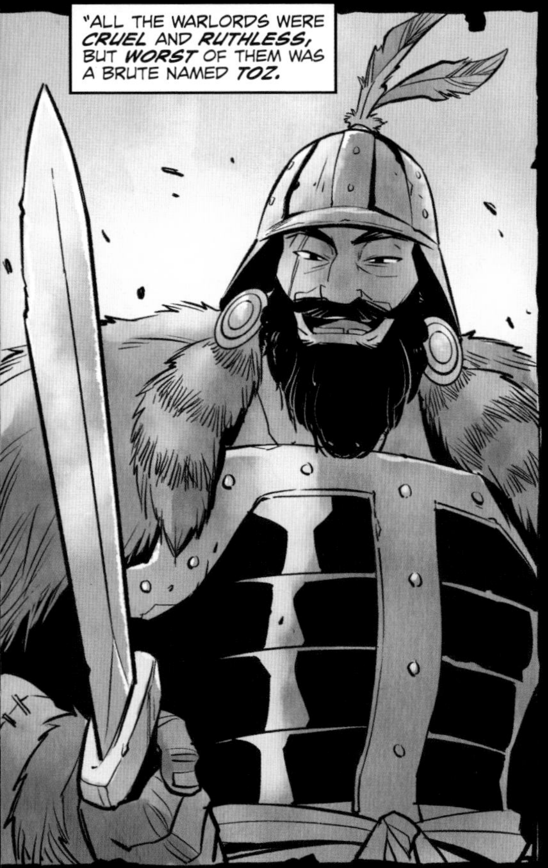
"ALL THE WARLORDS WERE CRUEL AND RUTHLESS, BUT WORST OF THEM WAS A BRUTE NAMED TOZ.
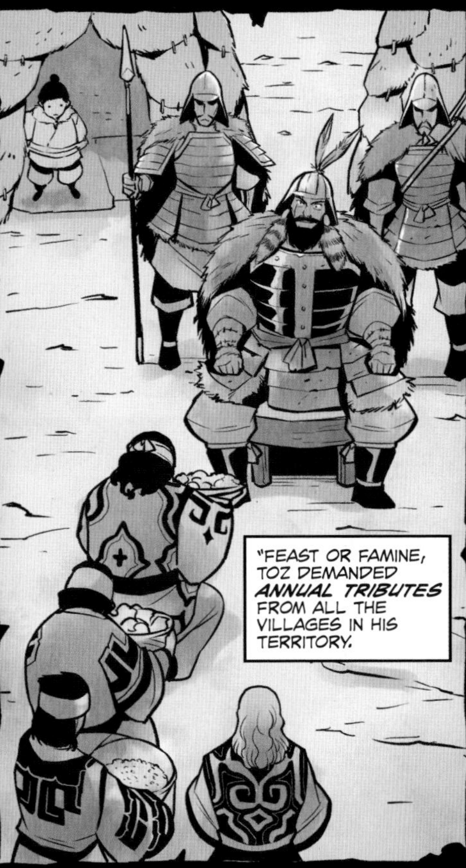
"FEAST OR FAMINE, TOZ DEMANDED ANNUAL TRIBUTES FROM ALL THE VILLAGES IN HIS TERRITORY.

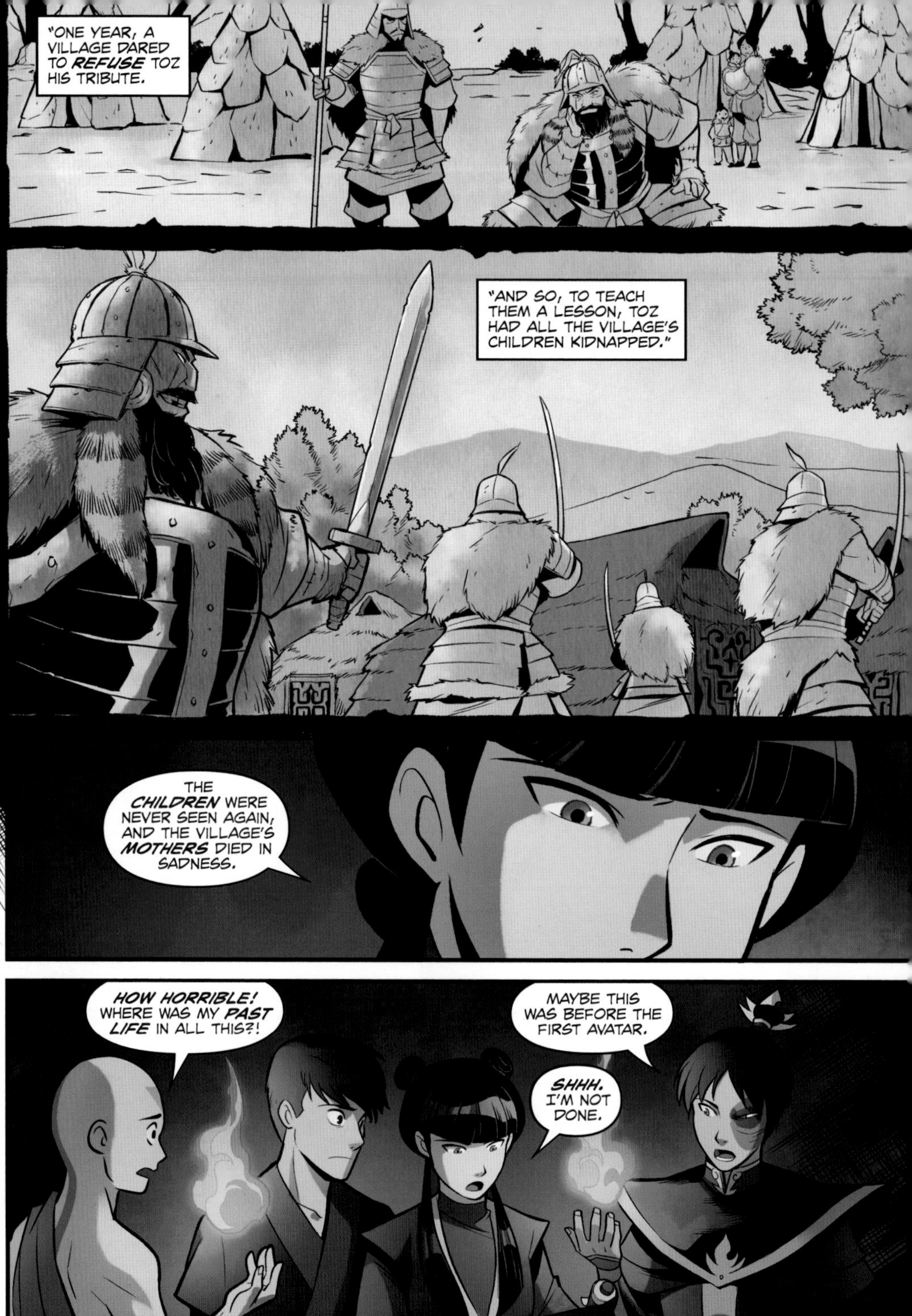
"ONE YEAR, A VILLAGE DARED TO REFUSE TOZ HIS TRIBUTE.
"AND SO, TO TEACH THEM A LESSON, TOZ HAD ALL THE VILLAGE'S CHILDREN KIDNAPPED."
THE CHILDREN WERE NEVER SEEN AGAIN, AND THE VILLAGE'S MOTHERS DIED IN SADNESS.
HOW HORRIBLE! WHERE WAS MY PAST LIFE IN ALL THIS?!
MAYBE THIS WAS BEFORE THE FIRST AVATAR.
SHHH. I'M NOT DONE.

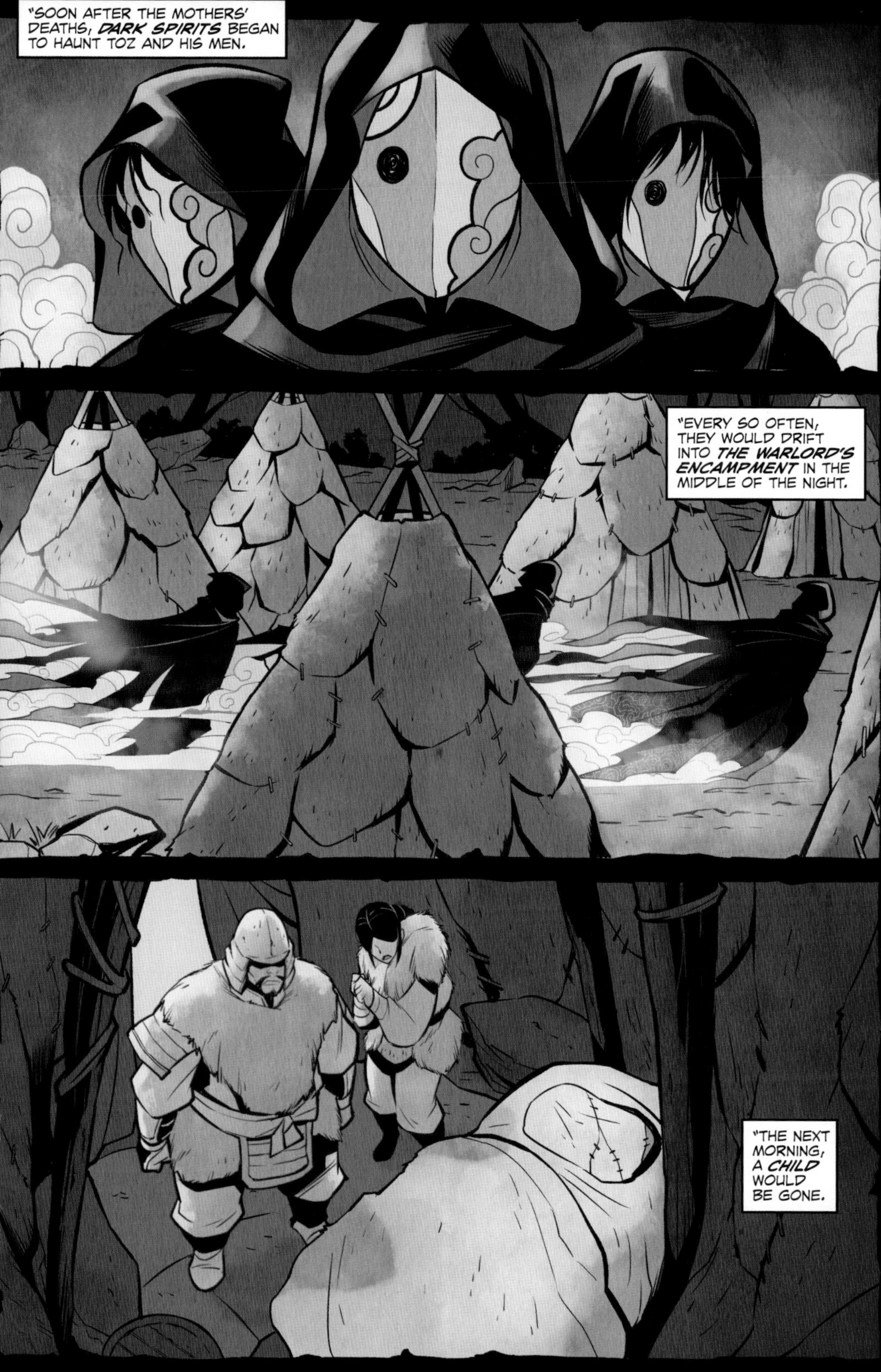
"SOON AFTER THE MOTHERS' DEATHS, DARK SPIRITS BEGAN TO HAUNT TOZ AND HIS MEN.
"EVERY SO OFTEN, THEY WOULD DRIFT INTO THE WARLORD'S ENCAMPMENT IN THE MIDDLE OF THE NIGHT.
"THE NEXT MORNING, A CHILD WOULD BE GONE.

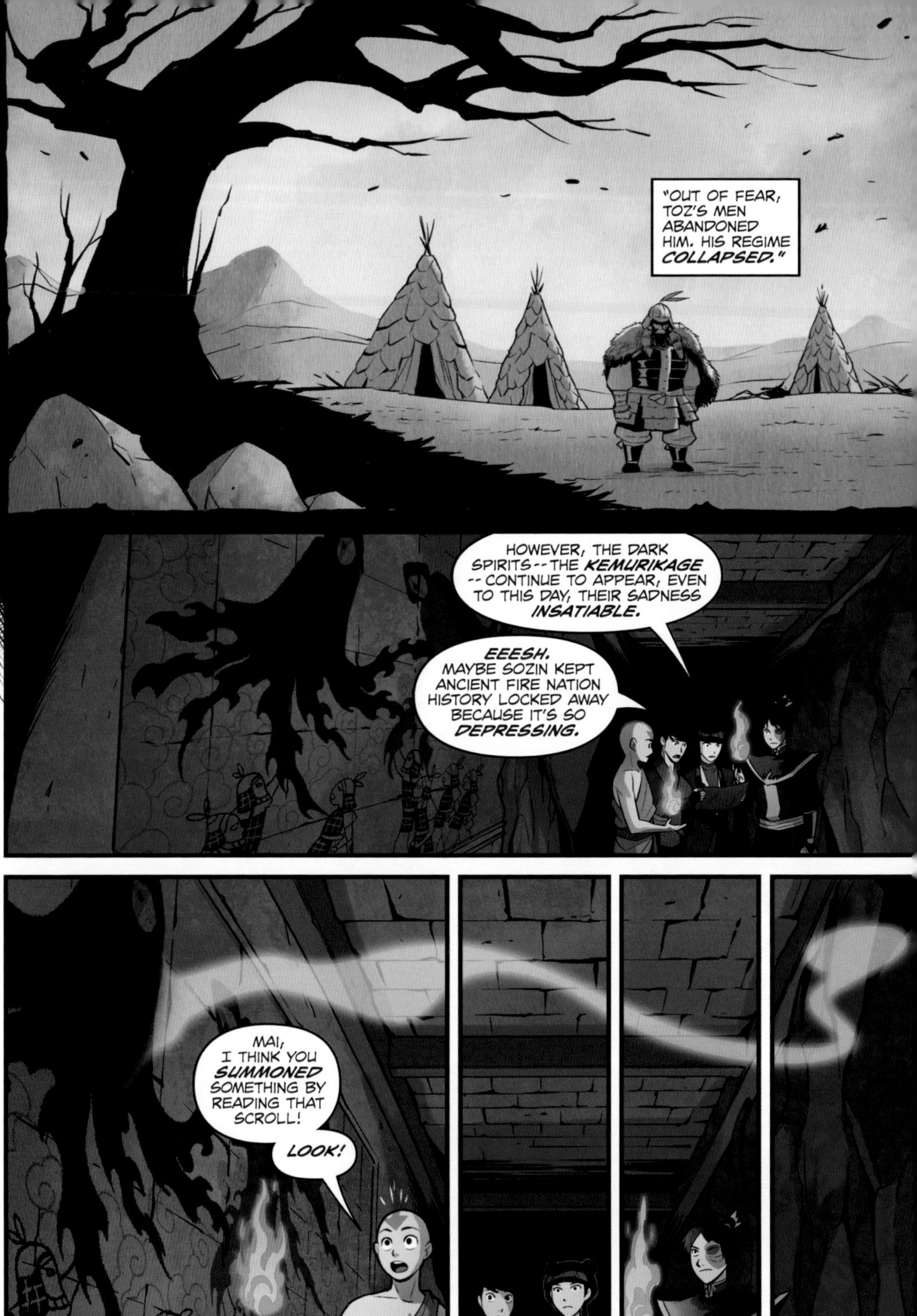
"OUT OF FEAR, TOZ'S MEN ABANDONED HIM. HIS REGIME COLLAPSED."
HOWEVER, THE DARK SPIRITS--THE KEMURIKAGE --CONTINUE TO APPEAR, EVEN TO THIS DAY, THEIR SADNESS INSATIABLE.
EEESH. MAYBE SOZIN KEPT ANCIENT FIRE NATION HISTORY LOCKED AWAY BECAUSE IT'S SO DEPRESSING.
MAI, I THINK YOU SUMMONED SOMETHING BY READING THAT SCROLL!
LOOK!

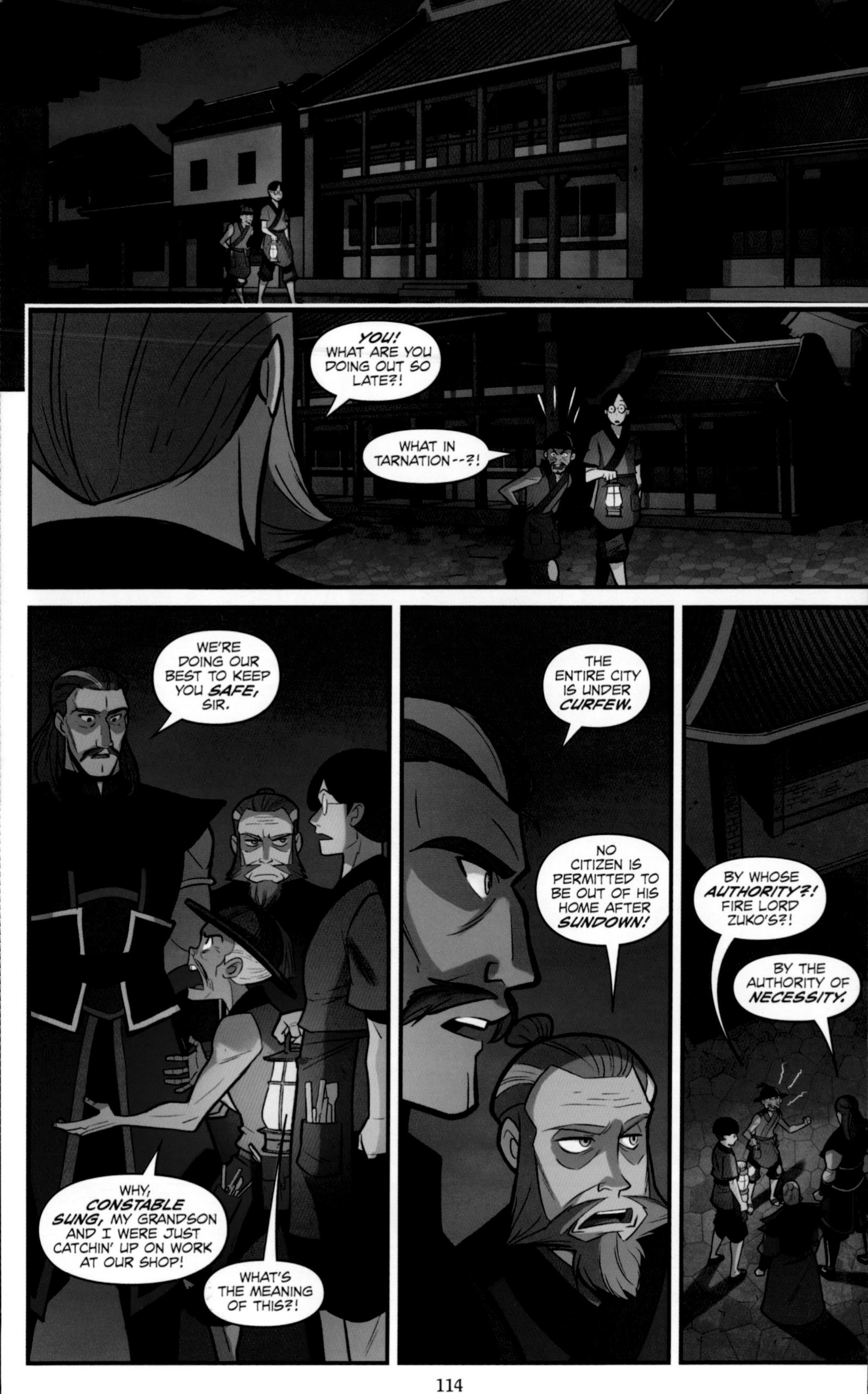
YOU! WHAT ARE YOU DOING OUT SO LATE?!
WHAT IN TARNATION--?!
WHY, CONSTABLE SUNG, MY GRANDSON AND I WERE JUST CATCHIN' UP ON WORK AT OUR SHOP!
WE'RE DOING OUR BEST TO KEEP YOU SAFE, SIR.
WHAT'S THE MEANING OF THIS?!
THE ENTIRE CITY IS UNDER CURFEW.
NO CITIZEN IS PERMITTED TO BE OUT OF HIS HOME AFTER SUNDOWN!
BY WHOSE AUTHORITY?! FIRE LORD ZUKO'S?!
BY THE AUTHORITY OF NECESSITY.

115

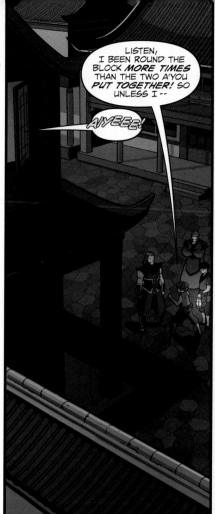

116

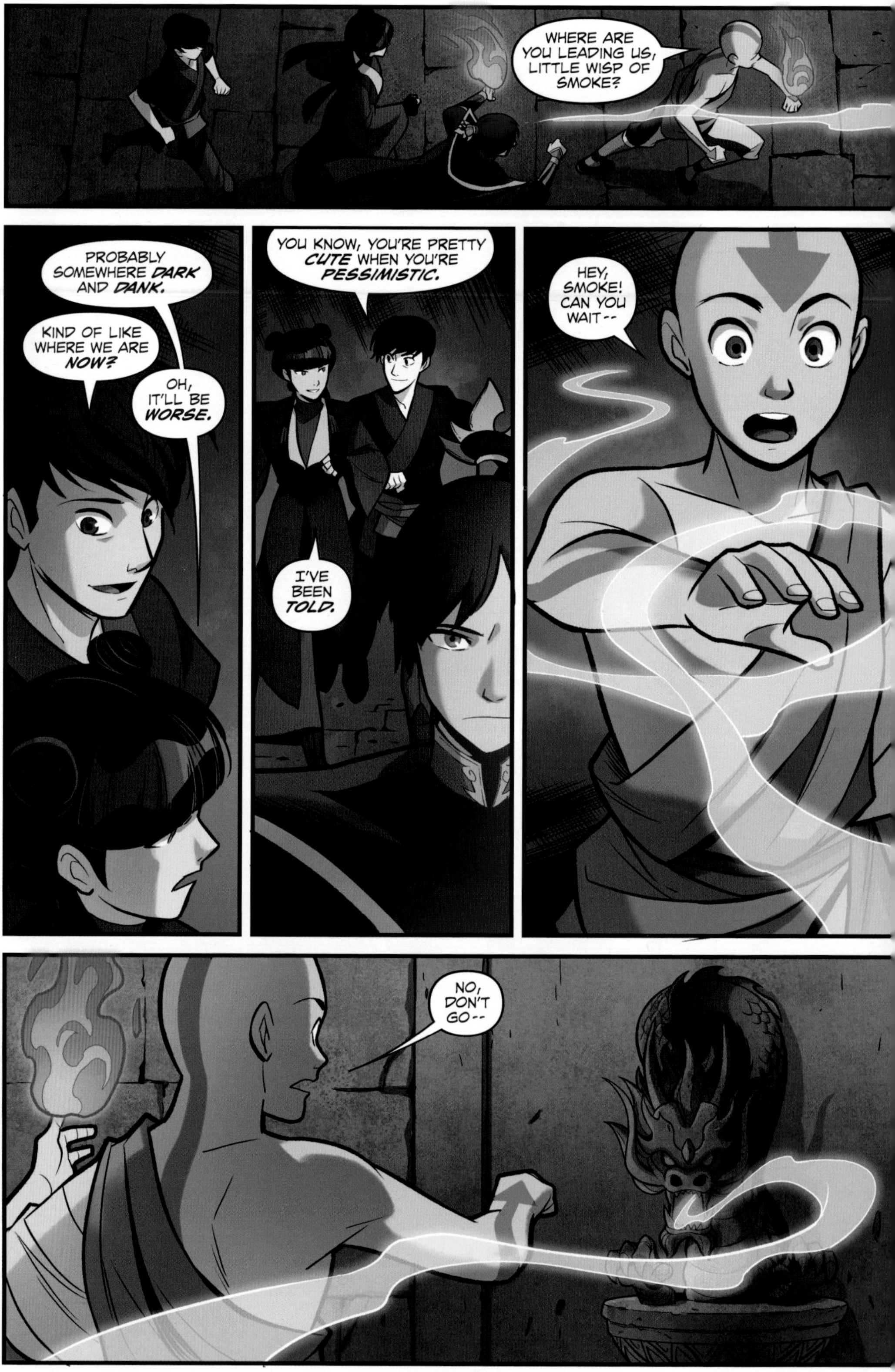
WHERE ARE YOU LEADING US, LITTLE WISP OF SMOKE?
PROBABLY SOMEWHERE DARK AND DANK.
KIND OF LIKE WHERE WE ARE NOW?
OH, IT'LL BE WORSE.
YOU KNOW, YOU'RE PRETTY CUTE WHEN YOU'RE PESSIMISTIC.
I'VE BEEN TOLD.
HEY, SMOKE! CAN YOU WAIT--
NO, DON'T GO--

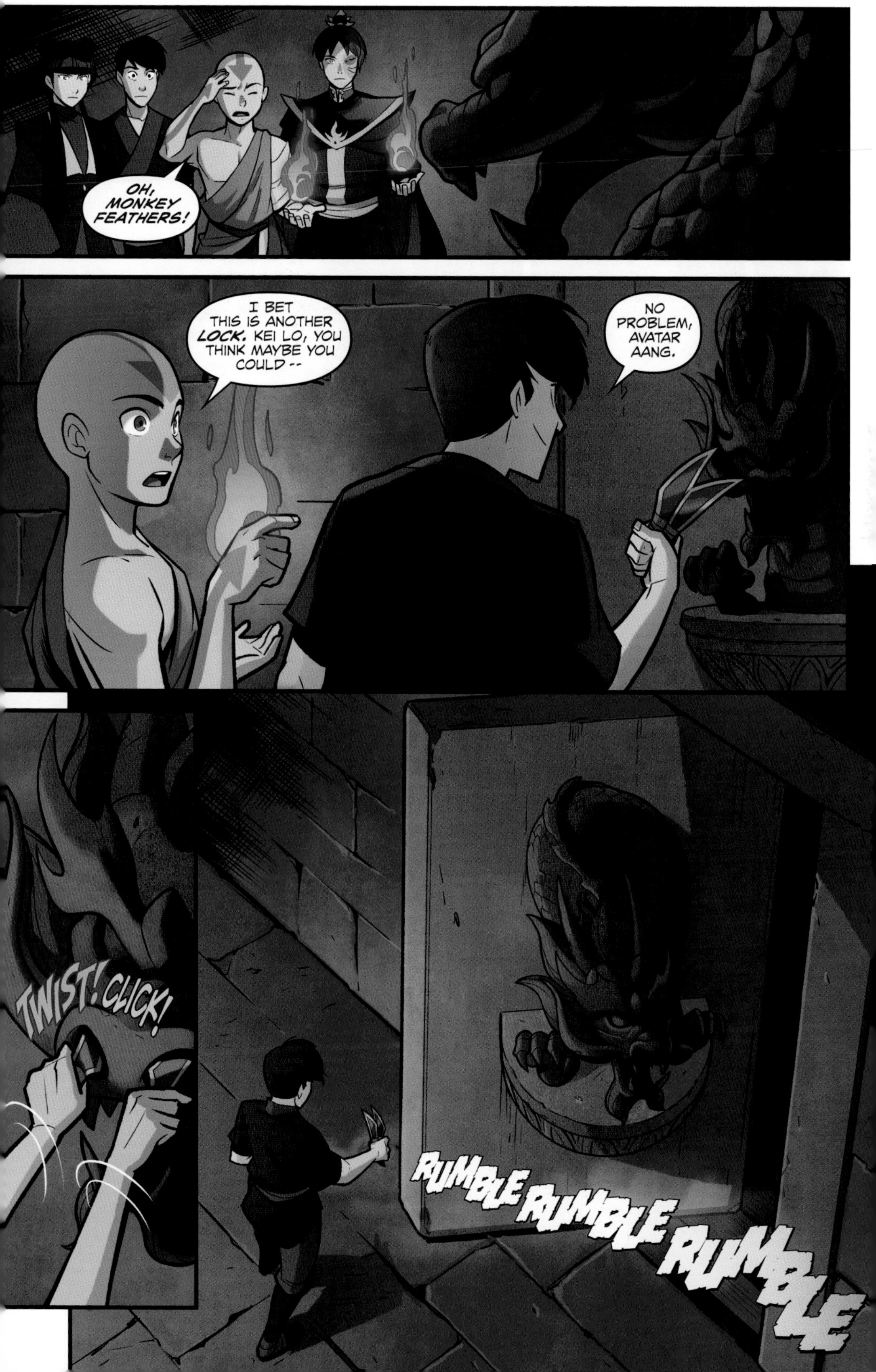
OH, MONKEY FEATHERS!
I BET THIS IS ANOTHER LOCK. KEI LO, YOU THINK MAYBE YOU COULD --
NO PROBLEM, AVATAR AANG.
TWIST! CLICK!
RUMBLE RUMBLE RUMBLE

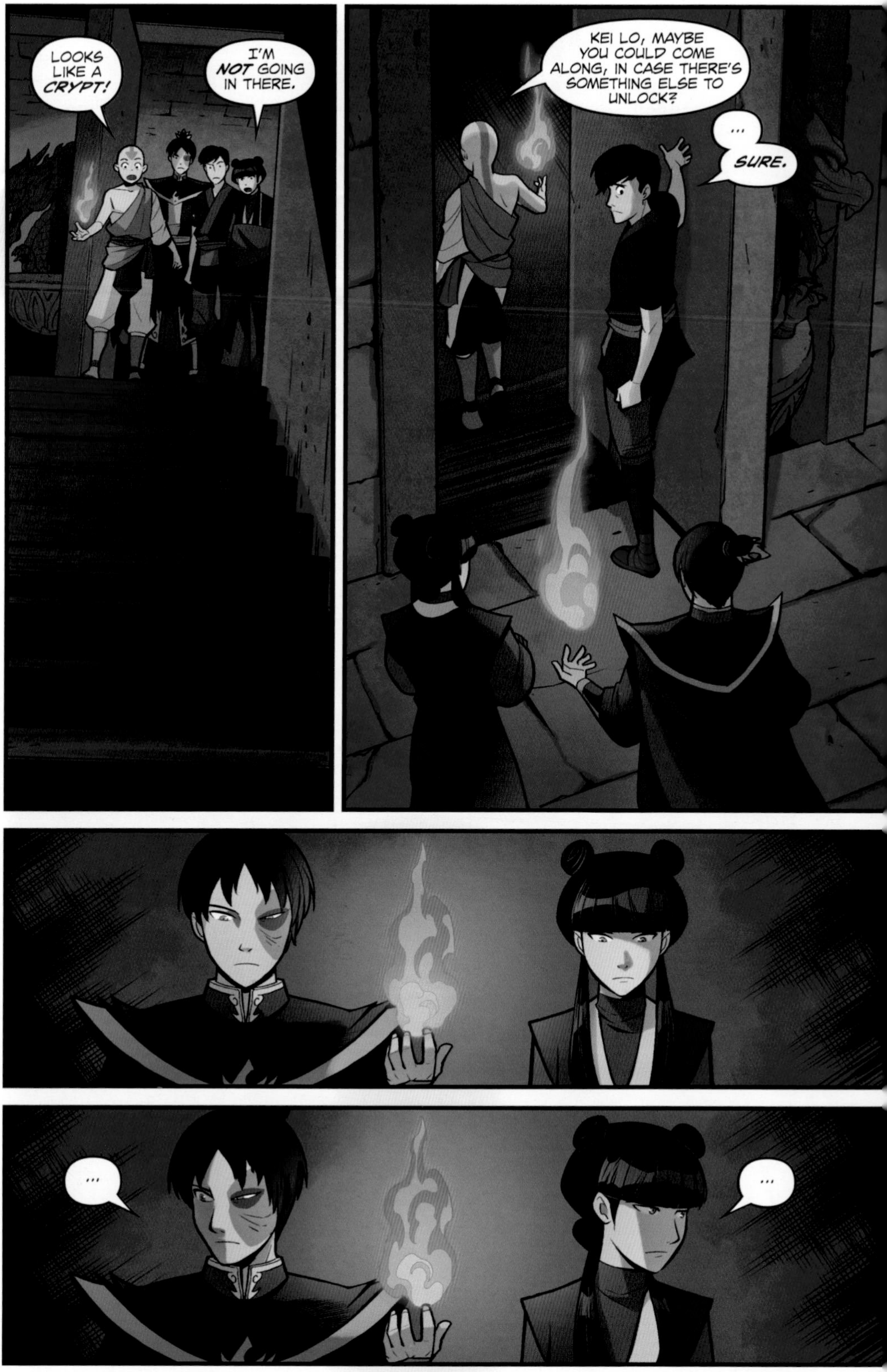
LOOKS LIKE A *CRYPT!*
I'M *NOT* GOING IN THERE.
KEI LO, MAYBE YOU COULD COME ALONG, IN CASE THERE'S SOMETHING ELSE TO UNLOCK?
... *SURE.*
...
...

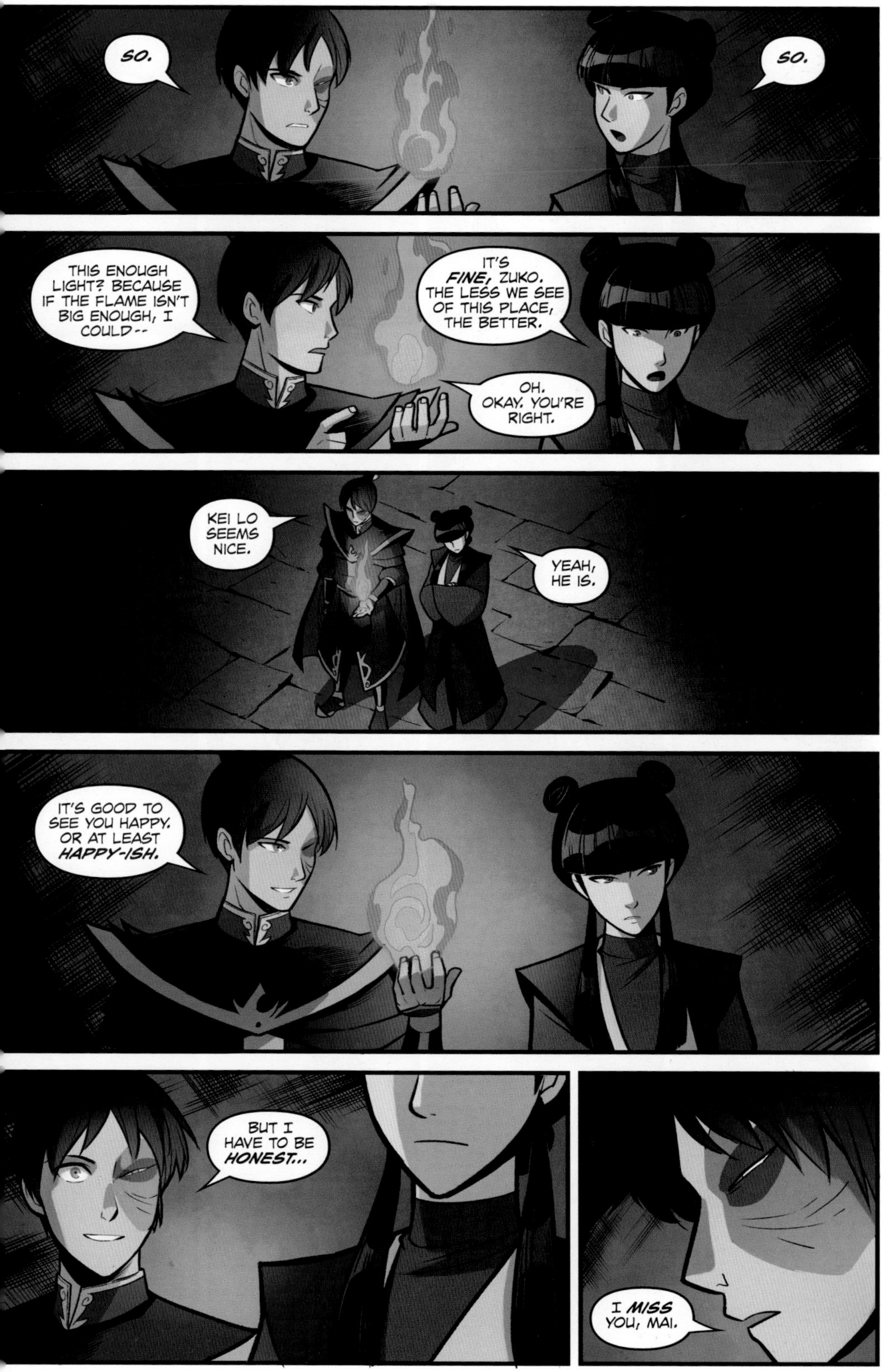
SO.
SO.
THIS ENOUGH LIGHT? BECAUSE IF THE FLAME ISN'T BIG ENOUGH, I COULD--
IT'S *FINE*, ZUKO. THE LESS WE SEE OF THIS PLACE, THE BETTER.
OH. OKAY. YOU'RE RIGHT.
KEI LO SEEMS NICE.
YEAH, HE IS.
IT'S GOOD TO SEE YOU HAPPY. OR AT LEAST *HAPPY-ISH*.
BUT I HAVE TO BE *HONEST*...
I *MISS* YOU, MAI.

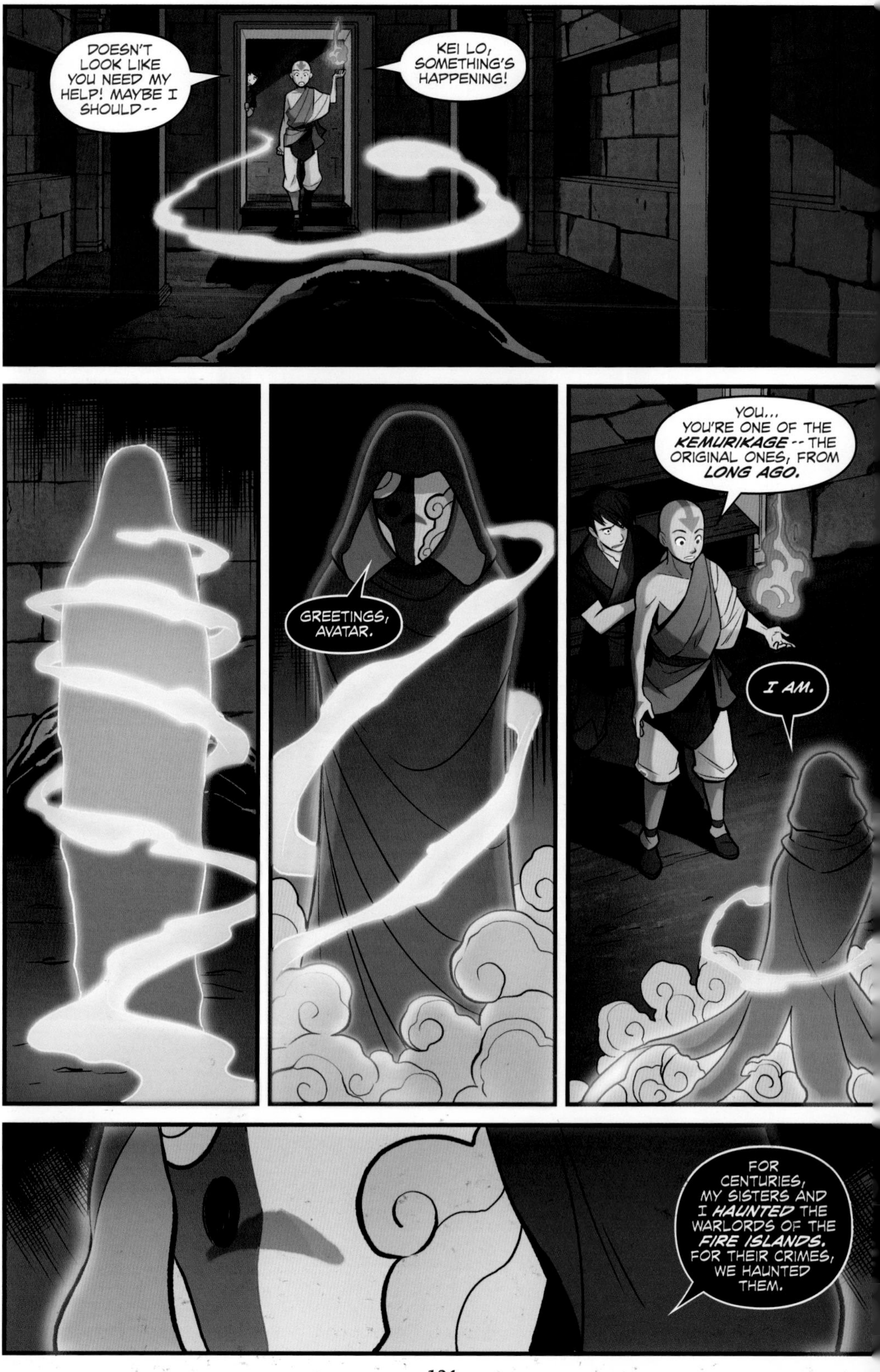

DOESN'T LOOK LIKE YOU NEED MY HELP! MAYBE I SHOULD--
KEI LO, SOMETHING'S HAPPENING!
GREETINGS, AVATAR.
YOU... YOU'RE ONE OF THE KEMURIKAGE--THE ORIGINAL ONES, FROM LONG AGO.
I AM.
FOR CENTURIES, MY SISTERS AND I HAUNTED THE WARLORDS OF THE FIRE ISLANDS. FOR THEIR CRIMES, WE HAUNTED THEM.

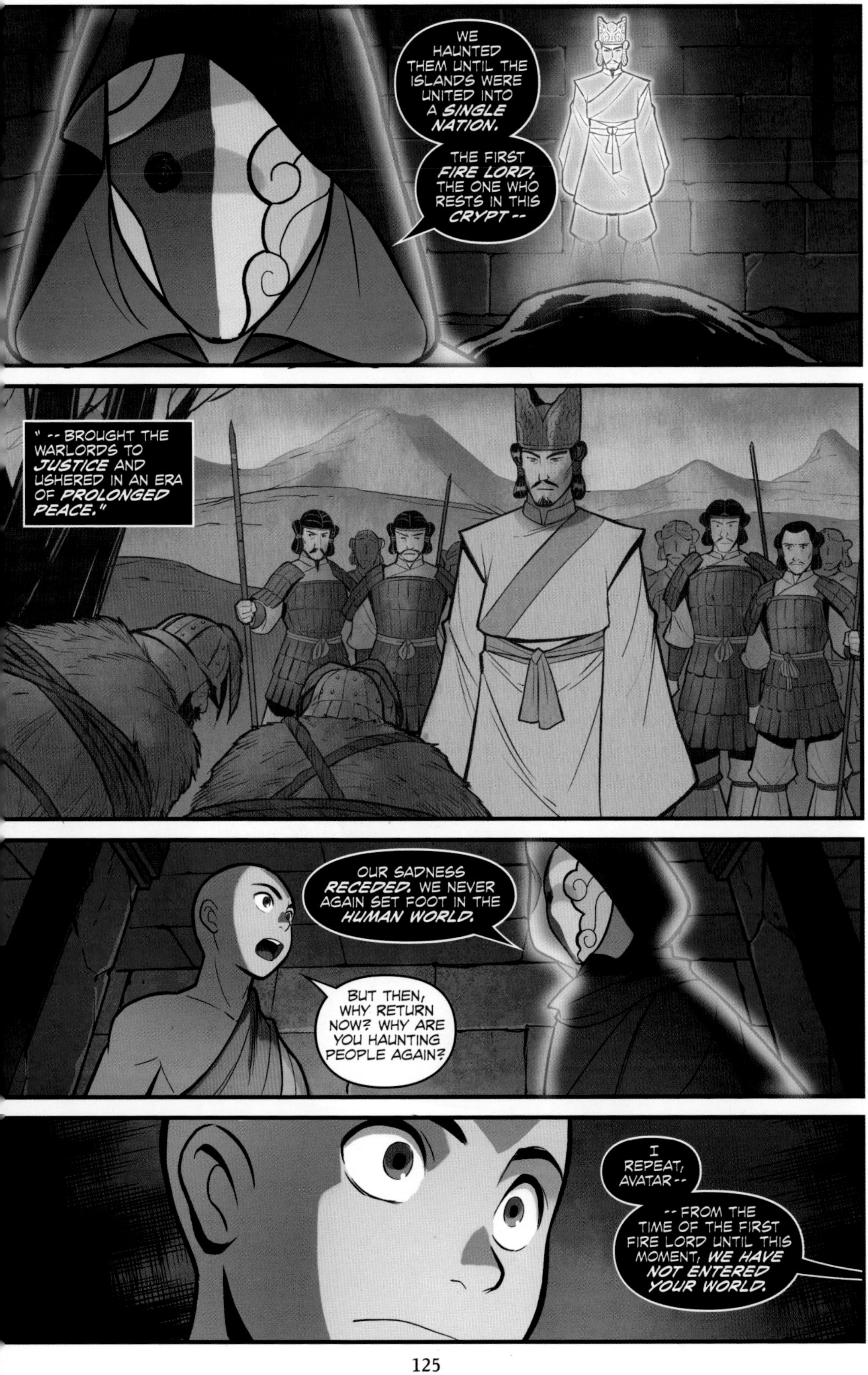
WE HAUNTED THEM UNTIL THE ISLANDS WERE UNITED INTO A SINGLE NATION.
THE FIRST FIRE LORD, THE ONE WHO RESTS IN THIS CRYPT --
" -- BROUGHT THE WARLORDS TO JUSTICE AND USHERED IN AN ERA OF PROLONGED PEACE."
OUR SADNESS RECEDED. WE NEVER AGAIN SET FOOT IN THE HUMAN WORLD.
BUT THEN, WHY RETURN NOW? WHY ARE YOU HAUNTING PEOPLE AGAIN?
I REPEAT, AVATAR --
-- FROM THE TIME OF THE FIRST FIRE LORD UNTIL THIS MOMENT, WE HAVE NOT ENTERED YOUR WORLD.

127

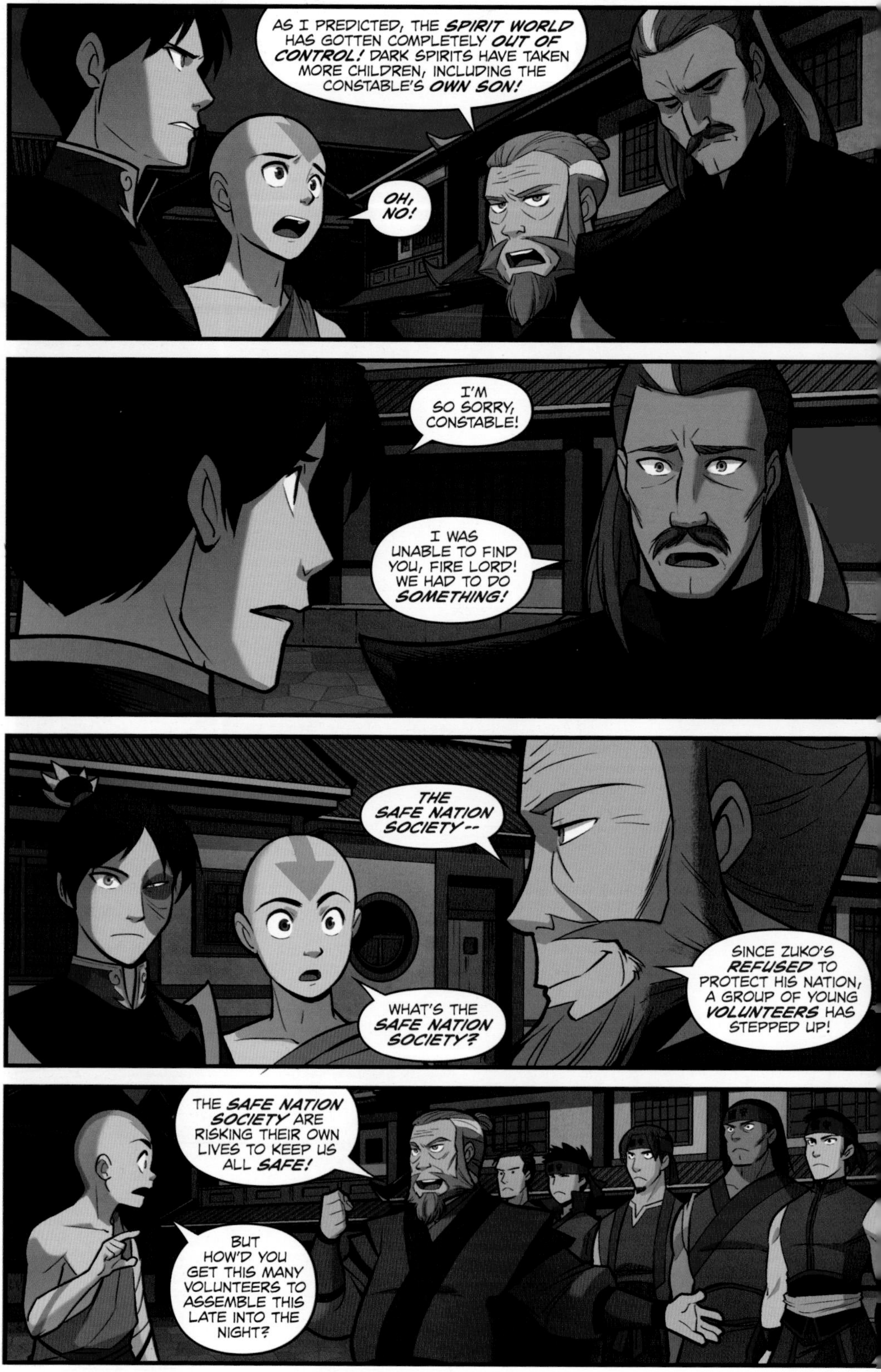
AS I PREDICTED, THE SPIRIT WORLD HAS GOTTEN COMPLETELY OUT OF CONTROL! DARK SPIRITS HAVE TAKEN MORE CHILDREN, INCLUDING THE CONSTABLE'S OWN SON!
OH, NO!
I'M SO SORRY, CONSTABLE!
I WAS UNABLE TO FIND YOU, FIRE LORD! WE HAD TO DO SOMETHING!
THE SAFE NATION SOCIETY--
WHAT'S THE SAFE NATION SOCIETY?
SINCE ZUKO'S REFUSED TO PROTECT HIS NATION, A GROUP OF YOUNG VOLUNTEERS HAS STEPPED UP!
THE SAFE NATION SOCIETY ARE RISKING THEIR OWN LIVES TO KEEP US ALL SAFE!
BUT HOW'D YOU GET THIS MANY VOLUNTEERS TO ASSEMBLE THIS LATE INTO THE NIGHT?

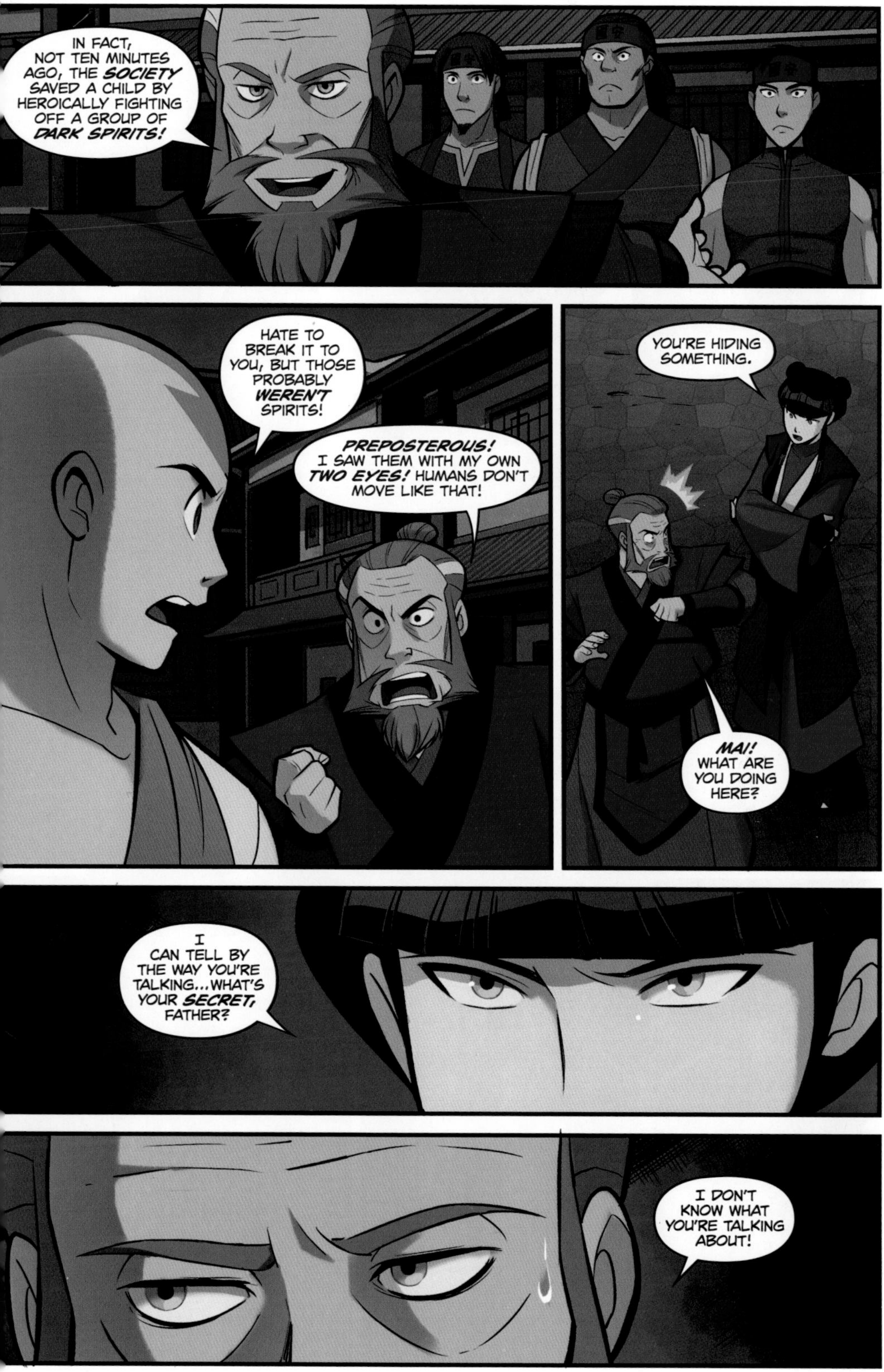
IN FACT, NOT TEN MINUTES AGO, THE SOCIETY SAVED A CHILD BY HEROICALLY FIGHTING OFF A GROUP OF DARK SPIRITS!
HATE TO BREAK IT TO YOU, BUT THOSE PROBABLY WEREN'T SPIRITS!
PREPOSTEROUS! I SAW THEM WITH MY OWN TWO EYES! HUMANS DON'T MOVE LIKE THAT!
YOU'RE HIDING SOMETHING.
MAI! WHAT ARE YOU DOING HERE?
I CAN TELL BY THE WAY YOU'RE TALKING... WHAT'S YOUR SECRET, FATHER?
I DON'T KNOW WHAT YOU'RE TALKING ABOUT!

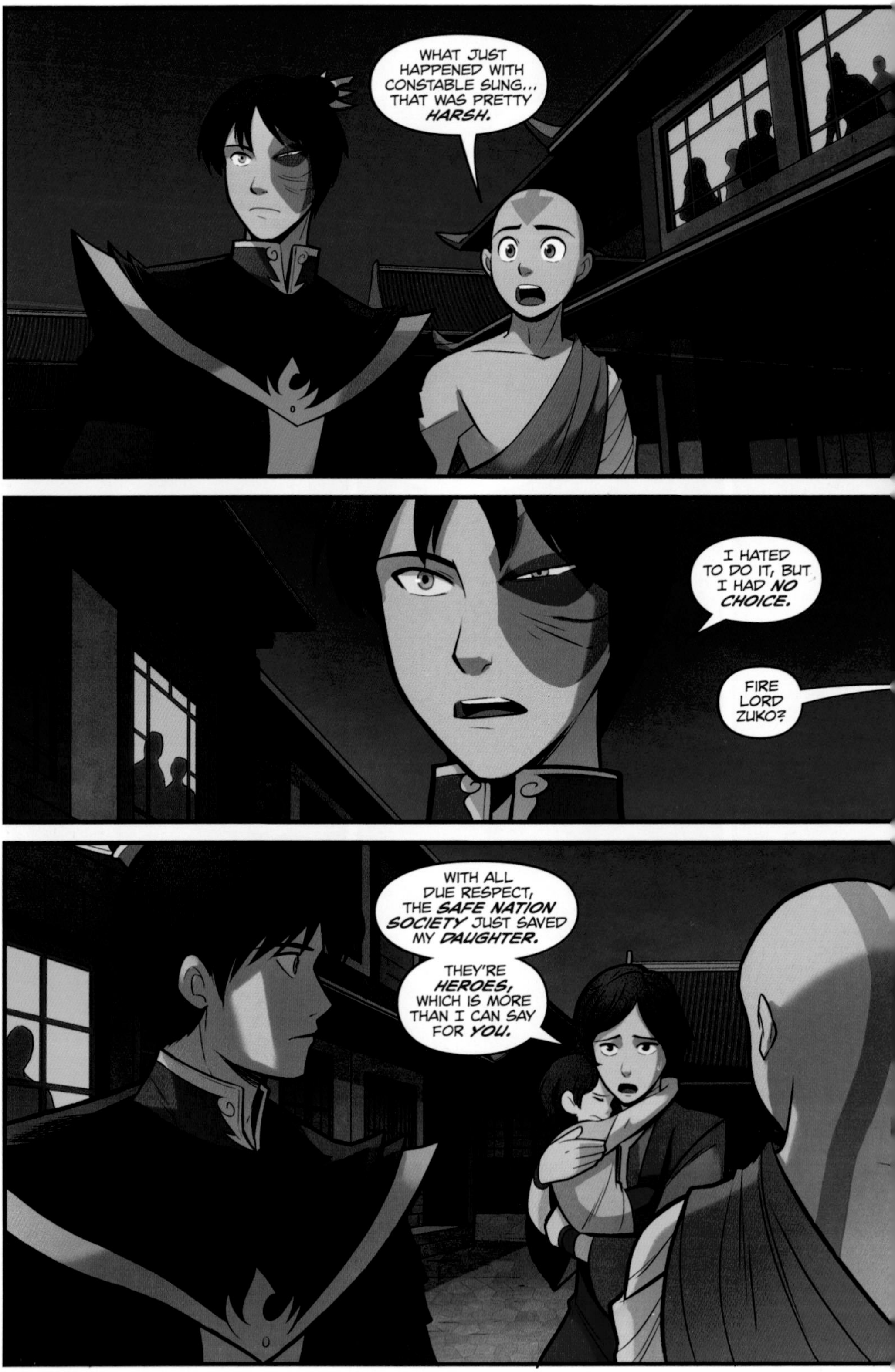
WHAT JUST HAPPENED WITH CONSTABLE SUNG... THAT WAS PRETTY *HARSH.*
I HATED TO DO IT, BUT I HAD *NO CHOICE.*
FIRE LORD ZUKO?
WITH ALL DUE RESPECT, THE *SAFE NATION SOCIETY* JUST SAVED MY *DAUGHTER.*
THEY'RE *HEROES,* WHICH IS MORE THAN I CAN SAY FOR *YOU.*

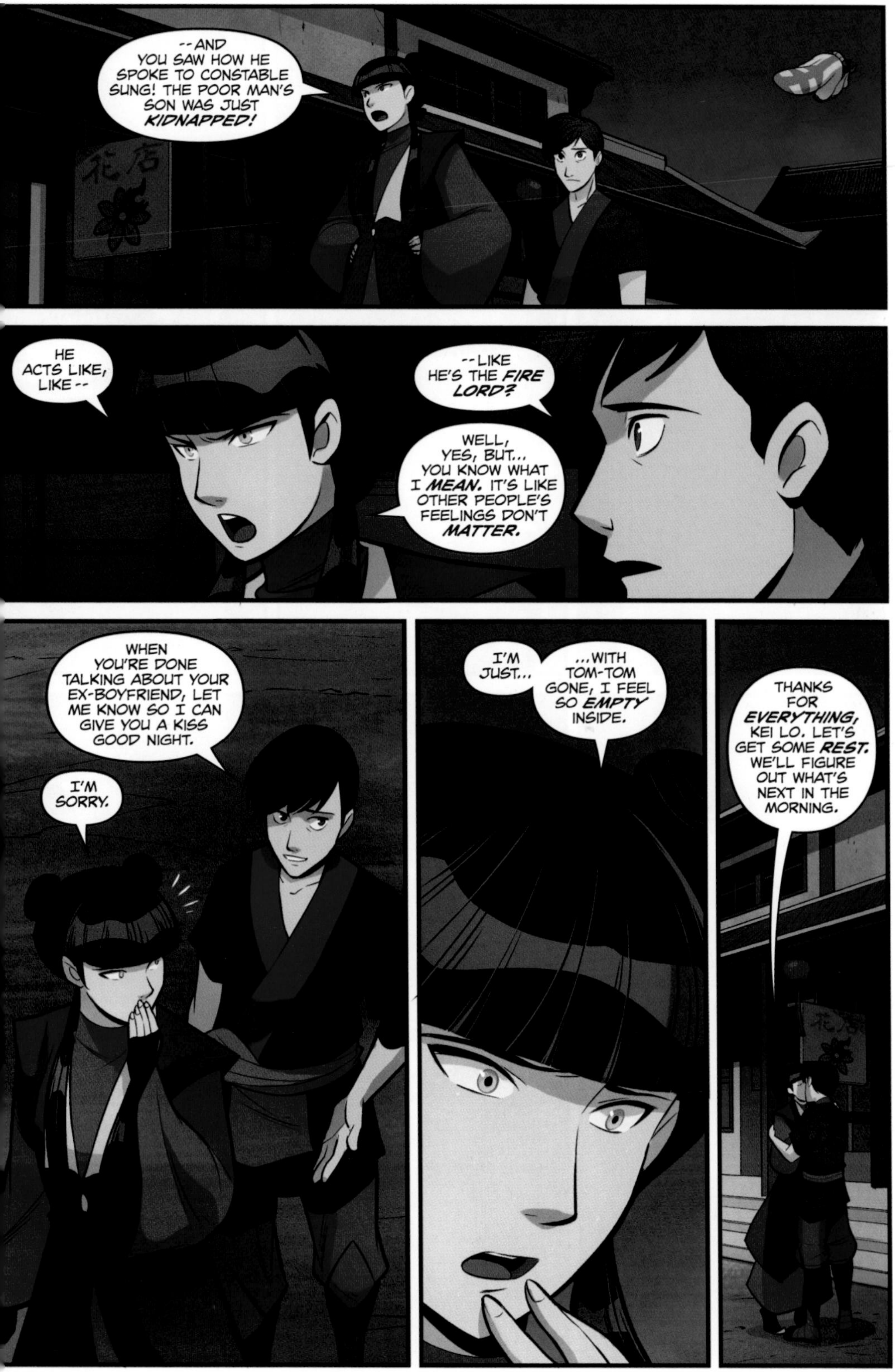
--AND YOU SAW HOW HE SPOKE TO CONSTABLE SUNG! THE POOR MAN'S SON WAS JUST KIDNAPPED!
HE ACTS LIKE, LIKE--
--LIKE HE'S THE FIRE LORD?
WELL, YES, BUT... YOU KNOW WHAT I MEAN. IT'S LIKE OTHER PEOPLE'S FEELINGS DON'T MATTER.
WHEN YOU'RE DONE TALKING ABOUT YOUR EX-BOYFRIEND, LET ME KNOW SO I CAN GIVE YOU A KISS GOOD NIGHT.
I'M SORRY.
I'M JUST...
...WITH TOM-TOM GONE, I FEEL SO EMPTY INSIDE.
THANKS FOR EVERYTHING, KEI LO. LET'S GET SOME REST. WE'LL FIGURE OUT WHAT'S NEXT IN THE MORNING.

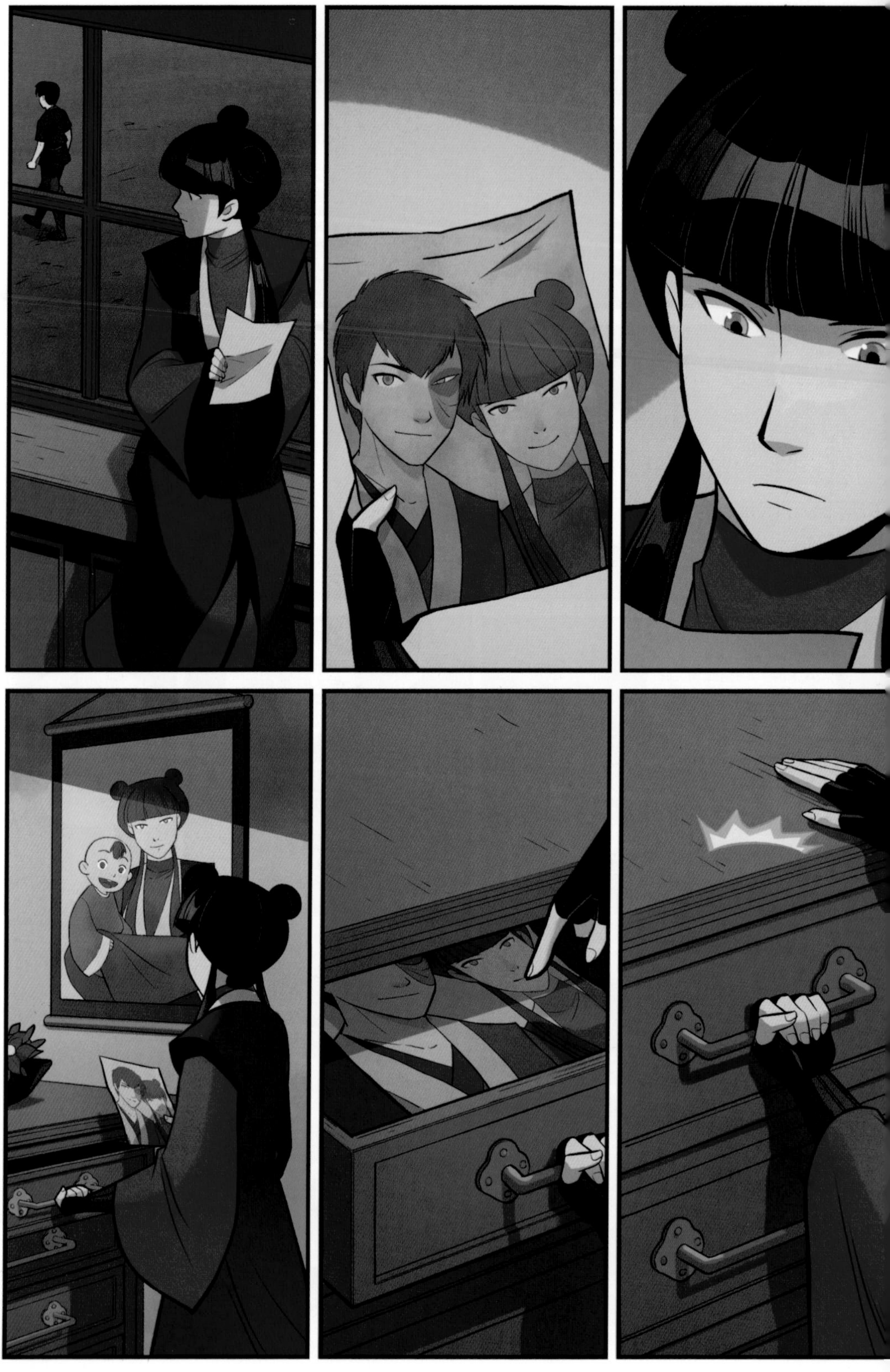

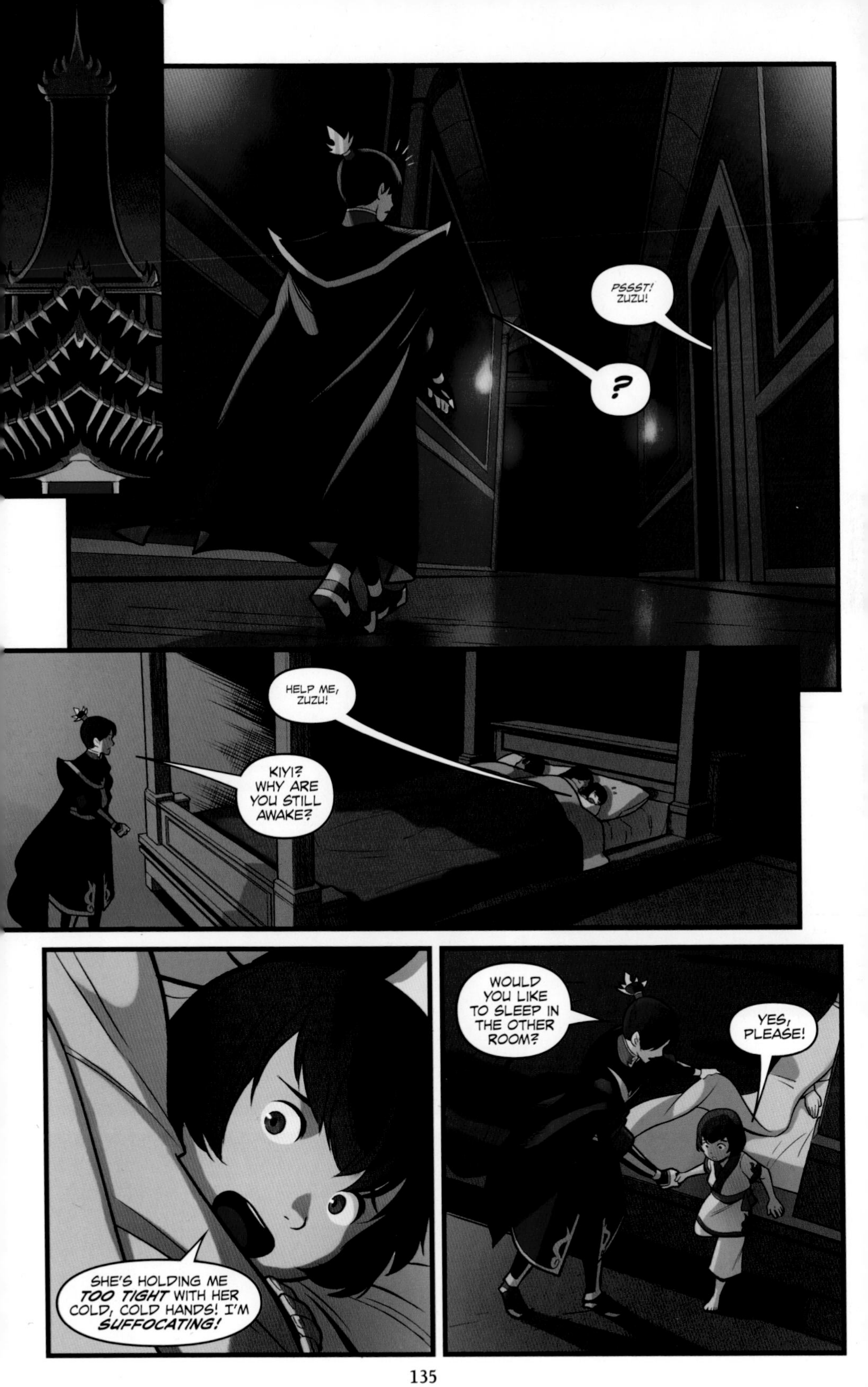
PSSST! ZUZU!
?
HELP ME, ZUZU!
KIYI? WHY ARE YOU STILL AWAKE?
SHE'S HOLDING ME TOO TIGHT WITH HER COLD, COLD HANDS! I'M SUFFOCATING!
WOULD YOU LIKE TO SLEEP IN THE OTHER ROOM?
YES, PLEASE!

136

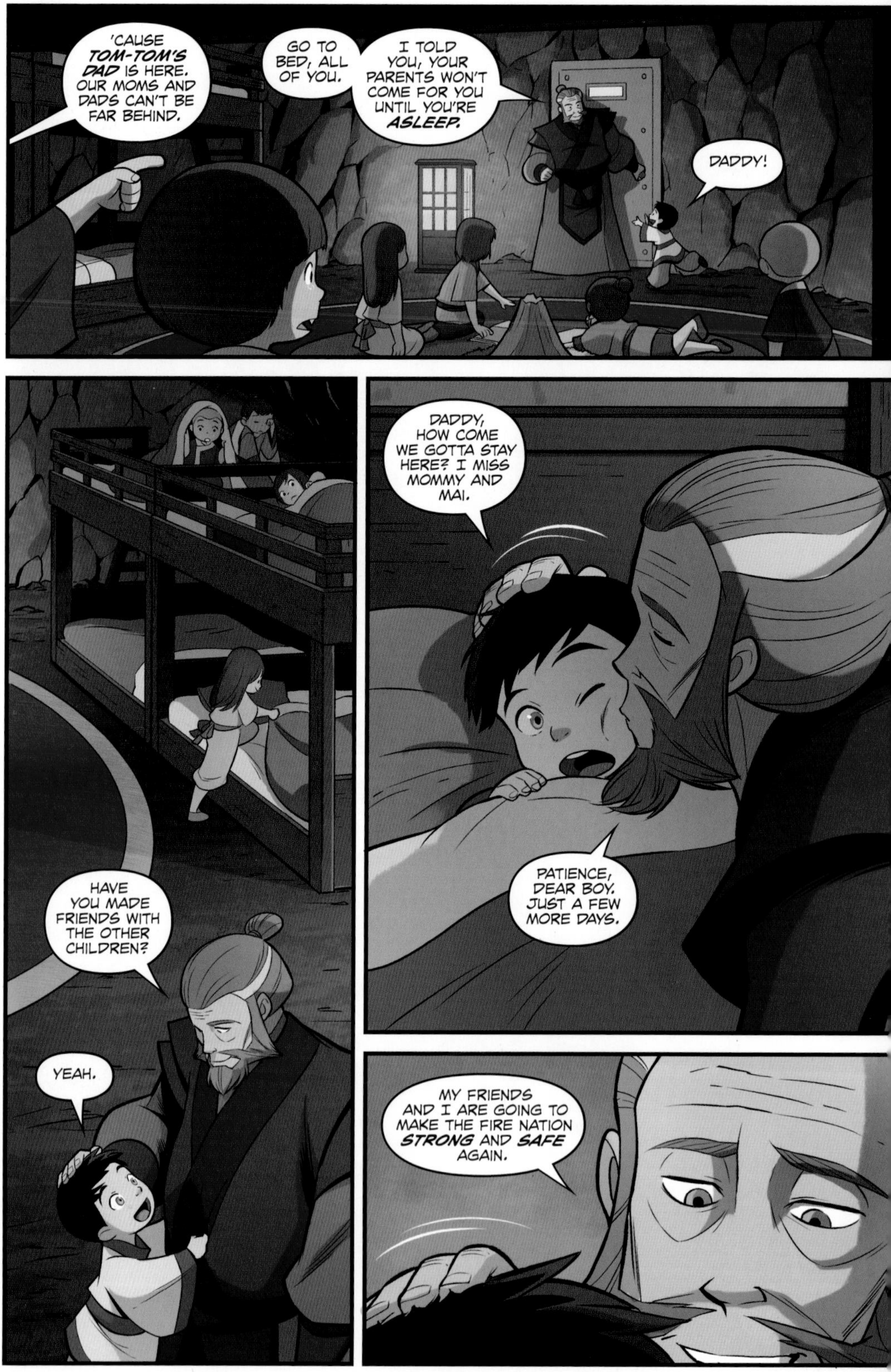
'CAUSE TOM-TOM'S DAD IS HERE. OUR MOMS AND DADS CAN'T BE FAR BEHIND.
GO TO BED, ALL OF YOU.
I TOLD YOU, YOUR PARENTS WON'T COME FOR YOU UNTIL YOU'RE ASLEEP.
DADDY!
HAVE YOU MADE FRIENDS WITH THE OTHER CHILDREN?
YEAH.
DADDY, HOW COME WE GOTTA STAY HERE? I MISS MOMMY AND MAI.
PATIENCE, DEAR BOY. JUST A FEW MORE DAYS.
MY FRIENDS AND I ARE GOING TO MAKE THE FIRE NATION STRONG AND SAFE AGAIN.

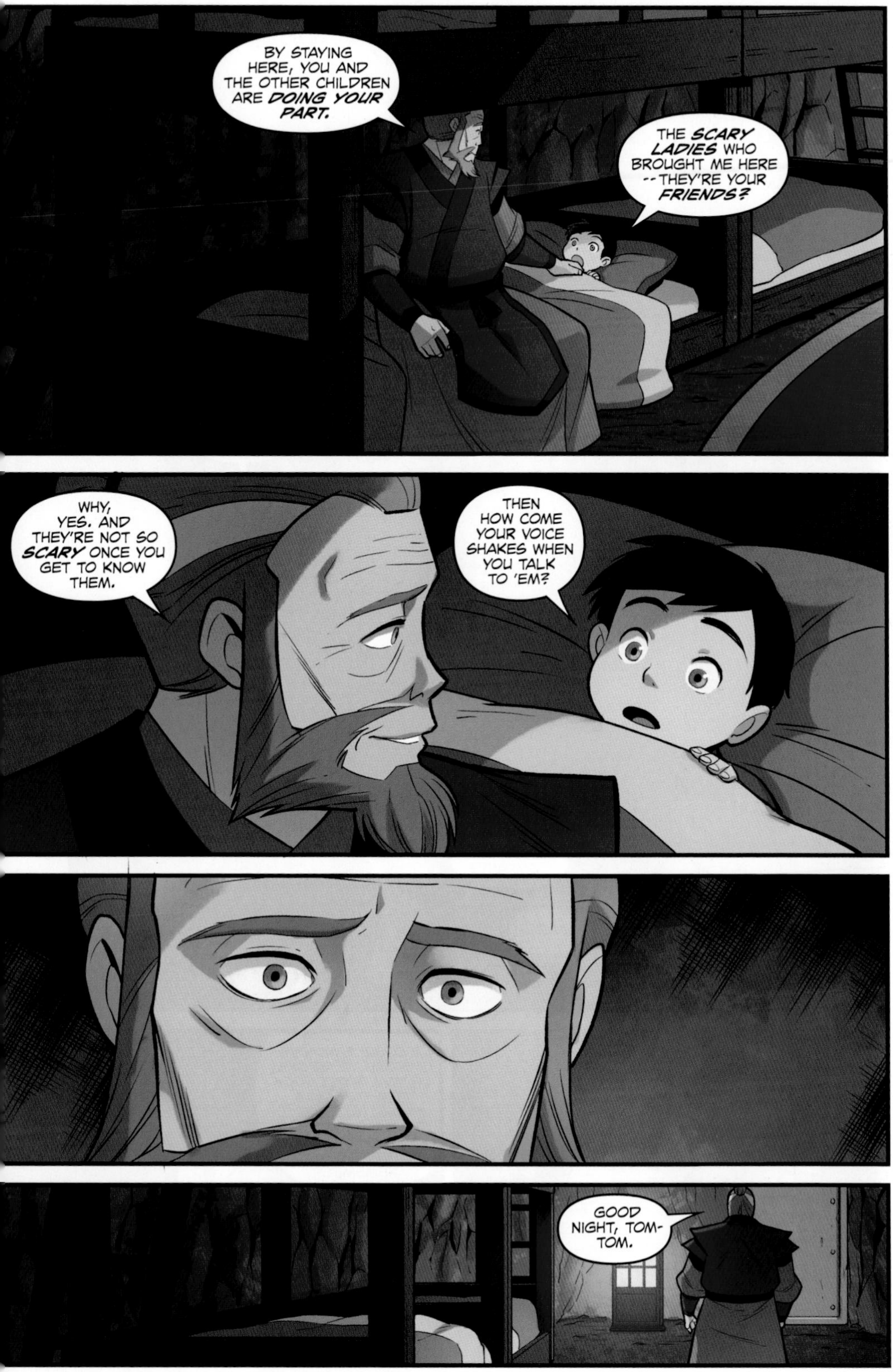
BY STAYING HERE, YOU AND THE OTHER CHILDREN ARE DOING YOUR PART.
THE SCARY LADIES WHO BROUGHT ME HERE -- THEY'RE YOUR FRIENDS?
WHY, YES. AND THEY'RE NOT SO SCARY ONCE YOU GET TO KNOW THEM.
THEN HOW COME YOUR VOICE SHAKES WHEN YOU TALK TO 'EM?
GOOD NIGHT, TOM-TOM.

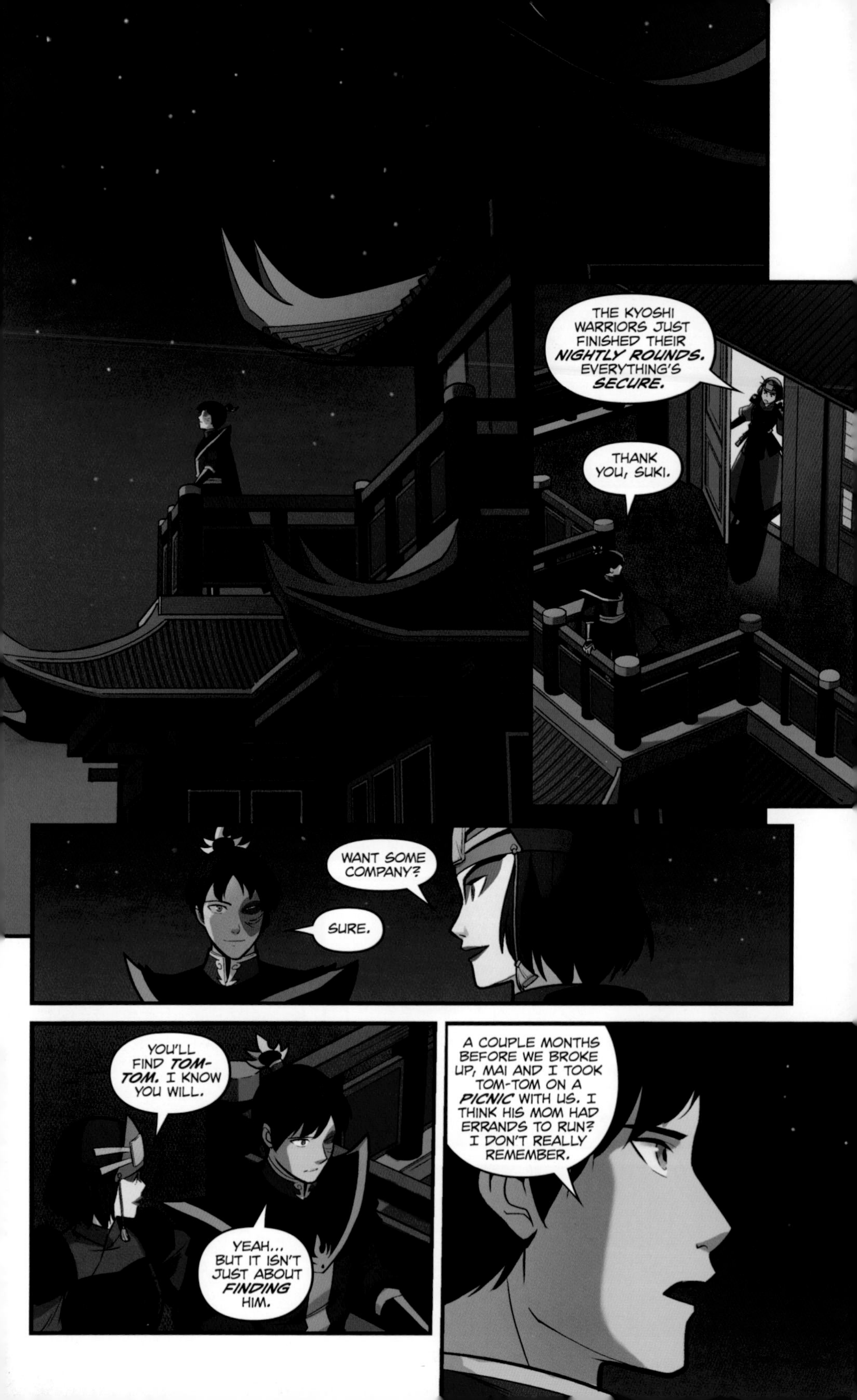

THE KYOSHI WARRIORS JUST FINISHED THEIR NIGHTLY ROUNDS. EVERYTHING'S SECURE.
THANK YOU, SUKI.
WANT SOME COMPANY?
SURE.
YOU'LL FIND TOM-TOM. I KNOW YOU WILL.
YEAH... BUT IT ISN'T JUST ABOUT FINDING HIM.
A COUPLE MONTHS BEFORE WE BROKE UP, MAI AND I TOOK TOM-TOM ON A PICNIC WITH US. I THINK HIS MOM HAD ERRANDS TO RUN? I DON'T REALLY REMEMBER.

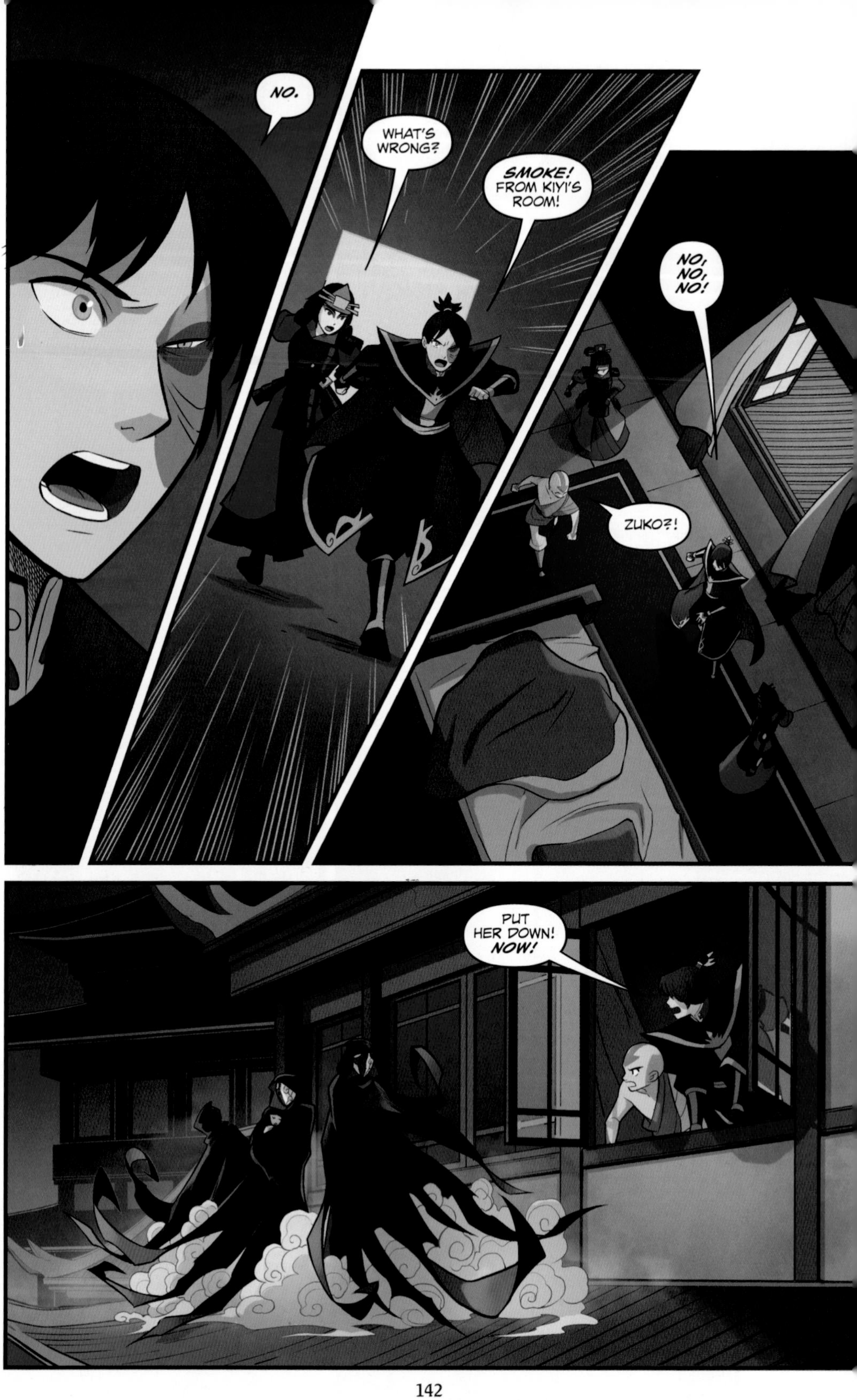
NO.
WHAT'S WRONG?
SMOKE! FROM KIYI'S ROOM!
NO, NO, NO!
ZUKO?!
PUT HER DOWN! NOW!

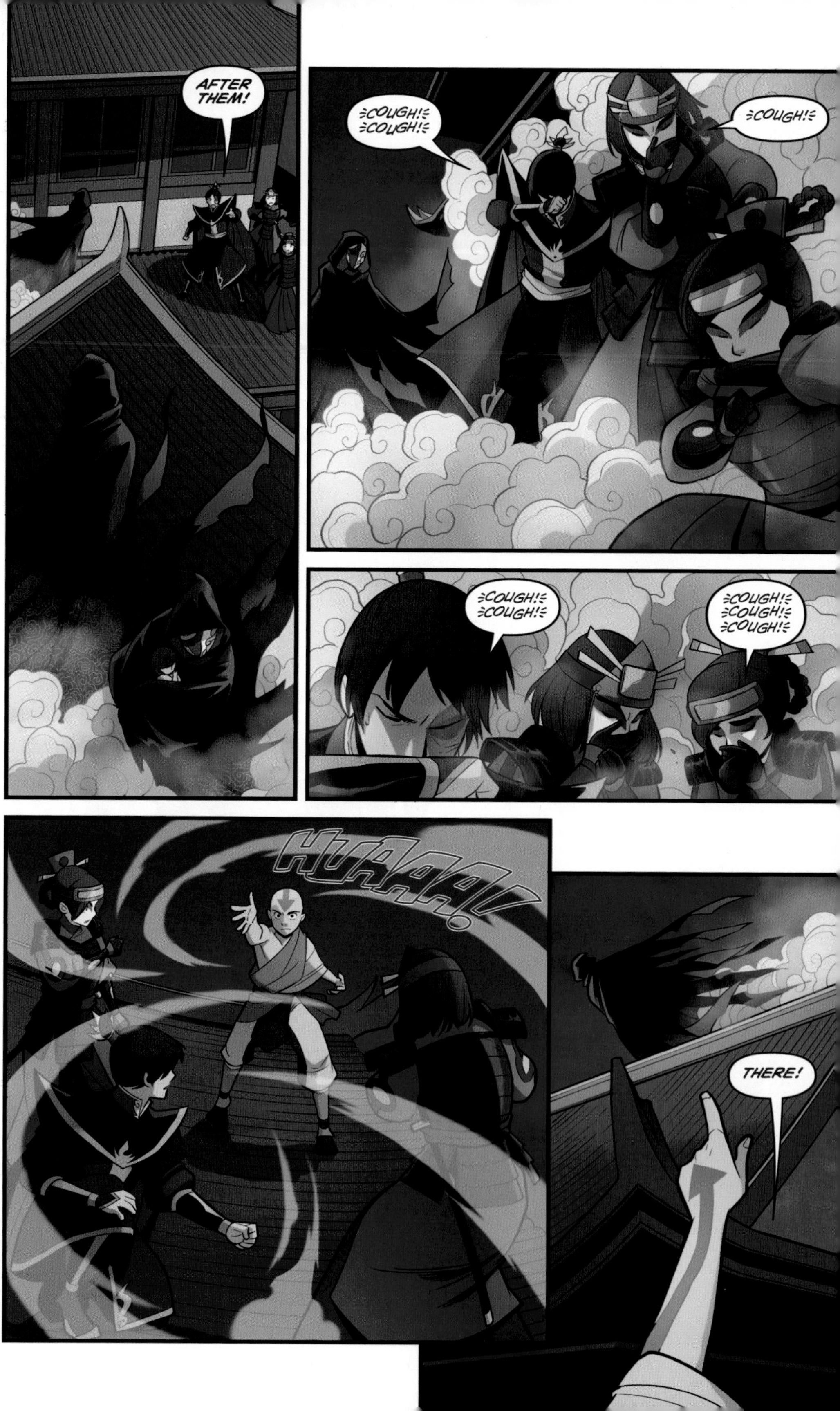
AFTER THEM!
COUGH! COUGH!
COUGH!
COUGH! COUGH!
COUGH! COUGH! COUGH!
HUAAA!
THERE!

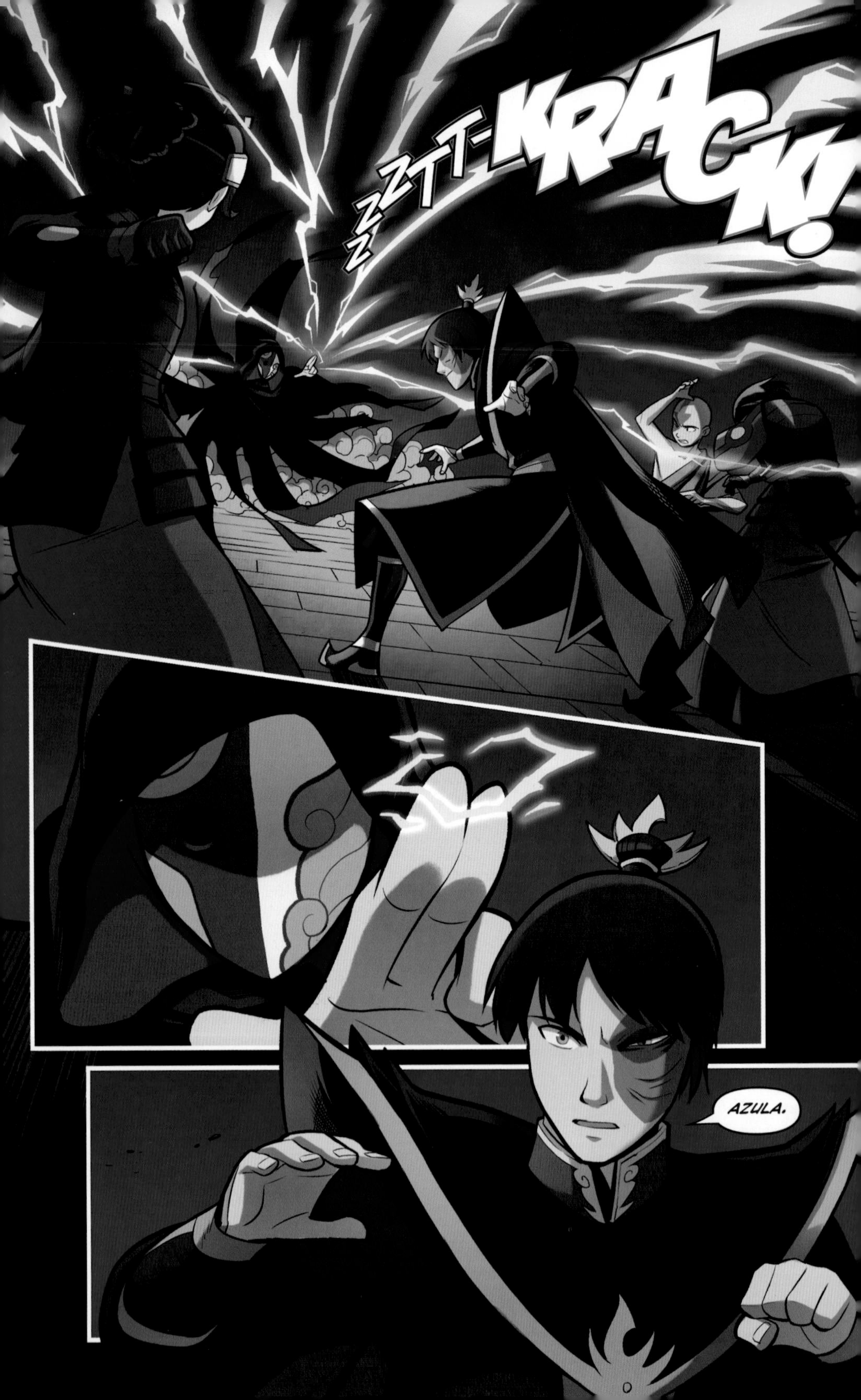
ZZZTT-KRACK!
AZULA.

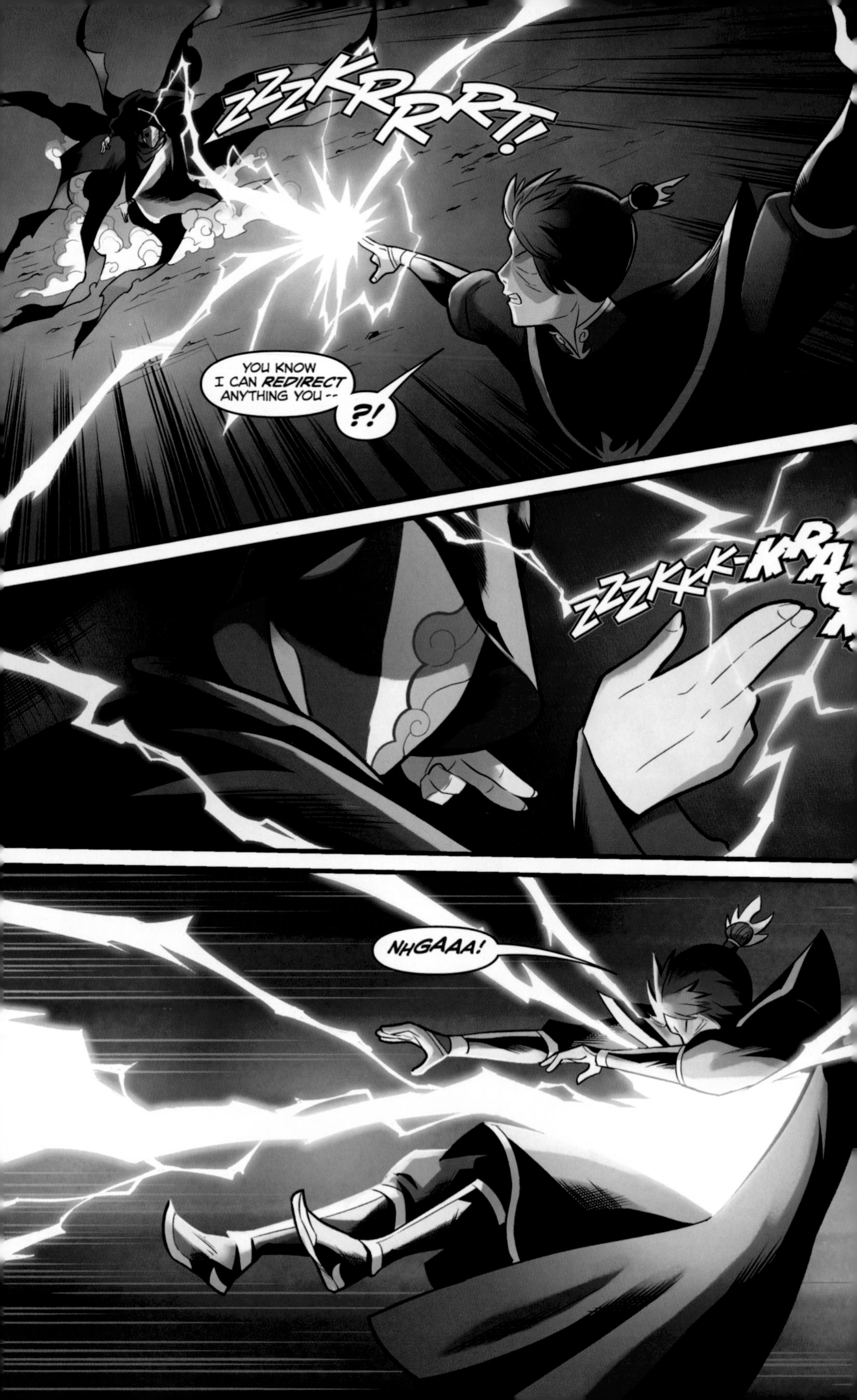
ZZZKRRRT!!
YOU KNOW I CAN *REDIRECT* ANYTHING YOU --
?!
ZZZKKK-KRAC
NHGAAA!

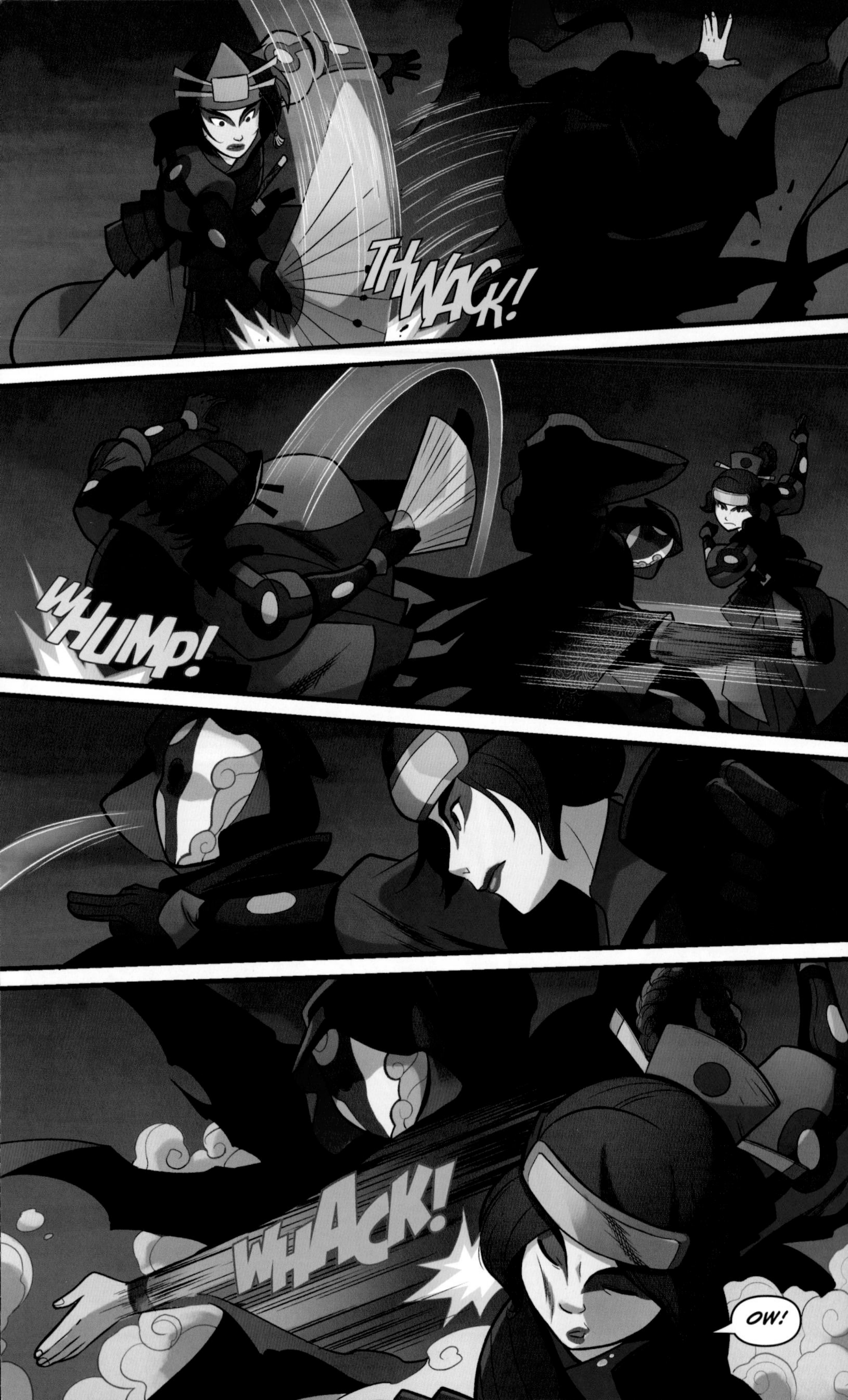
THWACK!
WHUMP!
WHACK!
OW!

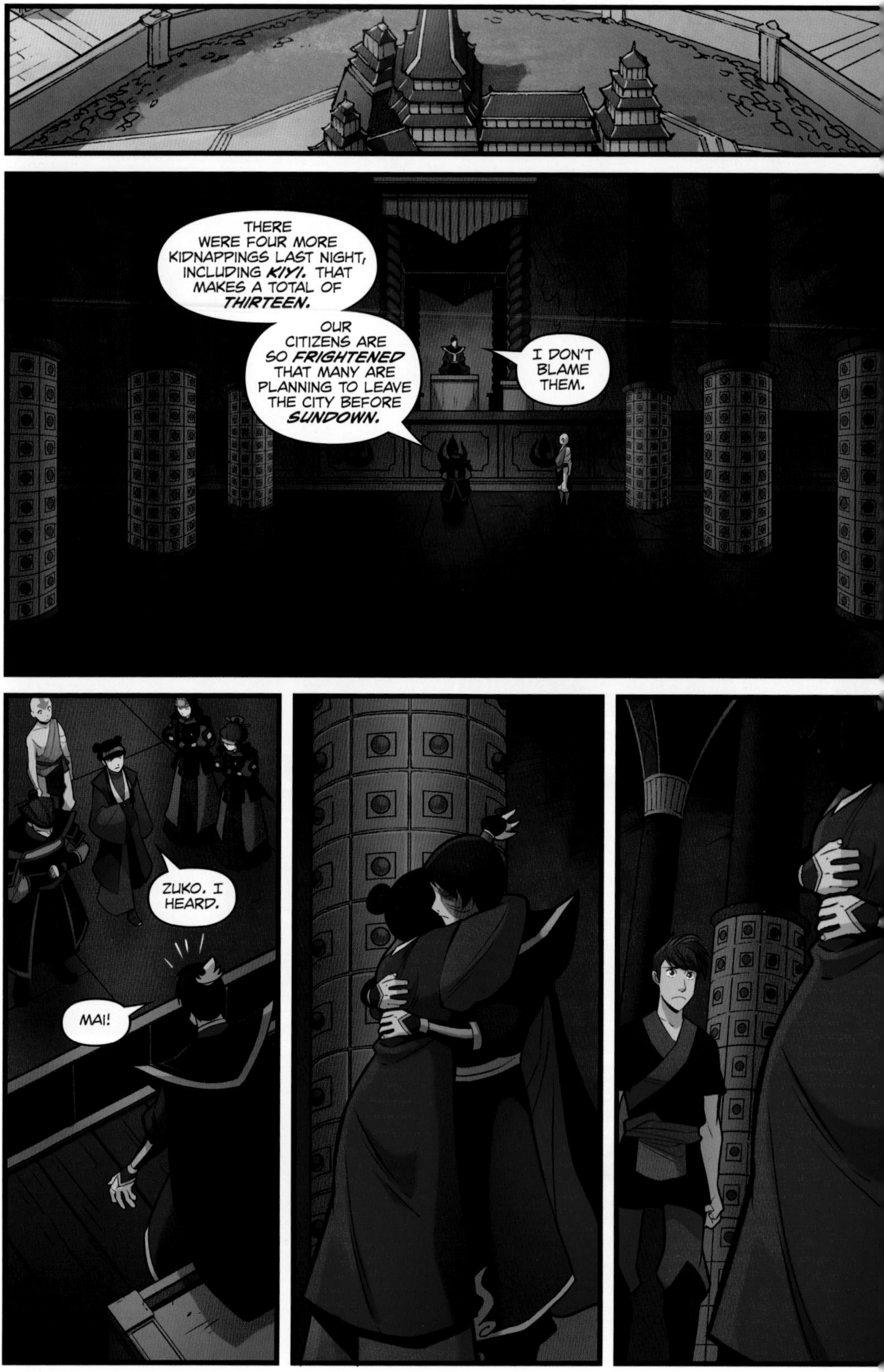
THERE WERE FOUR MORE KIDNAPPINGS LAST NIGHT, INCLUDING KIYI. THAT MAKES A TOTAL OF THIRTEEN.
OUR CITIZENS ARE SO FRIGHTENED THAT MANY ARE PLANNING TO LEAVE THE CITY BEFORE SUNDOWN.
I DON'T BLAME THEM.
ZUKO. I HEARD.
MAI!

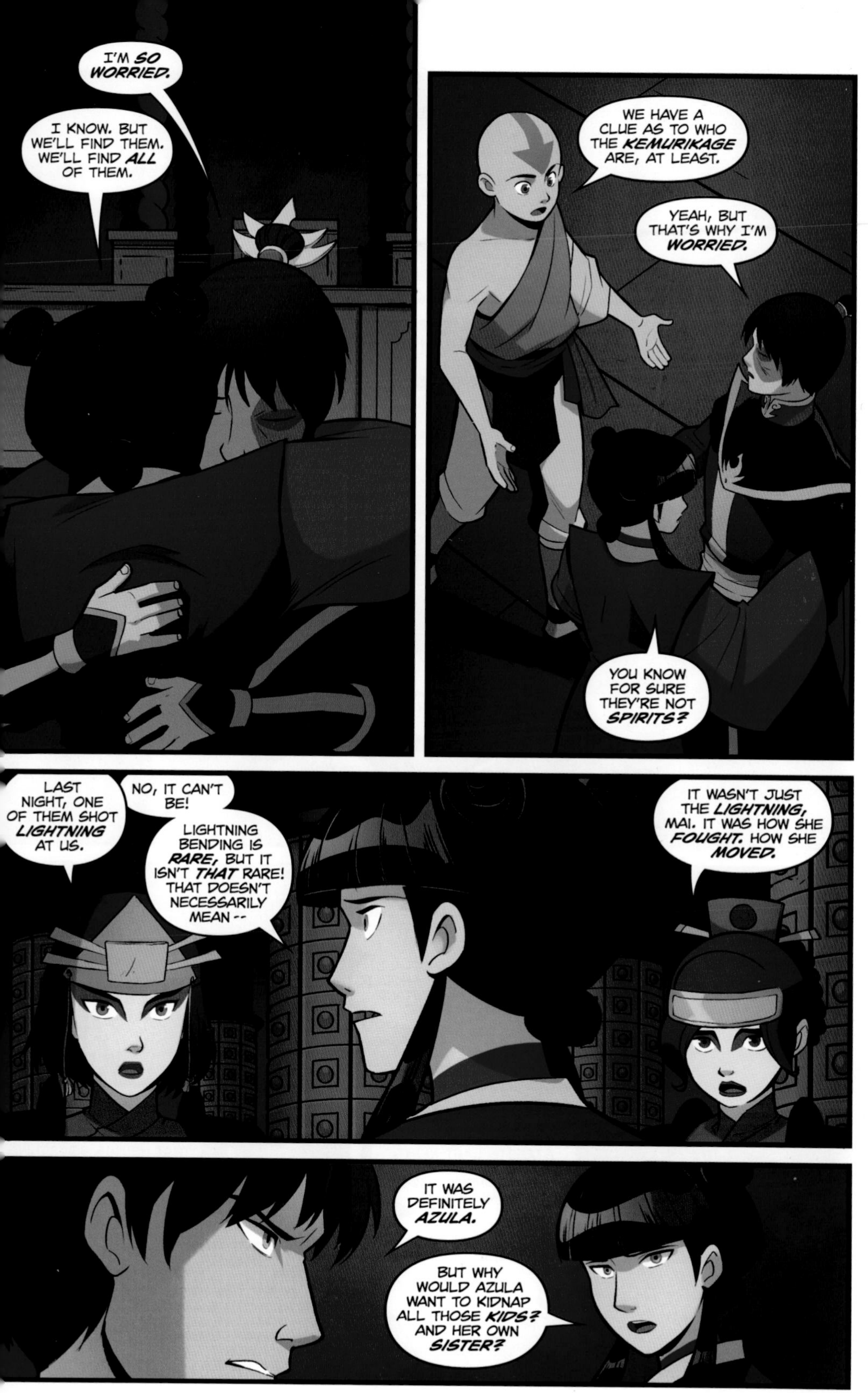
I'M SO WORRIED.
I KNOW. BUT WE'LL FIND THEM. WE'LL FIND ALL OF THEM.
WE HAVE A CLUE AS TO WHO THE KEMURIKAGE ARE, AT LEAST.
YEAH, BUT THAT'S WHY I'M WORRIED.
YOU KNOW FOR SURE THEY'RE NOT SPIRITS?
LAST NIGHT, ONE OF THEM SHOT LIGHTNING AT US.
NO, IT CAN'T BE!
LIGHTNING BENDING IS RARE, BUT IT ISN'T THAT RARE! THAT DOESN'T NECESSARILY MEAN --
IT WASN'T JUST THE LIGHTNING, MAI. IT WAS HOW SHE FOUGHT. HOW SHE MOVED.
IT WAS DEFINITELY AZULA.
BUT WHY WOULD AZULA WANT TO KIDNAP ALL THOSE KIDS? AND HER OWN SISTER?

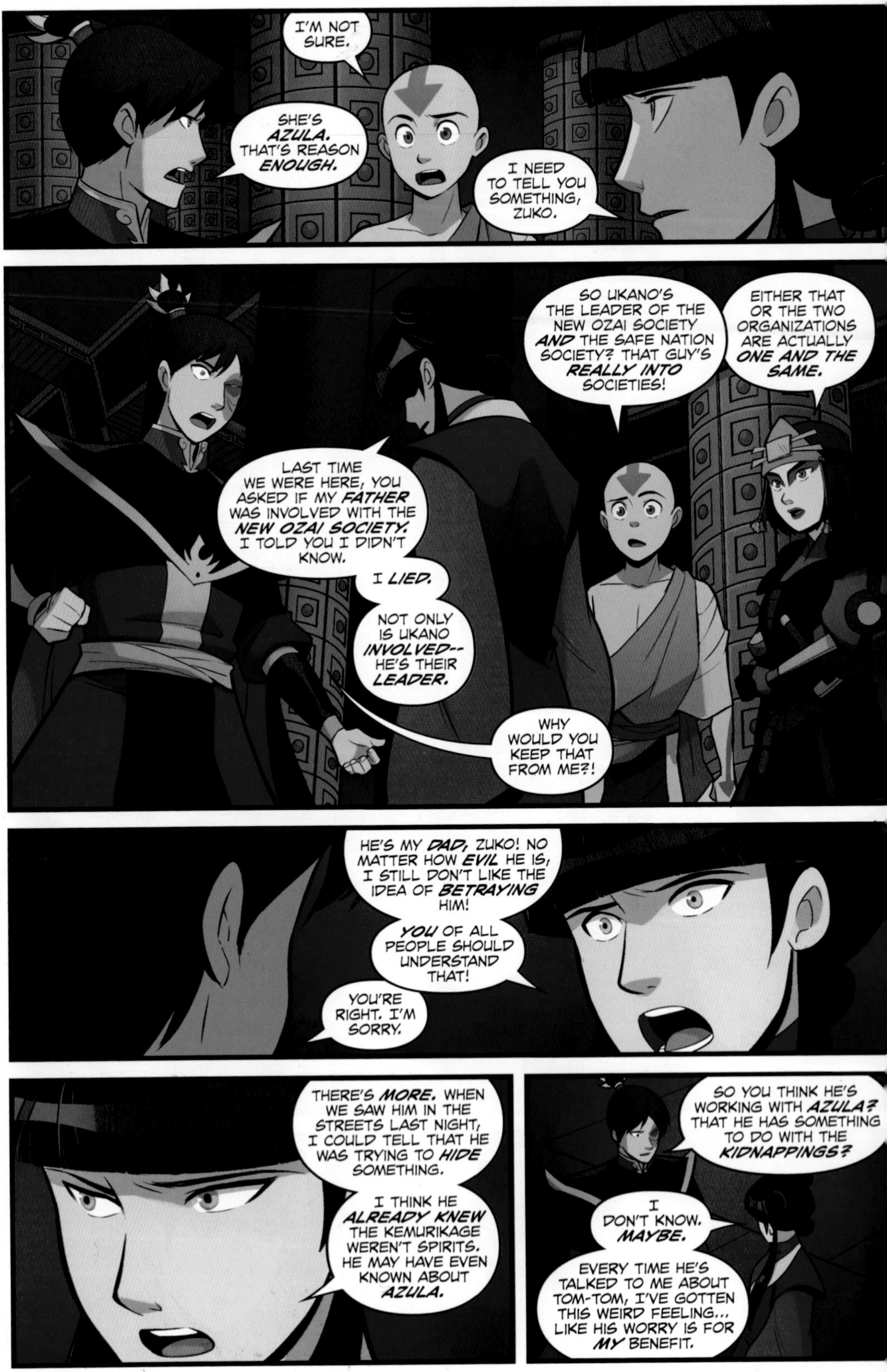

I'M NOT SURE.
SHE'S AZULA. THAT'S REASON ENOUGH.
I NEED TO TELL YOU SOMETHING, ZUKO.
SO UKANO'S THE LEADER OF THE NEW OZAI SOCIETY AND THE SAFE NATION SOCIETY? THAT GUY'S REALLY INTO SOCIETIES!
EITHER THAT OR THE TWO ORGANIZATIONS ARE ACTUALLY ONE AND THE SAME.
LAST TIME WE WERE HERE, YOU ASKED IF MY FATHER WAS INVOLVED WITH THE NEW OZAI SOCIETY. I TOLD YOU I DIDN'T KNOW.
I LIED.
NOT ONLY IS UKANO INVOLVED-- HE'S THEIR LEADER.
WHY WOULD YOU KEEP THAT FROM ME?!
HE'S MY DAD, ZUKO! NO MATTER HOW EVIL HE IS, I STILL DON'T LIKE THE IDEA OF BETRAYING HIM!
YOU OF ALL PEOPLE SHOULD UNDERSTAND THAT!
YOU'RE RIGHT. I'M SORRY.
THERE'S MORE. WHEN WE SAW HIM IN THE STREETS LAST NIGHT, I COULD TELL THAT HE WAS TRYING TO HIDE SOMETHING.
I THINK HE ALREADY KNEW THE KEMURIKAGE WEREN'T SPIRITS. HE MAY HAVE EVEN KNOWN ABOUT AZULA.
SO YOU THINK HE'S WORKING WITH AZULA? THAT HE HAS SOMETHING TO DO WITH THE KIDNAPPINGS?
I DON'T KNOW. MAYBE.
EVERY TIME HE'S TALKED TO ME ABOUT TOM-TOM, I'VE GOTTEN THIS WEIRD FEELING... LIKE HIS WORRY IS FOR MY BENEFIT.

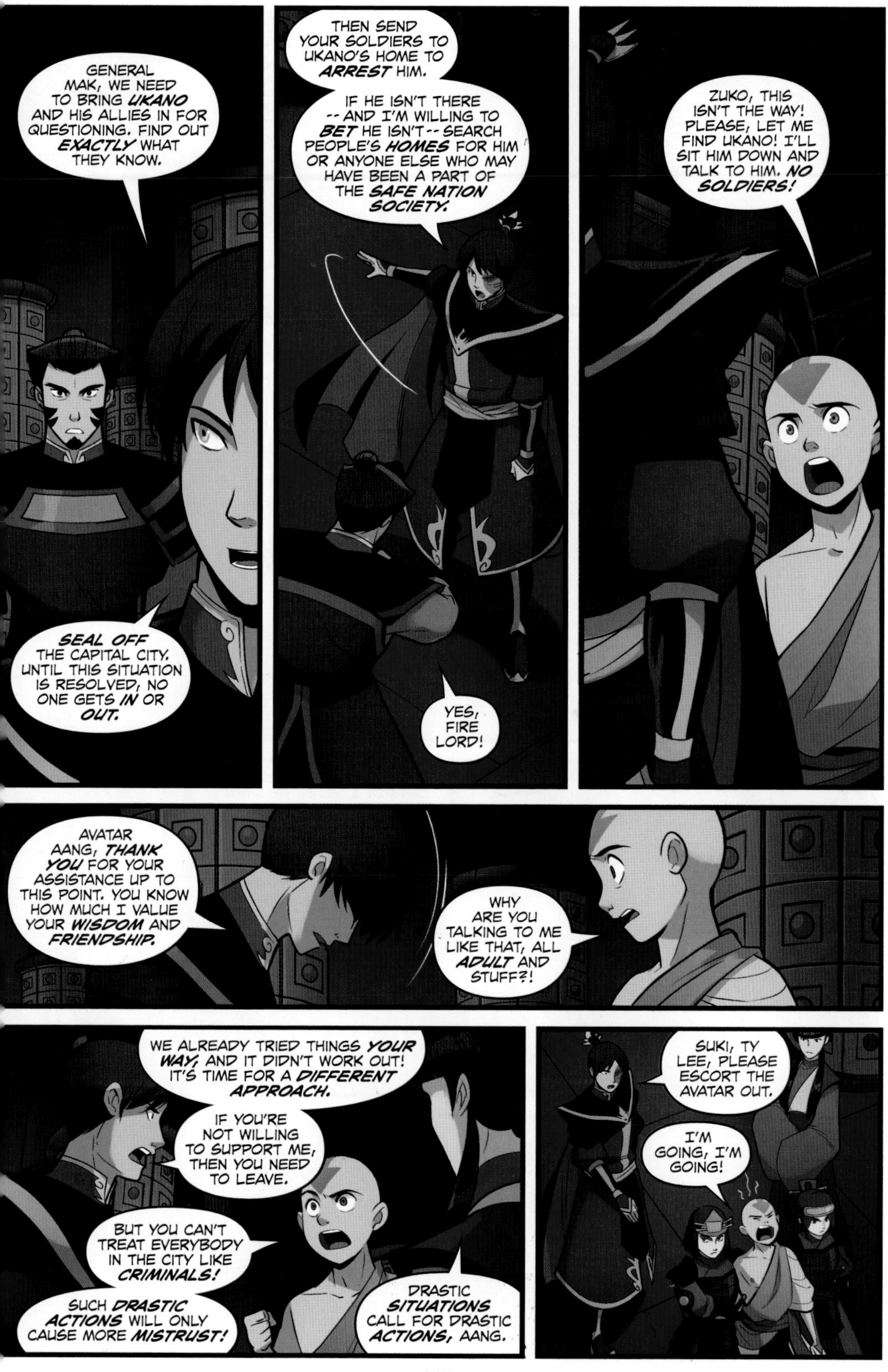
GENERAL MAK, WE NEED TO BRING UKANO AND HIS ALLIES IN FOR QUESTIONING. FIND OUT EXACTLY WHAT THEY KNOW.
SEAL OFF THE CAPITAL CITY. UNTIL THIS SITUATION IS RESOLVED, NO ONE GETS IN OR OUT.
THEN SEND YOUR SOLDIERS TO UKANO'S HOME TO ARREST HIM.
IF HE ISN'T THERE -- AND I'M WILLING TO BET HE ISN'T -- SEARCH PEOPLE'S HOMES FOR HIM OR ANYONE ELSE WHO MAY HAVE BEEN A PART OF THE SAFE NATION SOCIETY.
YES, FIRE LORD!
ZUKO, THIS ISN'T THE WAY! PLEASE, LET ME FIND UKANO! I'LL SIT HIM DOWN AND TALK TO HIM. NO SOLDIERS!
AVATAR AANG, THANK YOU FOR YOUR ASSISTANCE UP TO THIS POINT. YOU KNOW HOW MUCH I VALUE YOUR WISDOM AND FRIENDSHIP.
WHY ARE YOU TALKING TO ME LIKE THAT, ALL ADULT AND STUFF?!
WE ALREADY TRIED THINGS YOUR WAY, AND IT DIDN'T WORK OUT! IT'S TIME FOR A DIFFERENT APPROACH.
IF YOU'RE NOT WILLING TO SUPPORT ME, THEN YOU NEED TO LEAVE.
BUT YOU CAN'T TREAT EVERYBODY IN THE CITY LIKE CRIMINALS!
SUCH DRASTIC ACTIONS WILL ONLY CAUSE MORE MISTRUST!
DRASTIC SITUATIONS CALL FOR DRASTIC ACTIONS, AANG.
SUKI, TY LEE, PLEASE ESCORT THE AVATAR OUT.
I'M GOING, I'M GOING!

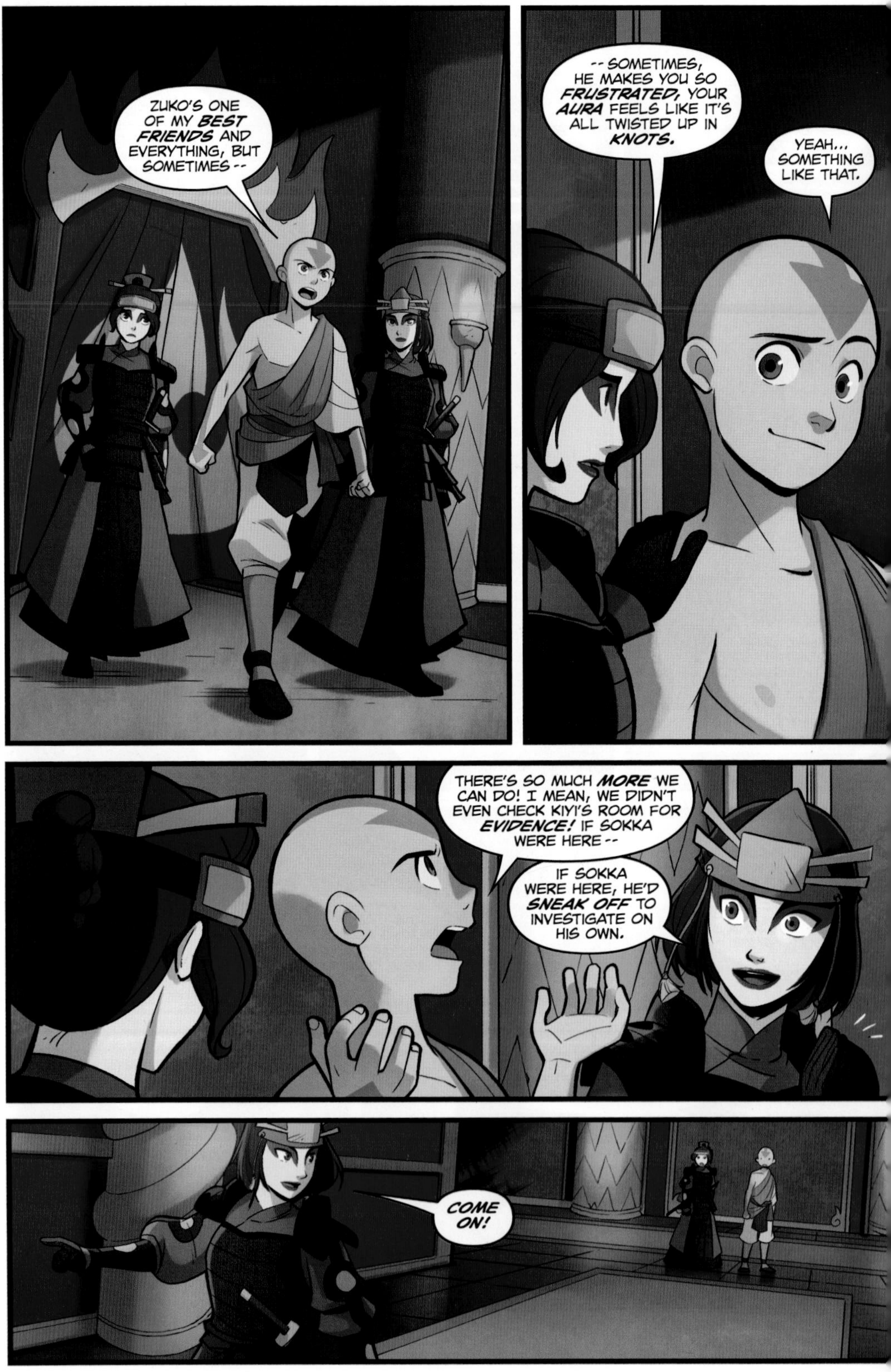
ZUKO'S ONE OF MY BEST FRIENDS AND EVERYTHING, BUT SOMETIMES --
-- SOMETIMES, HE MAKES YOU SO FRUSTRATED, YOUR AURA FEELS LIKE IT'S ALL TWISTED UP IN KNOTS.
YEAH... SOMETHING LIKE THAT.
THERE'S SO MUCH MORE WE CAN DO! I MEAN, WE DIDN'T EVEN CHECK KIYI'S ROOM FOR EVIDENCE! IF SOKKA WERE HERE --
IF SOKKA WERE HERE, HE'D SNEAK OFF TO INVESTIGATE ON HIS OWN.
COME ON!

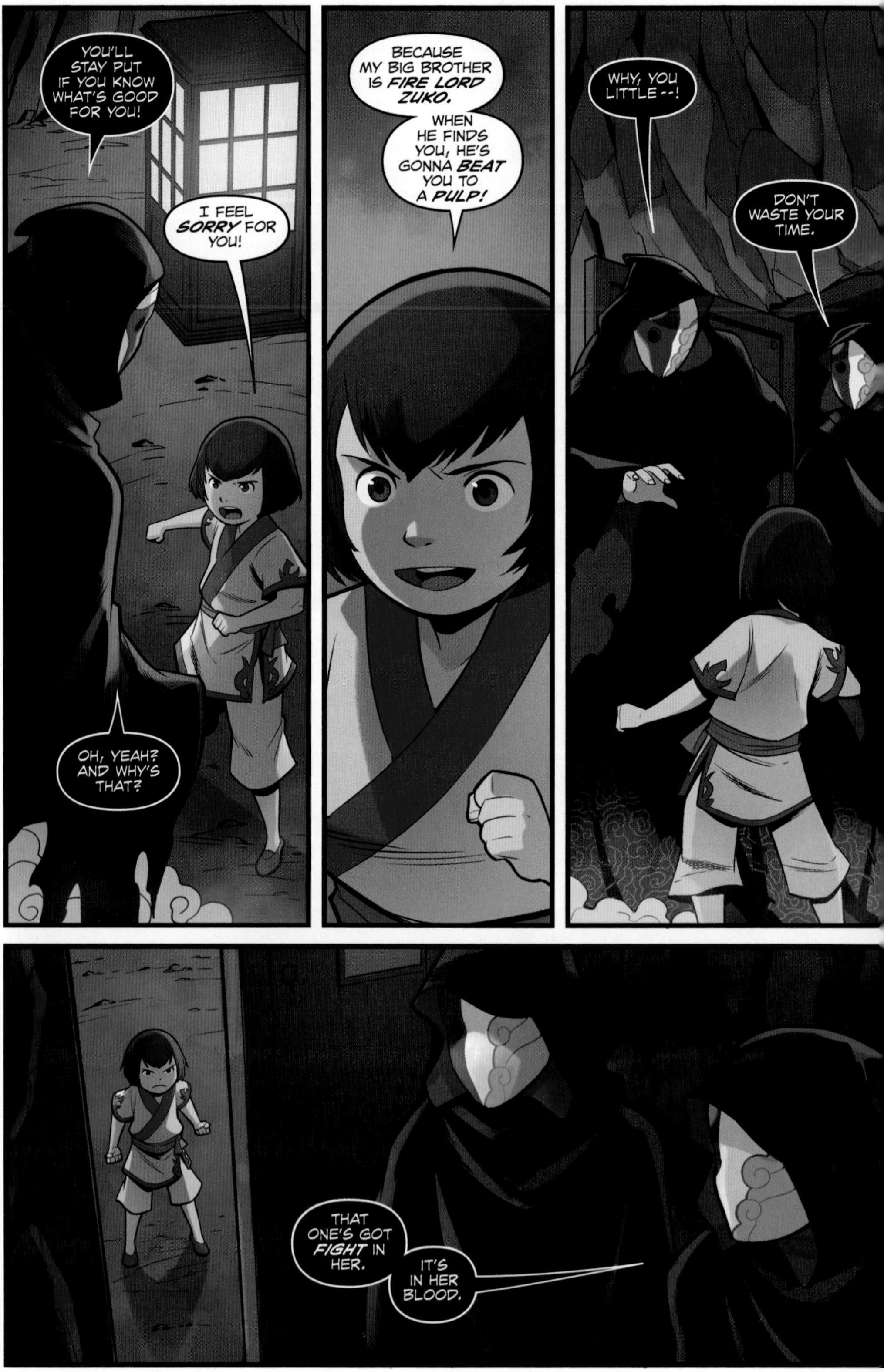
YOU'LL STAY PUT IF YOU KNOW WHAT'S GOOD FOR YOU!
I FEEL SORRY FOR YOU!
OH, YEAH? AND WHY'S THAT?
BECAUSE MY BIG BROTHER IS FIRE LORD ZUKO.
WHEN HE FINDS YOU, HE'S GONNA BEAT YOU TO A PULP!
WHY, YOU LITTLE --!
DON'T WASTE YOUR TIME.
THAT ONE'S GOT FIGHT IN HER.
IT'S IN HER BLOOD.

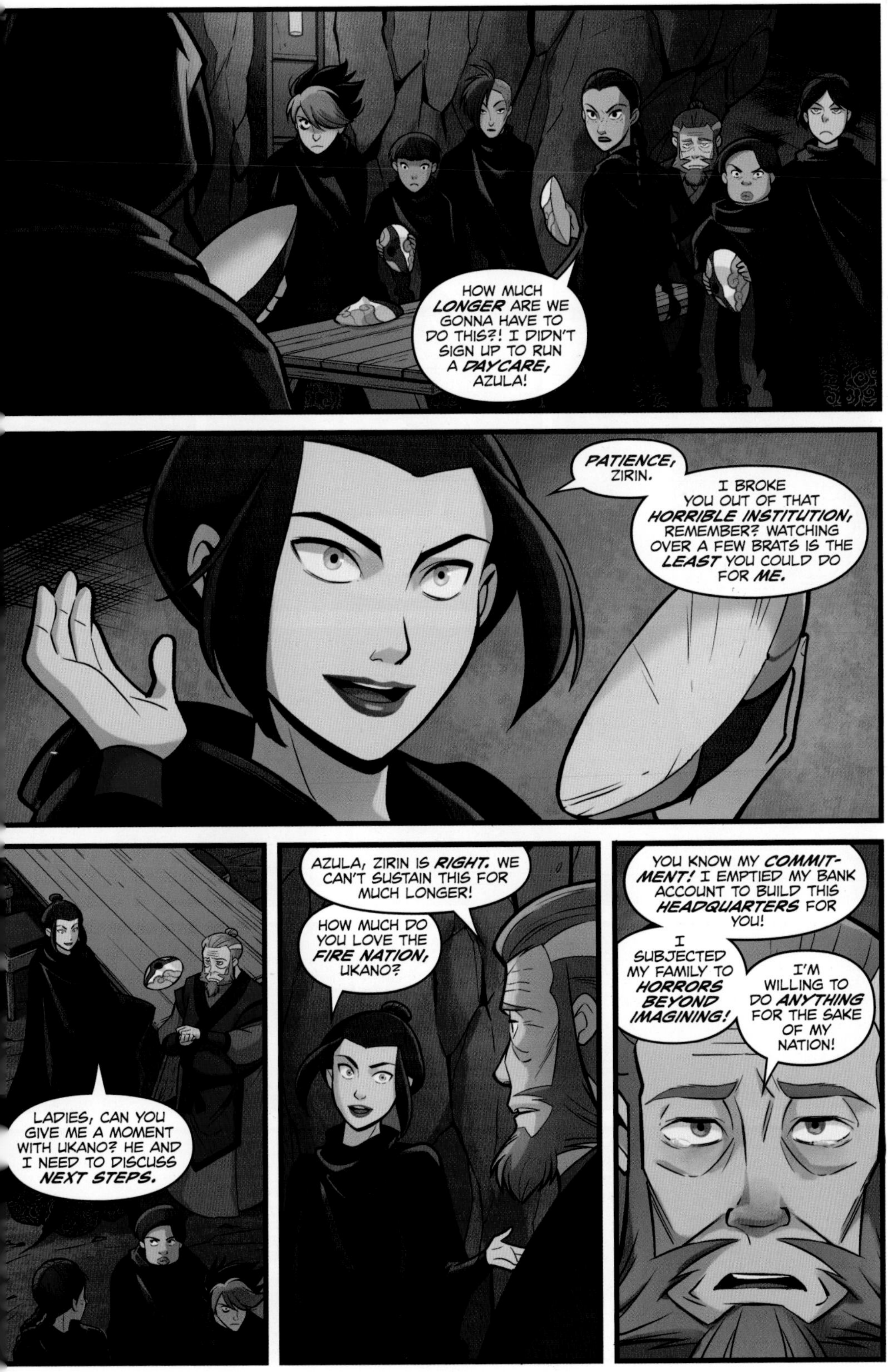
HOW MUCH LONGER ARE WE GONNA HAVE TO DO THIS?! I DIDN'T SIGN UP TO RUN A DAYCARE, AZULA!
PATIENCE, ZIRIN.
I BROKE YOU OUT OF THAT HORRIBLE INSTITUTION, REMEMBER? WATCHING OVER A FEW BRATS IS THE LEAST YOU COULD DO FOR ME.
LADIES, CAN YOU GIVE ME A MOMENT WITH UKANO? HE AND I NEED TO DISCUSS NEXT STEPS.
AZULA, ZIRIN IS RIGHT. WE CAN'T SUSTAIN THIS FOR MUCH LONGER!
HOW MUCH DO YOU LOVE THE FIRE NATION, UKANO?
YOU KNOW MY COMMIT-MENT! I EMPTIED MY BANK ACCOUNT TO BUILD THIS HEADQUARTERS FOR YOU!
I SUBJECTED MY FAMILY TO HORRORS BEYOND IMAGINING!
I'M WILLING TO DO ANYTHING FOR THE SAKE OF MY NATION!

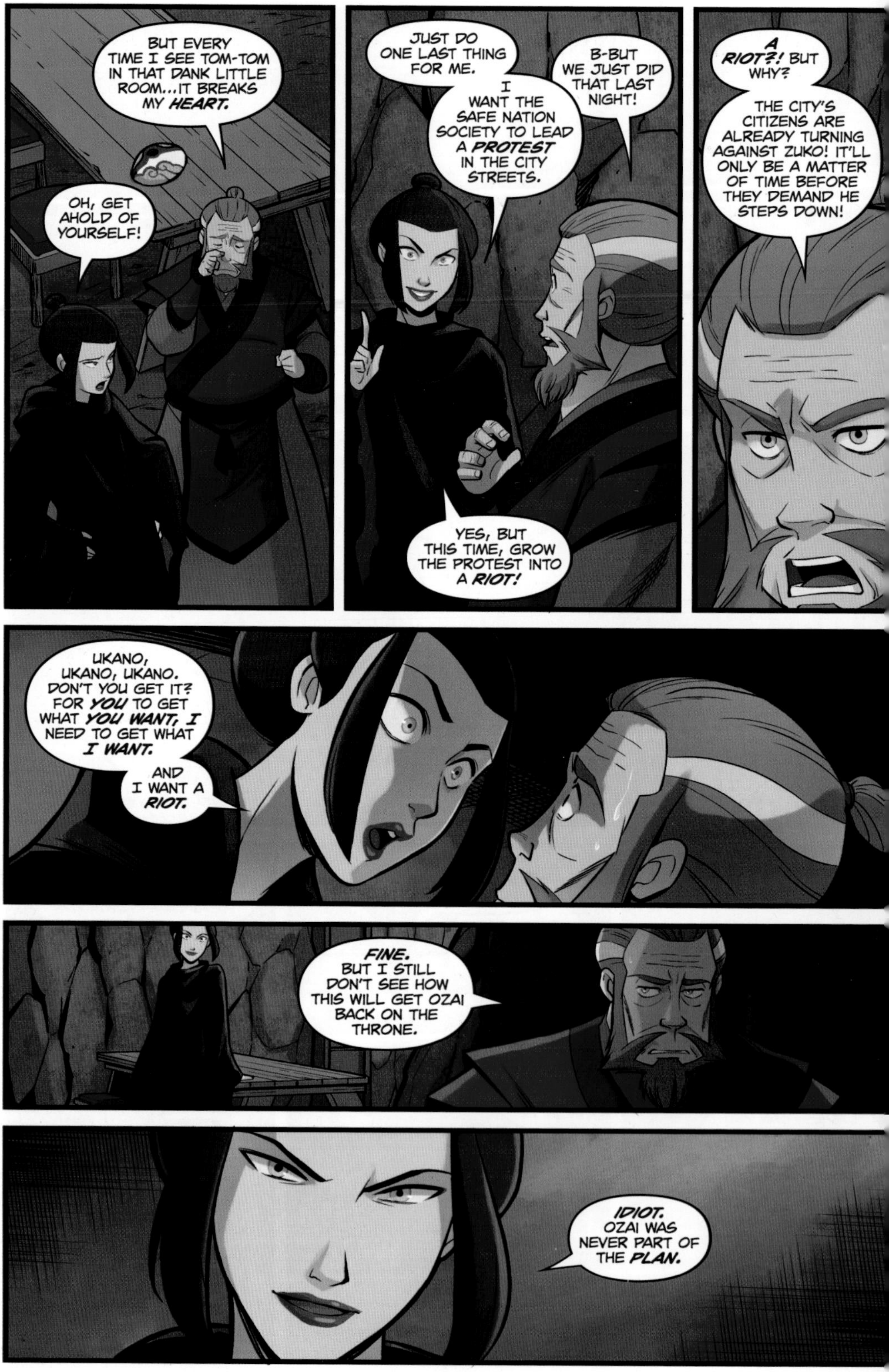
BUT EVERY TIME I SEE TOM-TOM IN THAT DANK LITTLE ROOM...IT BREAKS MY HEART.
OH, GET AHOLD OF YOURSELF!
JUST DO ONE LAST THING FOR ME.
I WANT THE SAFE NATION SOCIETY TO LEAD A PROTEST IN THE CITY STREETS.
B-BUT WE JUST DID THAT LAST NIGHT!
YES, BUT THIS TIME, GROW THE PROTEST INTO A RIOT!
A RIOT?! BUT WHY?
THE CITY'S CITIZENS ARE ALREADY TURNING AGAINST ZUKO! IT'LL ONLY BE A MATTER OF TIME BEFORE THEY DEMAND HE STEPS DOWN!
UKANO, UKANO, UKANO. DON'T YOU GET IT? FOR YOU TO GET WHAT YOU WANT, I NEED TO GET WHAT I WANT.
AND I WANT A RIOT.
FINE. BUT I STILL DON'T SEE HOW THIS WILL GET OZAI BACK ON THE THRONE.
IDIOT. OZAI WAS NEVER PART OF THE PLAN.

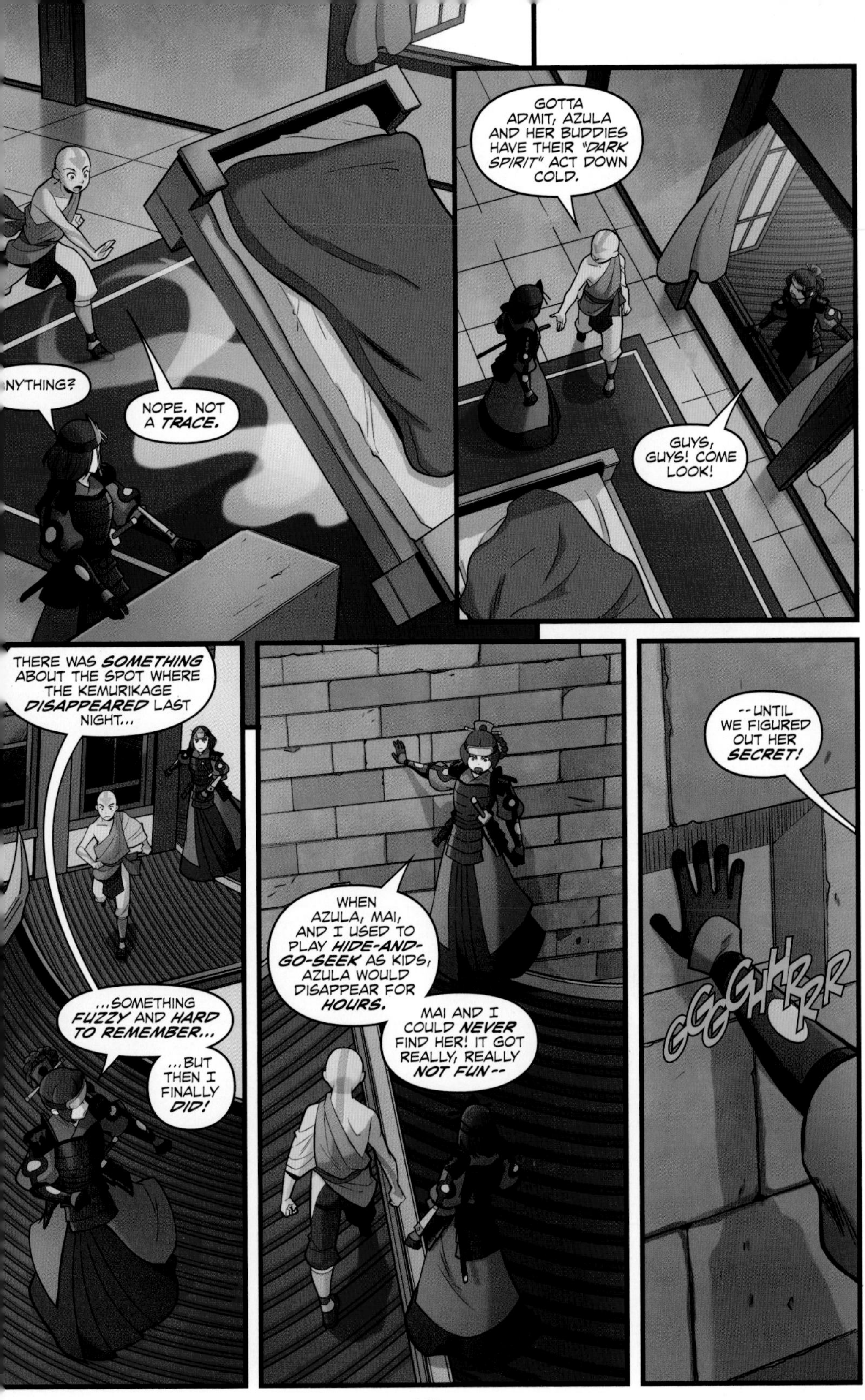
NYTHING?
NOPE. NOT A TRACE.
GOTTA ADMIT, AZULA AND HER BUDDIES HAVE THEIR "DARK SPIRIT" ACT DOWN COLD.
GUYS, GUYS! COME LOOK!
THERE WAS SOMETHING ABOUT THE SPOT WHERE THE KEMURIKAGE DISAPPEARED LAST NIGHT...
...SOMETHING FUZZY AND HARD TO REMEMBER...
...BUT THEN I FINALLY DID!
WHEN AZULA, MAI, AND I USED TO PLAY HIDE-AND-GO-SEEK AS KIDS, AZULA WOULD DISAPPEAR FOR HOURS.
MAI AND I COULD NEVER FIND HER! IT GOT REALLY, REALLY NOT FUN--
--UNTIL WE FIGURED OUT HER SECRET!
GGGGHHRRR

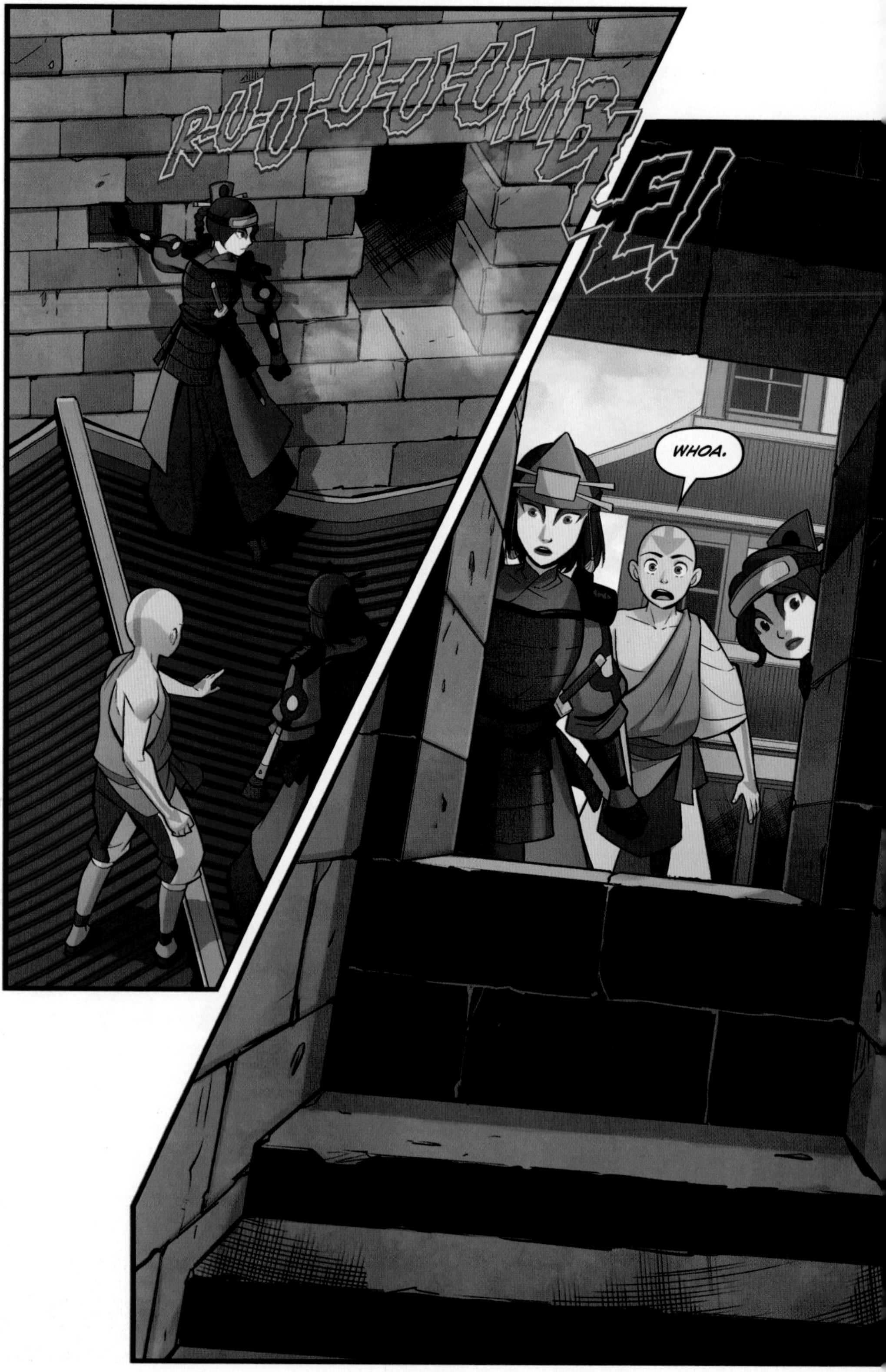
RU-U-U-U-UMBLE!
WHOA.

163

A STRONG NATION IS A SAFE NATION!

A STRONG NATION IS A SAFE NATION!

STOP! SAFE NATION SOCIETY, BY ORDER OF THE FIRE LORD, YOU ARE ALL *UNDER ARREST!*

BOO! BOO!

WHY DON'T YOU GO ATTACK THE *DARK SPIRITS* INSTEAD OF *YOUR OWN PEOPLE?!*

LEAVE THE HEROES ALONE!

THIS IS GOING TO BE EASIER THAN I THOUGHT.

CAN YOU BELIEVE THIS, SAFE NATION SOCIETY?!

WILL WE STAND FOR THIS *INJUSTICE?!*

WE ARE FIGHTING TO *PROTECT OUR CHILDREN,* AND INSTEAD OF THANKING US, FIRE LORD ZUKO TREATS US LIKE *COMMON CRIMINALS!*

NO!

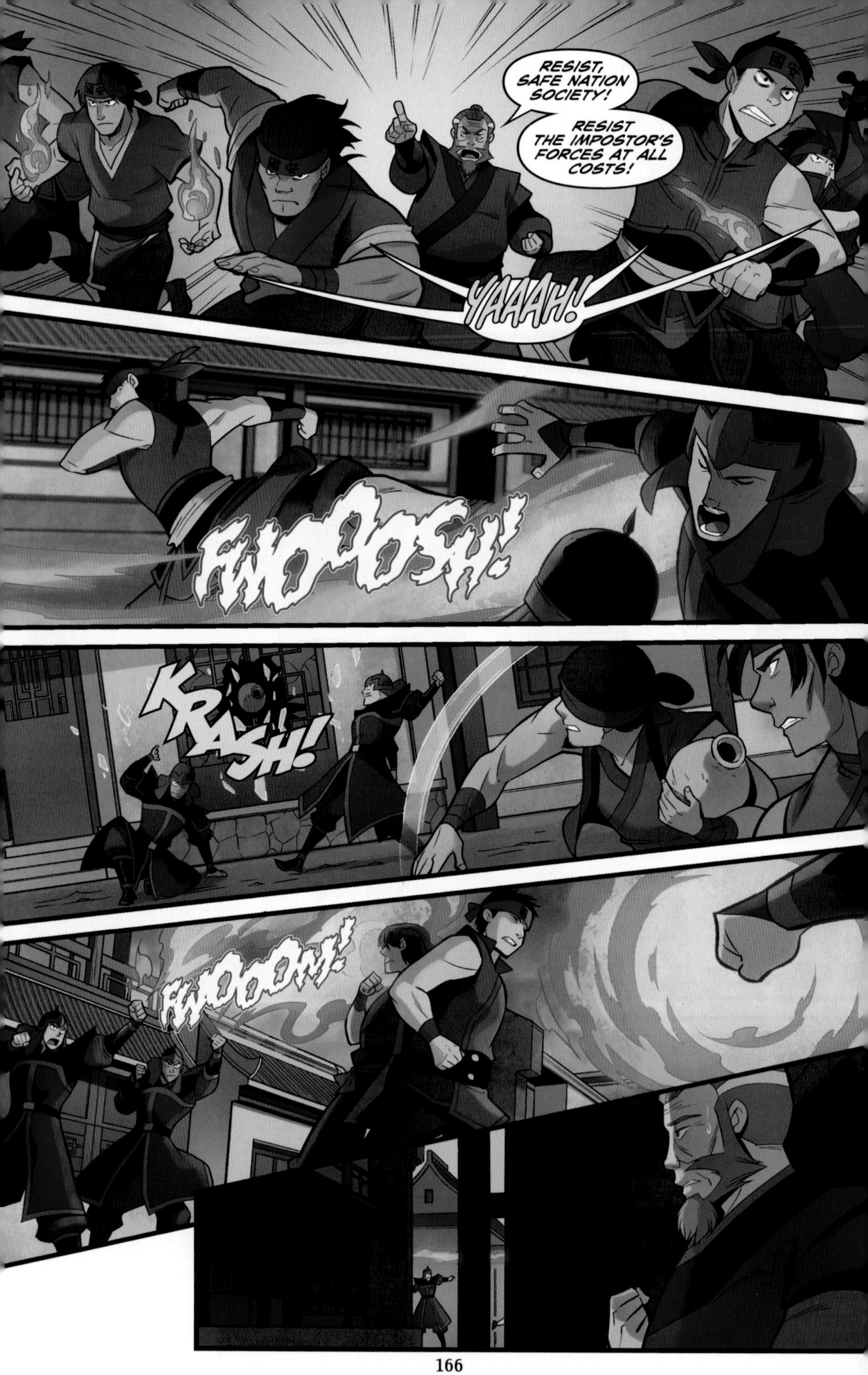
RESIST, SAFE NATION SOCIETY!
RESIST THE IMPOSTOR'S FORCES AT ALL COSTS!
YAAAH!
FWOOOSH!
KRASH!
FWOOOM!

I'M SORRY, KEI LO. MAI DIDN'T SAY WHERE SHE WAS GOING.

I HAVE AN IDEA. THANKS, MURA.

KRASH!

!

AllIEEE!

WHAT'S GOING ON OUT HERE?!

WATCH IT!

BUMP!

HING?

KEI LO, RUN! THEY'RE ARRESTING ANYONE CONNECTED TO UKANO!

BUT I'M NOT ANYMORE!

TRY TELLING THEM THAT!

YOU TWO! HANDS WHERE WE CAN SEE 'EM!

167

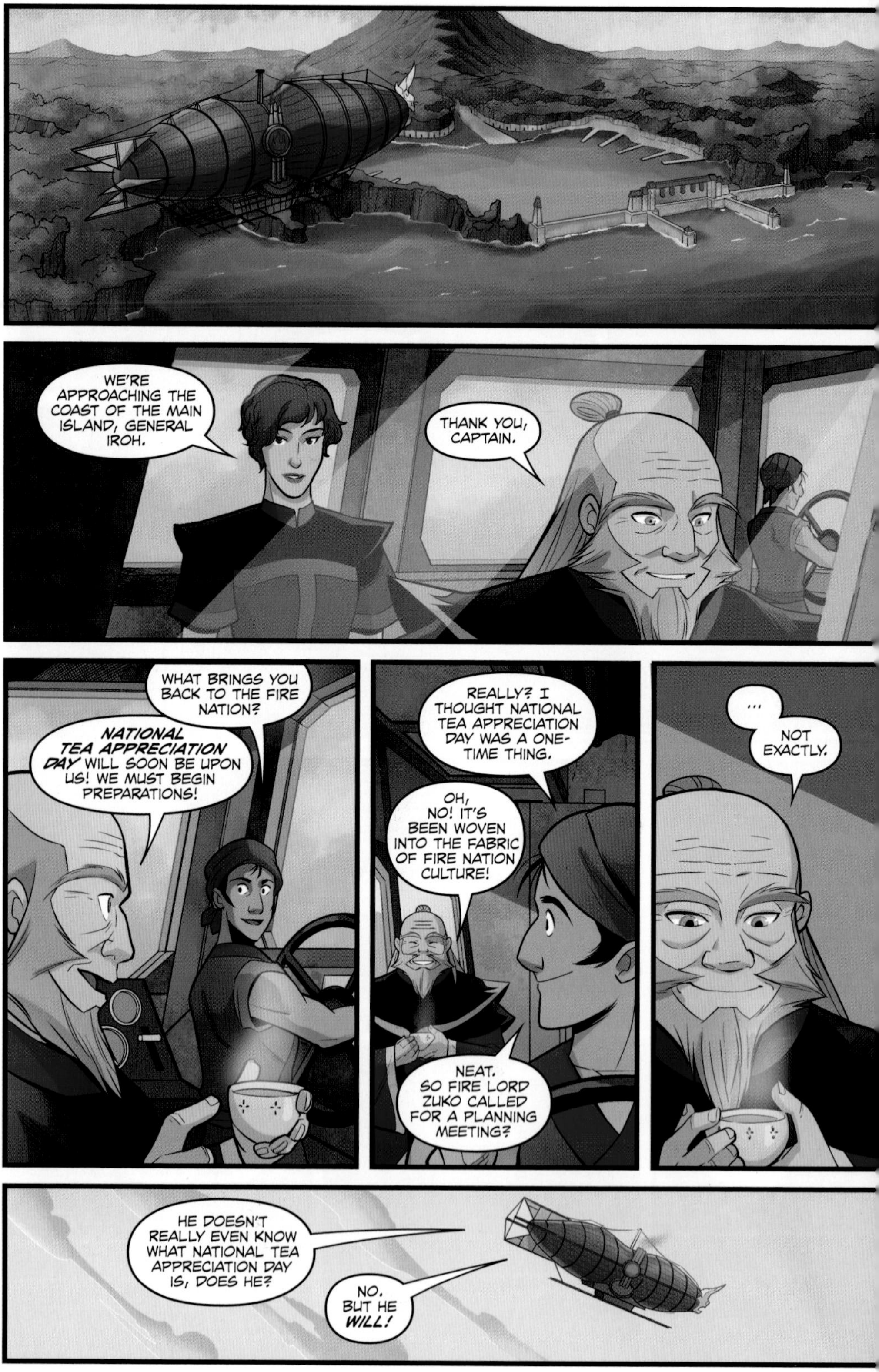
WE'RE APPROACHING THE COAST OF THE MAIN ISLAND, GENERAL IROH.
THANK YOU, CAPTAIN.
WHAT BRINGS YOU BACK TO THE FIRE NATION?
NATIONAL TEA APPRECIATION DAY WILL SOON BE UPON US! WE MUST BEGIN PREPARATIONS!
REALLY? I THOUGHT NATIONAL TEA APPRECIATION DAY WAS A ONE-TIME THING.
OH, NO! IT'S BEEN WOVEN INTO THE FABRIC OF FIRE NATION CULTURE!
NEAT. SO FIRE LORD ZUKO CALLED FOR A PLANNING MEETING?
...
NOT EXACTLY.
HE DOESN'T REALLY EVEN KNOW WHAT NATIONAL TEA APPRECIATION DAY IS, DOES HE?
NO. BUT HE WILL!

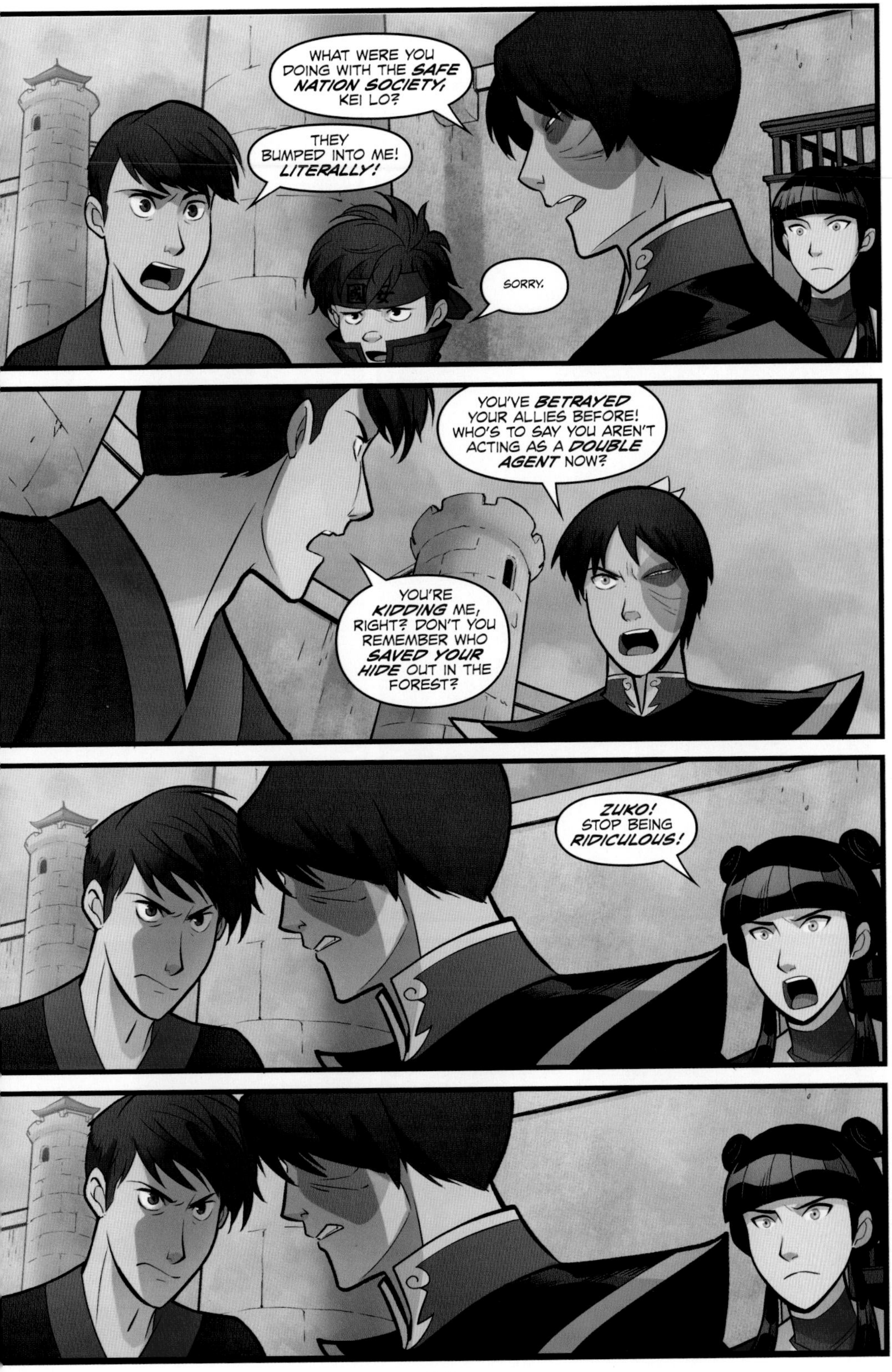

WHAT WERE YOU DOING WITH THE SAFE NATION SOCIETY, KEI LO?
THEY BUMPED INTO ME! LITERALLY!
SORRY.
YOU'VE BETRAYED YOUR ALLIES BEFORE! WHO'S TO SAY YOU AREN'T ACTING AS A DOUBLE AGENT NOW?
YOU'RE KIDDING ME, RIGHT? DON'T YOU REMEMBER WHO SAVED YOUR HIDE OUT IN THE FOREST?
ZUKO! STOP BEING RIDICULOUS!

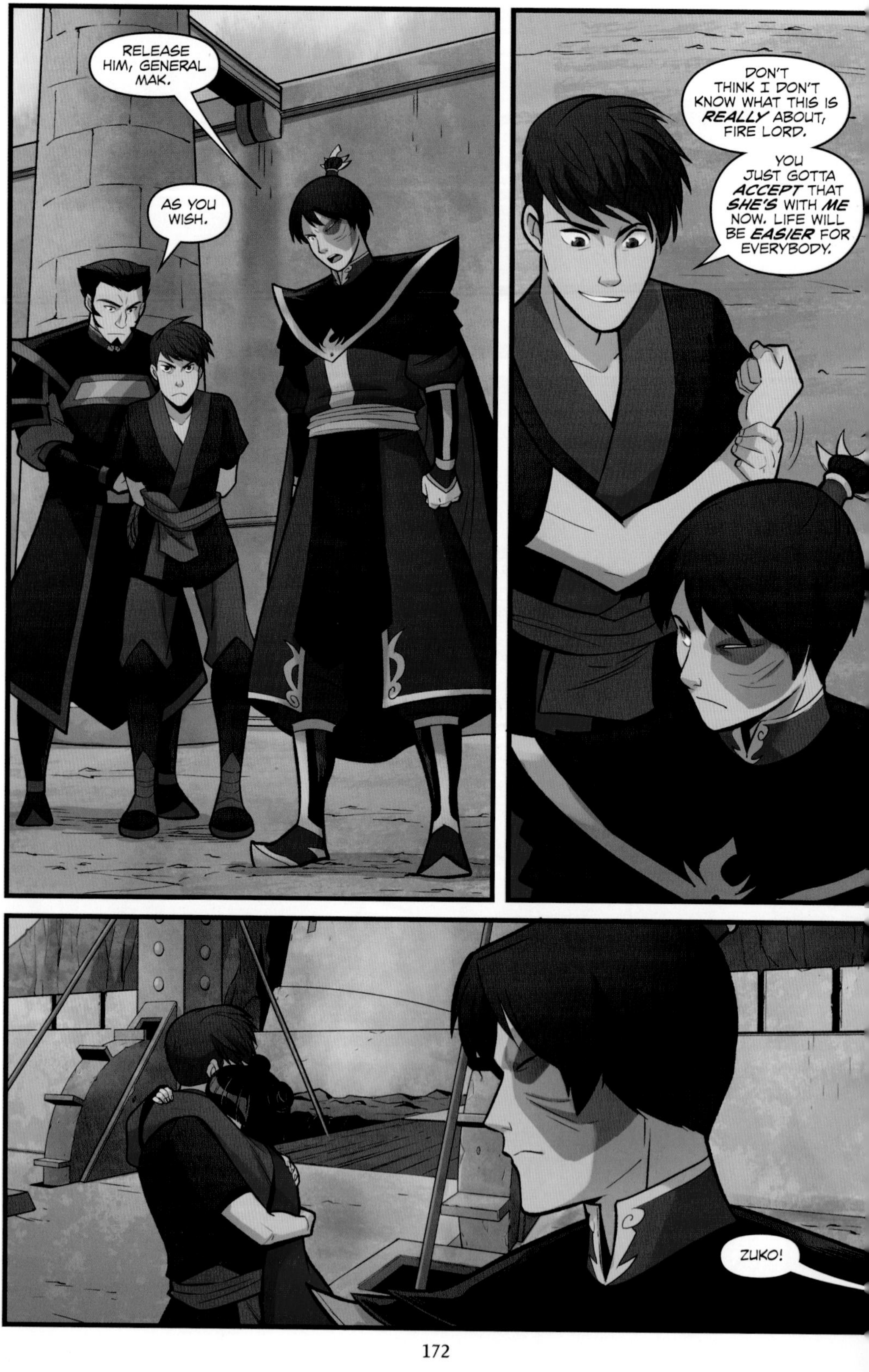
RELEASE HIM, GENERAL MAK.
AS YOU WISH.
DON'T THINK I DON'T KNOW WHAT THIS IS REALLY ABOUT, FIRE LORD.
YOU JUST GOTTA ACCEPT THAT SHE'S WITH ME NOW. LIFE WILL BE EASIER FOR EVERYBODY.
ZUKO!

FIRE LORD, THE SUN WILL **SET** BEFORE WE KNOW IT. WE NEED A **PLAN** OR OUR PEOPLE WILL **RISE UP** AGAIN.

WE'VE BEEN LOOKING ALL OVER FOR YOU!

AANG? I THOUGHT YOU LEFT.

WELL, YOU THOUGHT **WRONG,** BUDDY!

SUKI, TY LEE, AND I FOUND SOMETHING YOU GOTTA SEE! **COME ON!**

I'M SORRY, AANG, BUT GENERAL MAK IS RIGHT. LIKE I TOLD YOU, I NEED TO HANDLE THIS **MY WAY.**

EVEN IF YOUR WAY IS **STUPID?!**

STAND BACK.

WHAT ARE YOU DOING?

GETTING THE FIRE LORD'S **ATTENTION.**

WOOOOO!

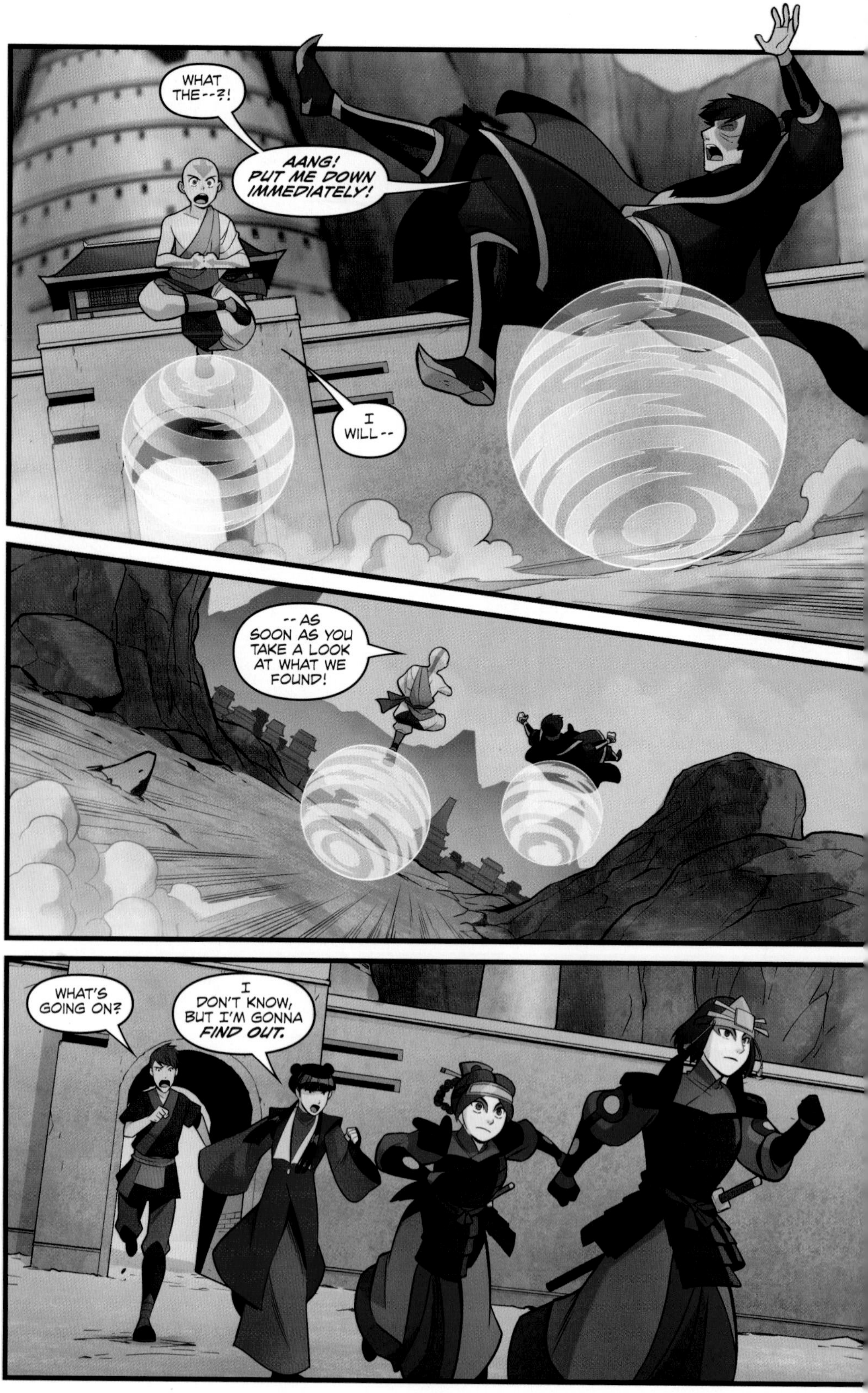
WHAT THE--?!
AANG! PUT ME DOWN IMMEDIATELY!
I WILL--
--AS SOON AS YOU TAKE A LOOK AT WHAT WE FOUND!
WHAT'S GOING ON?
I DON'T KNOW, BUT I'M GONNA FIND OUT.

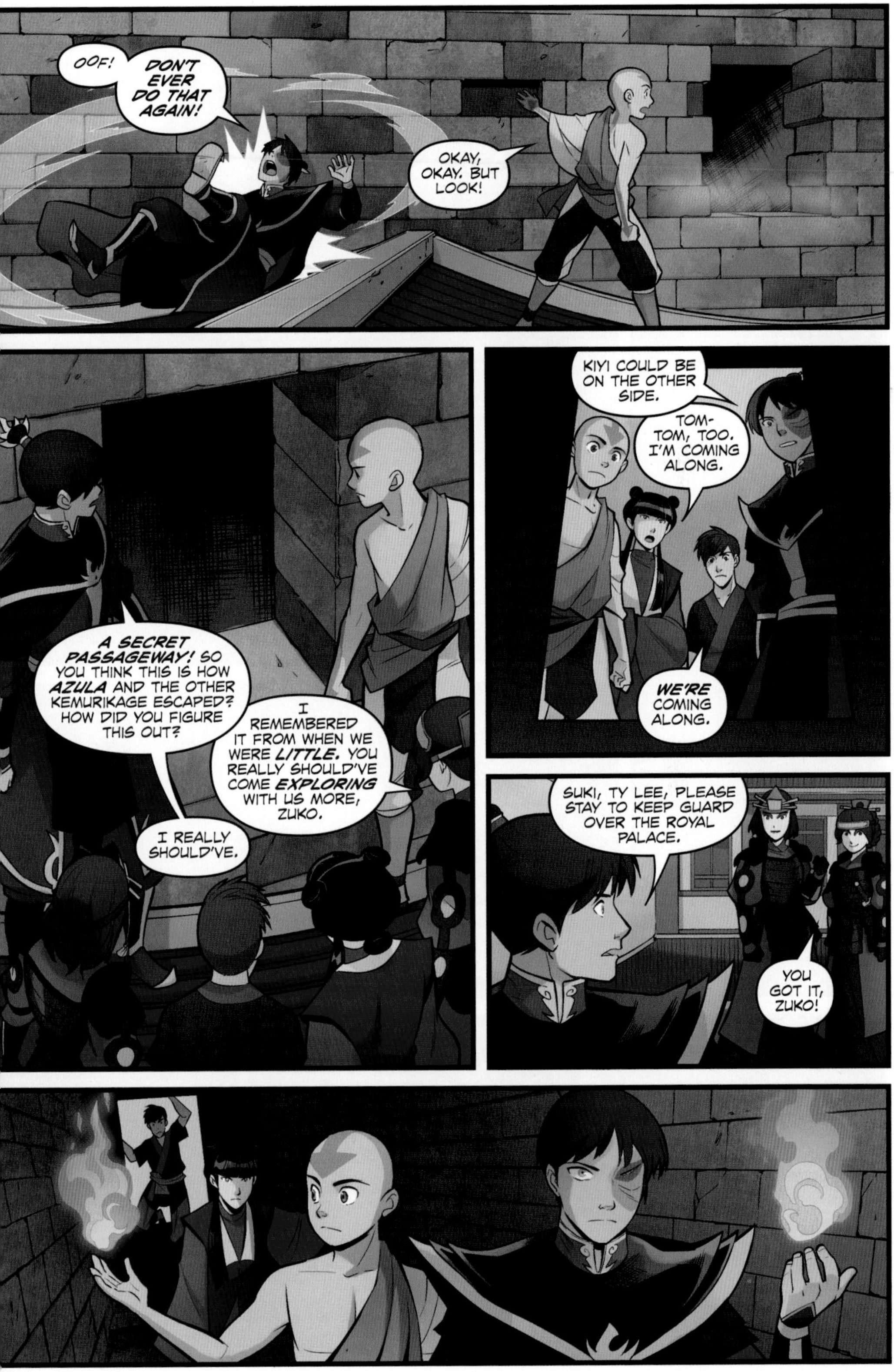
OOF!
DON'T EVER DO THAT AGAIN!
OKAY, OKAY. BUT LOOK!
A SECRET PASSAGEWAY! SO YOU THINK THIS IS HOW AZULA AND THE OTHER KEMURIKAGE ESCAPED? HOW DID YOU FIGURE THIS OUT?
I REMEMBERED IT FROM WHEN WE WERE LITTLE. YOU REALLY SHOULD'VE COME EXPLORING WITH US MORE, ZUKO.
I REALLY SHOULD'VE.
KIYI COULD BE ON THE OTHER SIDE.
TOM-TOM, TOO. I'M COMING ALONG.
WE'RE COMING ALONG.
SUKI, TY LEE, PLEASE STAY TO KEEP GUARD OVER THE ROYAL PALACE.
YOU GOT IT, ZUKO!

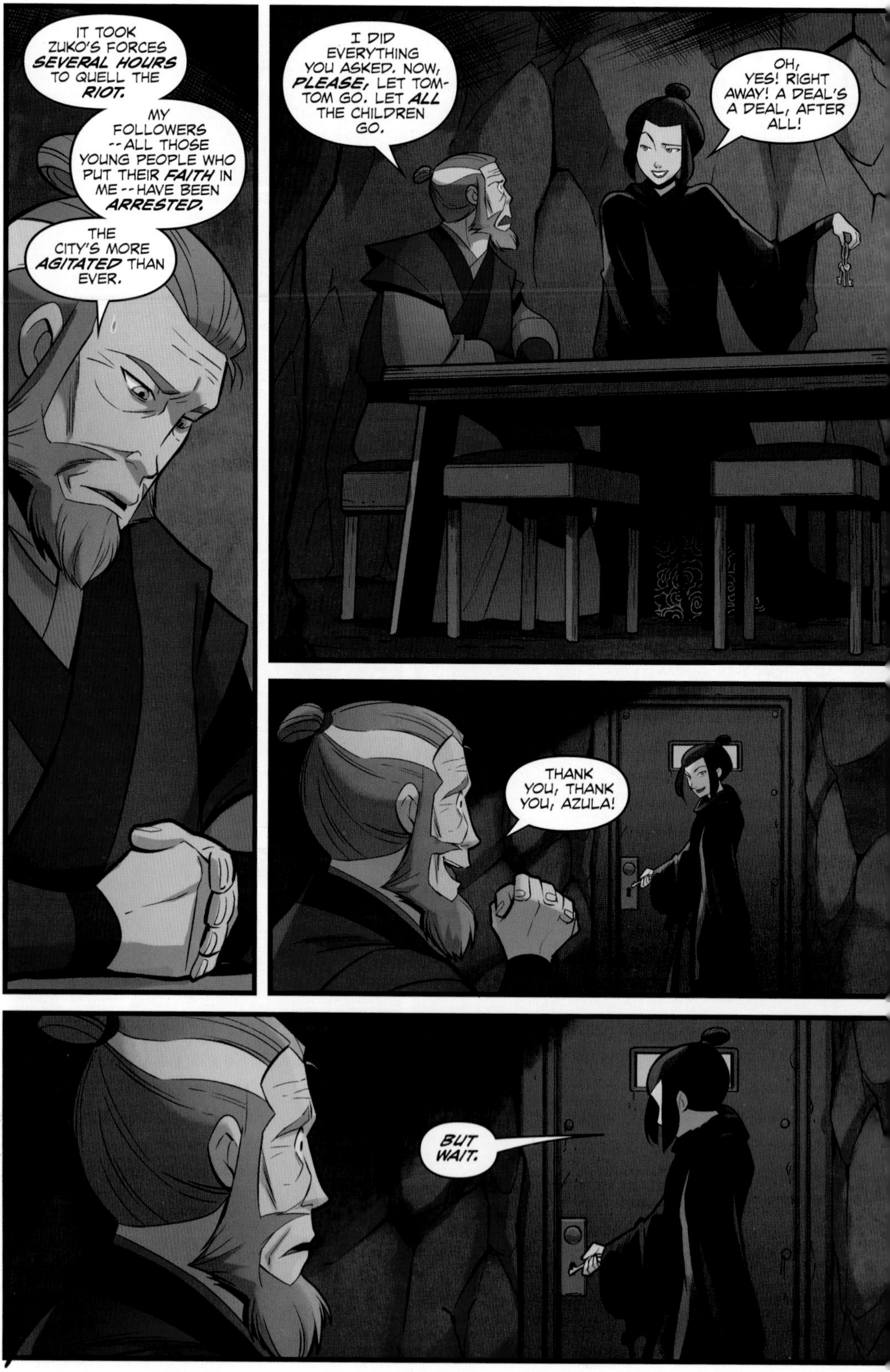
IT TOOK ZUKO'S FORCES SEVERAL HOURS TO QUELL THE RIOT.
MY FOLLOWERS --ALL THOSE YOUNG PEOPLE WHO PUT THEIR FAITH IN ME --HAVE BEEN ARRESTED.
THE CITY'S MORE AGITATED THAN EVER.
I DID EVERYTHING YOU ASKED. NOW, PLEASE, LET TOM-TOM GO. LET ALL THE CHILDREN GO.
OH, YES! RIGHT AWAY! A DEAL'S A DEAL, AFTER ALL!
THANK YOU, THANK YOU, AZULA!
BUT WAIT.

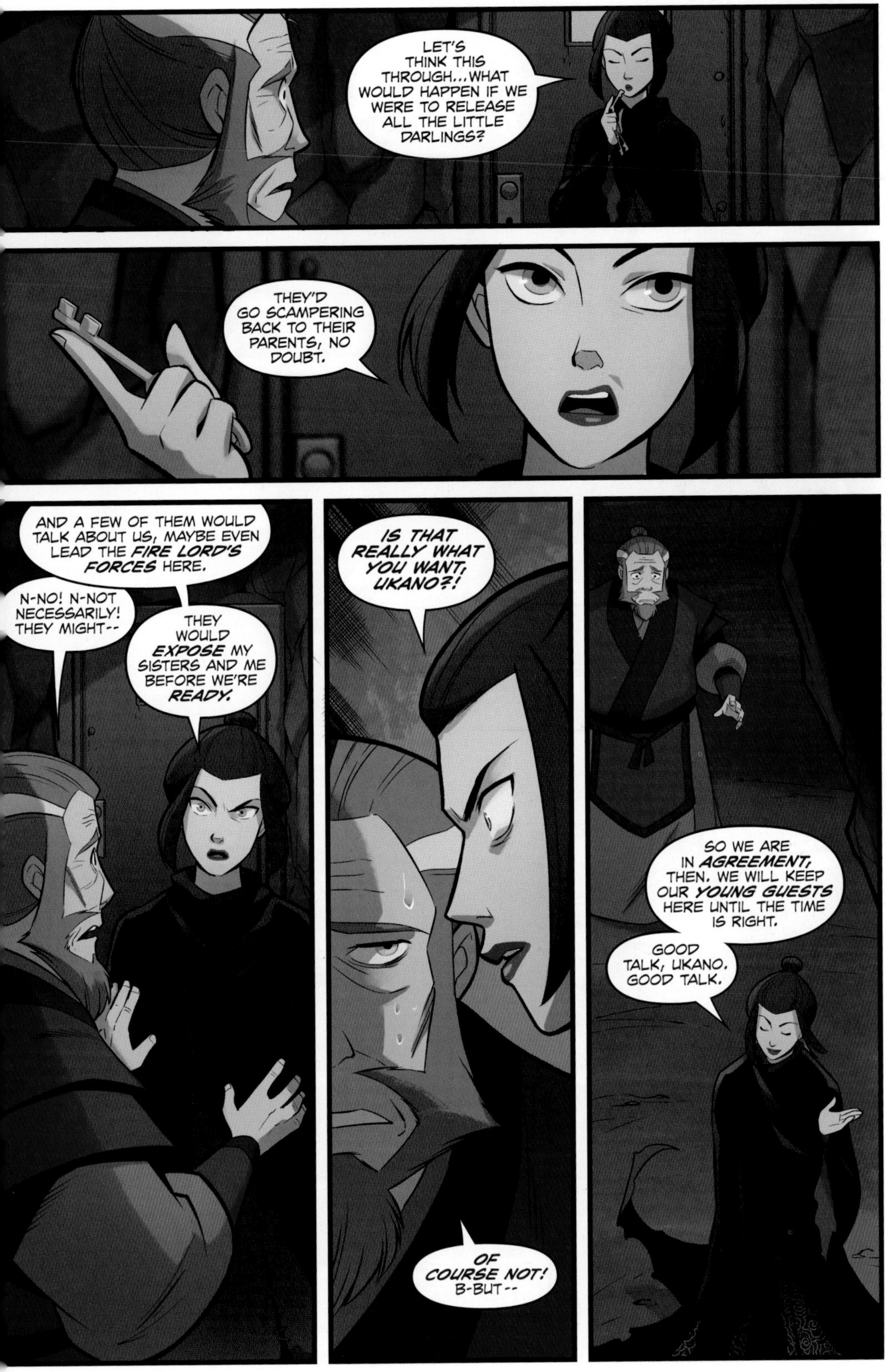
LET'S THINK THIS THROUGH...WHAT WOULD HAPPEN IF WE WERE TO RELEASE ALL THE LITTLE DARLINGS?
THEY'D GO SCAMPERING BACK TO THEIR PARENTS, NO DOUBT.
AND A FEW OF THEM WOULD TALK ABOUT US, MAYBE EVEN LEAD THE *FIRE LORD'S FORCES* HERE.
N-NO! N-NOT NECESSARILY! THEY MIGHT--
THEY WOULD *EXPOSE* MY SISTERS AND ME BEFORE WE'RE *READY.*
IS THAT REALLY WHAT YOU WANT, UKANO?!
OF COURSE NOT! B-BUT--
SO WE ARE IN *AGREEMENT,* THEN. WE WILL KEEP OUR *YOUNG GUESTS* HERE UNTIL THE TIME IS RIGHT.
GOOD TALK, UKANO. GOOD TALK.

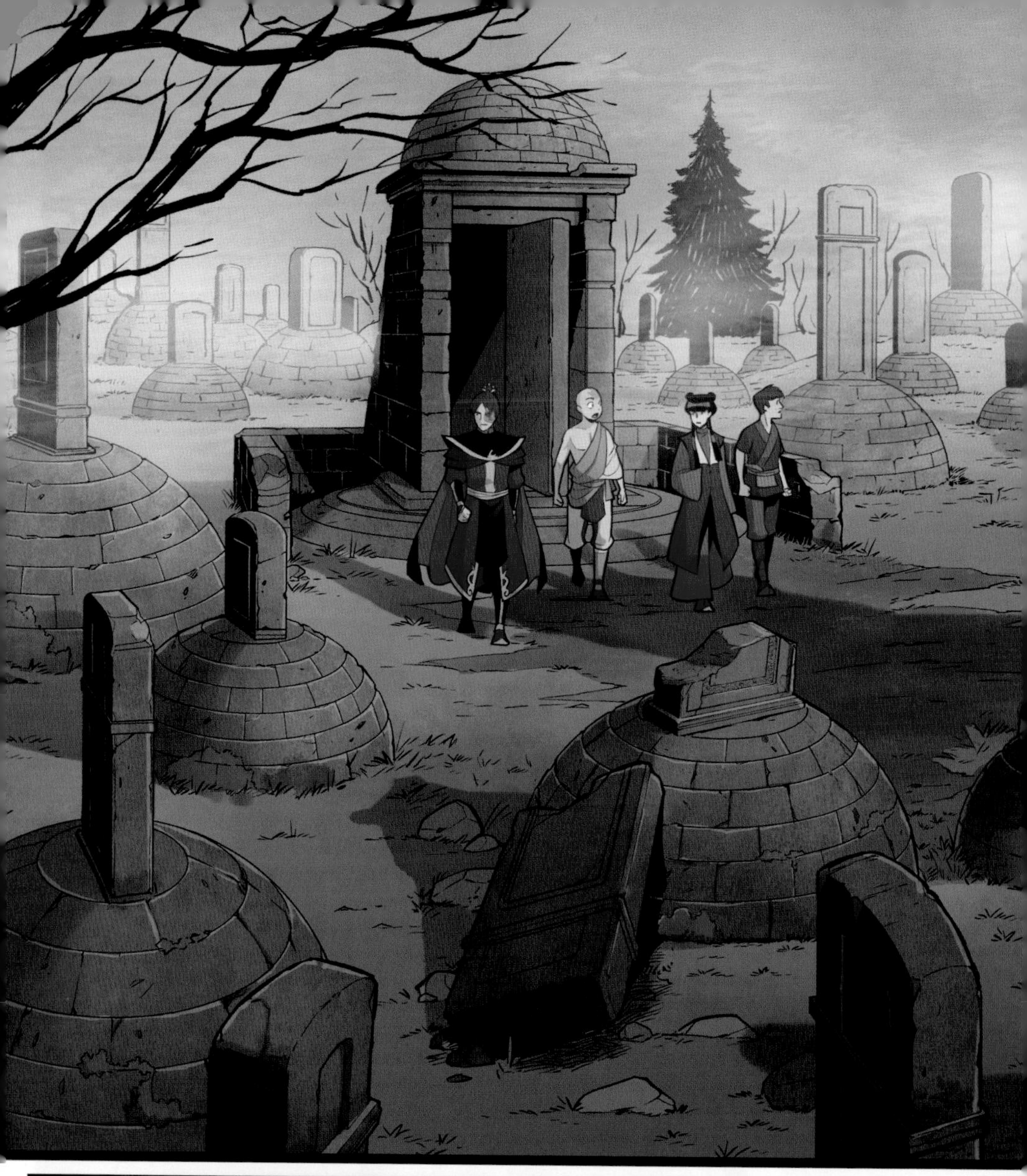

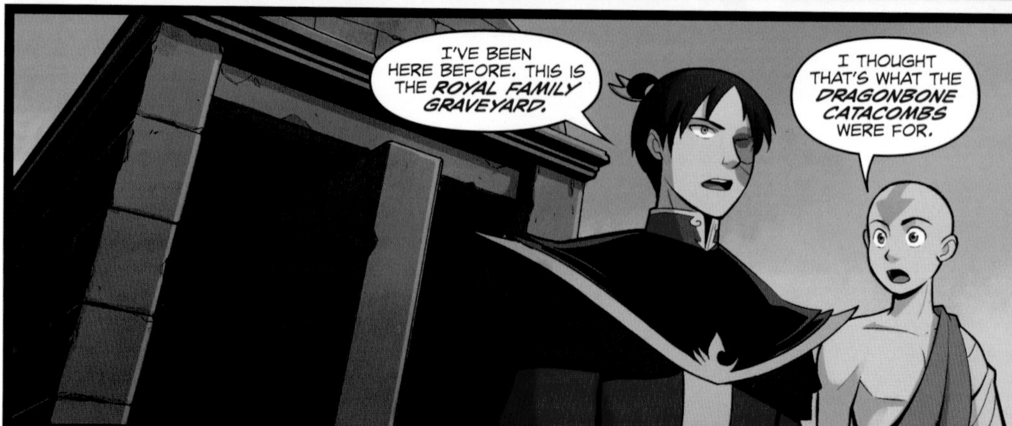
I'VE BEEN HERE BEFORE. THIS IS THE ROYAL FAMILY GRAVEYARD.
I THOUGHT THAT'S WHAT THE DRAGONBONE CATACOMBS WERE FOR.

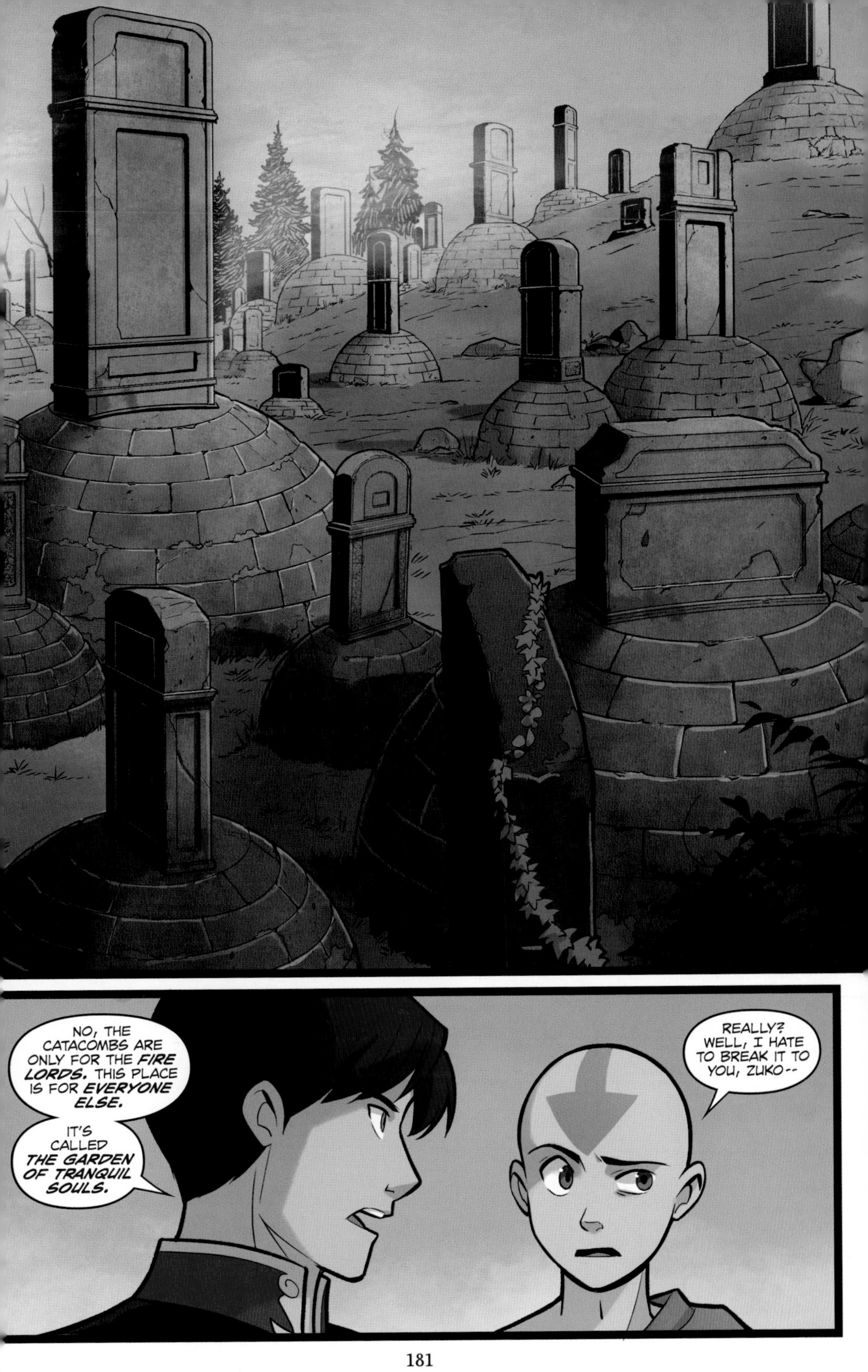
NO, THE CATACOMBS ARE ONLY FOR THE FIRE LORDS. THIS PLACE IS FOR EVERYONE ELSE.
IT'S CALLED THE GARDEN OF TRANQUIL SOULS.
REALLY? WELL, I HATE TO BREAK IT TO YOU, ZUKO--

HELLO? *HELLO!*
WHERE IS EVERYONE?
!

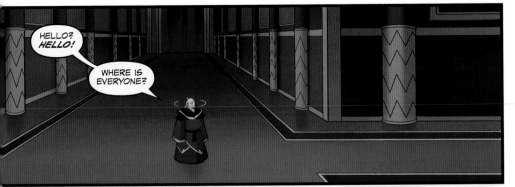

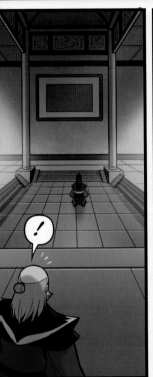

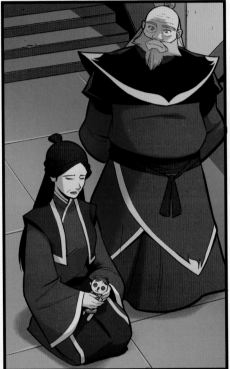

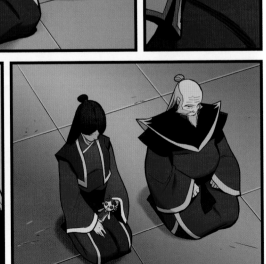

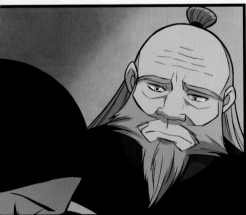

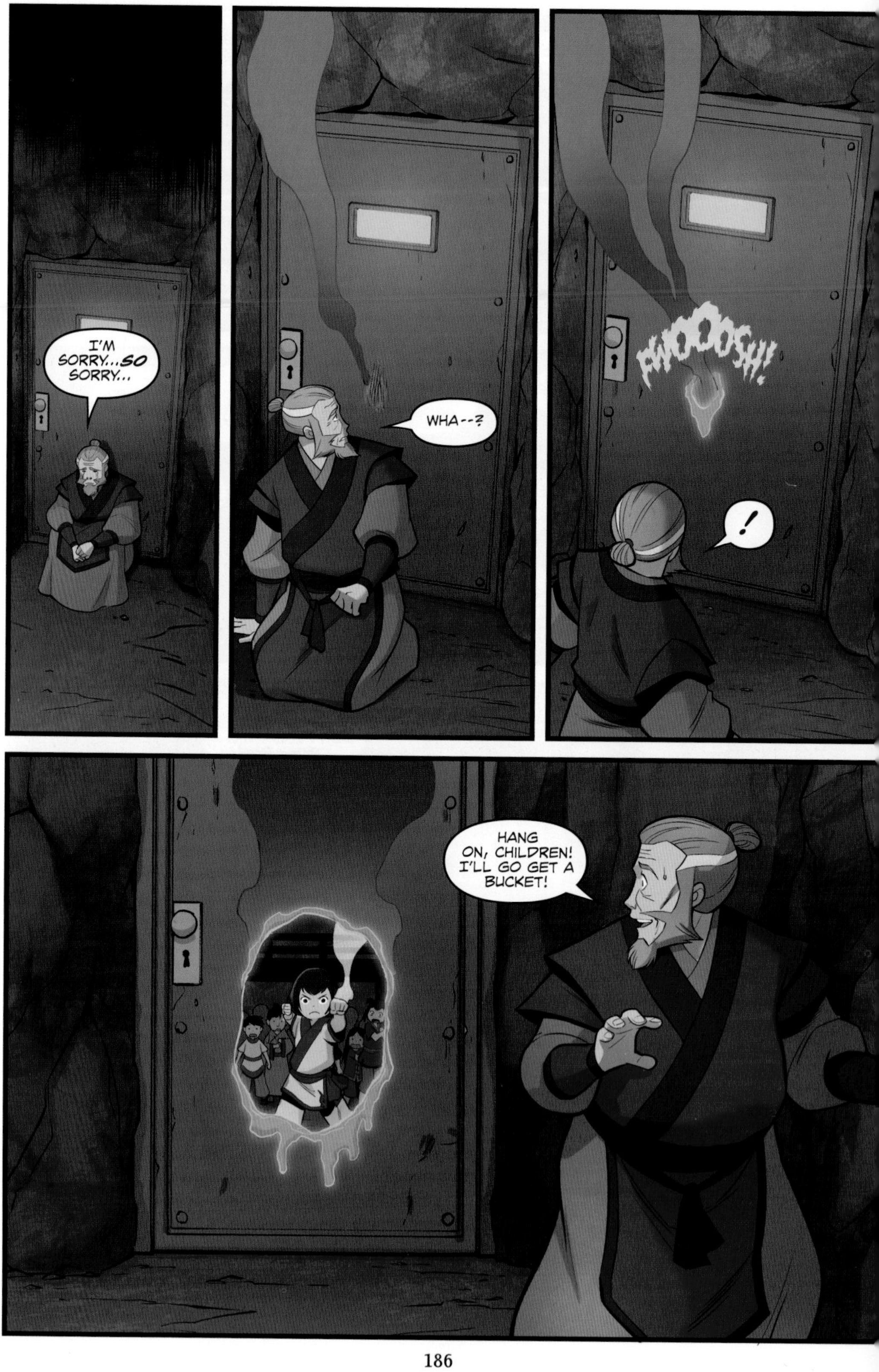
I'M SORRY...SO SORRY...
WHA--?
FWOOOSH!
!
HANG ON, CHILDREN! I'LL GO GET A BUCKET!

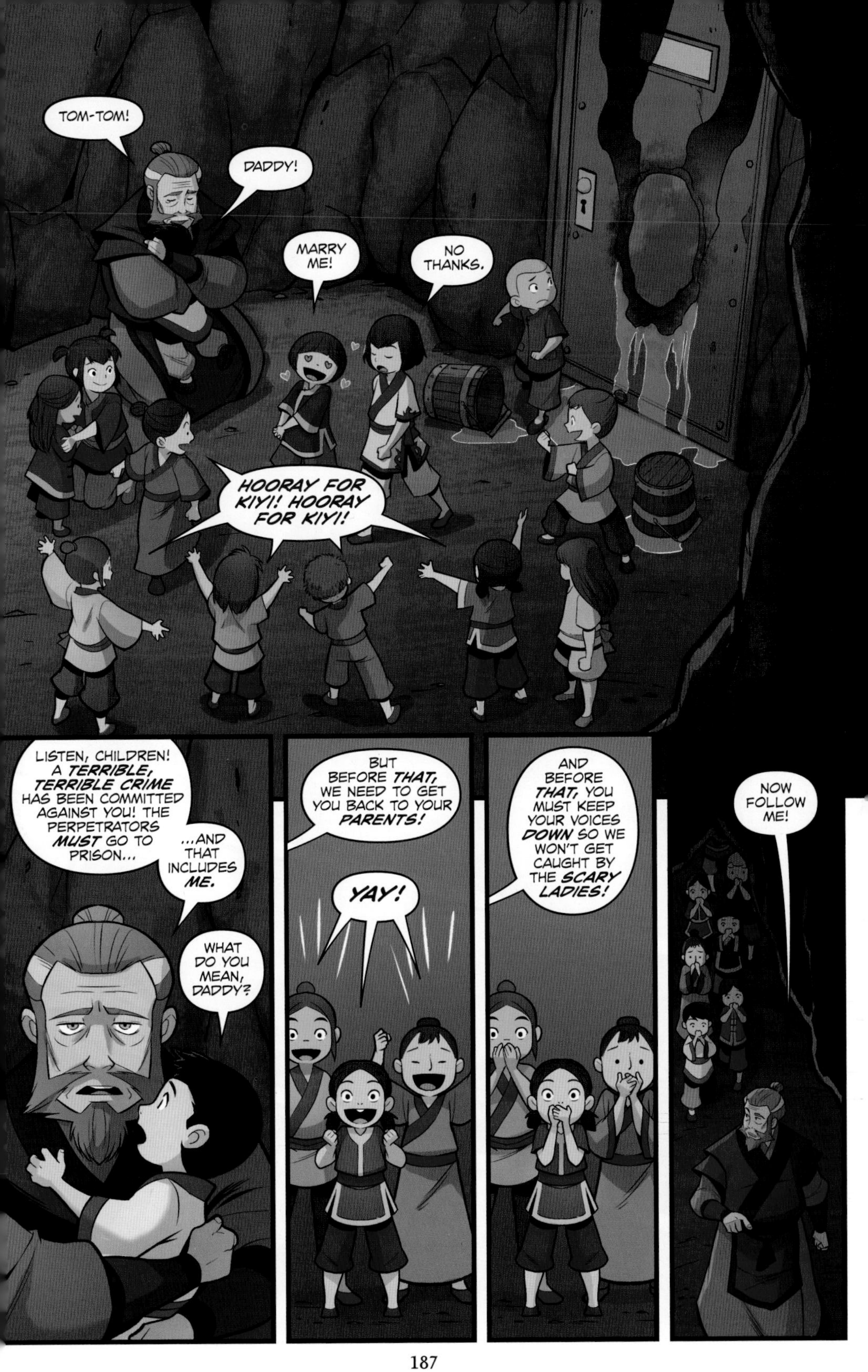
TOM-TOM!
DADDY!
MARRY ME!
NO THANKS.
HOORAY FOR KIYI! HOORAY FOR KIYI!
LISTEN, CHILDREN! A TERRIBLE, TERRIBLE CRIME HAS BEEN COMMITTED AGAINST YOU! THE PERPETRATORS MUST GO TO PRISON...
...AND THAT INCLUDES ME.
WHAT DO YOU MEAN, DADDY?
BUT BEFORE THAT, WE NEED TO GET YOU BACK TO YOUR PARENTS!
YAY!
AND BEFORE THAT, YOU MUST KEEP YOUR VOICES DOWN SO WE WON'T GET CAUGHT BY THE SCARY LADIES!
NOW FOLLOW ME!

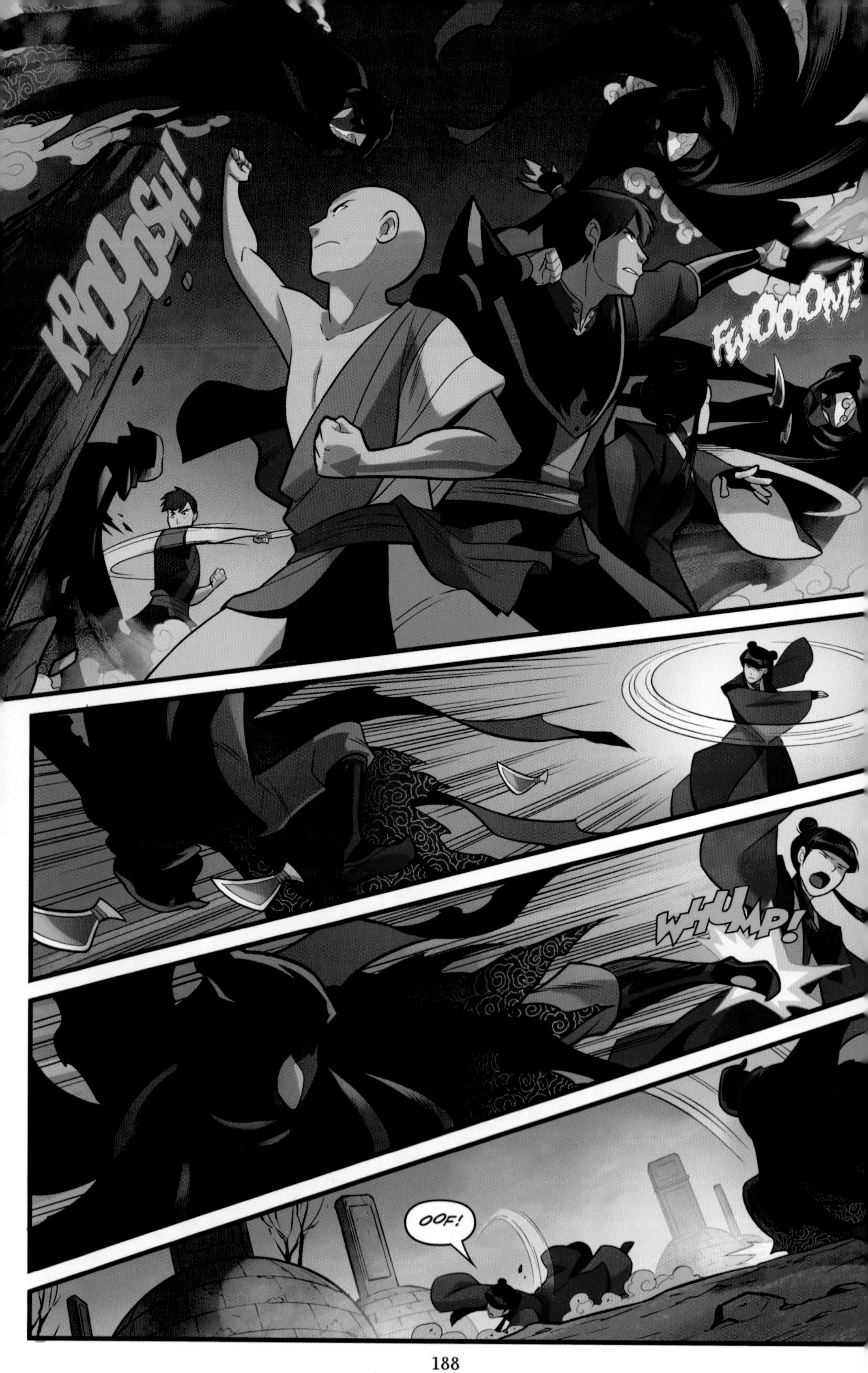
KROOOSH!
FWOOOM!
WHUMP!
OOF!

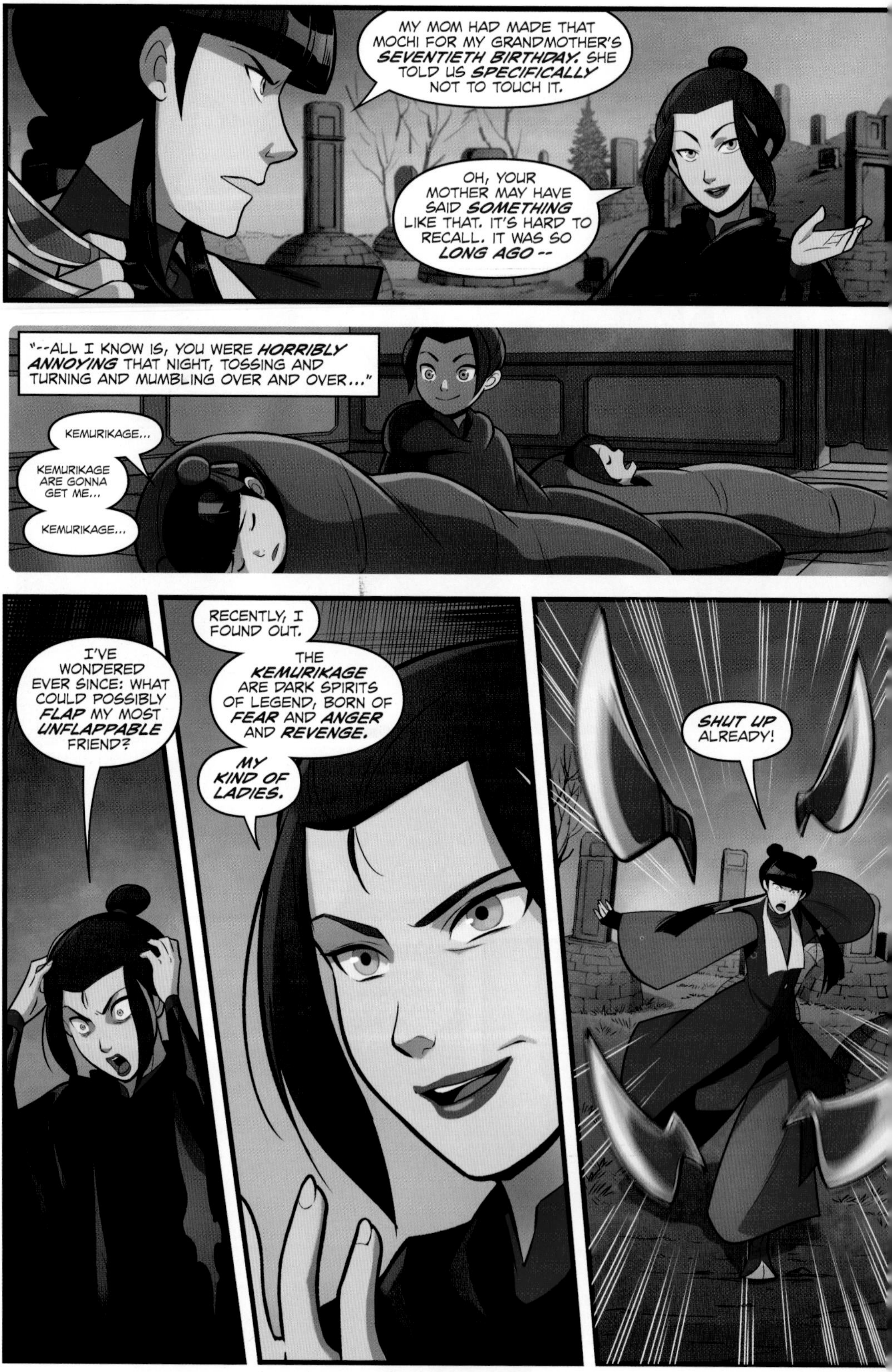
MY MOM HAD MADE THAT MOCHI FOR MY GRANDMOTHER'S SEVENTIETH BIRTHDAY. SHE TOLD US SPECIFICALLY NOT TO TOUCH IT.
OH, YOUR MOTHER MAY HAVE SAID SOMETHING LIKE THAT. IT'S HARD TO RECALL. IT WAS SO LONG AGO --
"--ALL I KNOW IS, YOU WERE HORRIBLY ANNOYING THAT NIGHT, TOSSING AND TURNING AND MUMBLING OVER AND OVER..."
KEMURIKAGE...
KEMURIKAGE ARE GONNA GET ME...
KEMURIKAGE...
I'VE WONDERED EVER SINCE: WHAT COULD POSSIBLY FLAP MY MOST UNFLAPPABLE FRIEND?
RECENTLY, I FOUND OUT.
THE KEMURIKAGE ARE DARK SPIRITS OF LEGEND, BORN OF FEAR AND ANGER AND REVENGE.
MY KIND OF LADIES.
SHUT UP ALREADY!

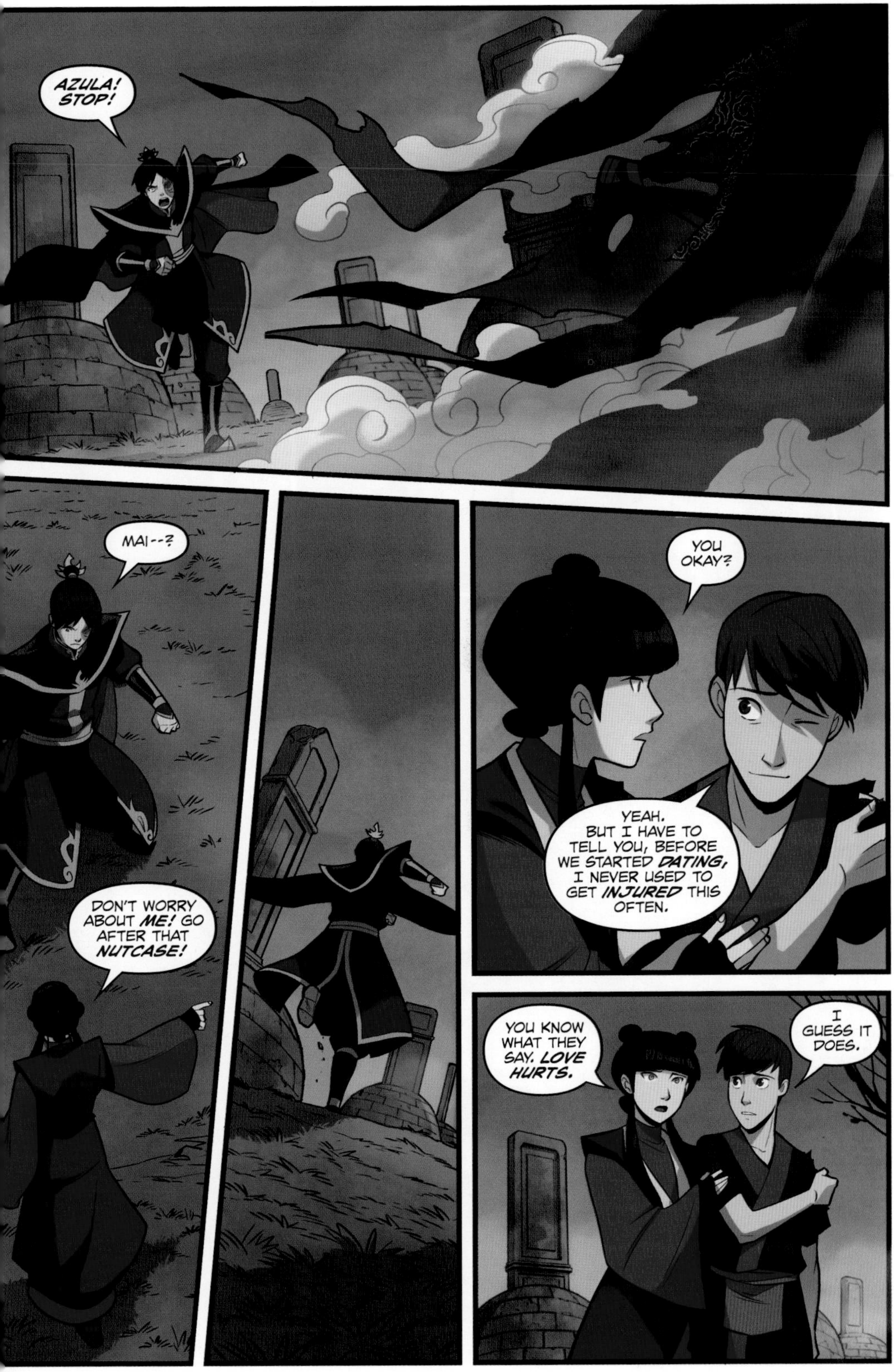

AZULA! STOP!
MAI--?
DON'T WORRY ABOUT ME! GO AFTER THAT NUTCASE!
YOU OKAY?
YEAH. BUT I HAVE TO TELL YOU, BEFORE WE STARTED DATING, I NEVER USED TO GET INJURED THIS OFTEN.
YOU KNOW WHAT THEY SAY. LOVE HURTS.
I GUESS IT DOES.

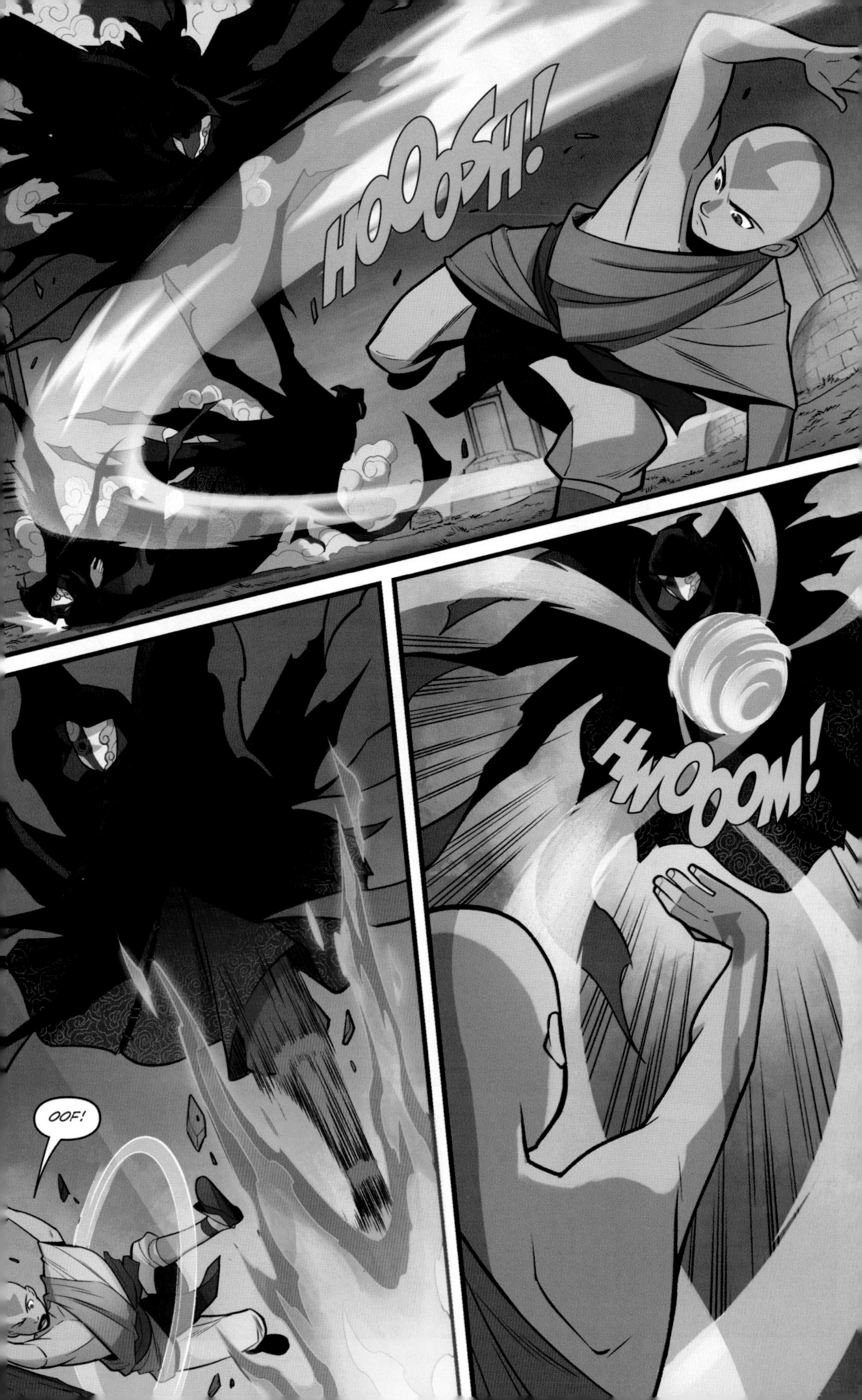
HOOOSH!
HWOOOM!
OOF!

KROOM!

ZUKO? MAI? KEI LO?

HEY! WHERE'D EVERYBODY GO?!

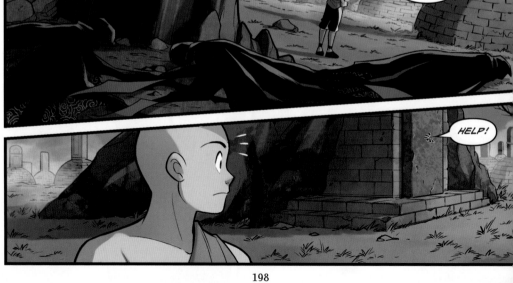

HELP!

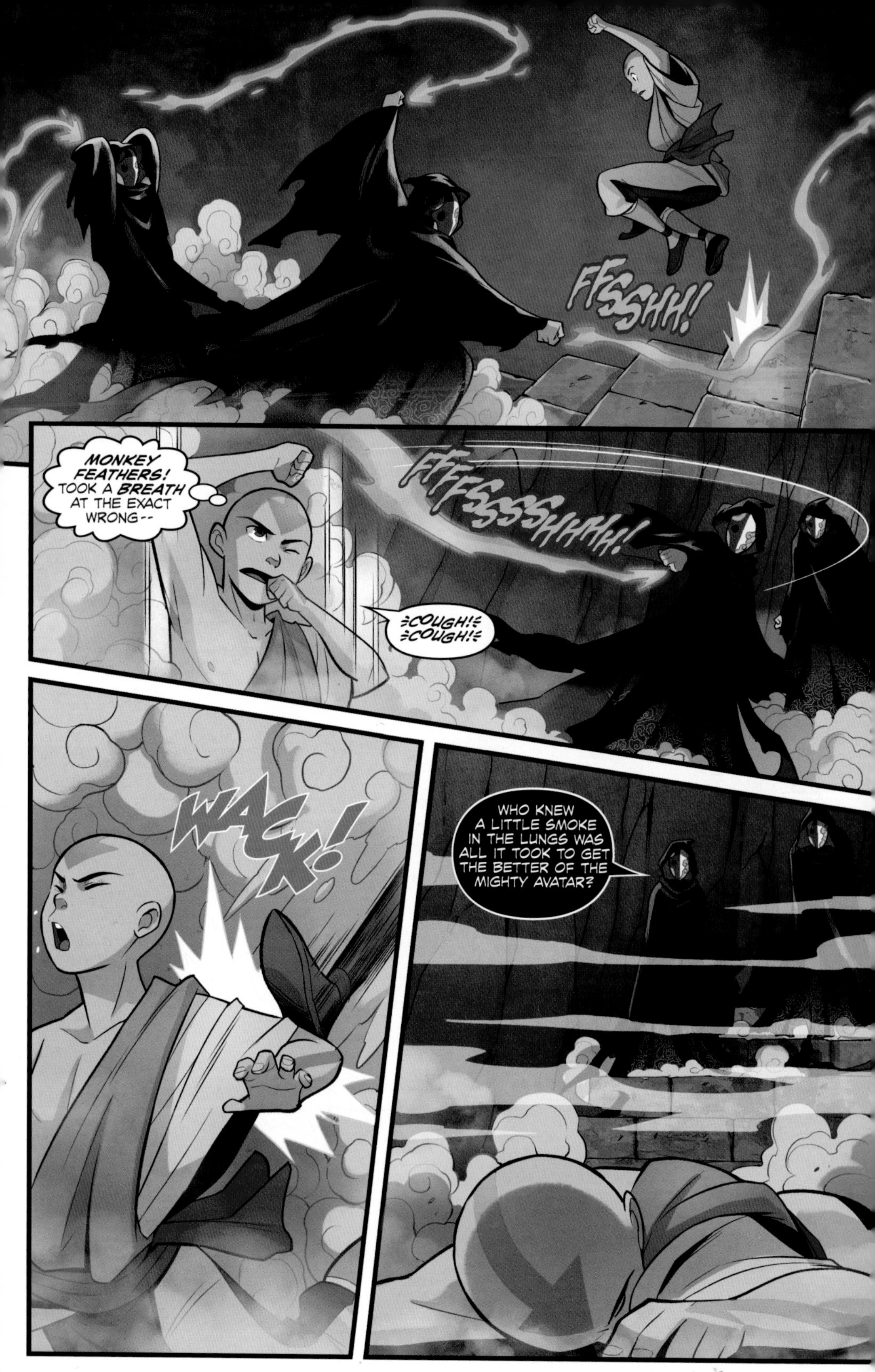
FFSSHH!
MONKEY FEATHERS! TOOK A BREATH AT THE EXACT WRONG--
FFFFSSSSHHHH!
COUGH! COUGH!
WACK!
WHO KNEW A LITTLE SMOKE IN THE LUNGS WAS ALL IT TOOK TO GET THE BETTER OF THE MIGHTY AVATAR?

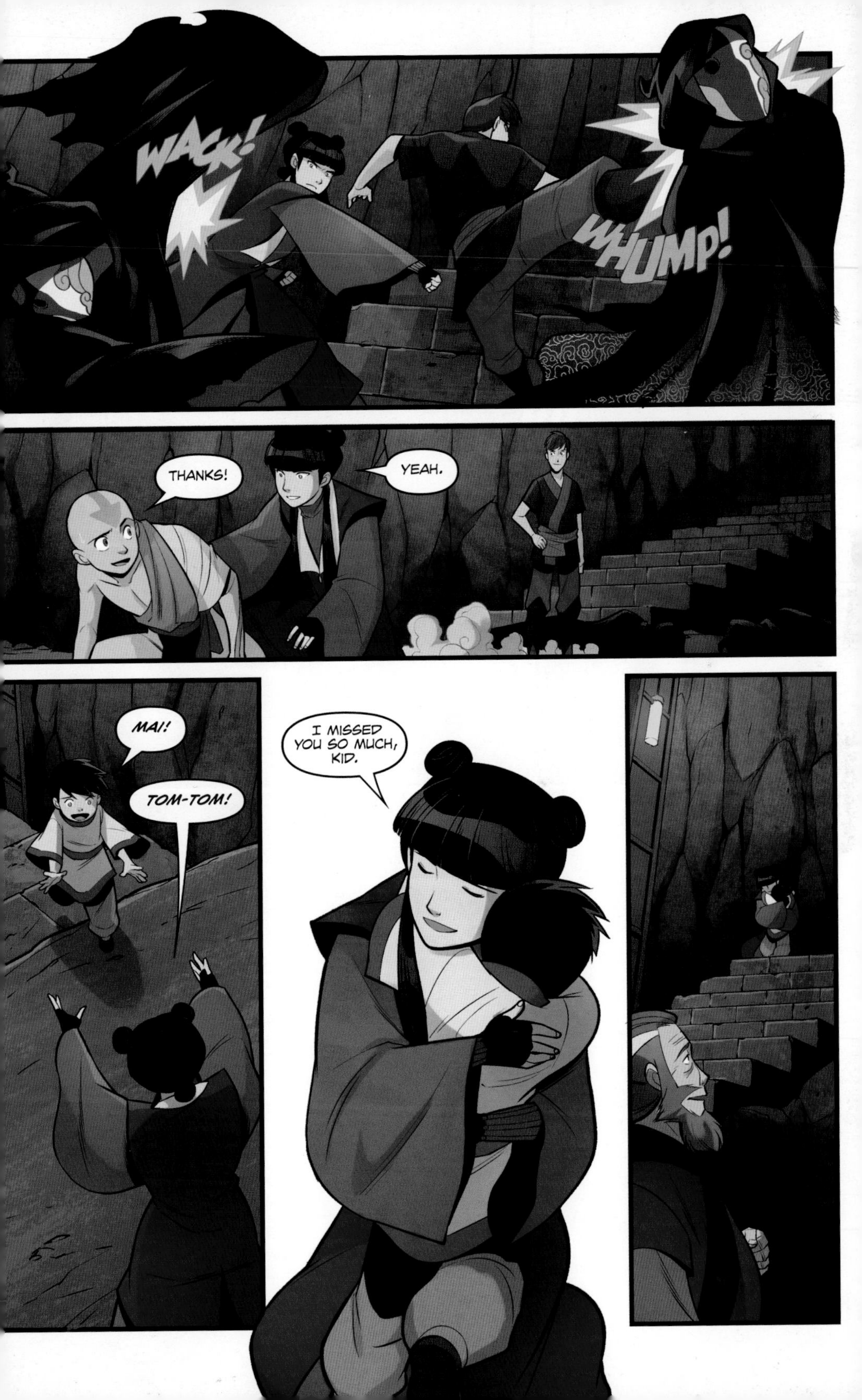
WACK!
WHUMP!
THANKS!
YEAH.
MAI!
TOM-TOM!
I MISSED YOU SO MUCH, KID.

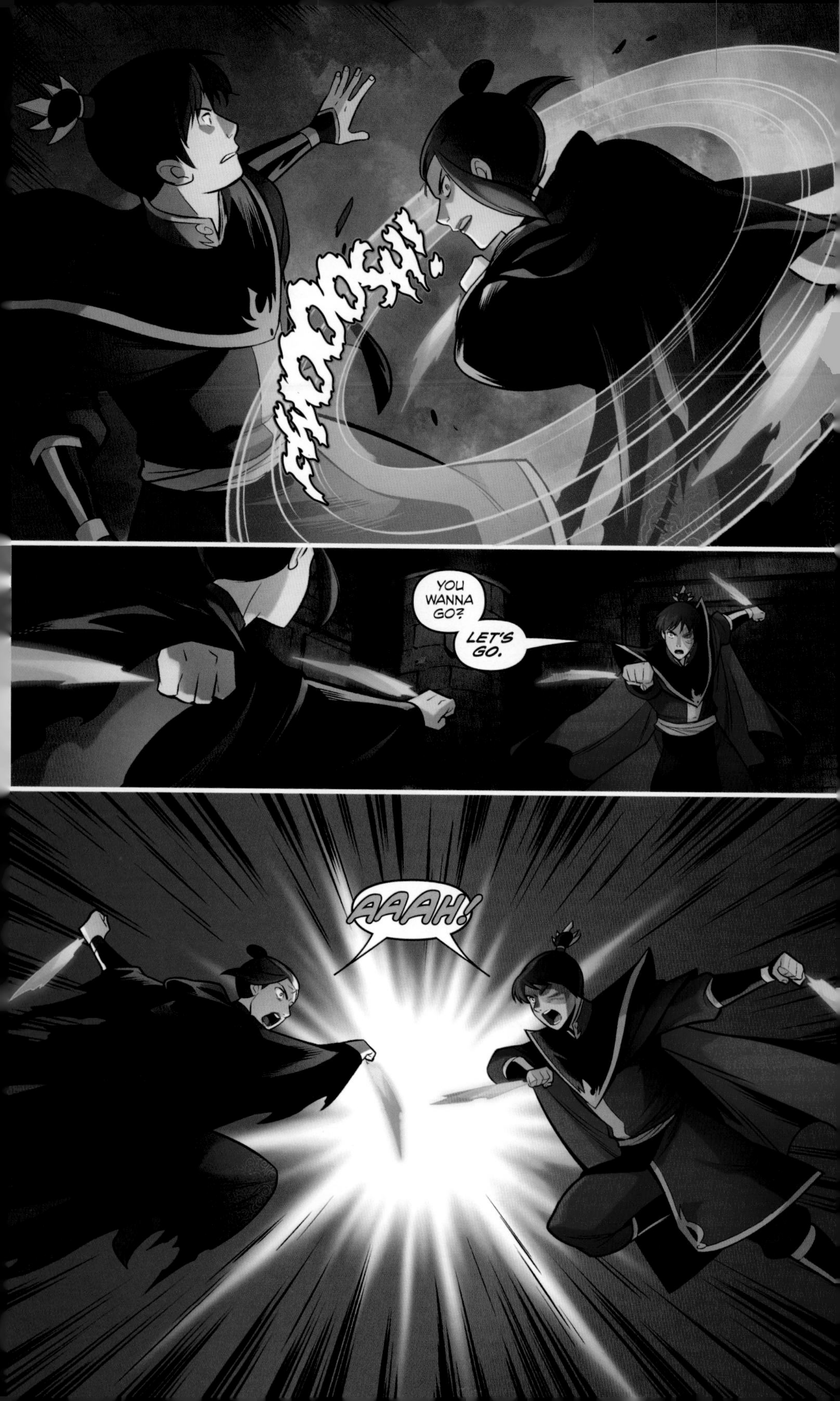
WHOOSH!
YOU WANNA GO?
LET'S GO.
AAAH!

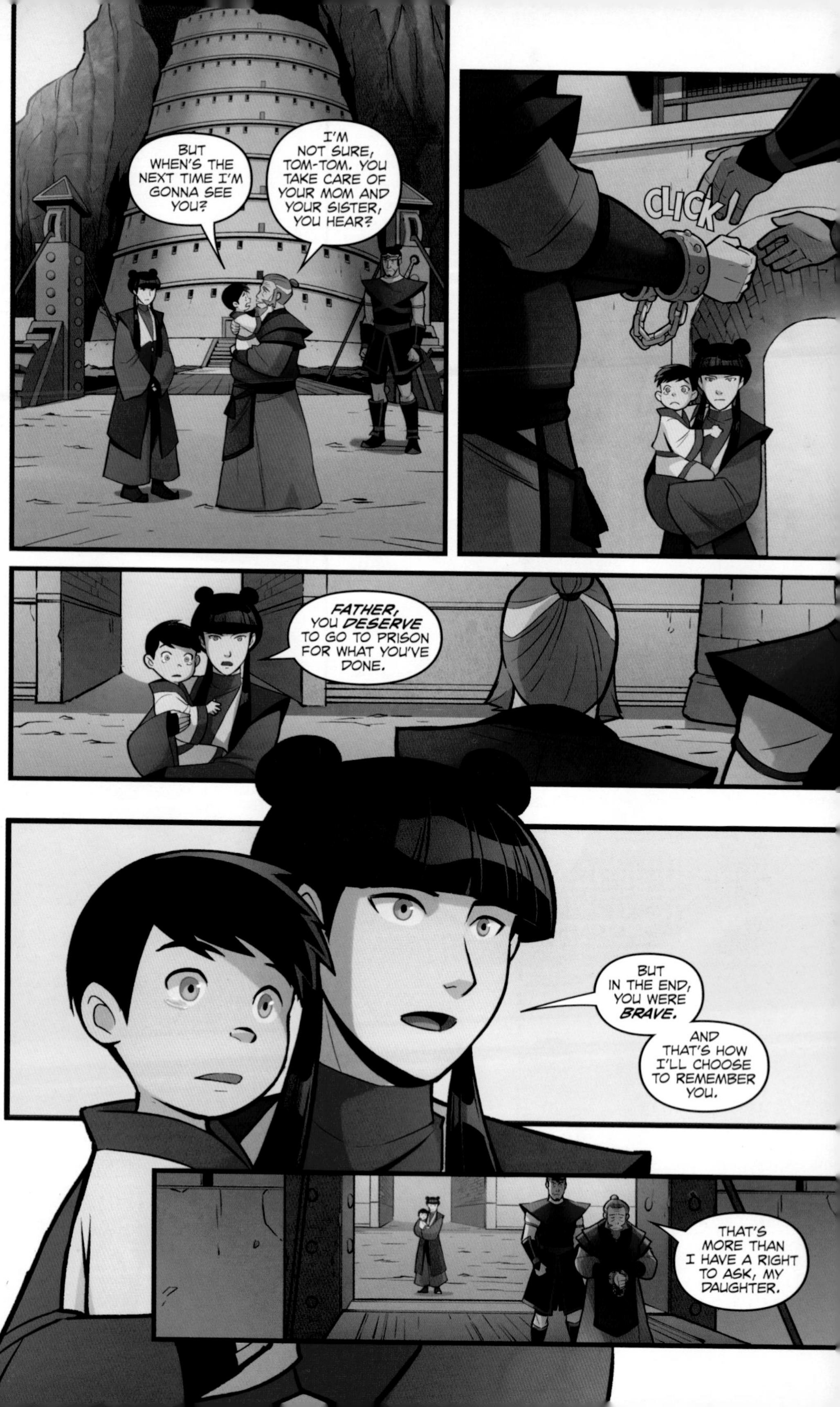
BUT WHEN'S THE NEXT TIME I'M GONNA SEE YOU?
I'M NOT SURE, TOM-TOM. YOU TAKE CARE OF YOUR MOM AND YOUR SISTER, YOU HEAR?
CLICK!
FATHER, YOU DESERVE TO GO TO PRISON FOR WHAT YOU'VE DONE.
BUT IN THE END, YOU WERE BRAVE.
AND THAT'S HOW I'LL CHOOSE TO REMEMBER YOU.
THAT'S MORE THAN I HAVE A RIGHT TO ASK, MY DAUGHTER.

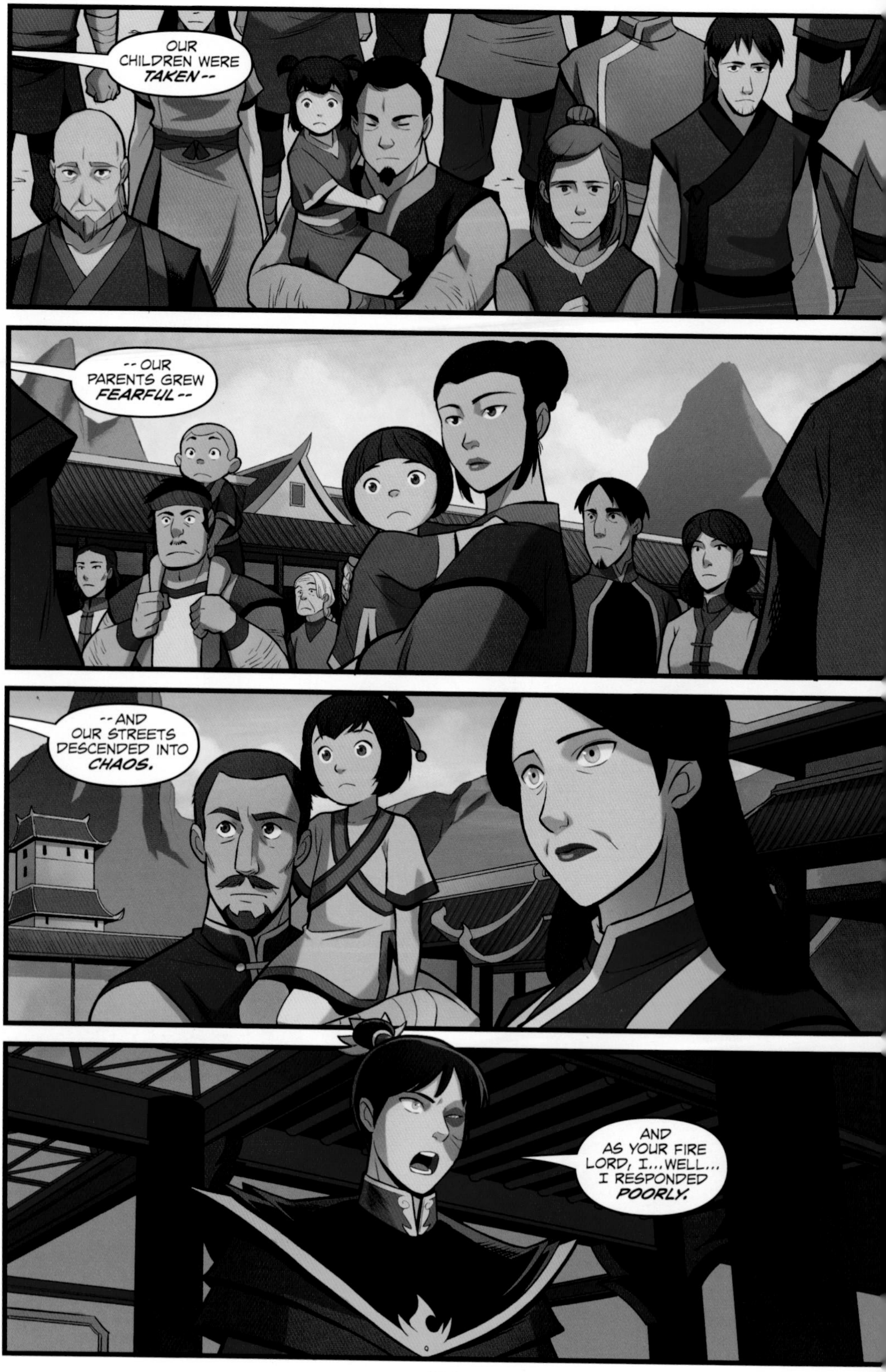
OUR CHILDREN WERE TAKEN--
--OUR PARENTS GREW FEARFUL--
--AND OUR STREETS DESCENDED INTO CHAOS.
AND AS YOUR FIRE LORD, I...WELL... I RESPONDED POORLY.

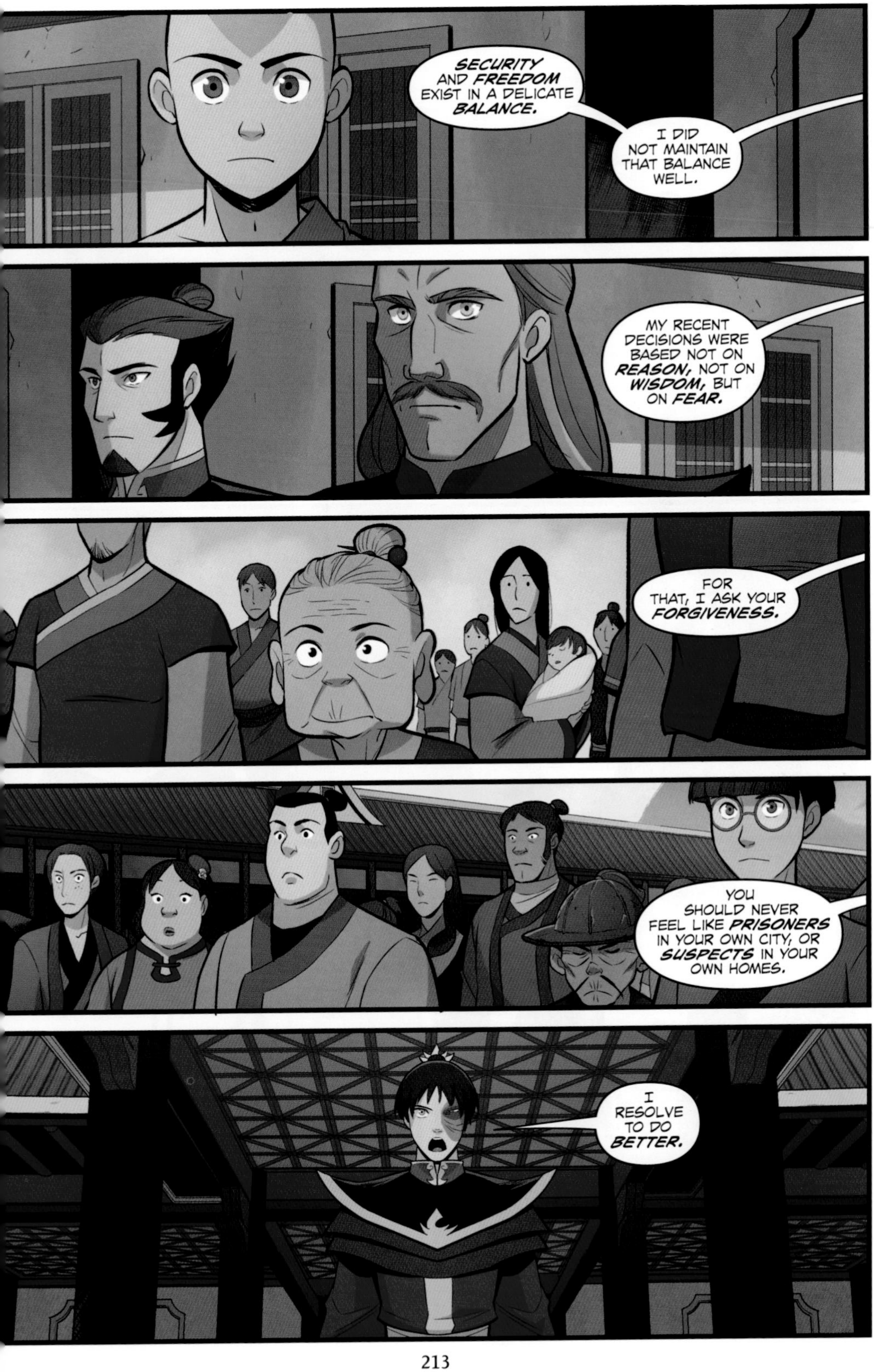
SECURITY AND FREEDOM EXIST IN A DELICATE BALANCE.
I DID NOT MAINTAIN THAT BALANCE WELL.
MY RECENT DECISIONS WERE BASED NOT ON REASON, NOT ON WISDOM, BUT ON FEAR.
FOR THAT, I ASK YOUR FORGIVENESS.
YOU SHOULD NEVER FEEL LIKE PRISONERS IN YOUR OWN CITY, OR SUSPECTS IN YOUR OWN HOMES.
I RESOLVE TO DO BETTER.

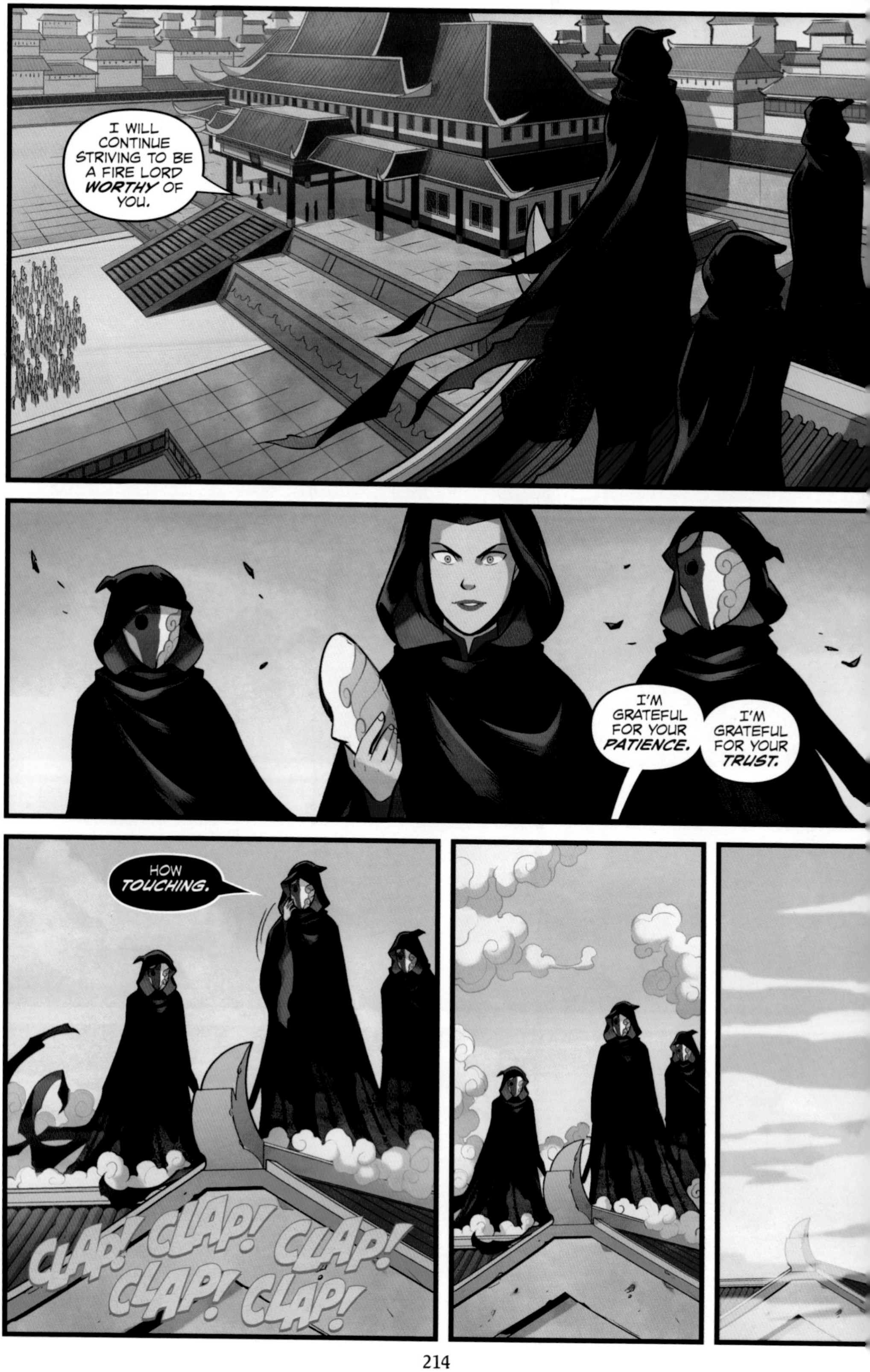
I WILL CONTINUE STRIVING TO BE A FIRE LORD WORTHY OF YOU.
I'M GRATEFUL FOR YOUR PATIENCE.
I'M GRATEFUL FOR YOUR TRUST.
HOW TOUCHING.
CLAP! CLAP! CLAP! CLAP! CLAP!

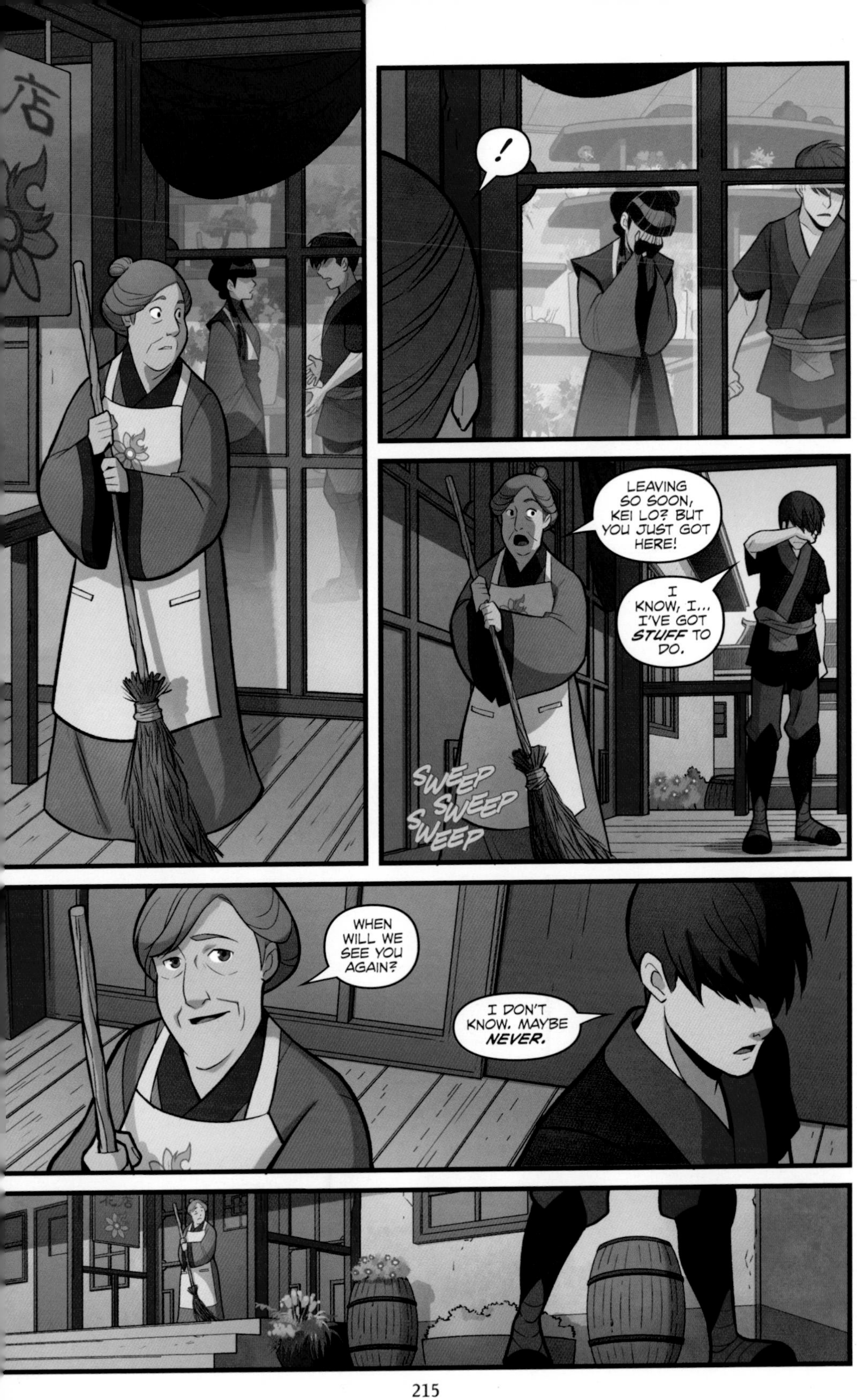
!
LEAVING SO SOON, KEI LO? BUT YOU JUST GOT HERE!
I KNOW, I... I'VE GOT STUFF TO DO.
SWEEP SWEEP SWEEP
WHEN WILL WE SEE YOU AGAIN?
I DON'T KNOW. MAYBE NEVER.

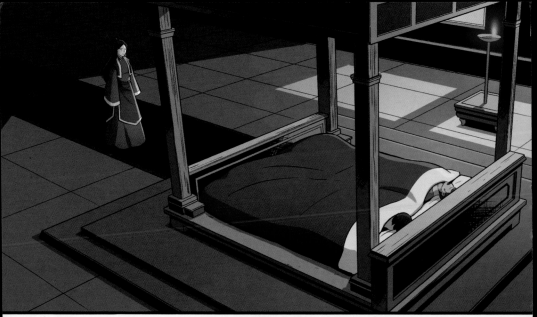

MOMMY... YOU'RE BACK.

I'M BACK.

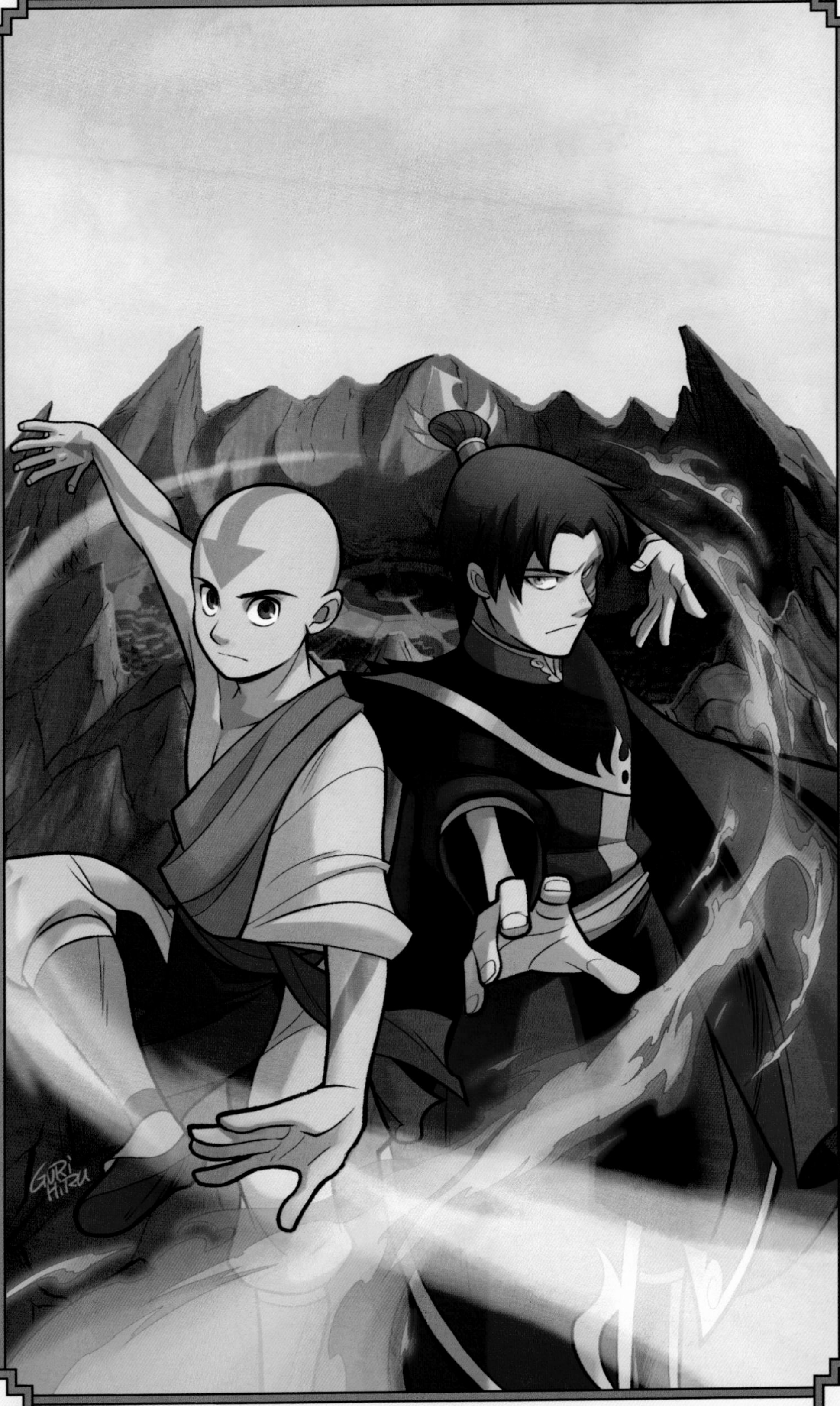
GURI HIRU

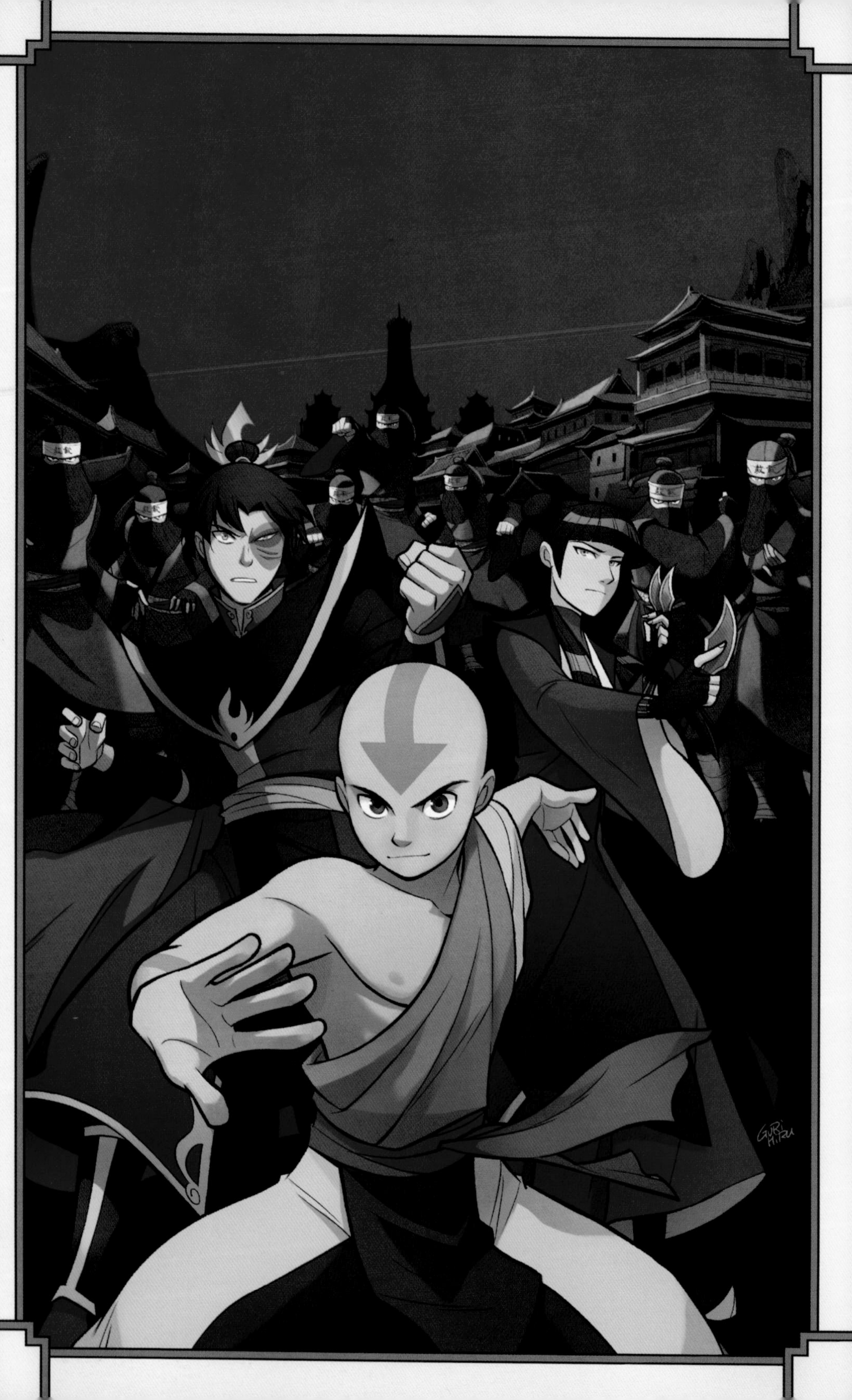
GURI HIRU

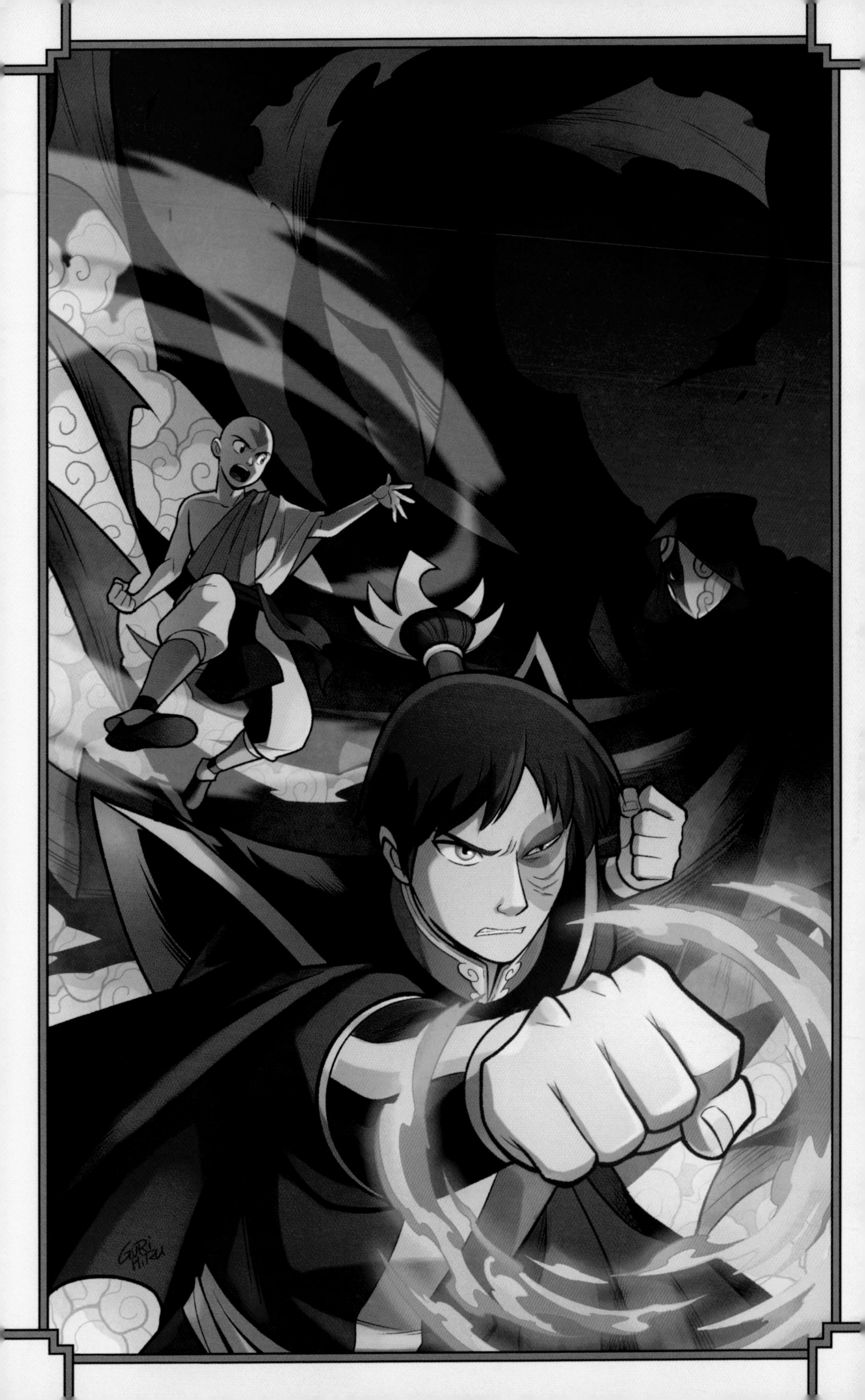
GURI HIRU

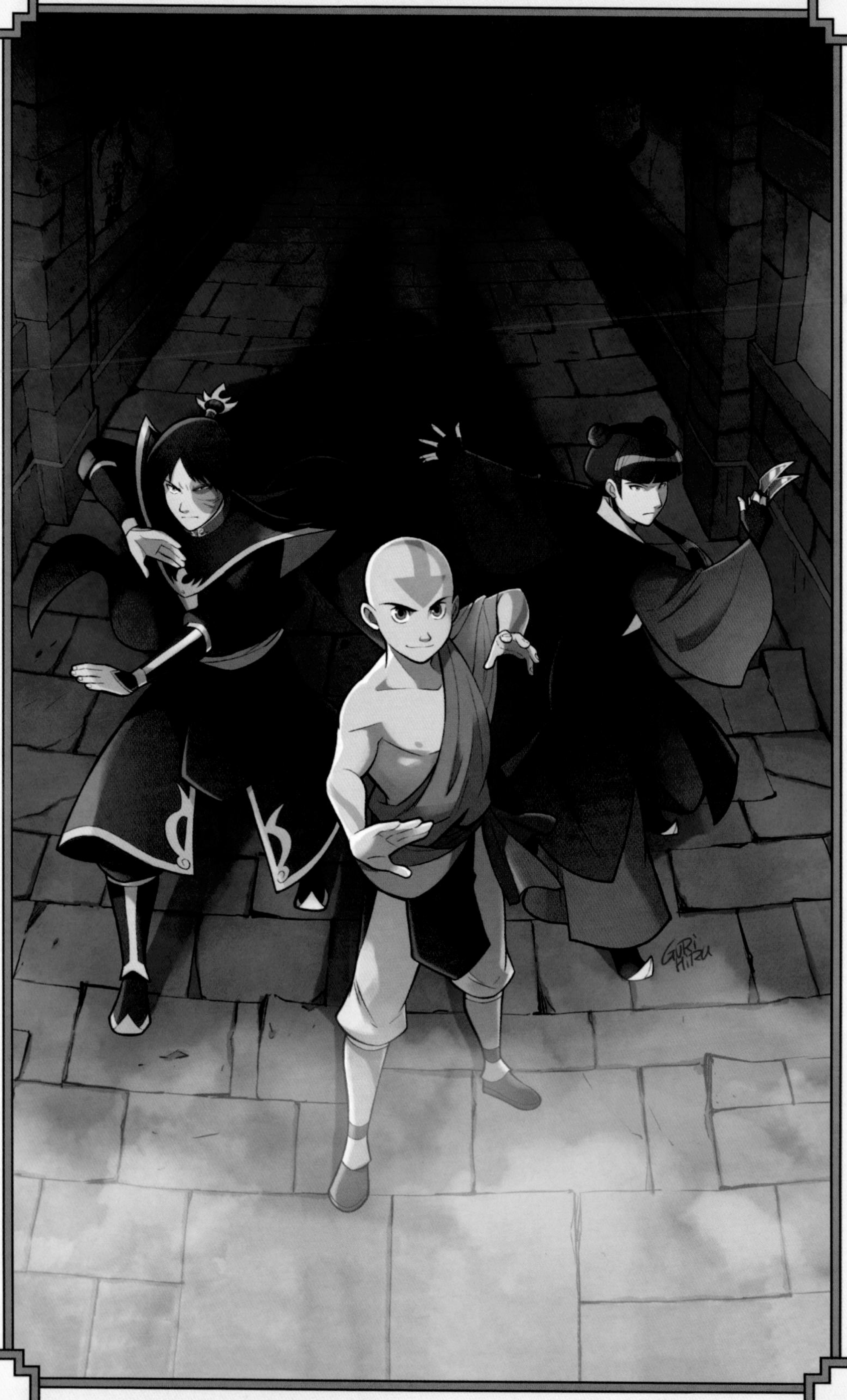
GURI HIRU

Avatar: The Last Airbender—Smoke and Shadow Sketchbook

Artwork and captions by Gurihiru

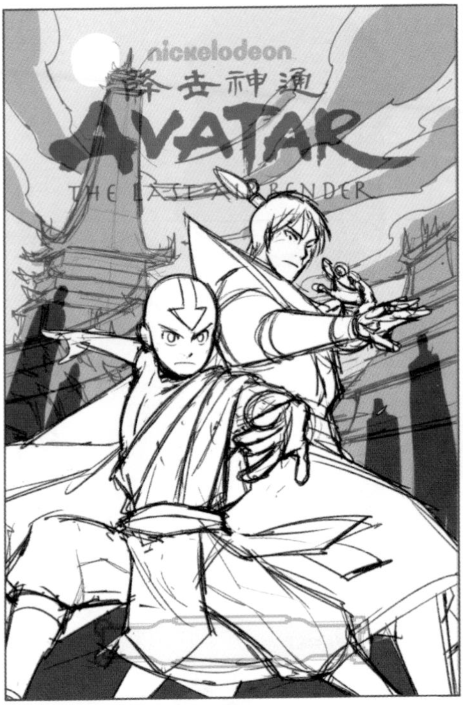
nickelodeon
AVATAR
THE LAST AIRBENDER

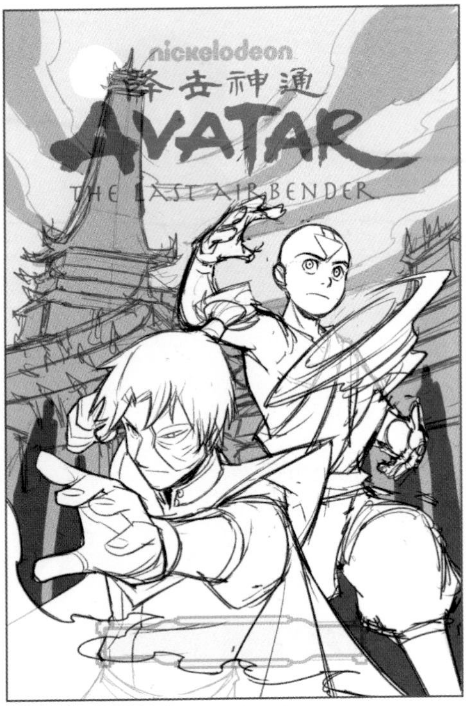
nickelodeon
AVATAR
THE LAST AIRBENDER

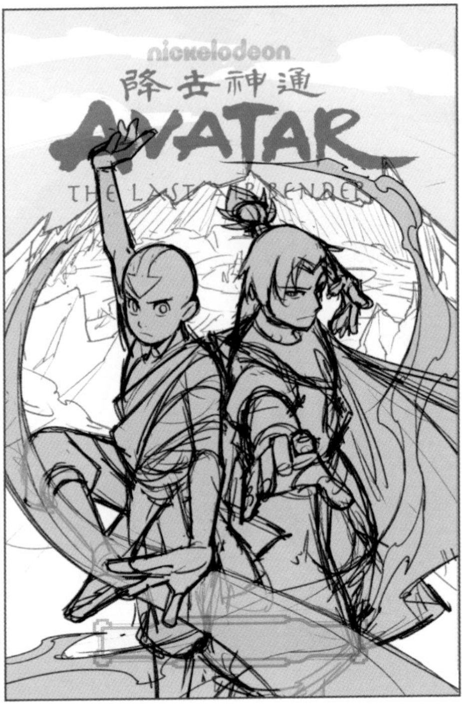
nickelodeon
AVATAR
THE LAST AIRBENDER

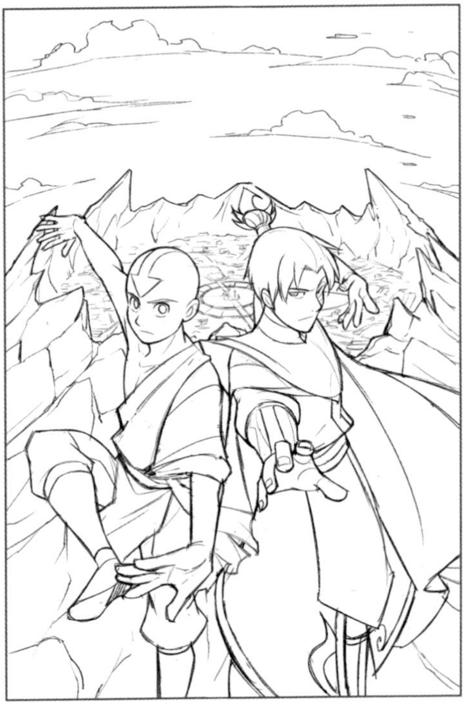

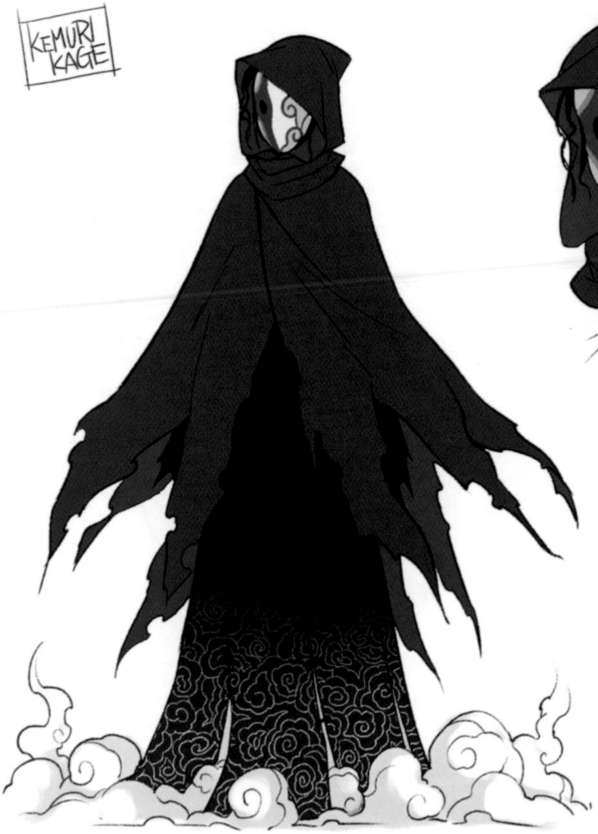
KEMURI
KAGE

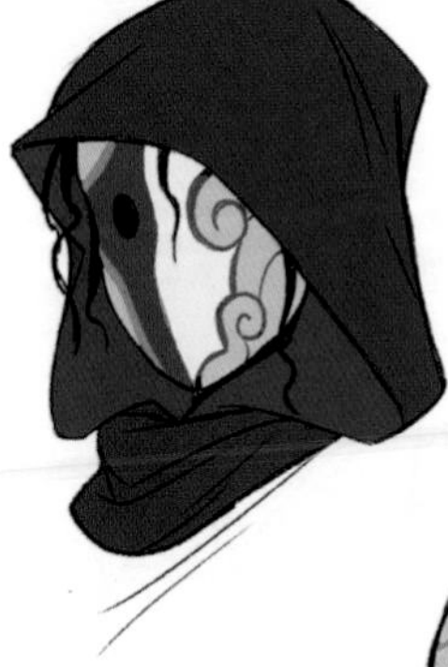

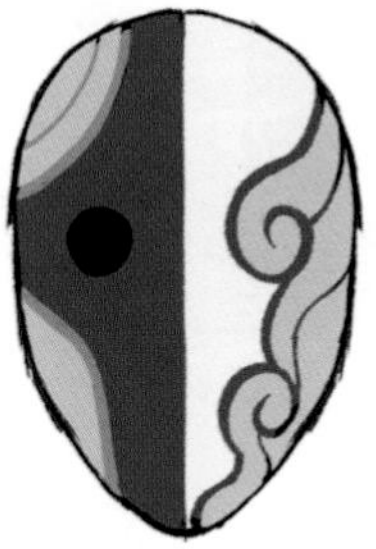

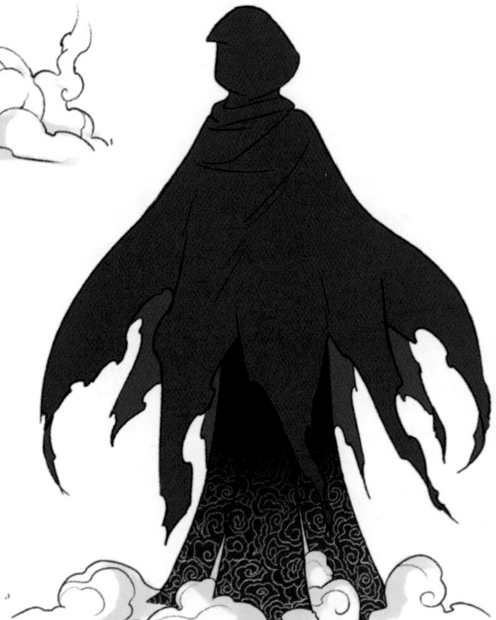

KEMURIKAGE

In Japanese, **kemuri** means "smoke," and **kage** means "shadow," so we designed the Kemurikage with dark cloaks and spooky, expressionless masks. The mask is asymmetrical, which evokes a sense of unease, and to make them look like spirits, smoke comes out from the bottom of the cloak.

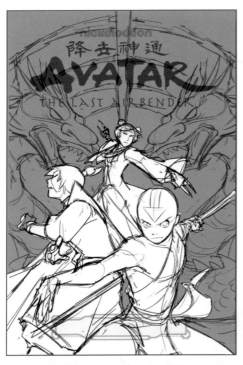

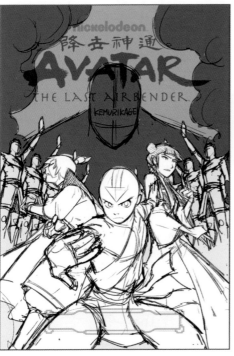

NEW OZAI SOCIETY

The members of the New Ozai Society wear Ozai's head-band, but in order to hide their identity, we designed it to cover half of their face. Since they work in the dark, we chose dark colors for their costumes.

The Ozai Society members

AVATAR

nickelodeon
AVATAR
THE LAST AIRBENDER

nickelodeon
AVATAR

AVATAR

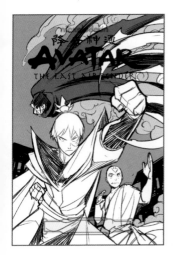

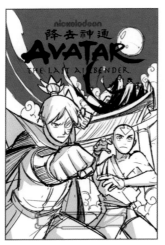

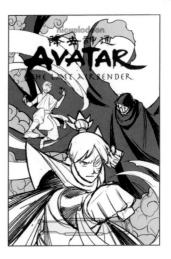

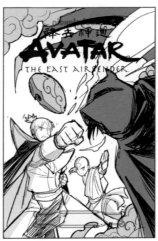

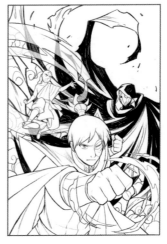

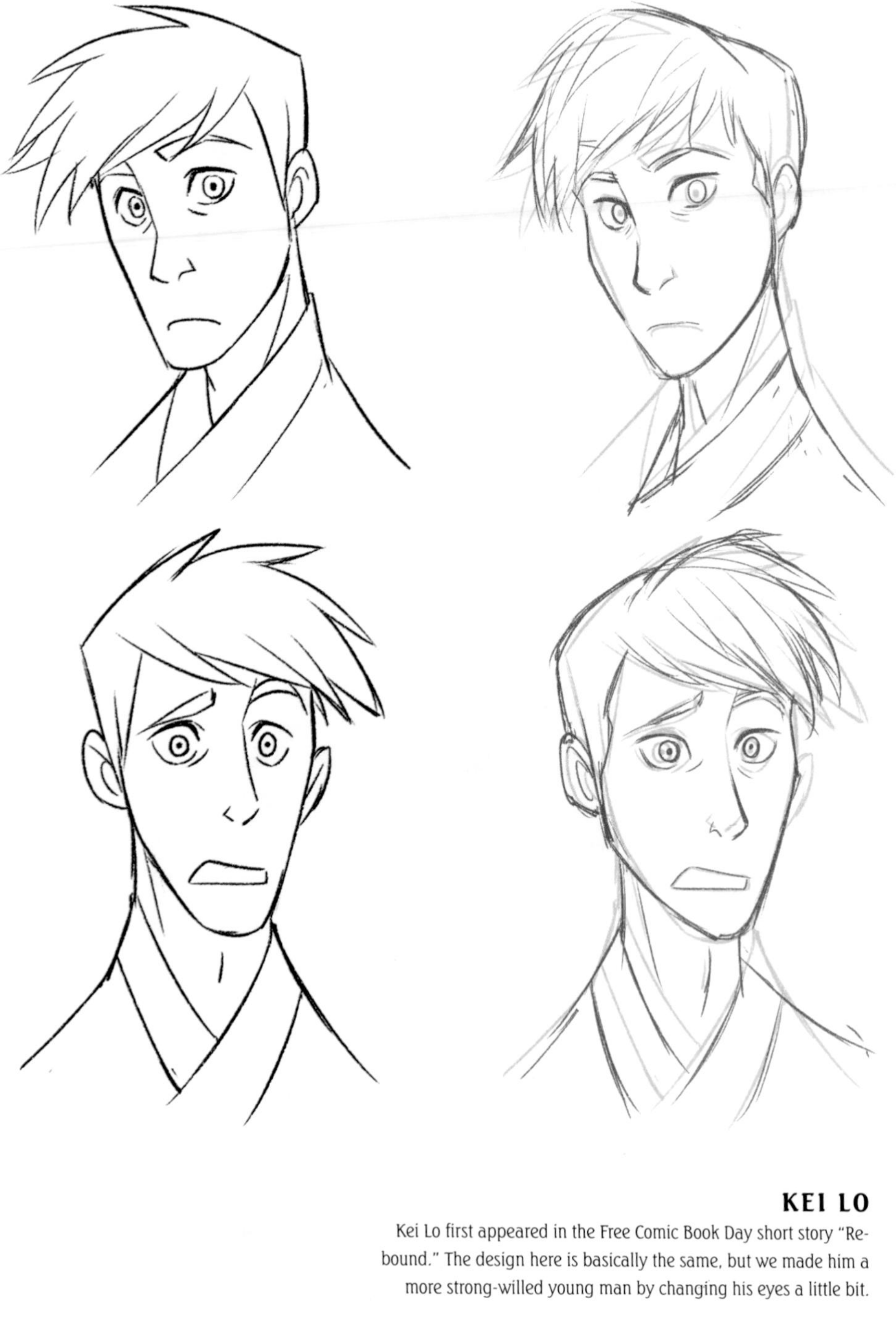

KEI LO

Kei Lo first appeared in the Free Comic Book Day short story "Rebound." The design here is basically the same, but we made him a more strong-willed young man by changing his eyes a little bit.

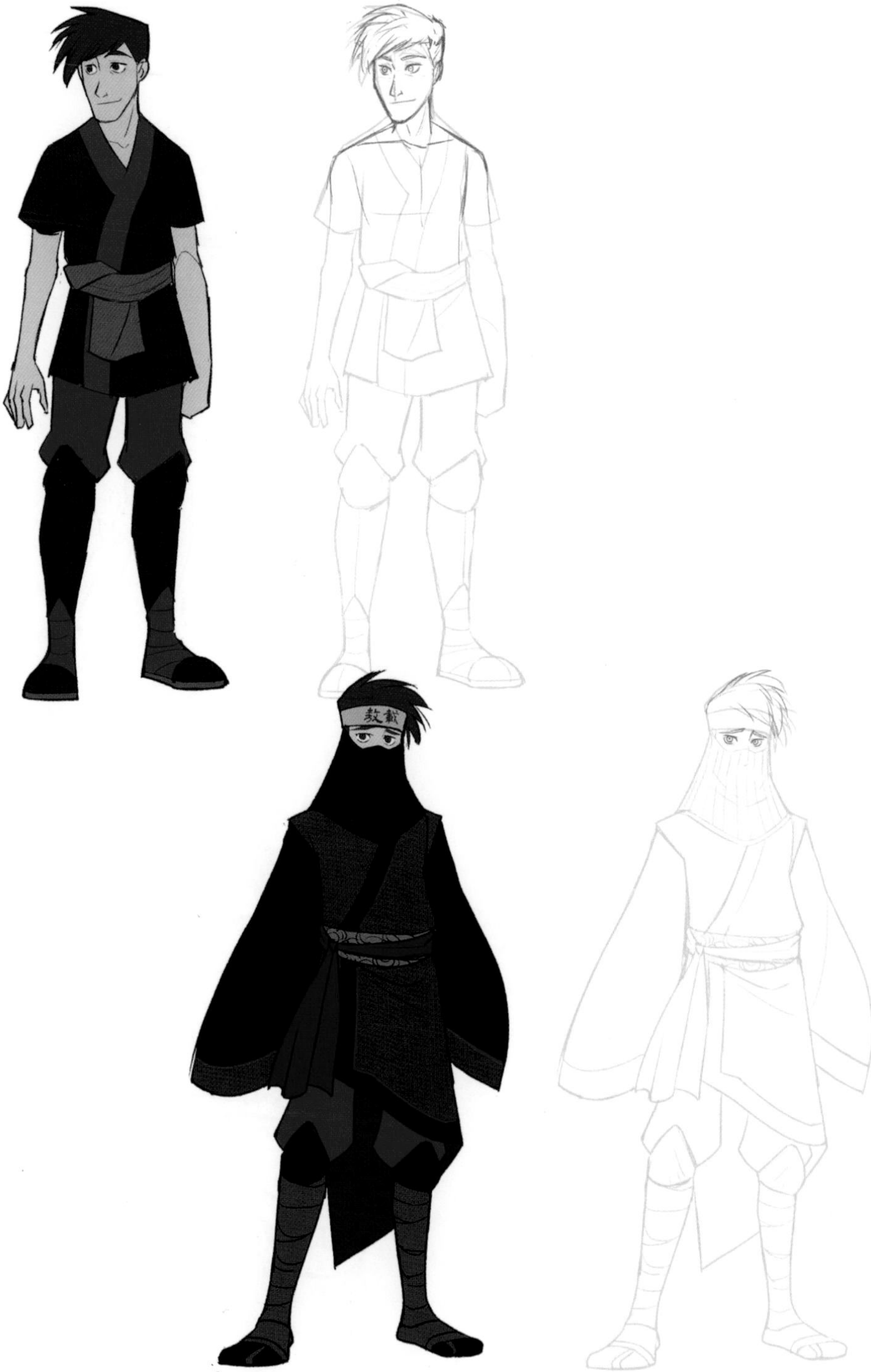

1

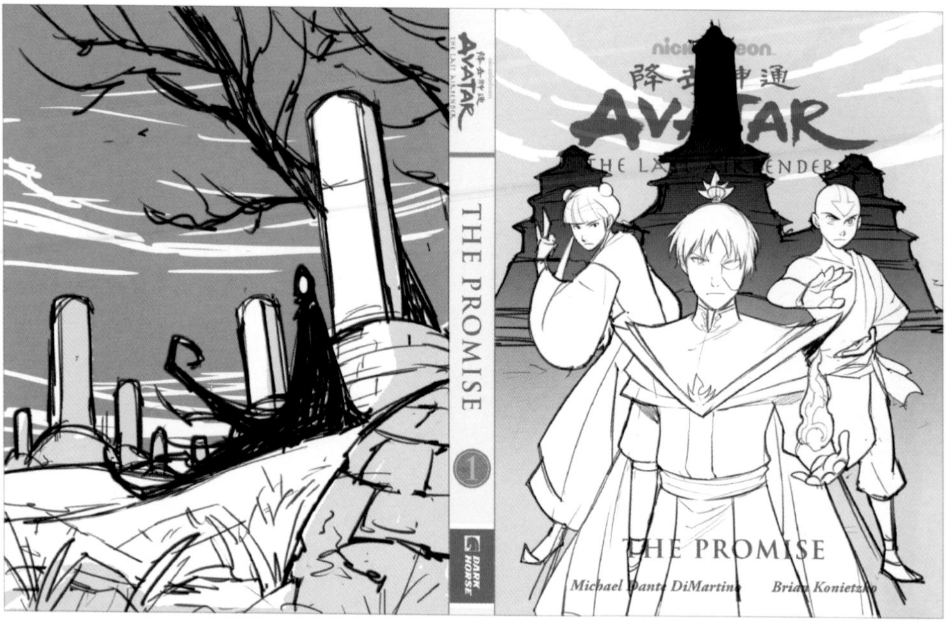
AVATAR
THE LAST AIRBENDER
THE PROMISE
1
DARK HORSE

2

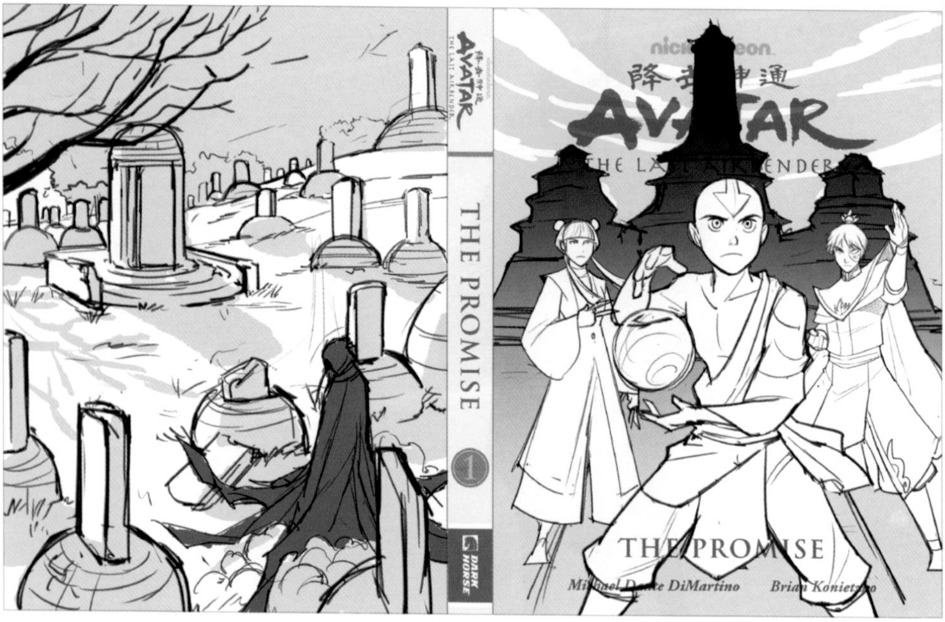
AVATAR
THE LAST AIRBENDER
THE PROMISE
1
DARK HORSE

3

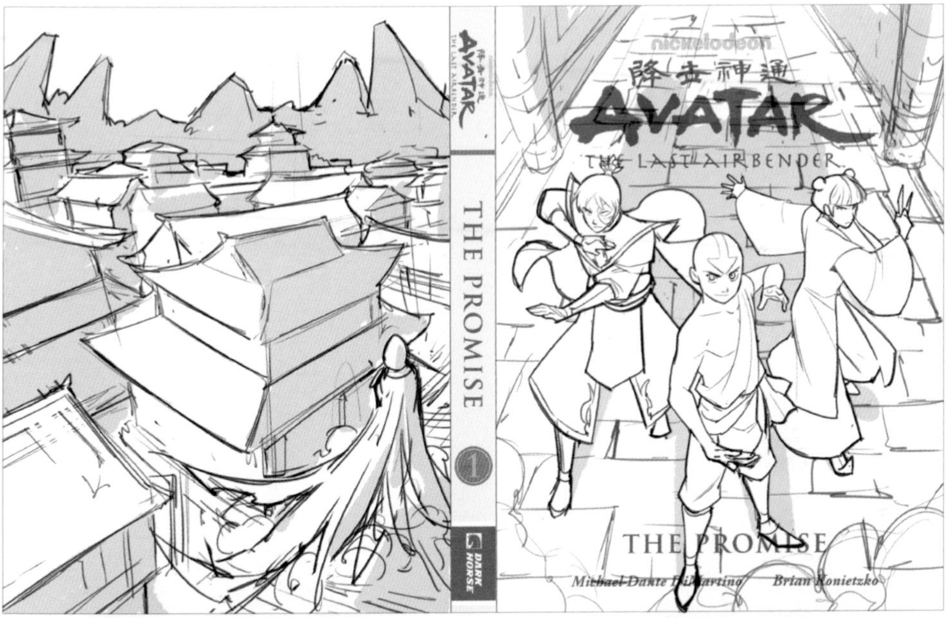
AVATAR
THE LAST AIRBENDER
THE PROMISE
1
DARK HORSE
nickelodeon
AVATAR
THE LAST AIRBENDER
THE PROMISE
Michael Dante DiMartino
Brian Konietzko

4

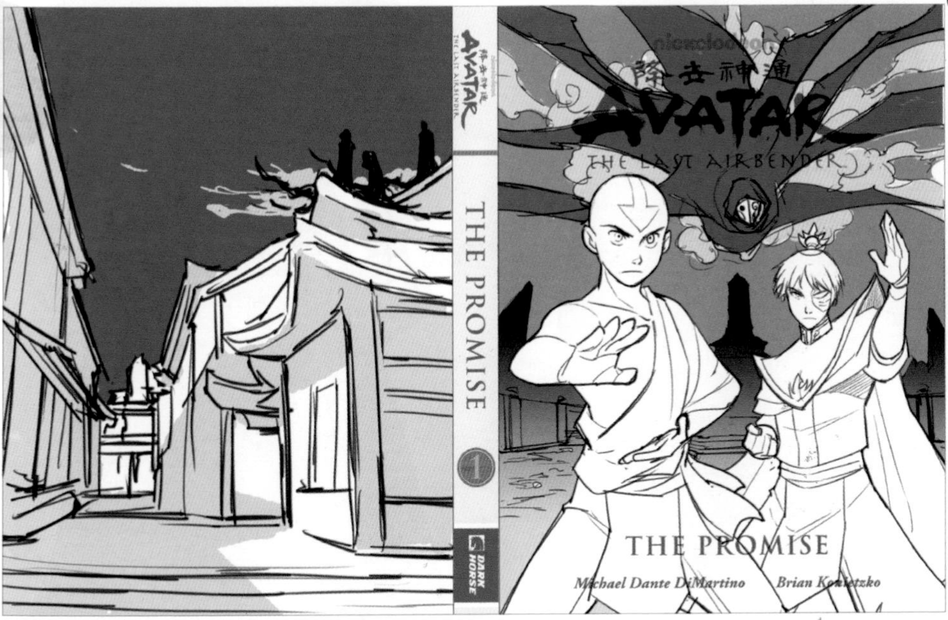
AVATAR
THE LAST AIRBENDER
THE PROMISE
1
DARK HORSE
nickelodeon
AVATAR
THE LAST AIRBENDER
THE PROMISE
Michael Dante DiMartino
Brian Konietzko

UKANO

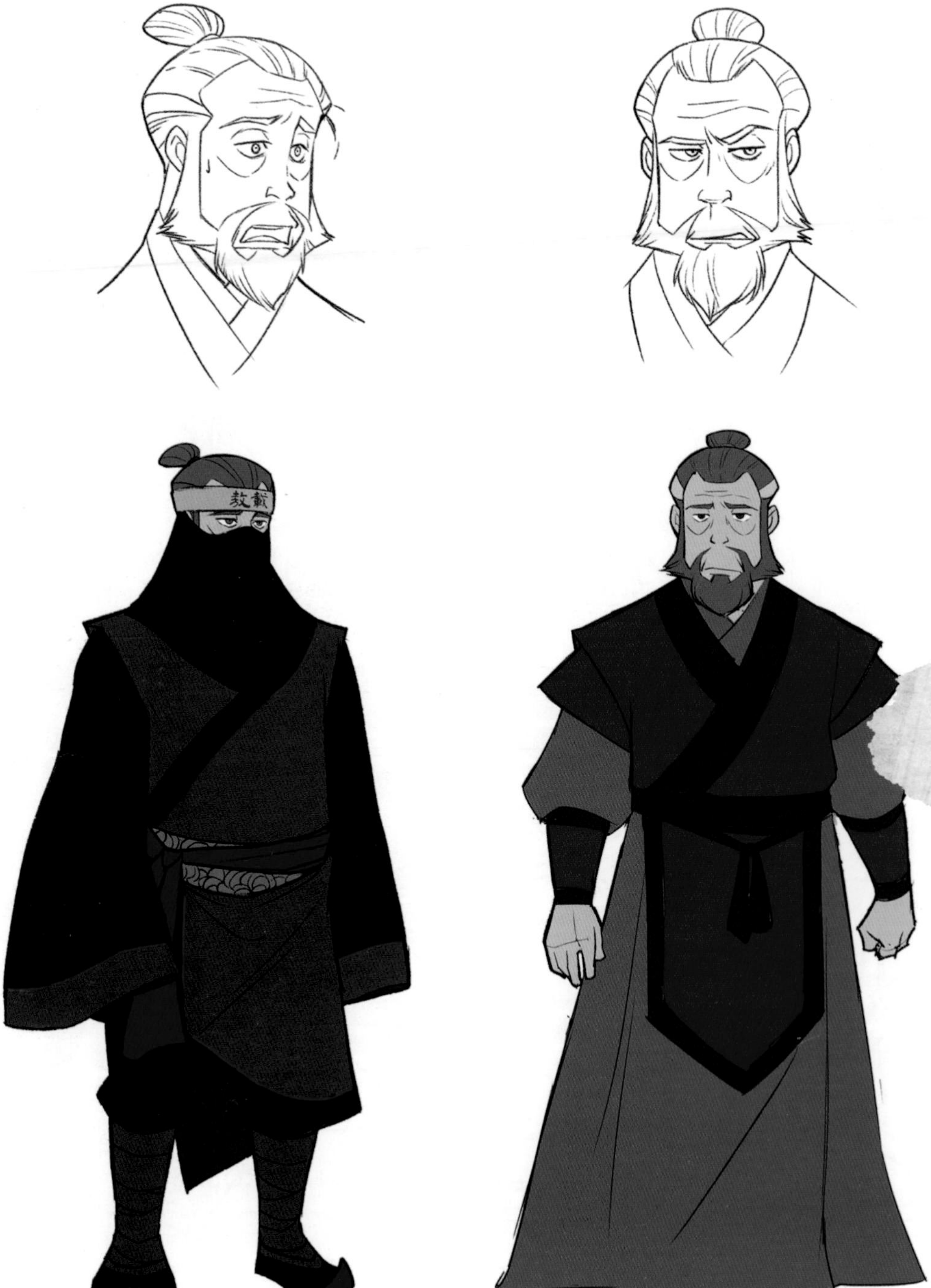